ERNEST D.W
The Wisdom Words

COPYCAT RECIPES
COOKBOOK
for beginners

All the Benefits of Cooking at Home with 500 delicious
Ideas, From Breakfast to Dinner

Gordon Benedict Richman and William Oliver Thomas

TABLE OF CONTENTS
BOOK 1: COPYCAT COOKBOOK

INTRODUCTION 17

CHAPTER 1
BENEFITS OF COOKING AT HOME 19

CHAPTER 2
PRACTICAL ADVICE FOR BEGINNERS ON THE CORRECT DISTRIBUTION OF MEALS DURING THE DAY, TO DIGEST WELL AND AVOID GAINING WEIGHT 25

CHAPTER 3
OLD AND MODERN BREAKFAST RECIPES 29

1. IHOP'S BUTTERMILK PANCAKE 30
2. STARBUCKS'S MARBLE POUND CAKE 31
3. IHOP'S SCRAMBLED EGG 32
4 .STARBUCKS'S CHOCOLATE CINNAMON BREAD 33
5. WAFFLE HOUSE'S WAFFLE 34
6. MIMI'S CAFÉ SANTA FÉ OMELET 35
7. ALICE SPRINGS CHICKEN FROM OUTBACK 36
8. ORIENTAL SALAD FROM APPLEBEE'S 37
9. BACON MUFFINS 38
10. BREAKFAST MUFFINS 38
11. BUTTERMILK BISCUITS 39
12. CHEESE ON SOFT TOAST 40
13. COOKIES WITH DARK CHOCOLATE 41
14. CORN PUDDING WITH BACON 42
15. EGG ROLLS 43
16. HASH BROWN CASSEROLE 44
17. CRANBERRY BLISS BARS (STARBUCKS) 45
18. EGG BITES (STARBUCKS) 46
19. CHICKEN NUGGETS (CHICK-FIL-A) 47
20. PRETZELS (AUNTIE ANNE'S) 48
21. CINNAMON ROLLS (CINNABON) 49
22. THE FRENCH TOASTS FROM DENNY'S 50
23. IHOP'S HEALTHY "HARVEST GRAIN 'N NUT" PANCAKES 51
24. MCDONALD'S SAUSAGE EGG MCMUFFIN 52
25. STARBUCKS' SPINACH AND FETA BREAKFAST WRAPS 53
26. JIMMY DEAN'S HOMEMADE PORK SAGE SAUSAGE 54
27. PANERA POWER BREAKFAST SANDWICH 55
28. MCDONALD'S MCGRIDDLE BREAKFAST SANDWICH 56
29. DIY CALIFORNIA A.M. CRUNCH WRAP 57
30. PANERA SPINACH AND CHEESE EGG SOUFFLÉ 58
31. YOUNG EGG FOO 59
32. CHEESE EGG SOUFFLE WITH SPINACH 60
33. STACK PANCAKES 61
34. PILLSBURY SWEET ROLL WITH

ORANGE JUICE — 62
35. WAFFLE WITH SPICY CHICKEN — 63
36. CHEESECAKE PANCAKES — 64
37. STARBUCKS LEMON BREAD — 65
38. BARREL CRACKER FRENCH TOAST — 66
39. EGG MCMUFFINS — 67
40. PUMPKIN PANCAKES — 68
41. FRITTATA — 69
42. RAGOUT — 70
43. BLUEBERRY PANCAKES — 71
44. BROWN SUGAR BACON — 72
45. STARBUCKS PUMPKIN BREAD — 73
46. DADDY'S BLUEBERRY BUTTERMILK PANCAKES — 74
47. AUNT BETTY'S BLUEBERRY MUFFINS — 74
48. BISCUITS AND SAUSAGE GRAVY — 75
49. TRUE BELGIAN WAFFLES — 75
50. THREE-CHEESE SOUFFLÉS — 76
51. CHICKEN-FRIED STEAK & GRAVY BOAT — 77
52. DELICIOUS POTATO DOUGHNUTS — 78
53. EGGS BENEDICT WITH HOMEMADE HOLLANDAISE — 79
54. BUTTERMILK PANCAKES5 — 80
55. HAM AND SWISS OMELET — 81

CHAPTER 4
ENERGIZING SMOOTHIE RECIPES — 83
56. MEGA MANGO SMOOTHIE — 84
57. ORANGE-A-PEEL SMOOTHIE — 84
58. ORANGE-C BOOSTER SMOOTHIE — 85
59. ORANGE CARROT KARMA SMOOTHIE — 85
60. ORANGE DREAM MACHINE SMOOTHIE — 86
61. PEACH MANGO SMOOTHIE — 86
62. PEACH PERFECTION SMOOTHIE — 87
63. PEACH PLEASURE SMOOTHIE — 87
64. PEANUT BUTTER MOO'D SMOOTHIE — 88
65. JAMBA JUICE POMEGRANATE PARADISE SMOOTHIE — 88
66. POMEGRANATE PICK-ME-UP SMOOTHIE — 89
67. PROTEIN BERRY WORKOUT SMOOTHIE — 89
68. RAZZAMATAZZ SMOOTHIE — 90
69. STRAWBERRY RASPBERRY BANANA SMOOTHIE — 90
70. MANGO-A-GO-GO SMOOTHIE — 91
71. JAMBA JUICE: PROTEIN BERRY WORKOUT — 91
72. JAMBA JUICE: RAZZAMATAZZ SMOOTHIE — 92
73. JAMBA JUICE: STRAWBERRY RASPBERRY BANANA — 92
74. JAMBA JUICE: STRAWBERRY SURF RIDER — 93
75. JAMBA JUICE: STRAWBERRY WHIRL SMOOTHIE — 93
76. JAMBA JUICE: STRAWBERRIES WILD — 94
77. JAMBA JUICE: TROPICAL HARVEST SMOOTHIE — 94
78. JAMBA JUICE: WHITE GUMMY BEAR — 95
79. NAKED JUICE: GREEN MACHINE — 95
80. NAKED JUICE: MIGHTY MANGO — 96
81. NAKED JUICE: RED MACHINE — 96
82. ORANGE JULIUS — 97

83. PANERA BREAD: PEACH & BLUEBERRY SMOOTHIE 97

84. PANERA BREAD: SUPER FRUIT SMOOTHIE WITH GREEK YOGURT 98

85. PANERA BREAD: GREEN PASSION SMOOTHIE 98

CHAPTER 5
MILK SHAKE RECIPES **99**

86. IN-N-OUT BURGER'S COPYCAT VANILLA SHAKE 100

87. WENDY'S COPYCAT CHOCOLATE FROSTY 100

88. JAMBA JUICE'S COPYCAT RAZZMATAZZ SMOOTHIE 101

89. TGI FRIDAY'S COPYCAT TROPICAL RUNNER SMOOTHIE 101

90. SHAKE SHACK'S COPYCAT PEANUT BUTTER SHAKE 102

91. SONIC'S COPYCAT STRAWBERRY SHAKE 102

92. DISNEY'S COPYCAT JELLY PEANUT B UTTER MILKSHAKE 103

93. ARBY'S COPYCAT JAMOCHA SHAKE 103

94. JACK IN THE BOX'S COPYCAT PUMPKIN PIE SHAKE 104

95. TROPICAL SMOOTHIE CAFÉ'S COPYCAT PEANUT PARADISE 104

96. MCDONALD'S COPYCAT SHAMROCK SHAKE 105

97. SMOOTHIE KING'S COPYCAT CARIBBEAN WAY 105

98. CHICK-FIL-A'S COPYCAT FROSTED LEMONADE 106

99. PANERA'S COPYCAT MANGO SMOOTHIE 106

100. DISNEY'S COPYCAT RED APPLE FREEZE 107

CHAPTER 6
SOUP RECIPES **109**

101. USHIO JIRU 110

102. JAPANESE TURNIP MISO SOUP 110

103. KENCHINJIRU 111

104. CORN POTAGE 112

105. TONJIRU 113

106. MATSUTAKE CLEAR SOUP 114

107. TOFU AND JAPANESE PUMPKIN SOUP 115

108. CHAMPON 116

109. SOBA NOODLES WITH SAKE-POACHED CHICKEN 117

110. SOBA NOODLES WITH MISO SALMON 118

111. EGG AND PORK CURRY SOUP WITH UDON NOODLES 119

112. CURRY UDON NOODLES 120

113. KITSUNE UDON 121

114. MOMOFUKU SOY SAUCE EGGS, CHILI CHICKEN, AND SOBA NOODLES 122

115. SOBA, PRAWN, AND LEMONGRASS SOUP 123

116. ANCIENT GRAINS SOUP 124

117. PIRANHA PALE ALE CHILI 125

118. CHICKEN TORTILLA SOUP 126

119. TUSCAN TOMATO BISQUE 127

120. BROCCOLI CHEDDAR SOUP 128

121. PF CHANG'S SPICY CHICKEN NOODLE SOUP 129

122. PF CHANG'S HOT AND SOUR SOUP 130

123. DISNEYLAND'S MONTEREY CLAM CHOWDER 131

124. OUTBACK'S BAKED POTATO SOUP 132

125. APPLEBEE'S TOMATO BASIL SOUP 133

126. CHICKEN ENCHILADA SOUP FROM CHILI' 134

127. PANERA'S BROCCOLI CHEDDAR SOUP 135

128. CHEESY WALKABOUT SOUP 136

129. OLIVE GARDEN CHICKEN GNOCCHI SOUP 137

130. PANERA BROCCOLI CHEESE SOUP 138

CHAPTER 7

APPETIZER RECIPES 139

131. BENNIGAN'S BROCCOLI BITES 140

132. CHI CHI'S SEAFOOD NACHOS 141

133. CHILI'S BONELESS BUFFALO WINGS 141

134. CHILI'S CHICKEN FAJITA NACHOS 142

135. CHILI'S SOUTHWESTERN EGGROLLS 142

136. CHILI'S TEXAS CHEESE FRIES 143

137. DAVE AND BUSTER'S PHILLY STEAK ROLLS 143

138. JOE'S CRAB SHACK CRAB NACHOS 144

139. JOHNNY CARINO'S ITALIAN NACHOS 144

140. OLIVE GARDEN BREAD STICKS 145

141. OLIVE GARDEN STUFFED MUSHROOMS 145

142. OLIVE GARDEN TOASTED RAVIOLI 146

143. OLIVE GARDEN TOMATO BASIL CROSTINI 146

144. OUTBACK STEAKHOUSE BLOOMIN' ONION 147

145. T.G.I. FRIDAY'S BAKED POTATO SKINS 148

146. PEI WEI'S CRAB WONTON 148

147. PEI WEI'S VIETNAMESE CHICKEN SALAD SPRING ROLL 149

148. TAKEOUT DRY GARLIC RIBS 150

149. ABUELO'S JALAPENO POPPERS 151

150. APPLEBEE'S BAJA POTATO BOATS 152

151. APPLEBEE'S CHICKEN WINGS 153

152. PANDA EXPRESS'S CHICKEN POTSTICKERS 154

153. PANDA EXPRESS'S CREAM CHEESE RANGOON 155

154. PANDA EXPRESS'S CHICKEN EGG ROLL 156

155. PANDA EXPRESS'S VEGGIE SPRING ROLL 157

156. PF CHANG'S HOT AND SOUR SOUP 158

157. PF CHANG'S LETTUCE WRAPS 159

158. PF CHANG'S SHRIMP DUMPLINGS 160

159. PF CHANG'S SPICY CHICKEN NOODLE 161

160. PEI WEI'S THAI CHICKEN SATAY 162

161. CHICKEN LETTUCE WRAPS 163

162. BBQ SPARE RIBS 164

163. CAULIFLOWER TEMPURA 165

164. DYNAMITE SHRIMP 166

165. NORTHERN-STYLE SPARE RIBS 167

166. CRISPY GREEN BEANS 168

167. PORK DUMPLINGS 169

168. RED SAUCE WONTON'S 170
169. CHARRED BRUSSELS SPROUTS 171
170. CHINA BISTRO BEEF LO MEIN 172
171. HOUSE-MADE PORK EGG ROLLS 173
172. CHILI-GARLIC GREEN BEANS 174
173. BUDDHA'S FEAST VEGETABLE STIR-FRY 175
174. COCONUT CURRY VEGETABLES 176
175. KOREAN CHICKEN STIR FRY 177

CHAPTER 8
OLD AND MODERN SAUCE AND DRESSING RECIPES **179**
176. DON PABLO'S PRAIRIE FIRE BEAN DIP 180
177. CAFÉ RIO'S PICO DE GALLO 181
178. CHIPOTLE'S REFRIED BEANS 182
179. ABUELO'S JALAPEÑO CHEESE FRITTERS 183
180. BAJA FRESH'S GUACAMOLE 184
181. CHIPOTLE'S GUACAMOLE 184
182. CHI CHI'S CHILI CON QUESO 185
183. CHIPOTLE'S QUESO DIP 185
184. DON PABLO'S WHITE CHILI 186
185. CHILI'S ORIGINAL CHILI 187
186. 2-INGREDIENT TAHINI PASTE 188
187. SPICY MEXICAN BARBECUE SAUCE 188
188. TANGY FRENCH REMOULADE SAUCE1 189
189. DUCK SAUCE 189
190. SPICY JAMAICAN JERK SAUCE 190
191. CREAMY MUSHROOM SAUCE 190
192. THAI SATAY PEANUT SAUCE 191
193. CARAMEL SAUCE 191
194. CARAMEL CREAM CHEESE SPREAD 192
195. BABA GHANOUSH 193

196. KRAFT THOUSAND ISLAND DRESSING 194
197. NEWMAN OWN'S CREAMY CAESAR SALAD DRESSING 194
198. BULL'S EYE ORIGINAL BBQ SAUCE 195
199. KRAFT MIRACLE WHIP 195
200. HELLMAN'S MAYONNAISE 196
201. HEINZ KETCHUP 196
202. HIDDEN VALLEY ORIGINAL RANCH DRESSING 197
203. SABRA HUMMUS 197
204. RONDELÉ GARLIC & HERBS CHEESE SPREAD 198
205. LIPTON ONION SOUP MIX 198
206. LAWRY'S TACO SEASONINGS 199
207. MRS. DASH SALT-FREE SEASONING MIX 200
208. OLD BAY SEASONING 201
209. LAWRY'S SEASONED SALT 202
210. KRAFT STOVE TOP STUFFING MIX 203
211. CHICK-FIL-A SAUCE 204
212. BURGER SAUCE 205
213. POLLO TROPICAL'S CURRY MUSTARD SAUCE 206
214. EL FENIX CHILI GRAVY 207
215. SWEET AND SMOKY CHIPOTLE VINAIGRETTE 208
216. BANG BANG SAUCE 209
217. SWEET CHILI SAUCE 210
218. BIG MAC SAUCE 211
219. CARAMEL SAUCE 212
220. PAULA DEEN BBQ SAUCE 213
221. CHORIZO QUESO FUNDIDO 214
222. ALFREDO SAUCE 215

CHAPTER 9
OLD AND MODERN LUNCH AND DINNER RECIPES 217

223. P.F. CHANG'S CRISPY HONEY CHICKEN 218
224. BOSTON MARKET'S CHICKEN POT PIE 219
225. P.F. CHANG'S BEEF AND BROCCOLI 220
226. OUTBACK'S SECRET SEASONING MIX FOR STEAKS 221
227. TACO BELL'S CHALUPA 222
228. CHILI'S BABY BACK RIBS 223
229. APPLEBEE'S HONEY BARBECUE SAUCE WITH RIBLETS 224
230. CRACKER BARREL'S GREEN B EANS WITH BACON 225
231. CAFÉ RIO'S PORK 226
232. RUTH CHRIS'S FILET MIGNON WITH BÉARNAISE SAUCE 227
233. P.F. CHANG'S SPARE RIBS 228
234. BOSTON MARKET'S MEATLOAF 229
235. BONEFISH GRILL COPYCAT BANG BANG SHRIMP 230
236. BLACK ANGUS STEAKHOUSE'S BBQ BABY BACK RIBS 231
237. TEXAS ROAD HOUSE'S MESQUITE GRILLED PORK CHOPS WITH CINNAMON APPLES 232
238. PANDA EXPRESS'S GRILLED TERIYAKI CHICKEN 233
239. PANDA EXPRESS'S SWEET FIRE CHICKEN BREAST 234
240. PANDA EXPRESS'S BLACK PEPPER CHICKEN 235
241. PANDA EXPRESS'S ZUCCHINI MUSHROOM CHICKEN 236
242. PANDA EXPRESS'S ORANGE CHICKEN 237
243. PF CHANG'S ORANGE PEEL CHICKEN 238
244. PF CHANG'S CRISPY CHICKEN 239
245. PF CHANG'S CHICKEN FRIED RICE 240
246. PF CHANG'S GINGER CHICKEN WITH BROCCOLI 241
247. PEI WEI'S SPICY CHICKEN 242
248. PEI WEI'S CHICKEN PAD THAI 243
249. PEI WEI'S SESAME CHICKEN 244
250. PEI WEI'S ASIAN DINER CARAMEL CHICKEN 245
251. PEI WEI'S KUNG PAO CHICKEN 246
252. PEI WEI'S CHICKEN LO MEIN 247
253. TUSCAN GARLIC CHICKEN 248
254. STUFFED CHICKEN MARSALA 249
255. CHICKEN PICCATA 250
256. CHICKEN ALFREDO 251
257. PARMESAN CRUSTED CHICKEN 252
258. CHICKEN GIARDINO 253
259. CHICKEN AND SAUSAGE MIXED GRILL 254
260. CHICKEN GNOCCHI VERONESE 255
261. CHICKEN PARMIGIANA 256
262. CHICKEN AND SHRIMP CARBONARA 257
263. CHICKEN MARSALA 258
264. CHICKEN SCAMPI 259
265. CHICKEN MARGHERITA 260
266. CHICKEN CARBONARA 261
267. STEAK GORGONZOLA ALFREDO 262
268. CRACKER BARREL'S CHICKEN FRIED CHICKEN 263
269. BROCCOLI CHEDDAR CHICKEN 264
270. GRILLED CHICKEN

TENDERLOIN	265
271. CHICKEN CASSEROLE	266
272. SUNDAY CHICKEN	267
273. CREAMY CHICKEN AND RICE	268
274. CAMPFIRE CHICKEN	269
275. CHICKEN AND DUMPLINGS	270
276. CHICKEN POT PIE	271
277. GREEN CHILI JACK CHICKEN	272
278. APPLE CHEDDAR CHICKEN	273
279. CORNFLAKE CRUSTED CHICKEN	274
280. TURKEY 'N STUFFING	275
281. FARM-RAISED CATFISH	276
282. LEMON PEPPER TROUT	277

CHAPTER 10
OLD AND MODERN BREAD RECIPES **279**

283. BLACK AND BLUE BURGER	280
284. THE MADLOVE BURGER	281
285. THE SOUTHERN CHARM BURGER	282
286. A.I. PEPPERCORN BURGER	283
287. BANZAI BURGER	284
288. BLEU RIBBON BURGER	285
289. BURNIN LOVE BURGER	286
290. RED ROBIN BURGER	287
291. SAUTÉED MUSHROOM BURGER	288
292. WHISKY RIVER BURGER	289
293. TUSCAN BUTTER BURGER	290
294. FOUR CHEESE MELT	291
295. PUB MAC N CHEESE ENTREE	292
296. THE BOSS BURGER	293
297. ALEX'S SANTA FE BURGER	294
298. CHILI'S AVOCADO BEEF BURGER	295
299. CHILI'S 1975 SOFT TACOS	296

300. SPICY SHRIMP TACOS	297
301. RANCHERO CHICKEN TACOS	298
302. BEEF BACON RANCH QUESADILLAS	299
303. CHICKEN ENCHILADAS	300
304. CHICKEN FAJITAS	301
305. MUSHROOM JACK CHICKEN 7 FAJITAS	302
306. GAME DAY CHILI	304
307. ROASTED TURKEY, APPLE AND CHEDDAR	305
308. TUNA SALAD SANDWICH	306
309. LENTIL QUINOA BOWL WITH CHICKEN	307
310. PANERA'S MAC & CHEESE	308
311. ASIAGO CHEESE BREAD	309
312. WILD BLUEBERRY MUFFIN	310
313. CINNAMON CRUNCH BAGEL	311
314. COBBLESTONE	312
315. CINNAMON CRUNCH SCONE	313
316. BROWN BETTY	314
317. PECAN BRAID	315

CONCLUSION **317**

BOOK 2: COPYCAT RECIPES

INTRODUCTION	**321**	TEXAS ROADHOUSE	347
CHAPTER 1		25. CHILI'S CHILI	348
SIDE SALAD RECIPES	**323**	26. HAM SALAD	349
1. EGGPLANT PARMESAN	324	27. ITALIAN B.M.T. ® SALAD	350
2. LASAGNA FRITTA	325	28. ROASTED CHICKEN SALAD	351
3. FRIED MOZZARELLA	326	29. ROAST BEEF SALAD	352
4. GNOCCHI WITH SPICY		30. STEAK & CHEESE SALAD	353
TOMATO AND WINE SAUCE	327	31. SUBWAY CLUB ® SALAD	354
5. BRUSSELS SPROUT N'		32. SUBWAY MELT ® SALAD	355
KALE SALAD	328	33. CHICKEN TERIYAKI SALAD	356
6. BREADED FRIED OKRA	329	34. TUNA SALAD	357
7. OLIVE GARDEN SALAD	330	35. TURKEY SALAD	358
8. ESPERANZA HOUSE SALAD	331	**CHAPTER 2**	
9. SPINACH APPLE SALAD	332	**OLD AND MODERN SWEET**	
10. ANYTHING AND		**AND SAVORY SNACK RECIPES**	**359**
EVERYTHING SALAD	333	36. ROADHOUSE MASHED P	
11. CHILI'S SALAD	334	OTATOES	360
12. CRACKER BARREL FRIED APPLES	335	37. SWEET POTATOES WITH	
13. HASH BROWN CASSEROLE	336	MARSHMALLOWS AND	
14. CUCUMBERS, TOMATOES,		CARAMEL SAUCE	361
AND ONIONS	337	38. SAUTÉED MUSHROOMS	362
15. OLD COUNTRY STORE		39. HAM AND CHEESE EMPANADAS	363
BABY CARROTS	338	40. ROADHOUSE GREEN BEANS	364
16. HOUSE SALAD AND DRESSING	339	41. ROADHOUSE CHEESE FRIES	365
17. SANTA FE CRISPERS SALAD	340	42. DINNER ROLLS	366
18. QUESADILLA EXPLOSION SALAD	341	43. TEXAS RED CHILI	367
19. CARIBBEAN SHRIMP SALAD	342	44. BONELESS BUFFALO WINGS	368
20. SOUTHWEST CAESAR SALAD	343	45. TATER SKINS	369
21. RED BEANS FROM POPEYE'S	344	46. FRIED PICKLES	370
22. CAFÉ RIO'S SWEET PORK		47. RATTLESNAKE BITES	371
BARBACOA SALAD	345	48. CACTUS BLOSSOM	372
23. ALMOND CRUSTED		49. CRISPY CHEESY CHIPS	373
SALMON SALAD	346	50. BRINED CHICKEN BITES	374
24. DEEP FRIED PICKLES FROM		51. BLOOMIN' ONION	375

52. PEPPERONI CHIPS 376

53. MAC 'N CHEESE 377

54. RED LOBSTER FUDGE OVERBOARD 378

55. CHOCOLATE WAVE 379

56. HOUSTON'S APPLE WALNUT COBBLER 380

57. PAPA JOHN'S CINNAPIE 381

58. OLIVE GARDEN'S CHEESE ZITI AL FORNO 382

59. CHIPOTLE'S REFRIED BEANS 383

60. LOW FAT VEGGIE QUESADILLA 384

61. GARLIC MASHED POTATOES 385

62. VEGETABLE MEDLEY 386

63. MEGA MANGO SMOOTHIE 387

64. LASAGNA WITH FETA AND BLACK OLIVES 388

65. EASY COPYCAT MONTEREY'S LITTLE MEXICO QUESO 389

66. FRIED KETO CHEESE WITH MUSHROOMS 390

67. MUSHROOM RECIPE STUFFED WITH CHEESE, SPINACH, AND BACON 391

68. SHRIMP NACHOS WITH AVOCADO AND TOMATO SALSA 392

69. MIMOSA EGGS WITH TRUFFLE 393

70. SHRIMP TEMPURA 394

71. COPYCAT CHILI'S SOUTHWEST EGG ROLLS 395

72. HAM AND CHEESE GRINDERS 396

73. MOZZARELLA CHEESE STICKS RECIPE 397

74. COPYCAT MAC AND CHEESE WITH SMOKED GOUDA CHEESE AND PUMPKIN 398

75. BAKED BUFFALO MEATBALLS 399

CHAPTER 3

OLD AND MODERN FRUIT SALAD RECIPES 401

76. APPLE POMEGRANATE SALAD: WENDY'S™ COPYCAT 402

77. CRANBERRY FRUIT SALAD: THE FAMOUS LUBY'S CAFETERIA™ COPYCAT 403

78. FUJI APPLE CHICKEN SALAD: PANERA BREAD™ COPYCAT 404

79. MARKET SALAD: CHICK-FIL-A™ COPYCAT 405

80. STRAWBERRY POPPYSEED SALAD: PANERA™ COPYCAT 406

81. SWEET CARROT SALAD: CHICK-FIL-A™ COPYCAT 407

82. WALDORF SALAD: TEXAS LUBY'S CAFETERIA™ COPYCAT 408

83. COTTAGE CHEESE AND POPPY SEED MOUSSE WITH CHERRY WATER 409

84. GOOD MOOD FRUIT SALAD 410

85. FRUIT SALAD WITH LEMON FOAM 411

86. VEGAN AMARANTH PUDDING WITH FRUIT SALAD 412

87. QUICK FRUIT SALAD WITH SABAYON 413

88. TROPICAL FRUIT SALAD WITH COCONUT CREAM 414

89. EXOTIC FRUIT SALAD WITH COCONUT-LIME YOGHURT 415

90. GINGER FRUIT SALAD WITH VANILLA SAUCE 416

91. FRUIT SALAD WITH VANILLA SAUCE 417

92. FRUIT SALAD WITH YOGHURT CREAM 418

CHAPTER 4
OLD AND MODERN
DESSERT RECIPES   **419**

93. MAPLE BUTTER BLONDIE   420
94. MAPPLE CHIMI CHEESECAKE   421
95. TRIPLE CHOCOLATE MELTDOWN   422
96. CHOCOLATE MOUSSE DESSERT SHOOTER   423
97. DEADLY CHOCOLATE SIN   424
98. ORANGE CREAMSICLE CAKE   425
99. CINNAMON APPLE TURNOVER   426
100. BURGER KING'S HERSHEY'S SUNDAE PIE   427
101. CHILI'S CHOCOLATE BROWNIE SUNDAE   428
102. BEN & JERRY'S CHERRY GARCIA ICE CREAM   429
103. P.F. CHANG'S COCONUT PINEAPPLE ICE CREAM WITH BANANA SPRING ROLLS   430
104. TGI FRIDAY'S OREO MADNESS   431
105. BEN & JERRY'S CHUNKY MONKEY ICE CREAM   432
106. JACK IN THE BOX'S OREO COOKIE SHAKE   433
107. DAIRY QUEEN'S CANDY CANE CHILL   434
108. DAIRY QUEEN'S BLIZZARD   435
109. APPLEBEE'S MAPLE BUTTER BLONDIE   436
110. HOUSTON'S APPLE WALNUT COBBLER   437
111. MELTING POT CHOCOLATE FONDUE   438
112. P.F. CHANG'S GINGER PANNA COTTA   439

113. STARBUCKS' CRANBERRY BLISS BARS   440
114. OLIVE GARDEN'S TIRAMISU   441
115. MAPLE BUTTER BLONDIE   442
116. CHEF JOHN'S ZABAGLIONE   443
117. CHOCOLATE MOUSSE DESSERT SHOOTER   444
118. CINNAMON APPLE TURNOVER   445
119. CHERRY CHOCOLATE COBBLER   446
120. PUMPKIN CUSTARD WITH GINGERSNAPS   447
121. BAKED APPLE DUMPLINGS   448
122. PEACH COBBLER   449
123. CAMPFIRE S'MORES   450
124. BANANA PUDDING   451
125. CHILI'S NEW YORK STYLE CHEESECAKE   452
126. STARBUCK'S COPYCAT CRANBERRY CHOCOLATE BLISS BARS   453
127. CHOCOLATE PECAN   454
128. PEANUT BUTTER KISSES   455
129. PEANUT BUTTER & PECAN NUT CHEESECAKE   456
130. THREE-INGREDIENT CHOCOLATE MACADAMIA FAT BOMBS   458
131. GOAT CHEESE WITH STEWED BLACKBERRIES   459
132. RHUBARB TART   461
133. SAFFRON PANNA COTTA   461

CHAPTER 5
OLD AND MODERN
PASTRY RECIPES   **463**

134. CHESS PIE   464
135. COCONUT CREAM PIE BARS   465
136. CREAMY HAZELNUT PIE   466
137. THE FAMOUS WOOLWORTH ICE BOX CHEESECAKE   467

138. FROZEN BANANA SPLIT PIE 468

139. FROZEN PEACH PIE 469

140. KEY LIME PIE 470

141. STRAWBERRY LEMONADE FREEZER PIE 471

143. SWEET POTATO PIE 472

143. BLUEBERRY SOUR CREAM POUND CAKE 473

144. CARROT CAKE DELIGHT 474

145. FOUR LAYER PUMPKIN CAKE WITH FROSTING 475

146. GEORGIA PEACH POUND CAKE 476

147. PINEAPPLE PECAN CAKE WITH FROSTING 477

148. RED VELVET CAKE 478

149. PUMPKIN CHEESECAKE 479

150. REESE'S PEANUT BUTTER CHOCOLATE CAKE CHEESECAKE 480

151. WHITE CHOCOLATE RASPBERRY SWIRL CHEESECAKE 482

152. CARROT CAKE CHEESECAKE 483

153. ORIGINAL CHEESECAKE 484

154. ULTIMATE RED VELVET CHEESECAKE 485

155. STRAWBERRY SHORTCAKE 487

156. LEMONCELLO CREAM TORTE 488

157. OREO COOKIE CHEESECAKE 489

158. BANANA CREAM CHEESECAKE 490

159. BLACKOUT CAKE 491

160. MOLTEN LAVA CAKE 492

161. WHITE CHOCOLATE RASPBERRY NOTHING BUNDT CAKES 494

162. CARAMEL ROCKSLIDE BROWNIES 495

163. CORNBREAD MUFFINS 496

164. CHOCOLATE MOUSSE CAKE 497

165. BLACKBERRY AND APPLES COBBLER 498

166. BLACK TEA CAKE 499

167. QUINOA MUFFINS 500

168. FIGS PIE 501

CHAPTER 6

SOFT DRINK RECIPES **503**

169. LEMON AND BERRY SLUSH 504

170. TACO BELL'S PENA COLADA DRINK 505

171. CHICK FIL-A LEMONADE 506

172. DAIRY QUEEN BLIZZARD 507

173. WATERMELON AND MINT LEMONADE 508

174. SONIC OCEAN WATER 509

175. RAINFOREST CAFÉ'S STRAWBERRY LEMONADE 510

176. CHICK-FIL-A'S FROZEN LEMONADE COPYCAT 511

177. DUNKIN DONUT'S MINT HOT CHOCOLATE COPYCAT 512

178. TIM HORTON'S HOT APPLE CIDER COPYCAT 513

179. NEW ORLEANS' FAMOUS HURRICANES COPYCAT 514

180. RUBY TUESDAY'S RASPBERRY ICED TEA COPYCAT 515

181. MIKE'S HARD LEMONADE COPYCAT 516

182. CHICK-FIL-A'S FROSTED LEMONADE COPYCAT 517

183.CRYSTAL LIGHT'S BERRY SANGRIA MIX COPYCAT 518

CHAPTER 7

PRACTICAL ADVICE FOR BEGINNERS TO CANNING AND PRESERVING YOUR FAVORITE FOODS **519**

CONCLUSION **523**

ERNEST D.W
The World of Words

COPYCAT
COOKBOOK

Make Your Favorite Restaurant Dishes at Home with these
Low Budget Recipes for Beginners.

Gordon Benedict Richman

Introduction

Dining out is one of the things we enjoy the most. There's also something about dining out that makes dining all the more fun, whether alone or with friends. Catching up with friends, going out on a hot date, a fast drive-through, or celebrating a family occasion revolve around food. Dining out, however, can be expensive and time-consuming. You may never think you can re-create the food you order at PF Chang's, Panda Express, or Pei Wei.

Yeah, you're going in there, standing in line for what seems to be an eternity, and then charging for food you know is way too overpriced. What more if you could make traditional restaurant food from the comfort of your home! Yet what if all this didn't have to go through? Do not leave the house, do not wait in line, and do not waste money on expensive food — just the delicious taste of your favorite restaurant dishes and the assurance that you can replicate them in your kitchen whenever you wish. Come to think of the money you can save and waiting in line all the time lost. You can make delicious meals without leaving your own house, plus you'll know what ingredients are being used. With simple copycat recipes from the most famous restaurants, you can create your favorite restaurant dishes at home!

Before you know it, you can start eating like a restaurant chef! And you'll save lots of time! The recipes chosen for this book are intended to tickle your taste buds just like their original counterpart. The best part about those recipes influenced by the restaurant is that you can tweak them to suit your tastes. The recipe can involve grilling meat, but instead, you can always bake it or cook it in a skillet. Want shrimps over beef or chicken, turn with the ingredient you want. Don't like any vegetable or the spiciness level? Only change the appropriate ingredients, and you and your family will be delighted with the meal.

What prompted me to look for those so-called 'secret recipes' is the fact that once I located the one for my favorite well-known dish, I could revel in it every time I desired proper at home.

Another motive I wanted to locate some eating place copycat recipes is because you can save numerous cash by cooking those dishes yourself. No transportation cost, no tipping, and you may enjoy the meal without getting all dressed up. Plus, getting to decide on my portion's length is excellent. I can definitely eat the entire Fonduta myself if I had the chance.

These copycat recipes are tested repeatedly to make sure that you are creating precise dishes from the restaurant. Expert cooks spend hours tweaking those recipes to get the taste just right. These recipes are as near the real thing as sitting your favorite restaurant proper in your kitchen.

If you have an own family and like to go out to restaurants, but do not enjoy the nasty charge tag related to a terrific meal, then those eating place copycat recipes are for you.

You oughtn't to be a trained chef to prepare your pleasant personal meals at home with restaurant copycat recipes. All you need are eating place copycat recipes, the components listed, and get admission to your kitchen.

Imagine impressing your buddies and own family with food that they have most effectively enjoyed at some restaurants, proper from your very own domestic comfort. Visualize how fulfilling it would be to show them that you created those masterpieces within your kitchen's comfort with restaurant copycat recipes!

Chapter 1

BENEFITS OF COOKING AT HOME

M eals in the restaurant can contain several unhealthy ingredients. There is also much more than what you lack when you feed on a take-outs.

These are some explanations of why you should consider having your cooking dinner tonight!

A Nutrient-Dense Plate

If prepared food arrives from outside the home, you typically have limited knowledge about salt, sugar, and processed oils. For a fact, we also apply more to our meal when it is served to the table. You will say how much salt, sugar, and oil are being used to prepare meals at home.

Increased Fruit and Vegetable Intake

The typical western diet loses both the weight and durability of plant foods we need to preserve. Many People eat only two fresh fruit and vegetables a day, while at least five portions are required. Tons of premade food, like restaurant food goods, restrict fruit and vegetable parts.

By supplying you with the convenience of cooking at home, you have complete control over your food. The message to note is that your attention will continue with the intake of more fruit and vegetables. Attach them to your cooking, snack them, or exchange them with your relatives on their way. Then take steps towards organic alternatives. It is always better to eat entire fruits and vegetables, whether or not organic, than processed foods.

Save Money and Use What You Have

Just because you haven't visited your local health food or food store this week doesn't mean you get stuck with taking in. Open your cupboard and fridge and see what you can make for a meal. It can be as easy as gluten-free rice, roasted tomatoes, carrots, frozen vegetables, and lemon juice. This simple meal is packed with fiber, protein, vitamins, and minerals. Best of all, in less than 30 minutes, it is delicious and can be prepared. You can save up your money in the long run and allows you sufficient food to share with or break the next day.

Sensible Snacking

Bringing premade snacks saves time, but everything goes back to what's in these products still. Don't worry, you can still have your guilty pleasures, but there is a way to make them more nutritious and often taste better. Swap your chips and dip the chopped vegetables into hummus. Create your snacks with bagged potato chips or carrots. Take a bowl and make your popcorn on top of your stove or in the popcorn machine. You can manage the amount of salt, sugar, and oil added.

Share Your Delicious Health

Once you make your recipes, you are so proud of your achievements. Furthermore, the food tastes amazing. Don't confuse me now–some of your inventive recipes won't taste the same thing, but friends and family will love your cuisine with constant practice and experimentation. You will see them enjoy the best nutritious food because of you and your faith in spreading health and love.

It gives you a chance to reconnect

Having that chance to cook together helps you reconnect with your partner and your loved ones. Cooking also has other benefits. The American Psychological Association says that working together with new things — like learning a new recipe— can help maintain a relationship.

It's proven to be healthier

Many researchers say that those who eat more often than not have a healthier diet overall. Such studies also show that in restaurants, menus, salt, saturated fat, total fat, and average calories are typically higher than in-house diets.
You have complete control over your food, whether you put fresh products together or shipped them straight to your door using a company like Plated. It can make a difference in your overall health.

It's easier to watch your calories

The average fast-food order is between 1,100 and 1,200 calories in total—nearly all the highly recommended daily calorie intake is 1,600 to 2,400 calories by a woman and almost two thirds (2,000 to 3,000 calories) a man daily. So, think again if you felt the independent restaurants so smaller chains would do well. Such products suck up an average of 1.327 calories per meal of additional calories.

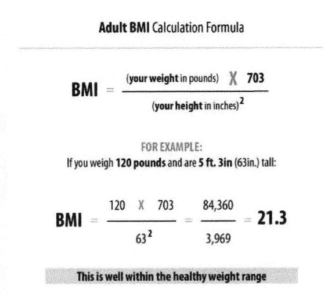

Adult BMI Calculation Formula

$$BMI = \frac{(\text{your weight in pounds}) \times 703}{(\text{your height in inches})^2}$$

FOR EXAMPLE:
If you weigh **120 pounds** and are **5 ft. 3in** (63in.) tall:

$$BMI = \frac{120 \times 703}{63^2} = \frac{84{,}360}{3{,}969} = 21.3$$

This is well within the healthy weight range

Creating your food ensures you can guarantee that the portion sizes and calories are where you want them. Recipes also come with nutritional information and tips for sizing, which ease this.

Body Mass Index Interpretation

BMI < 18.5:	Below normal weight
BMI >= 18.5 and < 25:	Normal weight
BMI >= 25 and < 30:	Overweight
BMI >= 30 and < 35:	Class I Obesity
BMI >= 35 and < 40:	Class II Obesity
BMI >= 40:	Class III Obesity

It's a time saver

Part of shopping is to wait for food to come or travel to get it. It may take much more time, depending on where you live, what time you order, and whether or not the delivery person is good at directions!
It doesn't have to take much time to cook at home if you don't want it. You remove the need to search for ingredients or foodstuffs by using a service like Plated. Everything you need is at your house, in the exact amount that you use.

It can be a money saver, too

In the long run, home-cooked food will save you money. A collection of basic ingredients also arrives at a lower price than a single dish. You can also consume more of a meal at home than if you buy a take-out or rest to work the next day. After a few weeks, you will see big savings starting to add up.

It's personalized

Cooking at home gives you the chance to enjoy the food you want, how you like it. For starters, with Plated, if you want your meat more well-done or less sweet, the formula includes suggested changes.

Cutting Costs

Nobody has to remind you that it's pricey to eat out. The disparity between a local restaurant sandwich and a kitchen sandwich is more than a feeling. The purchasing of packaged food in a restaurant typically costs far more than the buying of your products. Cooking at home helps you get more for your money by raising the excess expenses of cooking and servicing restaurants. The more often you make your food, the more money you save.

Enjoying the Process

Once you come back home from a busy day, there is little more enjoyable than disconnecting from work emails, voicemails, unfinished assignments, or homework. Cooking at home presents you with a break from your routine and space for imagination. Rather than listen to noisy messages, you should put on the radio, collect spices, and reflect on the sizzle's odors on the stove or roast vegetables. It may stun you on how much you might like it when you make a daily habit of preparing food.
If your breakfast is great, lunch soup, or fresh tomato sauce for dinner, home cooking is a worthy investment. In return for your time and energy in preparation, you will benefit richly— from cost savings to fun with friends.
And the more you enjoy cooking in the kitchen, the more you get to make fantastic food!

Try Plated

Ready to download and cook your smartphone? Plated is a kind of a meal kit delivery service that offers all the above and more positive features!
Choose from a weekly menu of designed recipes and get all you need right at your door. Pre-portioned foods are of the highest quality only and contain fresh, seasonal, organically, and sustainable seafood items and hormone-free meat.
Recipes vary from meals that require just 30 minutes to prepare, which is as demanding as its rewards. Where people find dinner a delight to consume and cook.

Chapter 2

PRACTICAL ADVICE FOR BEGINNERS ON THE CORRECT DISTRIBUTION OF MEALS DURING THE DAY, TO DIGEST WELL AND AVOID GAINING WEIGHT

Shifting to a healthy lifestyle seems to be intimidating. Being committed to your preferred diet, slowly and reasonably, will provide you lifelong changes and optimum health.

Start by selecting what seems doable to you. Follow your instincts when something piques your interest. You are the best at knowing what's right for you and what you will or will not eat or drink.

Be willing to trying something new because you will have to do something different, on purpose, if you want a different result. Don't worry about what you might give up. You don't have to decide to give up anything right now. Keep it easy. Once you go through the benefits of feeling better, having more energy, and looking better, it will be easier to embrace and maintain a healthy eating lifestyle.

The effortless mistake we've made by just only eating our food makes it a significant difference. It is vital to think that when it comes to our meals, timing is the key.

As for your breakfast, eating within 30 minutes of waking up is essential. 7 in the morning is the best time to have breakfast. Make sure to have your meal no later than 10 a.m. and always have protein in your breakfast.

Lastly, at 7 p.m., dinner is the perfect time to have your meal. It would be perfect for you to keep a 3 hours gap between dinner and bedtime. Have your meal before 10 p.m. because eating dinner close to bedtime might affect your good night's sleep. One way to adapt a healthy eating lifestyle is to add vegetables and fruit to what you already eat gradually.

- At breakfast, include bananas, blueberries, blackberries, strawberries, or raspberries. Add spinach, onions, or bell peppers to eggs or egg whites.
- At lunch, have a cup of vegetable soup or a salad with your meal.
- At dinner, include an extra serving or two of vegetables.

In between meals, try having a piece of fruit such as orange, peach, apple or pear, or vegetables like celery, cucumber, carrots, tomatoes, or bell pepper.

Meal dynamics is a way of saying that it's not just what you eat and when you eat that matters; how you eat matters, too! There are few variables in how one eats:

Your sequence: Main dish, salads, then dessert? How about having dessert first to guarantee that there is still room, instead of filling it all up? It is vital to deliberate on how customs lead us and to know whether it all makes sense. If you learn to yourself you want to have dessert, why not eat it first so you'll have time to relish it instead of stuffing it in when you're full?

Pace and duration: Are the meal more like a tweet or an essay? Is it more evocative of a furious choreography or ballroom dance? How long does it take to consume the meal?

Timing: If you have an AC eating schedule on your meals, do you eat your meal at the start of the eating window? Or at the end? Or do you nibble snack portion of foods through the window? Does it change anything if you eat carbohydrates first or last?

It can also be introduced that eating too heavy and too late promotes bad dreams, and the body focuses only on digestion and not on the regenerative processes of the body such as: skin renewal, treatment of infections and injuries of the body, hormones of satiety are not produced, the same as when you consume too much alcohol before going to bed.

Fast food may be adding to surplus fat in ways that go beyond being loaded with calories and engineered to have a compelling, appetite-stimulating taste and mouthfeel. Fast food is fast in another way: not only is it available quickly, but people tend to eat it and digest it promptly with complete absorption. The suitability of snacks such as burgers, smoothies, and fries helps you achieve your calorie intake worth for a day in those 10 minutes of eating them. With all of those calories flowing down to your throat, you won't be able to measure your calorie intake from the first bite of your meal. You just paid for the meal, so you eat every edge to get the maximum value. It may not be ideal, because those extra bites expand your stomach, so it will allow you to eat more food later on to have that same feeling of fullness. Stomach stretch is a viral sensation that helps you know when you've had enough; it prevents you from spraining your stomach by savoring those extra bites. You get your superior value by having those different bites later, if not necessary, getting rid of those excess calories is still better than stuffing it into your body. Be mindful of ordering meals to avoid left-overs.

To use meal dynamics as a tool, you:

1. Eat low-calorie, high-volume foods first: Soups and salads are great for this for reasons mentioned in the "Meal Composition" section. Besides soups and salads, you can snack on pickles, cucumbers, celery, carrots, grape tomatoes, and other low-calorie foods with high water content instead of concentrated calorie juice, nuts, chips, or rapidly digested foods. Remember the SuPeR-BCPs? (Sugars, pasta, rice, bread, cereal, and potatoes).
2. Nutrition experts say that you should focus on food by consciously sniffing and tasting so that your body can record the act of eating.

Take your time! Meals are not a pit stop where every second you reduce your eating time is an advantage for the daily rush.
Enjoy the aromas and the company of other people...

And if you have to eat alone, don't get tangled up in other activities at the same time. Do not chew or swallow hastily.
Bon appetite! If you take less than half an hour to eat, don't let your stomach and brain record everything you've eaten.

The dynamic of eating is to listen to your body and feel the natural feeling of satiety. Even if you eat fast food, you can correct your appetite by eating it slowly.

Chapter 3

OLD AND MODERN BREAKFAST RECIPES

1. IHoP's buTTermIlk PanCake

PREPARATION TIME: 5'

SERVINGS: 8-10

COOKING TIME: 8'

INGREDIENTS

- 1¼ cups all-purpose flour
- 1 teaspoon baking soda
- 1 teaspoon baking powder
- 1¼ cups granulated sugar
- 1 pinch salt
- 1 egg
- 1¼ cups buttermilk
- ¼ cup cooking oil

DIRECTIONS

1. Preheat your pan by leaving it over medium heat while you are preparing the pancake batter. Incorporate all the dry ingredients together, then combine all of your wet ingredients together as well.
2. Carefully combine the dry mixture into the wet mixture until everything is mixed together completely. Melt some butter in your pan.
3. Slowly pour batter into the pan until you have a 5-inch circle. Flip the pancake when its edges seem to have hardened. Cook the other side of the hotcake as well. Repeat steps six through eight until your batter is finished. Serve with softened butter and maple syrup.

NUTRITION: 180 Calories 7.9g Total Fat 23.2g Carbohydrates 4.1g Protein

2. STarbuCks's Marble Pound Cake

| PREPARATION TIME: | 10' | | SERVINGS: | 16 |

| COOKING TIME: | 1 h 30' |

INGREDIENTS

- 4½ cups cake flour
- 2 teaspoons baking powder
- 1/8 Teaspoon salt
- 6 ounces semisweet chocolate, finely chopped
- 2 cups unsalted butter, softened
- 3 cups granulated sugar
- 1 tablespoon vanilla
- 1 lemon, grated for zest
- 10 large eggs
- 2 tablespoons orange liquor OR milk

DIRECTIONS

1. Assemble your ingredients, and then: Preheat the oven to 350F; Grease a 10×4-inch tube pan;
2. Line the pan's bottom with greased wax paper, and Flour the entire pan. Sift together the cake flour, baking powder, and salt in a medium-sized bowl—this is your dry mixture.
3. Melt the chocolate in a medium-sized bowl, then beat in the butter. When it is smooth, mix in the sugar, lemon zest, and vanilla until the liquid mixture is uniform.
4. Beat eggs two at a time, until the mixture looks curdled.
5. Pour half of your dry mixture into your liquid mixture and mix until blended.
6. Add the orange liquor and the rest of the dry mixture. Continue beating the mixture.
7. When the mixture is blended, use a spatula to start folding it—this is your batter.
8. Set aside 4 cups of the batter. Whisk the softened chocolate with the batter.
9. Now that you have a light batter and a dark batter, place the batter into the tube pan by the spoonful, alternating between the two colors.
10. When the pan is full, shake it slightly to level the batter. Run a knife through the batter to marble it.
11. Put the dish within the stove and heat for an hour and 15 minutes. In case there are still a few damp pieces on the toothpick after you take it out, at that point, the cake is ready.
12. Remove the cake and leave it to rest overnight.

NUTRITION: 582 Calories 32g Total Fat 69g Carbohydrates 8.6g Protein

3. IHoP's Scrambled Egg

PREPARATION TIME: 5'	SERVINGS: 1

COOKING TIME: 5'

INGREDIENTS

- ¼ cup pancake mix
- 1–2 tablespoons butter
- 6 large eggs
- Salt and pepper, to taste

DIRECTIONS

1. Thoroughly beat the pancake mix and the eggs together until no lumps or clumps remain.
2. Butter a pan over medium heat. Add in the egg mixture in the middle of the pan. Add the salt and pepper and let the mixture sit for about a minute.
3. When the egg starts cooking, start pushing the edges of the mixture toward the middle of the pan. Continue until the entire mixture is cooked. Serve and enjoy.

NUTRITION: 870 Calories 54g Total Fat 9g Carbohydrates 69g Protein

4. Starbucks's Chocolate Cinnamon bread

PREPARATION TIME: 15'

SERVINGS: 16

COOKING TIME: 1 h

Ingredients

Bread:
- 1½ cups unsalted butter
- 3 cups granulated sugar
- 5 large eggs
- 2 cups flour
- 1¼ cups processed cocoa
- 1 tablespoon ground cinnamon
- 1 teaspoon salt
- ½ teaspoon baking powder
- ½ teaspoon baking soda
- ¼ cup water
- 1 cup buttermilk
- 1 teaspoon vanilla extract

Topping:
- ¼ cup granulated sugar
- ½ teaspoon cinnamon
- ½ teaspoon processed cocoa
- 1/8 Teaspoon ginger, ground
- 1/8 Teaspoon cloves, ground

Directions

1. Grease and preheat the oven to 350 degrees and line the bottoms of the pans with wax paper.
2. Cream the sugar by beating it with the butter. Beat the eggs into the mixture one at a time. Sift the flour, cocoa, cinnamon, salt, baking powder, and baking soda into a large bowl.
3. In another bowl, whisk together the water, buttermilk, and vanilla. Make a well in the dry mixture and start pouring in the wet mixtures a little at a time, while whisking.
4. When the mixture starts becoming doughy, divide it in two, and transfer it to the pans.
5. Combine together all the topping and sprinkle evenly on top of the mixture in both pans.
6. Bake until the bread has set.

NUTRITION: 370 Calories 14g Total Fat 59g Carbohydrates 7g Protein

5. Waffle House's Waffle

PREPARATION TIME: 5'

SERVINGS: 6

COOKING TIME: 20'

INGREDIENTS

- 1½ cups all-purpose flour
- 1 teaspoon salt
- ½ teaspoon baking soda
- 1 egg
- ½ cup + 1 tablespoon granulated white sugar
- 2 tablespoons butter, softened
- 2 tablespoons shortening
- ½ cup half-and-half
- ½ cup milk
- ¼ cup buttermilk
- ¼ teaspoon vanilla

DIRECTIONS

1. Prepare the dry mixture by sifting the flour into a bowl and mixing it with the salt and baking soda.
2. Lightly beat an egg until it becomes frothy, beat in the butter, sugar, and shortening. When the mixture is thoroughly mixed, beat in the half-and-half, vanilla, milk, and buttermilk. Continue beating the mixture until it is smooth.
3. While beating the wet mixture, slowly pour in the dry mixture, making sure to mix thoroughly and remove all the lumps.
4. Chill the batter overnight (optional but recommended; if you can't chill the mixture overnight, leave it for at least 15 to 20 minutes).
5. Take the batter out of the refrigerator. Preheat and grease your waffle iron.
6. Cook each waffle for three to four minutes. Serve with butter and syrup.

NUTRITION: 313 Calories 12g Total Fat 45g Carbohydrates 5.9g Protein

6. Mimi'sCafé SanTa fé OmeleT

PREPARATION TIME: 10'

SERVINGS: 1

COOKING TIME: 10'

INGREDIENTS

Chipotle Sauce:
* 1 cup marinara or tomato sauce
* ¾ cup water
* ½ cup chipotle in adobo sauce
* 1 teaspoon kosher salt

Omelet:
* 1 tablespoon onions, diced
* 1 tablespoon jalapeños, diced
* 2 tablespoons cilantro, chopped
* 2 tablespoons tomatoes, diced
* ¼ cup fried corn tortillas, cut into strips
* 3 eggs, beaten
* 2 slices cheese
* 1 dash of salt and pepper

Garnish:
* 2 ounces chipotle sauce, hot
* ¼ cup fried corn tortillas, cut into strips
* 1 tablespoon sliced green onions
* 1 tablespoon guacamole

DIRECTIONS

1. Cook butter over medium heat, making sure to coat the entire pan. Sauté the jalapeños, cilantro, tomatoes, onions, and tortilla strips for about a minute.
2. Pour the eggs, seasoning them with salt and pepper and stirring occasionally. Flip the omelet when it has set. Place the cheese on the top half.
3. When the cheese starts to become melty, fold the omelet in half and transfer to a plate. Garnish the omelet with chipotle sauce, guacamole, green onions, and corn tortillas.

NUTRITION: 519 Calories 32g Total Fat 60g Carbohydrates 14g Protein

7. aIICe SPrIngs CHICken from OuTbaCk

PREPARATION TIME: 5'	SERVINGS: 4

COOKING TIME: 2 H 30'

INGREDIENTS

Sauce:
- ½ cup Dijon mustard
- ½ cup honey
- ¼ cup mayonnaise
- 1 teaspoon fresh lemon juice

Chicken preparation:
- 4 chicken breast, boneless and skinless
- 2 tablespoons butter
- 1 tablespoon olive oil
- 8 ounces fresh mushrooms, sliced
- 4 slices bacon, cooked and cut into 2-inch pieces
- 2 ½ cups Monterrey Jack cheese, shredded
- Parsley for serving (optional)

DIRECTIONS

1. Preheat oven to 400 °F. Mix together ingredients for the sauce in a bowl.
2. Put the chicken in a Ziploc bag, then add the sauce into the bag until only ¼ cup is left. Keep the remaining sauce in a container, cover, and refrigerate. Make sure to seal the Ziploc bag tightly and shake gently until chicken is coated with sauce. Let it chill for 2 hours.
3. Cook butter in a pan over medium heat. Toss in mushrooms and cook for 5 minutes or until brown. Set aside, then transfer on a plate.
4. In an oven-safe pan, heat oil. Place marinated chicken flat in the pan and cook for 5 minutes on each side or until both sides turn golden brown.
5. Top with even amounts of mushroom, bacon, and cheese. Cover pan with oven-safe lid, then bake for 10 to 15 minutes until chicken is cooked through. Remove lid and bake an additional 1-3 minutes until the cheese is all melted.
6. Transfer onto a plate. Serve with remaining sauce on the side. Sprinkle chicken with parsley if desired

NUTRITION: 888 Calories 56g Total Fat 41g Carbohydrates 59g Protein

8. OrienTal Salad from aPPlebee's

PREPARATION TIME: 15'

SERVINGS: 6

COOKING TIME: 5'

INGREDIENTS

- 3 tablespoons honey
- 1½ tablespoons rice wine vinegar
- ¼ cup mayonnaise
- 1 teaspoon Dijon mustard
- 1/8 teaspoon sesame oil
- 3 cups vegetable oil, for frying
- 2 chicken breasts, cut into thin strips
- 1 egg
- 1 cup milk
- 1 cup flour
- 1 cup breadcrumbs
- 1 teaspoon salt
- ¼ teaspoon pepper
- 3 cups romaine lettuce, diced
- ½ cup red cabbage, diced
- ½ cup Napa cabbage, diced
- 1 carrot, grated
- ¼ cup cucumber, diced
- 3 tablespoons sliced almonds
- ¼ cup dry Chow Mein

DIRECTIONS

1. To make the dressing, add honey, rice wine vinegar, mayonnaise, Dijon mustard, and sesame oil to a blender. Mix until well combined. Store in refrigerator until ready to serve.
2. Cook oil over medium-high heat in a pan.
3. As the oil warms, whisk together egg and milk in a bowl. In another bowl, add flour, breadcrumbs, salt, and pepper. Mix well.
4. Dredge chicken strips in egg mixture, then in the flour mixture. Make sure the chicken is coated evenly on all sides. Shake off any excess.
5. Deep fry chicken strips for about 3 to 4 minutes until thoroughly cooked and lightly brown. Place onto a plate lined with paper towels to drain and cool. Work in batches, if necessary.
6. Chop strips into small bite-sized pieces once cool enough to handle.
7. Next, prepare the salad by adding romaine, red cabbage, Napa cabbage, carrots, and cucumber to a serving bowl. Top with chicken pieces, almonds, and chow Mein. Drizzle prepared dressing on top.
8. Serve immediately.

NUTRITION: 384 Calories 13g Total Fat 40g Carbohydrates 13g Sugar

9. baCon Mufflns

Preparation Time: 5'	Cooking Time: 15'	Servings: 4

Ingredients

- 12.7oz flour
- Salt Pepper
- Egg
- 1 tsp parsley
- Four bacon pieces
- 7.8fl oz milk
- Onion
- 2 tablespoons olive oil
- 3.5ounce Cheddar cheese
- 2 tsp powder

Directions

1. Preheat oven to 190C/170C fan forced. Line a 12-hole, 1/3 cup–capacity muffin pan with paper cases.
2. Heat oil over medium-high heat. Add bacon. Cook for 5 minutes or until crisp. Cool.
3. Combine sifted flour with pepper, cheese, chives, and bacon in a medium bowl. Make a well in the center. Add remaining ingredients, stirring until combined.
4. Spoon mixture into paper cases. Bake until golden and firm. Stand in pan for 5 minutes. Transfer to wire rack to cool.

Nutrition: 350 Calories 18g Fat 32g Carbohydrates16g Protein

10. breakfasT Mufflns

Preparation Time: 20'	Cooking Time: 20'	Servings: 2

Ingredients

- New Thyme 1.49fl oz almond milk
- Handfuls lettuce cooked veggies
- Salt Pepper
- 1 tbsp. coriander
- 3oz granola

Directions

1. Line and preheat the oven at 375 degrees. Transfer and whisk the eggs in a bowl until smooth.
2. Stir in the spinach, bacon, and cheese to the egg mixture to combine. Split the egg mixture evenly among the muffin cups. Bake until eggs are set.
3. Serve immediately. Garnish with diced tomatoes and parsley if desired.

Nutrition: 440 calories 28g Fat 28g Carbohydrates19g Protein

11. buTTermIlk bIsCulTs

PREPARATION TIME: 10'

SERVINGS: 4

COOKING TIME: 15'

INGREDIENTS

- 6.2ounces milk
- 1 tsp yeast
- 2 tbsp condensed milk
- 8.8ounce bread
- 1.4ounce butter
- 0.42-ounce milk powder
- Salt Sugar Herbs
- 1/2 cup cheddar cheese

DIRECTIONS

1. Grease and line the baking tray, then preheat the oven to 250 degrees. Bake until butter is melted.
2. Garnish with slices of cheese that cover the bread. Bake it again until the cheese is melted and golden brown.

NUTRITION: 60 Calories 1g Fat 7g Carbohydrates 12g Protein

12. Cheese on Soft Toast

PREPARATION TIME: 10'

SERVINGS: 4

COOKING TIME: 15'

INGREDIENTS

- 6.2ounces milk
- 1 tsp yeast
- 2 tbsp condensed milk
- 8.8ounce bread
- 1.4ounce butter
- 0.42-ounce milk powder
- Salt Sugar Herbs
- 1/2 cup cheddar cheese

DIRECTIONS

1. Grease and line the baking tray, then preheat the oven to 250 degrees. Bake until butter is melted.
2. Garnish with slices of cheese that cover the bread. Bake it again until the cheese is melted and golden brown.

NUTRITION: 60 Calories 1g Fat 7g Carbohydrates 12g Protein

13. Cookies with dark Chocolate

| PREPARATION TIME: | 10' | | SERVINGS: | 8 |

COOKING TIME: 10'

INGREDIENTS

- 10.6ounce bread Salt
- 4.4ounce butter
- 4.4ounce black chocolate
- 5.3ounce sugar
- 2 tsp vanilla essence
- 2 eggs
- 1 tbsp honey

DIRECTIONS

1. Heat oven to 325° F. baking sheets with parchment paper or lightly grease.
2. Soften 2/3 cup morsels in bowl on medium-high control the power for 30 seconds; Blend. Pieces may hold a few of their unique shape. Microwave at extra 10- to 15-second interims, blending fair until pieces are dissolved. Set aside.
3. Filter flour, cocoa, preparing pop, and salt in a bowl. Combine both sugar and butter until velvety. Include dissolved chocolate and blend well. Include egg and vanilla extricate, blending until well mixed, around 1 miniature. Include flour blend, blending fair until mixed. Mix in the remaining glass pieces. Drop mixture by level 1/4-cup degree 3 inches separated onto arranged preparing sheets.
4. Prepare for 16 to 18 minutes or until wooden choose embedded in the center comes out with damp scraps and the tops have a split appearance. Cool on preparing sheets for 5 minutes. Evacuate to wire rack to cool totally.

NUTRITION: 83 Calories 2g Fat 15g Carbohydrates 3g Protein

14. Corn Pudding with bacon

Preparation Time: 10'		Servings: 7

Cooking Time: 60'

Ingredients

- 4 tablespoons bacon
- 2 tsp garlic
- 1 tbsp butter
- 1 1/2 cup milk Onion
- 1/2 Bell-pepper
- Thyme leaves
- 1/2 cup lotions
- 2 tsp corn
- 1/4 cup lettuce
- 3 cups cubed bread
- 3 tablespoons Parmesan Salt Pepper
- 1 cup pasta

Directions

1. Grease baking dish with margarine, then preheat the oven to 325 degrees.
2. Cook 3 slices of bacon until crispy. Cut bacon into small pieces. Melt butter. Mix eggs, butter, and spices together in a bowl.
3. Mix in flour, creamed corn, light cream, & bacon until smooth.
4. Transfer the mixture to a baking dish. Bake for 1 hour and 30 minutes as it cools, the corn pudding deflates. Serve warm. Enjoy!

Nutrition: 360 Calories 21g Fat 60g Carbohydrates 23g Protein

15. Egg rolls

PREPARATION TIME: 5'

SERVINGS: 6

COOKING TIME: 7'

INGREDIENTS

- 0.35-pound beef
- 3/4 cup cabbage egg roll wrappers
- Spray to prevent sticking

DIRECTIONS

1. Warm the 2 teaspoons of vegetable oil in a huge dish over medium-high heat. Include the ground pork and season it with salt and pepper. Cook the pork with a spatula, until the meat is browned and cooked through. Include the garlic and ginger at that point, mix within the coleslaw blend and green onions.
2. Cook until cabbage is shriveled. Stir the soy sauce and sesame oil, at that point, evacuate from heat. Spoon roughly 2-3 tablespoons of filling into each egg roll wrapper and crease concurring to bundle headings.
3. Pour 2-3 inches of oil into a profound pot. Heat the oil to 350 degrees. Broil 3-4 egg rolls at a time, turning sometimes, until browned all over, roughly 3-5 minutes. Drain on paper towels, at that point, serve with plunging sauce of your choice.

NUTRITION: 140 Calories 16g Fat 2g Carbohydrates 2g Protein

16. HasH broWn Casserole

| Preparation Time: | 10' | | Servings: | 8 |

| Cooking Time: | 15' |

Ingredients

- 3 cups cauliflower stalks, shredded
- 1 cup sour cream
- 1/2 cup mayonnaise
- 1/2 cup Monterey jack cheese, shredded
- 1/2 cup cheddar cheese, shredded
- 4 tbsp butter
- 1 tbsp bouillon powder
- 1 tbsp onion, minced
- 1 tsp salt
- 1/2 tsp pepper
- cooking spray

Directions

1. Grease baking dish with a cooking spray. Put aside 1 tbsp each of the shredded cheese for topping. In a mixing bowl, combine all listed ingredients well. Pour the mixture into the greased baking dish. Sprinkle on top the reserved shredded cheeses.
2. Pre-heat the oven to 350 degrees F. Bake the casserole for 50 minutes until it turns bubbly and golden.

Nutrition: 271 Calories 3g Carbs 26g Fats 5g Protein

17. Cranberry bliss bars (STarbuCks)

PREPARATION TIME: 10'

SERVINGS: 16

COOKING TIME: 15'

INGREDIENTS

- 1/3 cup sweetener of your choice
- 1/4 cup coconut flour
- 1/4 cup almond flour
- 1/4 cup ground golden flax
- 1 cup fresh cranberries
- 6 tbsp butter, softened
- 1 tsp vanilla extract
- 1 tsp molasses
- 1 tsp baking powder
- 1/2 tsp orange extract
- 1/2 tsp pure stevia
- 2 eggs
- pinch salt
- cooking spray
- For the frosting:
- 1/2 cup powdered sweetener
- 1 tbsp butter, softened
- 4 oz cream cheese, softened
- 4 drops lemon extract

DIRECTIONS

1. Toss the fresh cranberries in a food processor together with the stevia. Grease baking dish with cooking spray.
2. Combine the sweetener and butter and cream them together. Add in the eggs, salt, orange and vanilla extracts, and molasses. Mix well.
3. Put in the dry ingredients and mix thoroughly. Fold the cranberries into the mixture. Pour mixture in a greased baking dish.
4. Pre-heat the oven to 350 degrees F. Bake the batter for 30 minutes until it turns golden brown. Set it aside to cool down, usually around 15 minutes.
5. In a mixing bowl, combine together the ingredients for frosting until the mixture becomes fluffy.
6. Lightly place the frosting evenly on top of the cooked bars. Be gentle enough that the bars will not crumble. Put in the fridge until cold and firm enough to be cut into small squares.

NUTRITION: 110 Calories 3g Carbs 10g Fats 2g Protein

18. egg bItes (STarbuCks)

PREPARATION TIME:	10'	SERVINGS:	12

COOKING TIME: 20'

INGREDIENTS

- 10 eggs
- 1 cup cheese of your choice, shredded
- 1 cup bacon, cooked
- 1/2 cup heavy whipping cream
- 1 red pepper, chopped
- 1 tsp salt
- 1 tsp pepper
- spray oil

DIRECTIONS

1. Prepare a muffin pan made of tin or silicone by spraying with cooking oil. Blend all the ingredients and mix well.
2. Pour the blended mixture into the muffin molds. Each mold should be 3/4 full, only to give some room for the batter to rise. Pre-heat the oven to 350 degrees F.
3. In the lowest rack of the oven, put a pan filled with 2 cups of water. Place the muffin pan with the egg bites on the rack in the middle of the oven. Bake the eggs bites for 20 minutes or until they turn golden brown.

NUTRITION: 145 Calories 1g Carbs 12g Fats 9g Protein

19. Chicken Nuggets (Chick-fil-a)

Preparation Time: 10'	Servings: 5

Cooking Time: 15'

Ingredients

- 1 lb. chicken breasts
- 1 1/2 cups pork rinds, crushed
- 1/2 cup pickle juice
- 1 egg, beaten
- 1/2 tsp garlic powder
- 1/2 tsp salt
- 1/4 tsp paprika
- A pinch of pepper

Directions

1. Slice the chicken breasts into 1-inch nuggets. Put the nuggets in a resealable plastic bag. Add in the pickle juice into the bag. Put in the fridge to marinate for at least 2 hours.
2. Put the pork rinds in a food processor. Pulse the pork rinds until they look like breadcrumbs. Transfer the pork rinds into a mixing bowl. Combine all the spices and stir well. Put the pork rind mixture in a resealable plastic bag.
3. Take the chicken nuggets out from the refrigerator. Transfer the nuggets into another resealable plastic bag. Put the egg into the plastic bag with the chicken nuggets. Squish the egg all over the nuggets and make sure that each nugget is completely coated with the egg.
4. Transfer the chicken nuggets into the plastic bag with the pork rind mixture. Use tongs when doing this step. Seal the bag. Squish the bag to make sure that each nugget is heavily coated with the pork rind mixture.
5. Arrange all the chicken nuggets on a roasting rack with a baking sheet lined with parchment paper underneath. Pre-heat the oven to 425 degrees F. Bake the nuggets for 20 minutes until they are golden brown.

Nutrition: 261 Calories 1g Carbs 9.4g Fats 44.6g Protein

20. Pretzels (auntie anne's)

PREPARATION TIME: 5'

SERVINGS: 8

COOKING TIME: 10'

INGREDIENTS

- 2 1/2 cups mozzarella cheese, shredded
- 1 cup almond flour
- 1 tbsp butter, melted
- 1 tbsp coarse salt
- 2 tsp xanthan gum
- 2 tsp baking powder
- 1/2 tsp table salt
- 2 eggs

DIRECTIONS

1. Put the mozzarella in a microwavable bowl. Microwave the mozzarella for 30 seconds to melt. Stir the cheese to avoid getting burnt. Microwave again for another 30 seconds, then stir again. Repeat the process as needed until the mozzarella has melted completely.
2. Add into the melted cheese the almond flour, table salt, xanthan gum, and baking powder. Mix well.
3. Put in the eggs. Mix until a dough is formed.
4. Microwave the dough for 20 seconds. Mix well after taking out from the microwave.
5. You will now have a very sticky dough, but still workable enough to make it into pretzels.
6. Divide the dough equally into 8 portions. Roll each portion into a thin log that is long enough to twist into a pretzel.
7. Fold the logs into pretzels. Arrange the pretzels on a cookie sheet lined with parchment paper.
8. Brush the pretzels with melted butter. Sprinkle the coarse salt on top of the pretzels.
9. Pre-heat the oven to 350 degrees F.
10. Bake the pretzels for 25 minutes or until they all golden brown. If the pretzels have turned brown before the 25-minute time is up, then cover with aluminum foil to continue cooking the insides of the pretzels.

NUTRITION: 226 Calories 3g Carbs 17g Fats 15g Protein

21. Cinnamon rolls (Cinnabon)

PREPARATION TIME: 15'

SERVINGS: 6

COOKING TIME: 20'

INGREDIENTS

For the rolls:
- 1 cup mozzarella cheese, shredded
- 1/2 cup almond flour
- 1-ounce cream cheese
- 2 tbsp Lakanto monk fruit
- 1 tbsp coconut flour
- 1 egg, beaten
- 1 tsp baking powder
- 1 tsp vanilla
- 1/4 tsp salt

For greasing:
- 2 tbsp butter, melted
- 1/2 tsp cinnamon powder
- For the filling:
- 3 tbsp butter, melted
- 1 1 /2 tsp cinnamon powder
- 2 tbsp Lakanto golden monk fruit

For the topping:
- 4 oz cream cheese, softened
- 1/4 cup powdered monk fruit
- 2 tbsp heavy whipping cream
- 2 tbsp butter, softened
- 1/2 tsp vanilla extract
- 1/4 tsp almond extract

DIRECTIONS

To make the rolls:
1. Make the cinnamon butter to be used for greasing. Mix the two ingredients listed for greasing in a small container. Get 3 small spring pans and grease them with the cinnamon butter.
2. In a mixing bowl, combine the almond flour, egg, monk fruit, vanilla, coconut flour, salt, and baking powder. Set aside.
3. In a microwave safe mixing bowl, put in the cream cheese and mozzarella cheese. Microwave the cheeses to melt (about 60 seconds). Stir well to combine.
4. Put the flour mixture into the melted cheese mixture. Use your hands to manually mix the dough. It will take some time for the two mixtures to combine. Just keep squishing them between your fingers, and they will eventually turn into dough.
5. Divide dough into 3 equal portions. Put them in the fridge to set for about 5 minutes.
6. Roll out dough into long logs. The circumference of the log is about the size of your thumb.

To make the filling:
7. In a mixing bowl, combine the cinnamon powder, monk fruit, and melted butter. Use a brush to paint the filling mixture on all sides of each log. Reserve a small amount of filling in the bowl to be used later.
8. Swirl each log into a greased spring pan. Paint the top of each swirled log with the reserved filling. Pre-heat the oven to 350 degrees F. Bake the rolls for 16 minutes.

To make the topping:
9. In another mixing bowl, put in the listed ingredients for the topping. Mix using hand beaters until the mixture becomes creamy. Spread on top of the rolls. Slice each roll into two and serve.

NUTRITION: 294 Calories 4g Carbs 28g Fats 7g Protein

22. The french Toasts from denny's

PREPARATION TIME: 10'

SERVINGS: 8

COOKING TIME: 12'

INGREDIENTS

Batter:
- 4 eggs
- 2/3 cup whole milk
- 1/3 cup flour
- 1/3 cup sugar
- ½ teaspoon vanilla extract
- ¼ teaspoon salt
- 1/8 teaspoon cinnamon

Other ingredients
- 6 slices bread loaf, sliced thick
- 3 tablespoons butter
- Powdered sugar for dusting
- Syrup as desired

DIRECTIONS

1. Mix in the ingredients for the batter in a bowl. Soak bread slices in batter one at a time for at least 30 seconds on both sides. Allow excess batter to drip off. Melt 1 tablespoon of butter in a pan, cook the battered bread over medium heat for 2 minutes, or until each side is golden brown. Move slice to a plate.
2. Repeat with the remaining slices of bread, adding more butter to the pan if needed.
3. Dust with powdered sugar, if desired, and with syrup poured on top.

NUTRITION: 264 Calories 11g Total Fat 33g Carbs 8g Protein

23. IHoP's HealTHy "HarvesT graln 'n nuT" PanCakes

PREPARATION TIME: 5'

SERVINGS: 4

COOKING TIME: 5'

INGREDIENTS

- 1 teaspoon olive oil
- ¾ cup oats, powdered
- ¾ cup whole wheat flour
- 2 teaspoons baking soda
- 1 teaspoon baking powder
- ½ teaspoon salt
- 1½ cup buttermilk
- ¼ cup vegetable oil
- 1 egg
- ¼ cup sugar
- 3 tablespoons almonds, finely sliced
- 3 tablespoons walnuts, sliced
- Syrup for serving

DIRECTIONS

1. Heat oil in a pan over medium heat. While the pan preheats, pulverize oats in a blender until powdered. Then, add to a large bowl with flour, baking soda, baking powder, and salt. Mix well.
2. Add buttermilk, oil, egg, and sugar in a separate bowl. Mix with an electric mixer until creamy. Mix in wet ingredients with dry ingredients, then add nuts. Mix everything together with the electric mixer.
3. Scoop ⅓ cup of batter and cook in the hot pan for at least 2 minutes or until both sides turn golden brown. Transfer onto a plate, then repeat for the remaining batter. Serve with syrup.

NUTRITION: 433 Calories 24g Total Fat 46g Carbs 12g Protein

24. McDonald's Sausage Egg McMuffin

| PREPARATION TIME: | 10' | | SERVINGS: | 4 |

| COOKING TIME: | 15' |

INGREDIENTS

- 4 English muffins, cut in half horizontally
- 4 slices American processed cheese
- ½ tablespoon oil
- 1-pound ground pork, minced
- ½ teaspoon dried sage, ground
- ½ teaspoon dried thyme
- 1 teaspoon onion powder
- ¾ teaspoon black pepper
- ¾ teaspoon salt
- ½ teaspoon white sugar
- 4 large ⅓-inch onion ring slices
- 4 large eggs
- 2 tablespoons water

DIRECTIONS

1. Preheat oven to 300°F. Cover one half of the muffin with cheese, leaving one half uncovered. Transfer both halves to a baking tray. Place in oven.
2. For the sausage patties, use your hands to mix pork, sage, thyme, onion powder, pepper, salt, and sugar in a bowl. Form into 4 patties. Make sure they are slightly larger than the muffins.
3. Heat oil in a pan. Cook patties on both sides for at least 2 minutes each or until all sides turn brown. Remove the muffin tray from the oven. Place cooked sausage patties on top of the cheese on muffins. Return tray to the oven.
4. In the same pan, position onion rings flat into a single layer. Crack one egg inside each of the onion rings to make them round. Add water carefully into the sides of the pan and cover. Cook for 2 minutes.
5. Remove the muffin tray from the oven. Add eggs on top of patties, then top with the other muffin half. Serve warm.

NUTRITION: 453 Calories 15g Total Fat 67g Carbs 15g Protein

25. Starbucks' Spinach and feta breakfast Wraps

PREPARATION TIME: 5'

SERVINGS: 6

COOKING TIME: 20'

Ingredients

- 10 ounces spinach leaves
- 1 14½-ounce can dice tomatoes, drained
- 3 tablespoons cream cheese
- 10 egg whites
- ½ teaspoon oregano
- ½ teaspoon garlic salt
- 1/8 teaspoon pepper
- 6 whole wheat tortillas
- 4 tablespoons feta cheese, crumbled
- Cooking Spray

Directions

1. Apply a light coating of cooking spray to a pan. Cook spinach leaves on medium-high heat for 5 minutes or until leaves wilt, then stir in tomatoes and cream cheese. Cook for an additional 5 minutes or until cheese is melted completely. Remove from pan and place into a glass bowl and cover. Set aside.
2. In the same pan, add egg whites, oregano, salt, and pepper. Stir well and cook at least 5 minutes or until eggs are scrambled. Remove from heat.
3. Microwave tortillas for 30 seconds or until warm. Place egg whites, spinach and tomato mixture, and feta in the middle of the tortillas. Fold sides inwards, like a burrito. Serve.

NUTRITION: 157 Calories 3g Total Fat 19g Carbs 14g Protein

26. Jimmy dean's Homemade Pork Sage Sausage

PREPARATION TIME: 5'

SERVINGS: 4

COOKING TIME: 20'

INGREDIENTS

- 1-pound ground pork
- 1 teaspoon salt
- ½ teaspoon dried parsley
- ¼ teaspoon rubbed sage
- ¼ teaspoon black pepper, ground
- ¼ teaspoon dried thyme
- ¼ teaspoon coriander
- ¼ teaspoon seasoned salt

DIRECTIONS

1. Mix all ingredients in a bowl. Shape into patties. Then, cook in a pan on medium heat until meat is brown on both sides and cooked through. Serve.

NUTRITION: 313 Calories 24g Total Fat 4g Carbs 19g Protein

27. Panera Power breakfast Sandwich

PREPARATION TIME: 10'	SERVINGS: 1

COOKING TIME: 7'

INGREDIENTS

- 2 egg whites
- 1 teaspoon butter, divided in half
- 1 bagel thin, cut in half
- Mustard
- ¼ avocado, sliced
- 1 large tomato slice
- 4 spinach leaves
- 1 slice Swiss cheese

DIRECTIONS

1. Cook egg whites for about 1 minute in a small tightly covered custard cup in the microwave. Apply ½ teaspoon butter to both thin halves of the bagel. Coat inside of top bagel half with mustard and the other with avocado. Place egg whites, tomato, spinach leaves, and cheese on the bottom bagel thin. Top with another thin half of bagel.
2. Coat a heated pan with a thin layer of cooking spray, pan fry sandwich on medium-high heat for 3 minutes on each side or until golden brown and cheese is melted. I use a panini press for this step. Serve immediately.

NUTRITION: 277 Calories 10g Total Fat 30g Carbs 22g Protein

28. mcDonald's mcGriddle breakfast sandwich

PREPARATION TIME: 1 H

SERVINGS: 4

COOKING TIME: 15'

INGREDIENTS

- ½ cup maple syrup
- 1 cup flour
- 1 teaspoon baking powder
- ½ teaspoon baking soda
- 1 cup buttermilk
- 2 tablespoons butter, melted
- 1 egg
- Softened butter to grease the mold
- 4 slices American cheese
- 4 eggs, scrambled
- 4 strips bacon, cooked and cut in half

DIRECTIONS

1. Line a baking tray with parchment paper and set aside.
2. Add maple syrup to a pot and bring to a boil over medium heat while stirring often. Keep stirring the syrup even when already boiling. At about 230 °F, after about a minute of boiling, the syrup will appear a bit darker, and the boiling will lessen to some degree. Cook for about 2 more minutes or until the syrup becomes darker and begins to smell a bit like caramel. It is ready to be removed from heat once it reaches 265 °F.
3. Pour maple syrup onto the prepared baking sheet. Spread evenly in a thin layer with a spatula. Refrigerate until cool. Flip the syrup over, with parchment paper now on top. Then peel off the paper and break the solidified syrup into tiny pieces.
4. To make the pancakes, combine flour, baking powder, and baking soda in a large bowl. Set aside.
5. In another bowl, add buttermilk, butter, and egg. Mix together until fully combined. Then pour onto dry ingredients and mix well until incorporated.
6. Preheat electric griddle to medium-high heat.
7. Coat insides of round molds with softened butter, then place on a hot griddle coated with butter over medium heat. Add about 2 tablespoons pancake batter into each mold, then sprinkle maple crystals on top. Afterward, add 2 more tablespoons of pancake batter on top, sandwiching the maple crystals inside the pancakes.
8. Once bubbles form and edges look cooked, remove molds and flip pancakes. Cook for an additional 1 to 2 minutes.
9. To assemble the sandwiches, add cheese, scrambles egg, and bacon on pancake, then top with another pancake. Serve immediately.

NUTRITION: 419 calories 15g total fat 55g carbs 24g sugar

29. dIy CalIfornIa a.m. CrunCH WraP

PREPARATION TIME: 10'	SERVINGS: 4

COOKING TIME: 20'

INGREDIENTS

- 4 frozen hash brown patties
- 5 large eggs
- 1 tablespoon milk
- Salt and pepper, to taste
- 4 large tortillas
- 1 cup cheddar cheese, shredded
- 4 strips of thick cut bacon, cooked and crumbled
- 2 ripe California avocados, peeled and pitted
- 4 tablespoons Pico de Gallo

DIRECTIONS

1. Cook hash brown patties until crisp, based on package instructions. Add eggs, milk, salt, and pepper in a bowl. Mix well until combined. Then pour onto a skillet and cook until scrambled. Set aside.
2. Heat two different-sized (one smaller than the other) heavy bottomed pans over medium heat. Once heated, place tortillas into the bigger pan and, in even amounts, add cheese, a hash brown patty, eggs, bacon, avocado, and Pico de Gallo in the center of the tortilla in that order.
3. Using a wheel pattern, fold the tortilla around the filling with the edge facing up. Place heated smaller pan (such as a cast iron skillet) on top for about 20 seconds or until browned. Serve immediately.

NUTRITION: 933 calories 51g total fat 91g carbs 1g sugar

30. Panera Spinach and Cheese Egg Soufflé

Preparation Time: 15'	Servings: 4

Cooking Time: 25'

Ingredients

- 1 tube butter flake crescent rolls
- 6 eggs, divided
- 2 tablespoons milk
- 2 tablespoons heavy cream
- ¼ cup cheddar cheese, grated
- ¼ cup jack cheese, grated
- 1 tablespoon Parmesan cheese
- 3 tablespoons fresh spinach, minced
- 4 slices of bacon, cooked and crumbled
- Cooking spray
- ¼ teaspoon salt
- ¼ cup Asiago cheese, grated, divided

Directions

1. Preheat oven to 375°F.
2. Add 5 eggs, milk, heavy cream, cheddar cheese, jack cheese, parmesan cheese, spinach, bacon, and salt to a nonreactive bowl. Mix well until combined, then heat in the microwave for about 30 seconds. Stir, then microwave for another 20 seconds. Repeat about 5 times or until egg mixture is a bit thicker but still runny and uncooked.
3. Roll out crescent roll dough. Make 4 rectangles by pressing together the triangles. Then, using a rolling pin, stretch them out until they are 6in x 6in square.
4. Coat ramekin with cooking spray and place flattened roll inside, making sure the edges are outside the ramekin. Add 1/3 cup egg mixture and then about 1/8 cup Asiago cheese. Wrap edges of the roll-on top. Repeat for remaining rolls.
5. Whisk remaining egg with salt lightly in a bowl then, with a pastry brush, brush on top of each crescent roll dough. Place ramekins in the oven and bake for 20 minutes or until brown. Serve.

Nutrition: 303 calories 25g total fat 4g carbs

31. Young egg foo

PREPARATION TIME: 10'

SERVINGS: 6

COOKING TIME: 5'

INGREDIENTS

- 1/2 cup of green bell pepper
- 1/4 cup of bean sprouts cut in half
- 1 tablespoon of light soy sauce
- 8 large eggs
- 1/2 yellow onion
- 1/2 cup of carrots chunks
- 1/4 cup of green peas
- 3 tablespoons of sesame oil, divided

DIRECTIONS

1. Add the onion, eggs, mushroom, bell pepper, soy sauce, and bean sprouts together in a bowl. Whisk to combine. Heat 1 teaspoon of sesame oil at a time for each and cook on medium heat in a large skillet.
2. Add 1/3 cup of the mixture per pancake. Cook on the first side for 3 to 4 minutes and on the second side for 1 to 2 minutes. Serve and enjoy.

NUTRITION: 170 calories 13g total fat 2g Carbohydrates

32. Cheese Egg Souffle with Spinach

Preparation Time:	15'	**Servings:**	4

Cooking Time: 20'

Ingredients

- 1/4 cup of shredded sharp cheddar cheese
- 1/4 cup of shredded Monterey Jack cheese
- 1 tablespoon of Parmesan cheese
- 1 (8 ounces) tube Pillsbury butter flake crescent rolls
- 6 large eggs (keep 1 aside so you can use it to brush the tops of the crescent rolls)
- 2 tablespoons of milk
- 2 tablespoons of heavy cream
- 3 tablespoons fresh spinach
- 4 slices bacon
- 1/4 teaspoon of salt
- 1/4 cup of shredded Asiago cheese

Directions

1. Preheat the oven to 375 degrees F. Combine milk, 5 eggs, heavy cream, Monterey Jack cheese, cheddar cheese, spinach, Parmesan cheese, salt, and bacon in a small microwaveable bowl. Mix them all together, and microwave the mixture for about 30 seconds. Stir the mixture, then microwave for about 4 to 5 minutes in 20 seconds intervals. You want the egg mixture to get just a tad thickened. It'll be uncooked and very runny, the fact it just a tiny bit thicker, which will assist hold up the crescent roll dough when you fold it over the top. Unroll the crescent roll dough. Separate it into 4 rectangles. To make the rectangles, press the perforated triangles together. Roll out each rectangle for about 6 by 6 square until it is in. Use cooking spray to spray four souffle or ramekin dishes (about 4 to 5 inches in diameter). Lay a rolled-up crescent roll in each of the dishes, with the edges hanging over the sides.

2. Pour 1/3 cup of egg mixture on top of each crescent roll dough. On top of the egg mixture, sprinkle the Asiago cheese, dividing the cheese between the 4 ramekins. Over the egg mixture, fold the crescent roll dough. Take the eggs left and lightly beat in a small dish. Brush the egg on top of the crescent roll dough using a pastry brush. Bake until browned on top, at 375 degrees for about 20 minutes. Serve and enjoy.

Nutrition: 513 Calories 37g Total fat: 24g Carbohydrates 21g Protein

33. STaCk PanCakes

| PREPARATION TIME: | 10' | | SERVINGS: | 6 |

| COOKING TIME: | 15' |

INGREDIENTS

- 1 cup all-purpose flour
- 1 teaspoon baking powder
- 1/2 tablespoon sugar
- 1/2 teaspoon salt
- 1 large egg
- 3/4 cup milk
- 1/4 teaspoon vanilla extract
- 1 tablespoon butter, melted
- 1 teaspoon butter for the pan

DIRECTIONS

1. In a large bowl, whisk together the flour, baking powder, sugar, and salt.
2. In another bowl, beat the egg and then whisk in the milk, vanilla, and melted butter.
3. Pour the wet ingredients into the dry ingredients and mix until just incorporated. If the batter seems too thick, add more of the milk, a little at a time.
4. Melt the butter in a large skillet or griddle over medium heat.
5. Ladle about 3/4 cup of the batter onto the skillet to make a pancake.
6. Cook until bubbles break the surface of the pancake, and the underside is golden brown, about 3 minutes.
7. Flip with a spatula and cook about 1 minute more on the second side. Remove from the pan and place on a plate.
8. Repeat until all the batter is used up.
9. Serve with your favorite toppings: butter, syrup, fruit, or any other topping you desire.

NUTRITION: 684 Calories 37g Total fat: 83g Carbohydrates 7g Protein

34. Pillsbury Sweet Roll with Orange Juice

Preparation Time: 3'	Servings: 15

Cooking Time: 30'

Ingredients

Dough
- 2 1/4 teaspoons active dry yeast
- 1/2 cup warm water
- fresh orange zest; from 1 medium-sized orange
- 1/2 cup orange juice
- 1/4 cup sugar
- 1 teaspoon salt
- 1 large egg
- 2 Tablespoons unsalted butter; softened to room temperature
- 3 to 3.5 cups all-purpose flour

Filling
- 2 Tablespoons sugar
- 2 teaspoons ground cinnamon
- 1 Tablespoon unsalted butter; softened to room temperature

Glaze
- 1 cup confectioners' sugar
- 1 Tablespoon orange juice
- fresh orange zest; from 1 medium orange
- 1 teaspoon vanilla extract

Directions

Make the Dough:
1. Dissolve the yeast in 1/2 cup warm water for about 1 minute. No need to use a thermometer for the water's temperature, but to be precise: about 105-115F degrees. Stir the yeast/water around. Then add orange zest, orange juice, sugar, salt, egg, butter, and 1.5 cups of flour. Beat everything together on low with a handheld mixer, scraping down the sides as needed. (A mixer is definitely needed to break up all the butter and beat everything to the proper consistency.) With a wooden spoon, stir in enough of the remaining flour to make a dough easy to handle - about 1.5 - 2 more cups. You are looking for a dough that is not sticky and will spring back when poked with a finger.
2. Transfer the dough to a lightly floured surface and knead it with your hands for about 5-6 minutes. Form the dough into a ball and transfer it to a lightly greased bowl. Cover the dough and let sit in a warm place until doubled in size, about 1.5 hours.
3. Line the bottom of a 9x13 inch baking dish with parchment paper, leaving room on the sides. Turn the dough out onto a lightly floured work surface and, using a rolling in, roll into a 15x9 inch rectangle. I used a ruler for accuracy. Make sure the dough is smooth and evenly thick, even at the corners.

For the Filling:
4. In a small bowl, mix together sugar and cinnamon. Spread the dough rectangle with softened butter and sprinkle generously with all the cinnamon-sugar mixture. Tightly roll up the dough and cut into 16 even rolls (1 inch in width each) with a very sharp knife. Arrange them in the prepared baking pan, cut sides up. Cover the rolls and let them rise in a warm place for about 30 minutes - 1 hour.
5. Preheat the oven to 375F degrees. Cover the rolls with aluminum foil and bake for about 25-30 minutes, until they are lightly golden in color. Transfer the pan to a rack to cool for about 15 minutes.

Make the Glaze:
6. In a small bowl, mix together all the glaze ingredients and drizzle over rolls before serving.

Nutrition: 374 Calories 5.8g Total fat 70.1g Carbohydrates

35. Waffle with Spicy Chicken

Preparation Time: 2 H

Servings: 4

Cooking Time: 10'

Ingredients

Sweet Hot Maple Glaze:
- 1 cup honey
- 1 cup maple syrup
- 1 teaspoon chili powder
- 1 teaspoon paprika
- 1 teaspoon ground black pepper
- 1 teaspoon apple cider vinegar
- 1/4 teaspoon cayenne
- 1/2 teaspoon kosher salt

Waffles:
- 2 cups all-purpose flour
- 1 cup shredded sharp Cheddar
- 2 tablespoons sugar
- 2 teaspoons baking powder
- 3 to 4 scallions, chopped, whites and greens separated
- 7 to 8 dashes hot sauce
- 2 teaspoons kosher salt, plus a pinch
- 2 large eggs
- 2 cups whole milk
- 8 tablespoons (1 stick) unsalted butter, melted
- Nonstick cooking spray, for the waffle iron

Fried Chicken:
- Vegetable or canola oil, for frying
- 8 boneless, skin-on chicken thighs
- 1 cup buttermilk
- 2 cups all-purpose flour
- 1 teaspoon garlic powder
- 1 teaspoon onion powder
- 1 teaspoon paprika
- 1 teaspoon ground black pepper
- 1/2 teaspoons kosher salt, plus more for seasoning

Directions

1. For the glaze: Combine the honey, maple syrup, chili powder, paprika, black pepper, vinegar, cayenne, and salt in a small saucepot. Bring just to a simmer. Remove from the heat and let steep for 20 minutes, then strain into a clean container.
2. For the waffles: Preheat the oven to 250 degrees F and place a rack in the middle of the oven. Place a baking sheet fitted with a wire rack in the oven.
3. Whisk together the flour, Cheddar, sugar, baking powder, hot sauce, scallion whites, and salt in a large bowl and set aside.
4. In another large bowl, whisk the eggs and a pinch of salt until just broken up, then add the milk and whisk. Pour in the melted butter and whisk until combined.
5. Add the wet ingredients to the dry ingredients and stir with a rubber spatula until the flour is just incorporated and no streaks remain (the batter may have a few lumps).
6. Preheat a Belgian waffle iron to medium heat according to the manufacturer's instructions. Spray with nonstick cooking spray, add some batter, close the lid, and cook until the steam starts to diminish (open the top and peek for doneness after a few minutes). Transfer the waffle to the wire rack in the oven to keep warm. Repeat with the remaining batter to make 8 waffles.
7. For the chicken: Pour 5-inches of oil in a heavy-bottomed pot. Heat over medium-high heat until a deep-frying thermometer inserted in the oil reaches 360 degrees F.
8. Place the chicken thighs and buttermilk in a bowl. In a separate bowl, add the flour, garlic powder, onion powder, paprika, pepper, and salt, and mix to combine. Dredge each thigh in the flour mix, then shake off any excess flour and carefully place in the oil. Fry until golden, 7 to 8 minutes. Remove the chicken to a paper bag or paper towels to drain excess grease and immediately season with salt.
9. Place each piece of fried chicken on top of a waffle and top each with some glaze and scallion greens to serve.

Nutrition: 1168 Calories 49.1g Total fat 94.7g Carbohydrates

36. CHeeseCake PanCakes

PREPARATION TIME: 10'	SERVINGS: 12

COOKING TIME: 6'

INGREDIENTS

- Pancakes
- 1 package (8 oz) cream cheese
- 2 cups Original Bisquick™ mix
- ½ cup graham cracker crumbs
- ¼ cup sugar
- 1 cup milk
- 2 eggs
- Strawberry Syrup
- 1 cup sliced fresh strawberries
- ½ cup strawberry syrup for pancakes

DIRECTIONS

1. Slice cream cheese lengthwise into four pieces. Place on ungreased cookie sheet; cover and freeze 8 hours or overnight. Brush griddle or skillet with vegetable oil, or spray with cooking spray; heat griddle to 375°F or heat skillet over medium heat.
2. Cut cream cheese into bite-size pieces; set aside. In a large bowl, stir Bisquick mix, graham cracker crumbs, sugar, milk, and eggs with whisk or fork until blended. Stir in cream cheese.
3. For each pancake, pour slightly less than 1/3 cup batter onto hot griddle. Cook until edges are dry. Turn; cook other sides until golden brown.
4. In a small bowl, mix strawberries and syrup; top pancakes with strawberry mixture.

NUTRITION: 132 Calories 5.3g Total fat 18.7g Carbohydrates

37. Starbucks Lemon Bread

Preparation Time: 15'

Servings: 2

Cooking Time: 50'

Ingredients

- 1 1/2 cups all-purpose flour
- 1/2 teaspoon baking powder
- 1/4 teaspoon baking soda
- 1/4 teaspoon salt
- 1/2 cup unsalted butter softened
- 1 cup granulated sugar
- 3 large eggs
- 1/2 teaspoon vanilla extract
- 1 teaspoon lemon extract*
- zest of 1 large lemon or use 1 and 1/2 lemons if you don't have lemon extract
- 2 tablespoons lemon juice
- 1/3 cup buttermilk sour cream works too
- Lemon Icing
- 1 cup powdered sugar add more until desired consistency is reached
- 1 tablespoon lemon juice
- 1 tablespoon cream or milk

Directions

Lemon Loaf
1. Preheat the oven to 350F degrees. Grease and flour an 8 x 4-inch loaf pan, or line with parchment paper.
2. In a medium bowl, whisk together the flour, baking powder, baking soda & salt.
3. In a separate bowl, beat together the butter and sugar until fluffy - this will take at least 3 minutes.
4. Mix in the eggs 1 at a time. Then mix in the vanilla extract, optional lemon extract, lemon zest, and lemon juice.
5. With the mixer on low speed, mix in about 1/2 of the flour mixture followed by about 1/2 of the buttermilk. Turn off the mixer and scrape down the sides of the bowl.
6. Repeat the process with the rest of the flour mixture and buttermilk.
7. Pour the batter into the prepared pan and bake for 50-60 minutes. It will be done when an inserted toothpick comes out clean, and the top feels firm to the touch. If after about 30-40 minutes the top is browning too much, tent a piece of aluminum foil over top and continue baking.
8. Cool the loaf fully before icing (otherwise, the icing will melt through the cake and run off the sides).

Lemon Icing
9. In a medium bowl, whisk together the powdered sugar, lemon juice, and cream/milk until smooth. Add in more powdered sugar or cream as needed for the desired consistency.
10. Remove the cooled loaf from the pan and drizzle or pour over top.

Nutrition: 477 Calories 20g Total fat 70.8g Carbohydrates

38. barrel CraCker frenCH ToasT

<table>
<tr><td>PREPARATION TIME: 1'</td><td>SERVINGS: 1</td></tr>
</table>

COOKING TIME: 5'

INGREDIENTS

- 8 slices Texas Toast (or Sourdough bread)
- 4 eggs
- 1 cup Milk
- 2 Tablespoons Sugar
- 4 teaspoons Vanilla extract
- 2 pinches of salt

DIRECTIONS

1. Whisk eggs, milk, sugar, vanilla, and salt together in a large bowl.
2. Heat griddle to 350 (or heat a skillet on medium heat). Grease with butter/ margarine or non-stick cooking spray.
3. Dip each slice of bread in the egg mixture for 30 seconds on each side.
4. Place slices on the griddle and cook for 4-5 minutes, or until golden brown.
5. Serve with a pat of butter and your favorite syrup!

NUTRITION: 1312 Calories 30.5g Total fat 191g Carbohydrates 54.1g Protein

39. Egg McMuffins

| PREPARATION TIME: | 5' | SERVINGS: | 2 |

COOKING TIME: 10'

INGREDIENTS

- 1 tablespoon unsalted butter (1/2 ounce; 15g), softened, divided
- 1 English muffin, split
- 1 slice high-quality Canadian bacon
- Nonstick cooking spray
- 1 large egg
- Kosher salt and freshly ground black pepper
- 1 slice American, cheddar, Swiss, or Jack cheese

DIRECTIONS

1. Spread 1 teaspoon butter on each half of the English muffin and place halves in a 10-inch nonstick or cast-iron skillet over medium heat. Cook, swirling muffin halves and pressing gently to get good contact with the pan, until both pieces are well browned, about 4 minutes. Transfer to a sheet of aluminum foil, split side up.
2. Melt remaining 1 teaspoon butter in the now-empty skillet and increase heat to medium-high. Add bacon and cook, turning frequently, until browned and crisp around the edges, about 1 1/2 minutes. Transfer bacon to lower muffin half.
3. Place the lid of a quart-sized, wide-mouthed Mason jar (both the lid and the sealing ring) upside down in the now-empty skillet. (The side the jar screws onto should be facing up.) Spray the inside with nonstick cooking spray and break the egg into it. Poke the egg yolk with a fork to break it and season with salt and pepper. Pour 3/4 cup (180ml) water into the skillet, cover, and cook until egg is set, about 2 minutes.
4. Using a thin spatula, transfer Mason jar lid to a paper towel-lined plate. Pour excess water out of the skillet and return it to the stovetop with the heat off. Flip Mason jar lid over and gently remove it to release the egg. Place egg on top of bacon and top with cheese slice. Close sandwich, wrap in aluminum foil and return to the now-empty skillet. Let it warm up in the skillet for 2 minutes with the heat off, flipping occasionally. Unwrap and serve immediately.

NUTRITION: 96 Calories 2.7g Total fat 12.8g Carbohydrates 5.3g Protein

40. Pumpkin Pancakes

| Preparation Time: | 10' | | Servings: | 9 |

| | Cooking Time: | 10' |

Ingredients

- 1 ½ cups milk
- 1 cup pumpkin puree
- 1 egg
- 2 tablespoons vegetable oil
- 2 tablespoons vinegar
- 2 cups all-purpose flour
- 3 tablespoons brown sugar
- 2 teaspoons baking powder
- 1 teaspoon baking soda
- 1 teaspoon ground allspice
- 1 teaspoon ground cinnamon
- ½ teaspoon ground ginger
- ½ teaspoon salt

Directions

1. In a bowl, mix together the milk, pumpkin, egg, oil, and vinegar. Combine the flour, brown sugar, baking powder, baking soda, allspice, cinnamon, ginger, and salt in a separate bowl. Stir into the pumpkin mixture just enough to combine.
2. Heat a lightly oiled griddle or frying pan over medium-high heat. Pour or scoop the batter onto the griddle, using approximately 1/4 cup for each pancake. Brown on both sides and serve hot.

Nutrition: 134 Calories 5g Total fat 18g Carbohydrates

41. frITTaTa

PREPARATION TIME:	5'	SERVINGS:	6

COOKING TIME:	20'

INGREDIENTS

- 6 large eggs, enough to cover the ingredients
- 1/4 cup heavy cream
- 1 teaspoon kosher salt, divided
- 4 slices thick-cut bacon (8 ounces), chopped (optional)
- 2 small Yukon gold potatoes, peeled and thinly sliced
- 1/4 teaspoon freshly ground black pepper
- 2 cups baby spinach (2 ounces)
- 2 cloves garlic, minced
- 2 teaspoons fresh thyme leaves
- 1 cup shredded cheese, such as Gruyère, Fontina, or cheddar (optional)

DIRECTIONS

1. Heat the oven. Arrange a rack in the middle of the oven and heat to 400°F.
2. Whisk the eggs and cream together. Whisk the eggs, heavy cream, and 1/2 teaspoon salt together in a small bowl; set aside.
3. Cook the bacon. Place the bacon in a cold 10- to 12-inch nonstick oven safe frying pan or cast-iron skillet, then turn the heat to medium-high. Cook the bacon, stirring occasionally, until crisp, 8 to 10 minutes. Remove the bacon with a slotted spoon to a paper towel-lined plate and pour off all but 2 tablespoons of the fat. (If omitting the bacon, heat 2 tablespoons oil in the skillet, then proceed with adding the potatoes).
4. Sauté the potatoes in bacon fat. Return the pan to medium heat, add the potatoes and sprinkle with the pepper and the remaining 1/2 teaspoon salt. Cook, stirring occasionally, until tender and lightly browned, 4 to 6 minutes.
5. Wilt the spinach with the garlic and thyme. Pile the spinach into the pan with the garlic and thyme, and cook, stirring, for 30 seconds to 1 minute or until spinach wilts. Add the bacon back to the pan and stir to evenly distribute.
6. Add the cheese. Spread the vegetables into an even layer, flattening with a spatula. Sprinkle the cheese on top and let it just start to melt.
7. Pour the egg mixture into the skillet. Pour the egg mixture over the vegetables and cheese. Tilt the pan to make sure the eggs settle evenly over all the vegetables. Cook for a minute or two until you see the eggs at the edges of the pan beginning to set.
8. Bake the frittata for 8 to 10 minutes. Bake until the eggs are set, 8 to 10 minutes. To check, cut a small slit in the center of the frittata. If raw eggs run into the cut, bake for another few minutes; if the eggs are set, pull the frittata from the oven. For a browned, crispy top, run the frittata under the broiler for a minute or two at the end of cooking.
9. Cool and serve. Cool in the pan for 5 minutes, then slice into wedges and serve.

NUTRITION: 324 Calories 25g Total fat 2g Carbohydrates 19g Protein

42. ragouT

PREPARATION TIME: 2'	SERVINGS: 2

COOKING TIME: 15'

INGREDIENTS

- 2 tablespoons extra-virgin olive oil, divided
- 2 lb. chuck roast, cut into 2" cubes
- Kosher salt
- Freshly ground black pepper
- 1 medium yellow onion, chopped
- 5 cloves garlic, thinly sliced
- 1/2 tsp. fennel seeds
- 1/4 tsp. red pepper flakes
- 2 tablespoons tomato paste
- 1/4 c. red wine
- 1 (28 oz.) can whole peeled tomatoes
- 1/4 c. water
- 3 sprigs thyme
- 1 bay leaf
- 2 teaspoons balsamic vinegar
- Parmesan, for serving
- Freshly chopped parsley, for serving

DIRECTIONS

1. In a large stockpot over medium heat, heat 1 tablespoon oil. Season chuck roast with salt and pepper and sear, in batches if needed, until browned on all sides, 10 minutes. Remove into a large bowl.
2. Heat remaining oil, still over medium heat. Add onion and cook until soft, 6 minutes. Add garlic, fennel seeds, and red pepper flakes and cook until fragrant, 1 minute more.
3. Add tomato paste and cook until it is darkened in color, 1 to 2 minutes more. Deglaze the pot with wine, scraping any brown bits up at the bottom of your pot with a wooden spoon.
4. Add whole peeled tomatoes, water, thyme, bay leaf, balsamic vinegar, and seared pot roast and season with salt and pepper. Stir to combine and reduce heat to low. Cover and simmer, stirring occasionally, until meat easily shreds, 2 to 2 1/2 hours. Use a wooden spoon to break up tomatoes and meat, and remove bay leaf. Serve over your favorite pasta or polenta. Top with parmesan and parsley before serving.

NUTRITION: 180 Calories 14.1g Total fat 13.8g Carbohydrates

43. blueberry PanCakes

PREPARATION TIME: 5'   SERVINGS: 1

COOKING TIME: 15'

INGREDIENTS

- 2 cups all-purpose flour
- 2 tablespoons baking powder
- 1 teaspoon kosher salt
- 3 tablespoons light brown sugar
- 2 eggs
- 1 teaspoon vanilla
- 1 1/2 cups milk
- 5 tablespoons butter, melted
- 2 cups fresh blueberries
- butter for frying

DIRECTIONS

1. In a large bowl, whisk the flour, baking powder, salt, and brown sugar together.
2. In a separate bowl, whisk the eggs, vanilla, and milk together.
3. Add the wet ingredients into the dry and mix until just combined. Lastly, mix in the melted butter and stir until combined, the batter will be slightly lumpy. Set the batter aside while you heat your griddle to medium-low heat. Melt a small pat of butter on the griddle and then scoop out 1/4 cup of pancake batter onto the hot griddle and top evenly with blueberries, as many or few as you prefer.
4. Cook until the edges are set, and bubbles form on top of the pancake. Flip and cook until browned.
5. Serve warm.

NUTRITION: 45 Calories 0.1g Total fat 11.9g Carbohydrates

44. broWn Sugar baCon

PREPARATION TIME: 5'

SERVINGS: 11

COOKING TIME: 20'

INGREDIENTS

- 1/4 cup firmly packed brown sugar
- 2 teaspoons chili powder
- 8 slices thick-cut bacon

DIRECTIONS

1. Preheat oven to 400 degrees F. Line a rimmed baking sheet with aluminum foil. Set a cooling rack inside the prepared pan and set aside.
2. In a shallow dish, combine the brown sugar and chili powder. Dredge the bacon slices in the brown sugar mixture and arrange the bacon on the rack. Bake in the preheated oven until crisp, about 20 minutes. Transfer to a serving plate and serve.

NUTRITION: 157 Calories 11g Total fat 3g Carbohydrates 11g Protein

45. Starbucks Pumpkin bread

Preparation Time: 15'

Servings: 11

Cooking Time: 1 H 10'

Ingredients

- 1 ½ cups all-purpose flour
- 1 teaspoon baking soda
- 1 teaspoon ground nutmeg
- 1 teaspoon ground cinnamon
- 1 teaspoon ground cloves
- ½ teaspoon baking powder
- ½ teaspoon salt
- 4 large eggs
- 1 cup white sugar
- ¼ cup light brown sugar
- ½ teaspoon vanilla extract
- ¾ cup canned pumpkin
- ¾ cup vegetable oil

Directions

1. Preheat oven to 350 degrees F (175 degrees C). Grease an 8-1/2x4-1/2-inch loaf pan.
2. Combine flour, baking soda, nutmeg, cinnamon, cloves, baking powder, and salt together in a large bowl.
3. Beat eggs, white sugar, brown sugar, and vanilla extract in a large bowl with an electric mixer on high speed until combined, about 30 seconds. Beat in pumpkin and oil. Add flour mixture; mix until batter is blended and smooth.
4. Pour batter into the prepared loaf pan. Bake in the preheated oven until the top is dark brown and a toothpick inserted into the center of the bread comes out clean, about 70 minutes. Let cool in the pan, about 30 minutes. Invert onto a wire rack and slice it into 1-inch thick slices.

Nutrition: 429.6 Calories 23.6g Total fat: 50.1g Carbohydrates

46. daddy's blueberry buTTermIlk PanCakes

| PREPARATION TIME: | 15' | COOKING TIME: | 10' | SERVINGS: | 12 |

INGREDIENTS

- 1 cup all-purpose flour.
- 3 tbsps. Cornmeal.
- 3 tablespoons quick-cooking oats.
- 3 tbsps. Sugar.
- 1 teaspoon baking powder.
- 1/2 tsp cooking soda.
- 1/2 tsp sodium.
- Dash ground nutmeg.
- 1 sizable egg.
- 1-1/2 cups buttermilk.
- 2 tbsps. Canola oil.
- 1 teaspoon vanilla remove.
- 1 cup new or even frosted blueberries.

DIRECTIONS

1. In a big bowl, whip the 1st 8 ingredients. In one more dish, whip egg, buttermilk, oil, and vanilla up until blended.
2. Add to flour mixture; stir only till moistened (batter is going to be lumpy). Permit cool for 15 mins.
3. Lightly grease a frying pan or huge nonstick skillet; heat over tool heat.
4. Rouse blueberries batter right in. Put the batter on griddle or frying pan by 1/4 cups. Cook before blisters start to blister ahead.
5. The bottoms stick out and become brown gold. Switch; cook brown until edge 2.

NUTRITION: 332 calories 10g fat 52g carbohydrate 18g sugars

47. aunT beTTy's blueberry MuffIns

| PREPARATION TIME: | 15' | COOKING TIME: | 20' | SERVINGS: | 1 dOzen |

INGREDIENTS

- 1/2 cup out-of-date oatmeal.
- 1/2 cup orange extract.
- 1 huge egg, room temperature.
- 1/2 cup canola oil.
- 1/2 cup sugar.
- 1-1/2 mugs all-purpose flour.
- 1-1/4 teaspoons cooking powder.
- 1/2 teaspoon salt.
- 1/4 teaspoon cooking soda.
- 1 cup clean or frosted blueberries.
- Topping:
- 2 tablespoons sugar.
- 1/2 teaspoon ground cinnamon.

DIRECTIONS

1. Combine the oats and orange juice in a wide bowl; let stand 5 Moments. Beat in the egg, olive oil, and sugar until mixed. Merge the Cover with flour, baking powder, salt, and baking soda; add oat mixture
2. Just until they're moist. Blueberries fold in. Fill two-thirds full of muffin cups wrapped in greased or parchment. Merge the topping ingredient; brush over the batter. Bake at 20-25 ° C minutes or until a toothpick is inserted in the middle.
3. Remove from pan to wire rack for 5 minutes before cooling. Serve warm.

NUTRITION: 208 calories, 10g excess fat 18mg cholesterol 28g carb

48. bisCuiTs and Sausage gravy

PREPARATION TIME: 15'

SERVINGS: 2

COOKING TIME: 10'

INGREDIENTS

- 1/4 extra pound bulk pig bratwurst
- 2 tbsps. butter
- 2 to 3 tablespoons all-purpose flour
- 1/4 teaspoon salt
- 1/8 teaspoon pepper
- 1-1/4 to 1-1/3 cups entire milk
- Warm cookies

DIRECTIONS

1. In a little skillet, chef bratwurst over tool warmth until no longer pink; drain. Add butter and heat energy until thawed.
2. Add the pepper, flour, and sodium; chef and stir until combined. Gradually add the milk, mixing regularly. Take to a boil; chef and mix up until expanded, concerning 2 moments. Serve with biscuits.

NUTRITION: 337 calories, 27g fat 10g protein.

49. True belgian Waffles

PREPARATION TIME: 30'   COOKING TIME: 15'   SERVINGS: 10

INGREDIENTS

- 2 cups all-purpose flour.
- 3/4 cup sugar.
- 3-1/2 teaspoons cooking particle.
- 2 huge eggs, separated.
- 1-1/2 cups whole milk.
- 1 cup butter, melted.
- 1 tsp vanilla extract.
- Chopped fresh strawberries or syrup.

DIRECTIONS

1. In a bowl, combine flour, sugar, and cooking powder. In one more dish, softly beat egg yolks. Add butter, milk, and vanilla; mix effectively.
2. Stir into dry out ingredients just till incorporated. Beat egg whites up until thick tops develop; layer right into the concoction.
3. Bake in a preheated waffle iron depending on to producer's Directions, until golden brownish. Serve with strawberries or even syrup.

NUTRITION: 696 calories 41g fat 72g carb

50. THree-CHeeseSoufflés

<table>
<tr><td>PREPARATION TIME:</td><td>40'</td><td>SERVINGS:</td><td>8</td></tr>
</table>

COOKING TIME: 40'

INGREDIENTS

- 1/3 cup butter, cubed.
- 1/3 cup all-purpose flour.
- 2 cups whole milk.
- 1 teaspoon Dijon mustard.
- 1/4 tsp salt.
- Dashboard hot pepper sauce.
- 1/2 cups cut Swiss cheese.
- 1 cup cut cheddar cheese.
- 1/4 cup shredded Parmesan cheese.
- 6 huge eggs1/2 tsp cream of tartar.

DIRECTIONS

1. Liquefy butter over a warm machine in a tiny saucepan.
2. Mix well into the flour until smooth; cook for 1 minute.
3. Progressively whip the milk, pepper, mustard, and salt in the dressing. Offer a boil, stirring continuously; cook and stir for 1-2 mins or even until thickened.
4. Reduce warm to medium-low; blend until thawed in cheeses. Transfer onto a large platter.
5. Eggs Exclusive. Place the egg whites in a layered bowl; let stand at room temperature for 30 minutes.
6. Beat egg yolk bags in a tiny dish until they are thick and lemon-colored for about 4 minutes.
7. Mix boiling cheese mixture in 1/3 cup; add everything to the remaining mixture, blend consistently. Composed wholly, about 30 moments.
8. Preheat to 325 °. Place eight 8-oz unfed. Cooking ramekins with clean beaters in a frying pan, hammer the egg whites with tartar lotion on top Speed till tight however not dry out.
9. With a rubber spatula, gently stir a fourth of the egg whites into the cheese mixture.
10. Fold up in continuing to be whites. Move to packed ramekins. For baking, apply 1 inch of warm water to the frying pan.
11. Cook 40-45 mins or even until bests are gold brownish. Serve right away. Freeze option: Securely wrap unbaked soufflés with aluminum foil and freeze.
12. Preheat stove to 325 ° to use. Remove foil in a baking pan, and mark frosted soufflés; add 1 in. Bigger pot of warm tea. Cook 60-65 minutes or even gold-brown until heated through and leads.

NUTRITION: 317 calories 223mg cholestero l9g carb

51. Chicken-fried Steak & gravy boat

Preparation Time: 30'

Servings: 4

Cooking Time: 20'

Ingredients

- 1-1/4 mugs versatile flour, divided
- 2 big eggs
- 1-1/2 cups 2% milk, split
- 4 beef cube steaks (6 ozs each).
- 1-1/4 teaspoons salt, divided.
- 1 tsp pepper, broken down.
- Oil for panning fry.
- 1 cup water.

Directions

1. Add 1 cup of flour in a shallow platter. Toss eggs and 1/2 cup milk in a separate small pot, until mixed.
2. Sprinkle steaks with 3/4 tsp each sodium and pepper. Dip in flour to coat each side; get away from excess.
3. Plunge in egg mixture, at that point once again in flour. Warm 1/4 in. In a large skillet of oil over warm substance.
4. Remove steaks; cook until golden brownish, and a thermostat reads on each side through 160 °, 4-6 mins.
5. Remove the towels from the pot; drain abstractly. Hold warm.
6. Remove about 2 tablespoons oil from pot. Stir in the staying 1/4 cup flour, 1/2 tsp salt, and 1/4 teaspoon pepper until smooth; chef and stir over medium heat up until golden brown, 3-4 moments.
7. Progressively whip in water and continue with the milk.
8. Offer a boil, stirring continuously; prepare and mix up until expanded, 1-2 mins. Serve with steaks.

Nutrition: 563 calories 28g fat 29g carbohydrate

52. deliClous PoTaTo dougHnuTs

| PREPARATION TIME: | 20' | | SERVINGS: | 4 |

| COOKING TIME: | 40' |

INGREDIENTS

- 2 mugs warm mashed potatoes (with included milk and butter).
- 2-1/2 cups sweets.
- 2 mugs buttermilk.
- 2 big eggs, softly beaten.
- 2 tbsps. Butter, melted.
- 2 teaspoons baking soda.
- 2 teaspoons cooking particle.
- 1 teaspoon sodium.
- 1 tsp ground nutmeg.
- 6-1/2 to 7 mugs all-round flour.
- Oil for deep-fat frying.

Fast Fudge Frosting:
- 3-3/4 cups confectioners' glucose.
- 1/2 cup baking chocolate.
- 1/4 tsp sodium.
- 1/3 cup boiling water.
- 1/3 cup butter, liquefied.
- 1 tsp vanilla extract.

DIRECTIONS

1. In a big bowl, mix the potatoes, glucose, buttermilk, and eggs. Mix in the butter, baking soda, cooking powder, sodium, nutmeg, and enough of the flour to establish a smooth dough.
2. Turn onto a lightly floured surface; tap bent on 3/4-in. fullness. Reduce with a 2-1/2-in. floured doughnut cutter machine.
3. In an electricity frying pan, warm 1 in. of oil to 375 °. Pan fry the doughnuts for 2 mins on each edge or even until browned.
4. Place on towels made from paper for frosting, combine the confectioners' sweets, cocoa, and sodium in a big dish. Stir in the water, butter, and vanilla. Plunge leadings of hot pastries in the frosting.

NUTRITION: 226 calories 15mg cholestero l35g carb

53. Eggs benedICT WITH Homemade Hollandalse

PREPARATION TIME: 30'

SERVINGS: 8

COOKING TIME: 10'

INGREDIENTS

- 4 big egg yolk sacs
- 2 tbsps. water
- 2 tablespoons lemon juice
- 3/4 cup butter, thawed
- Dash white colored pepper
- 8 big eggs
- 4 English buns, crack and cooked
- 8 pieces Canadian bacon, heated Paprika

DIRECTIONS

1. For the white sauce, whisk egg yolk packets, water, and lemon juice until blended in top of a double central heating boiler or even steel fantastic churning water, chef up until the mixture is thick enough to cover a steel spoon and temperature exceeds 160 °, mixing consistently.
2. Take off fire. Gradually drizzle excessively in soft melted oil, whisking continuously. Blend with chili pepper. Switch to a small bowl if need be. Place dish in a comfortable water bowl far larger than this.
3. Just keep dry, rousing occasionally, about 30 minutes till all set to serve. Spot 2-3 in. of water in a huge saucepan or even a frying pan with high sides. Offer a boil; readjust heat to sustain a gentle simmer. Crack 1 egg right into a small dish, having dish closed next to the water, slide the egg into the water.
4. Repeat with 3 additional eggs.
5. Chef, exposed, 2-4 moments, or whites are completely formed, and bags of yolk are not yet difficult to enlarge. Take eggs out of the water using a slotted spoon;
6. Repeat with 4 eggs in the process. Cover one-half of each muffin with a slice of bacon, a poached egg, and 2 teaspoons of sauce; sprinkle with paprika. Serve forthwith.

NUTRITION: 345 calories 26g fat 15g carbohydrate

54. buTTermIlk PanCakes

PREPARATION TIME: 5′	SERVINGS: 2 dOzen

COOKING TIME: 10′

INGREDIENTS

- 4 cups versatile flour.
- 1/4 cup sugar.
- 2 teaspoons cooking soda.
- 2 teaspoons salt.
- 1-1/2 teaspoons cooking grain.
- 4 large eggs, room temperature.
- 4 cups buttermilk.

DIRECTIONS

1. In a large bowl, combine the flour, sweets, cooking soft drink, salt, and cooking particle.
2. In an additional bowl, whisk the eggs and buttermilk until mixed; mix them into dry-out ingredients simply till dampened.
3. Pour batter by 1/4 cups onto a lightly buttered scorching griddle; turn when blisters form on top. Cook until the 2nd side is golden brown.
4. Freeze alternative: Freeze cooled down hot cakes between levels of waxed paper in a freezer container.
5. To make use of side hot cakes on an ungreased flat pan, cover with aluminum foil and reheat in a preheated 375 ° stove 6-10 moments.
6. Or place a stack of 3 hot cakes on a microwave-safe layer and microwave on high for 45-90 seconds or even up until warmed.

NUTRITION: 270 calories 3g fat 48g carb

55. Ham and SWISS OmeleT

PREPARATION TIME: 20′	SERVINGS: 2

COOKING TIME: 10′

INGREDIENTS

- 1 tablespoon butter
- 3 eggs
- 3 tbsps. water
- 1/8 teaspoon sodium
- 1/8 teaspoon pepper
- 1/2 cup cubed fully cooked ham
- 1/4 cup cut Swiss cheese

DIRECTIONS

1. In a little nonstick skillet, liquefy butter over medium-high temperature. Blend the eggs, pepper, water, and sodium. Add egg mixture to skillet (mixture must set quickly at edges).
2. As eggs prepared, press cooked sides toward the midpoint, allowing raw section circulation below.
3. When the eggs are established, place ham on one edge and sprinkle with cheese; fold the opposite side over the filling. Slide omelet onto a layer.

NUTRITION: 530 calories 726mg cholesterol 4g carb

Chapter 4

energIzIng SmOOtHIe r ecIPes

56. Mega Mango SmooTHIe

| PREPARATION TIME: 5' | COOKING TIME: 0' | SERVINGS: 2 |

INGREDIENTS

- 1 cup frozen mangos
- 1 cup frozen strawberries
- ½ cup orange juice
- ½ cup pineapple juice
- 1 cup ice

DIRECTIONS

1. Blend all the ingredients until smooth consistency.

NUTRITION: 590 calories 35g fats 8g protein

57. Orange-a-Peel SmooTHIe

| PREPARATION TIME: 10' | COOKING TIME: 0' | SERVINGS: 2 |

INGREDIENTS

- ½ banana, sliced
- 1 cup frozen strawberries
- 1 cup orange juice
- ½ cup vanilla nonfat frozen yogurt
- 1 cup ice

DIRECTIONS

1. Blend all the ingredients until smooth consistency.

NUTRITION: 529 calories 34g fats 6g protein

58. Orange-C booster SmooTHIe

PREPARATION TIME: 10'	COOKING TIME: 0'	SERVINGS: 2

INGREDIENTS

- ½ banana, sliced
- ½ cup frozen peaches
- 1 cup orange juice
- 1 cup orange sherbet
- 1 cup ice
- Antioxidant Power Boost
- Immunity Boost

DIRECTIONS

1. Put all the ingredients and fill it to the max water line, then blend until smooth

NUTRITION: 550 calories 29g fats 4.9g protein

59. Orange CarroT Karma SmooTHIe

PREPARATION TIME: 10'	COOKING TIME: 0'	SERVINGS: 2

INGREDIENTS

- ½ banana, sliced
- ½ cup frozen mangos
- 1 cup carrot juice
- 1 cup orange juice
- 1 cup ice

DIRECTIONS

1. Put all the ingredients and fill it to the max water line, then blend until smooth.

NUTRITION: 603 calories 24g fats 5g fiber

60. Orange dream MaCHIne SmooTHIe

| PREPARATION TIME: | 5' | COOKING TIME: | 20' | SERVINGS: | 4 |

INGREDIENTS

- ½ cup orange juice
- ½ cup soy milk
- 1 cup vanilla nonfat frozen yogurt
- 1 cup orange sherbet
- 1 cup ice
- Lemon Zest

DIRECTIONS

1. Put all the ingredients and fill it to the max water line, then blend until smooth.

NUTRITION: 491 calories 29g fats 2g fiber

61. PeaCH mango SmooTHIe

| PREPARATION TIME: | 5' | COOKING TIME: | 0' | SERVINGS: | |

INGREDIENTS

- 1 cup frozen mangos
- 1 cup frozen peaches
- ½ cup peach juice
- ½ cup soy milk
- 1 cup ice
- Balance Boost
- Lean Advantage Boost

DIRECTIONS

1. Put all the ingredients and fill it to the max water line, then blend until smooth.

NUTRITION: 449 calories 28g fats 5g fiber

62. PeaCH PerfeCTIon SmooTHIe

PREPARATION TIME: 5'	COOKING TIME: 0'	SERVINGS: 2

INGREDIENTS

- ½ cup frozen mangos
- 1 cup frozen peaches
- ½ cup frozen strawberries
- ¼ cup apple juice
- ½ cup peach juice
- ¼ cup strawberry juice
- 1 cup ice

DIRECTIONS

1. Put all the ingredients and fill it to the max water line, then blend until smooth.

NUTRITION: 509 calories 31g fats 4g fiber

63. PeaCH Pleasure SmooTHIe

PREPARATION TIME: 5'	COOKING TIME: 0'	SERVINGS: 1

INGREDIENTS

- ½ banana, sliced
- 1 cup frozen peaches
- 1 cup peach juice
- ½ cup orange sherbet
- 1 cup ice

DIRECTIONS

1. Put all the ingredients and fill it to the max water line, then blend until smooth.

NUTRITION: 501 calories 31g fats 6g fiber

64. Peanut butter moo'd Smoothie

| PREPARATION TIME: | 12' | COOKING TIME: | 0' | SERVINGS: | 2 |

INGREDIENTS

- ½ banana, sliced
- ½ cup peanut butter
- ½ cup chocolate milk
- 1 cup soy milk
- ½ cup vanilla nonfat frozen yogurt
- 1 cup ice

DIRECTIONS

1. Put all the ingredients and fill it to the max water line, then blend until smooth.

NUTRITION: 489 calories 26g fats 3.9g fiber

65. Jamba Juice Pomegranate Paradise Smoothie

| PREPARATION TIME: | 5' | COOKING TIME: | 0' | SERVINGS: | |

INGREDIENTS

- ½ cup frozen mangos
- ½ cup frozen peaches
- 1 cup frozen strawberries
- 1 cup pomegranate juice
- 1 cup ice

DIRECTIONS

1. Put all the ingredients and fill it to the max water line, then blend until smooth.

NUTRITION: 481 calories 23g fats 7g protein

66. Pomegranate Pick-me-up Smoothie

Preparation Time: 5'	Cooking Time: 0'	Servings: 2

Ingredients

- ½ cup frozen blueberries
- ½ cup frozen strawberries
- ½ cup mixed berry juice
- ½ cup pomegranate juice
- 1 cup raspberry sherbet
- 1 cup ice

Directions

1. Put all the ingredients and fill it to the max water line, then blend until smooth.

Nutrition: 501 calories 26g fats 4g fiber

67. Protein berry Workout Smoothie

Preparation Time: 5'	Cooking Time: 0'	Servings: 2

Ingredients

- ½ banana, sliced
- 1 cup frozen strawberries
- 1 cup soy milk
- 1 cup ice
- Whey Protein Boost

Directions

1. Put all the ingredients and fill it to the max water line, then blend until smooth.

Nutrition: 440 calories 28g fats 6g fiber

68. razzamaTazz SmooTHIe

| PREPARATION TIME: | 10' | COOKING TIME: | 0' | SERVINGS: | 2 |

INGREDIENTS

- ½ banana, sliced
- 1 cup strawberries
- 1 cup raspberry juice
- 1 cup orange sherbet
- 1 cup ice

DIRECTIONS

1. Put all the ingredients and fill it to the max water line, then blend until smooth.

NUTRITION: 491 calories 29g fats 8g fiber

69. STraWberry rasPberry banana SmooTHIe

| PREPARATION TIME: | 5' | COOKING TIME: | 0' | SERVINGS: | 2 |

INGREDIENTS

- ½ banana, sliced
- ½ cup frozen raspberries
- ½ cup frozen strawberries
- ½ cup apple juice
- ½ cup strawberry juice
- ½ cup soy milk
- 1 cup ice

DIRECTIONS

1. Put all the ingredients and fill it to the max water line, then blend until smooth.

NUTRITION: 488 calories 29g fats 4g protein

70. mango-a-go-go SmooTHIe

PREPARATION TIME:	5'	COOKING TIME:	0'	SERVINGS:	2

INGREDIENTS

- 1 cup frozen mangos
- 1 cup passion fruit-mango juice
- 1 cup pineapple sherbet
- 1 cup ice

DIRECTIONS

1. Put all the ingredients and fill it to the max water line, then blend until smooth.

NUTRITION: 501 calories 28g fats 4g fiber

71. Jamba JuICe: ProTeIn berry WorkouT

PREPARATION TIME:	5'	COOKING TIME:	0'	SERVINGS:	2

INGREDIENTS

- 1 cup vanilla soy milk
- 1 scoop vanilla protein powder, desired brand
- 1 cup frozen strawberries
- 1 frozen banana, sliced (slice before freezing)
- 1 cup ice

DIRECTIONS

1. Put all the ingredients and fill it to the max water line, then blend until smooth.

NUTRITION: 418 calories 24g fats 5g fiber

72. Jamba Juice: razzamaTazz SmooTHie

PREPARATION TIME: 5'	COOKING TIME: 0'	SERVINGS: 2

INGREDIENTS

- 1 cup fresh orange juice
- ½ cup coconut yogurt
- ¼ cup shredded purple cabbage
- ½ cup frozen raspberries
- ½ cup frozen strawberries
- ½ small banana, sliced
- 2-3 ice cubes

DIRECTIONS

1. Put all the ingredients and fill it to the max water line, then blend until smooth.

NUTRITION: 501 calories 5g fiber 12g protein

73. Jamba Juice: STrawberry rasPberry banana

PREPARATION TIME: 5'	COOKING TIME: 0'	SERVINGS: 2

INGREDIENTS

- ½ cup apple juice
- ½ cup almond milk
- ¾ cup frozen strawberries
- ½ cup fresh raspberries
- ½ small banana, sliced
- 1 cup ice

DIRECTIONS

1. Put all the ingredients and fill it to the max water line, then blend until smooth.

NUTRITION: 410 calories 31g fats 6g protein

74. Jamba Juice: Strawberry Surf Rider

PREPARATION TIME: 5'	COOKING TIME: 0'	SERVINGS: 2

INGREDIENTS

- 1 cup lemonade
- 2 tablespoons lime juice
- ½ cup non-fat frozen yogurt
- 1 cup strawberries
- 1 cup of ice cubes

DIRECTIONS

1. Put all the ingredients and fill it to the max water line, then blend until smooth.

NUTRITION: 440 calories 29g fats 4g protein

75. Jamba Juice: Strawberry Whirl Smoothie

PREPARATION TIME: 0'	COOKING TIME: 5'	SERVINGS: 2

INGREDIENTS

- 1 cup lemonade
- 2 tablespoons lime juice
- ½ cup non-fat frozen yogurt
- 1 cup strawberries
- 1 cup of ice cubes

DIRECTIONS

1. Put all the ingredients and fill it to the max water line, then blend until smooth.

NUTRITION: 501 calories 6g fiber 18g fats

76. Jamba Juice: Strawberries Wild

Preparation Time: 5'	Cooking Time: 0'	Servings: 2

Ingredients

- ¼ cup frozen strawberries
- ¼ cup fresh forest strawberries
- ¼ cup organic apple juice
- ¼ cup almond yogurt or Greek yogurt
- 1 small banana, sliced
- Ice, as desired

Directions

1. Put all the ingredients and fill it to the max water line, then blend until smooth.

Nutrition: 490 calories 12g fats 6g fiber

77. Jamba Juice: Tropical Harvest Smoothie

Preparation Time: 5'	Cooking Time: 0'	Servings: 2

Ingredients

- 1 small frozen peach, sliced
- ½ cup lemon sorbet
- ¼ cup frozen mango chunks
- ½ cup yellow vegetable juice
- ¼ cup passion fruit pulp
- ½ cup of ice cubes

Directions

1. Put all the ingredients and fill it to the max water line, then blend until smooth.

Nutrition: 391 calories 31g fats 4g fiber

78. Jamba Juice: WHIte gummy bear

PREPARATION TIME:	5'	COOKING TIME:	0'	SERVINGS:	2

INGREDIENTS

- ½ cup white peach juice
- ½ cup almond milk
- 3 strawberries, sliced
- ½ scoop pineapple sherbet
- ½ scoop lime sherbet
- ½ scoop orange sherbet
- ½ scoop non-fat frozen yogurt
- ¼ cup frozen raspberries
- Ice, as desired

DIRECTIONS

1. Put all the ingredients and fill it to the max water line, then blend until smooth.

NUTRITION: 502 calories 16g fats 6g fiber

79. naked Juice: green maCHIne

PREPARATION TIME:	5'	COOKING TIME:	0'	SERVINGS:	2

INGREDIENTS

- 2 green apples, peeled and cored
- ¾ cup fresh broccoli florets
- ½ cup frozen mango chunks
- 1 cup pineapple juice
- ¼ cup apple juice
- 1 cup baby spinach
- 4 kale leaves, stems removed
- 1 kiwi, peeled, sliced
- 1 small frozen banana, sliced

DIRECTIONS

1. Put all the ingredients and fill it to the max water line, then blend until smooth.

NUTRITION: 391 calories 5g fiber 19g fats

80. naked JuICe: mIgHTy mango

PREPARATION TIME:	5′	COOKING TIME:	0′	SERVINGS:	2

INGREDIENTS

- 2 cups frozen mango chunks
- ½ small frozen banana, sliced (slice before freezing)
- 1/3 cup fresh orange juice
- ¼ cup fresh lemonade
- 1 small green apple, cored, peeled

DIRECTIONS

1. Put all the ingredients and fill it to the max water line, then blend until smooth.

NUTRITION: 339 calorie 16g fats 8g fiber

81. naked JuICe: red maCHIne

PREPARATION TIME:	0′	COOKING TIME:	5′	SERVINGS:	2

INGREDIENTS

- 1 red apple, peeled, cored, and chopped
- ½ cup raspberries
- ½ frozen banana, sliced (slice before freezing)
- ¼ cup fresh pomegranate juice
- ¼ cup blood orange juice
- 4 fresh cranberries
- ¼ cup red grapes
- 3-4 ice cubes

DIRECTIONS

1. Put all the ingredients and fill it to the max water line, then blend until smooth.

NUTRITION: 601 calories 14g fats 3g fiber

82. Orange Jullus

PREPARATION TIME:	5'	COOKING TIME:	0'	SERVINGS:	2

INGREDIENTS

- 3oz. frozen orange juice concentrate
- ½ cup water
- 2 tablespoons coconut sugar or maple syrup
- ½ cup almond milk
- ½ teaspoon vanilla paste or extract
- 1 cup of ice cubes

DIRECTIONS

1. Put all the ingredients and fill it to the max water line, then blend until smooth.

NUTRITION: 501 calories 12g fats 3.9g fiber

83. Panera bread: PeaCH & blueberry SmooTHIe

PREPARATION TIME:	5'	COOKING TIME:	0'	SERVINGS:	2

INGREDIENTS

- ¼ cup frozen blueberries
- 1 small frozen peach, pitted and sliced (slice before freezing)
- ½ frozen banana, sliced (slice before freezing)
- ¾ cup unsweetened almond milk
- ½ cup fresh orange juice

DIRECTIONS

1. Put all the ingredients and fill it to the max water line, then blend until smooth.

NUTRITION: 600 calories 19g fats 6g fiber

84. Panera bread: Super fruit Smoothie with greek Yogurt

| PREPARATION TIME: 5' | COOKING TIME: 0' | SERVINGS: 2 |

INGREDIENTS

- 1 ½ cups fresh strawberries, sliced
- ½ cup frozen raspberries
- 1 cup vanilla Greek yogurt
- ¼ cup coconut milk
- 1 tablespoon maple syrup
- 2-3 ice cubes

DIRECTIONS

1. Put all the ingredients and fill it to the max water line, then blend until smooth.

NUTRITION: 412 calories 15g fats 4g fiber

85. Panera bread: green Passion Smoothie

| PREPARATION TIME: 5' | COOKING TIME: 0' | SERVINGS: |

INGREDIENTS

- 1 cup frozen mango chunks
- ½ cup passion fruit pulp
- ½ cup passion fruit juice
- ½ cup white grape juice
- 2 medium peaches, pitted and sliced
- 2 cups baby spinach
- 1 cup ice

DIRECTIONS

1. Put all the ingredients and fill it to the max water line, then blend until smooth.

NUTRITION: 531 calories 18g fats 7g fiber

Chapter 5

MILK SHAKE RECIPES

86. In-n-Out burger's CopyCat Vanilla Shake

| PREPARATION TIME: | 10′ | COOKING TIME: | 0′ | SERVINGS: | 2 |

INGREDIENTS

- ½ cup whole milk
- 2 cups French vanilla ice cream
- 1 tablespoon Smucker's caramel topping

DIRECTIONS

1. Add the milk and ice cream to a blender or food processor. Blend for 30 seconds until the mixture is smooth. Add the caramel and blend again until mixed well.
2. Pour the mixture into a 12-ounce glass and serve chilled. Alternatively, place the blender in the freezer for 30 minutes and serve after stirring a bit if you like a thicker version.

NUTRITION: 680 calories 37g total fats 9g protein

87. Wendy's CopyCat Chocolate frosty

| PREPARATION TIME: | 1 H 20′ | COOKING TIME: | 0′ | SERVINGS: | 2 |

INGREDIENTS

- ½ cup chocolate syrup
- 2 cups whole milk
- 1 (7-ounce) can sweetened condensed milk
- ½ teaspoon vanilla extract
- ½ cup heavy cream

DIRECTIONS

1. Combine the chocolate syrup, whole milk, and condensed milk in a mixing bowl. Refrigerate for 1 hour until chilled.
2. To another mixing bowl, add the heavy cream and vanilla. Beat well until soft peaks form. Chill in the refrigerator.
3. Ready your ice cream maker and add the chocolate mixture to the ice cream making bowl. Prepare ice cream as per instructions (it will take about 15–20 minutes to churn it). Turn off the machine, take out the paddles, and add the cream mixture to the bowl. Combine well. Serve chilled, or place in the freezer until frozen to the desired consistency.

NUTRITION: 509 calories 29g fats 8g protein

88. Jamba Juice's CoPyCaT razzmaTazz SmooTHIe

| PREPARATION TIME: 5' | COOKING TIME: 0' | SERVINGS: 2 |

INGREDIENTS

- 1 cup frozen strawberries
- ½ banana, sliced
- 1 cup orange sherbet
- 1 cup raspberry juice
- 1 cup ice

DIRECTIONS

1. Add the ice and other ingredients to a blender or food processor. Blend until the mixture is smooth. Serve chilled.

NUTRITION: 590 calories 34g fats 6g protein

89. Tgl friday's CoPyCaT TroPICal runner SmooTHIe

| PREPARATION TIME: 10' | COOKING TIME: 0' | SERVINGS: 2 |

INGREDIENTS

- 1 (8-ounce) can crushed pineapple, with juice
- 1 banana
- ½ cup orange sherbet
- ½ cup liquid Piña Colada mix
- 2 cups ice

DIRECTIONS

1. Cut the banana in half, then make ¼-inch slices. Set aside two slices. Add the remaining slices, pineapple with juice, Piña Colada mix, orange sherbet, and ice to a blender or food processor.
2. Blend until the mixture is smooth. Pour into two glasses. Garnish with banana slices and serve chilled.

NUTRITION: 670 calories 29g fats 10g protein

90. SHake SHaCk's CoPyCaT PeanuT buTTer SHake

| PREPARATION TIME: | 5' | COOKING TIME: | 0' | SERVINGS: | 3 |

INGREDIENTS

- 2 cups vanilla ice cream
- 1 cup milk
- 2 tablespoons sugar
- ½ cup peanut butter

DIRECTIONS

1. Blend all the ingredients until smooth. Pour into chilled glasses and serve.

NUTRITION: 681 calories 36g fats 7g protein

91. SonIC's CoPyCaT STraWberry SHake

| PREPARATION TIME: | 5' | COOKING TIME: | 0' | SERVINGS: | 2 |

INGREDIENTS

- 1½ cups vanilla ice cream
- 1/3 cup 2% milk
- 1 tablespoon strawberry preserves
- ½ cup frozen strawberries

DIRECTIONS

1. Blend all the ingredients until smooth. Pour into chilled glasses and serve.

NUTRITION: 649 calories 35g fats 8g protein

92. dIsney's CoPyCaT Jelly PeanuT buTTer mIlksHake

PREPARATION TIME: 5'	COOKING TIME: 0'	SERVINGS: 2

INGREDIENTS

- 3 cups vanilla ice cream
- ¼ cup peanut butter
- 3–4 tablespoons grape jelly
- ¼–1/3 cup milk

DIRECTIONS

1. Combine the jelly and peanut butter in a bowl. Add the ice cream, jelly mix, and milk to a blender or food processor and blend to make a smooth mixture. Serve chilled.

NUTRITION: 688 calories 33g fats 11g protein

93. arby's CoPyCaT JamoCHa SHake

PREPARATION TIME: 10'	COOKING TIME: 0'	SERVINGS: 3-4

INGREDIENTS

- 3 tablespoons sugar
- 3 cups vanilla ice cream
- 1 cup cold coffee
- 1 cup milk, low-fat
- 3 tablespoons chocolate syrup

DIRECTIONS

1. Add the milk, coffee, and sugar to a blender or food processor. Blend for about 15–20 seconds until the sugar dissolves, and the mixture is smooth. Mix in the ice cream and chocolate syrup; blend until the mixture is creamy. Pour into two 16-ounce glasses and serve chilled.

NUTRITION: 669 calories 34g fats 8g protein

94. Jack In The box's Copycat Pumpkin Pie Shake

Preparation Time: 10'	Cooking Time: 0'	Servings: 2

Ingredients

- 3 tablespoons sugar
- ¾ cup whole milk
- 3 cups vanilla ice cream
- ¾ teaspoon pumpkin pie spice
- ¾ cup canned pumpkin
- 2 maraschino cherries and whipped cream to garnish

Directions

1. Add the milk and sugar to a mixing bowl; mix well until the sugar dissolves. Add the pumpkin, pumpkin pie spice, ice cream, and milk mixture to a blender or food processor.
2. Blend until the mixture is smooth. Pour into two 16-ounce glasses. Serve topped with whipped cream and cherry.

Nutrition: 664 calories 34g fats 8g protein

95. Tropical Smoothie Café's Copycat Peanut Paradise

Preparation Time: 5'	Cooking Time: 0'	Servings: 1

Ingredients

- 2 tablespoons nonfat milk powder
- 1 tablespoon honey
- 1 medium ripe banana
- ½ cup plain yogurt
- 1 tablespoon creamy peanut butter
- 2 ice cubes

Directions

1. Add the ice cubes and other ingredients to a blender or food processor.
2. Blend for about 30 seconds until the mixture is smooth, and the ice is crushed completely. Pour into serving glass; serve chilled.

Nutrition: 679 calories 31g fats 7g protein

96. mcDonald's CoPyCaT SHamroCk SHake

| PREPARATION TIME: 5' | COOKING TIME: 0' | SERVINGS: 2 |

INGREDIENTS

- 1¼–1½ cups vanilla ice cream
- 3 tablespoons 2% milk
- Dash of peppermint extract or 3 tablespoons crème de menthe
- 7 thin mint cookies
- Green food coloring (optional)

DIRECTIONS

1. Blend all the ingredients until smooth. Pour into serving glasses; serve chilled.

NUTRITION: 684 calories 34g fats 7.9g protein

97. SmooTHIe KIng's CoPyCaT CarIbbean Way

| PREPARATION TIME: 10' | COOKING TIME: 0' | SERVINGS: 4 |

INGREDIENTS

- 2 cups frozen strawberries
- 1 cup orange juice
- ¾ cup strawberry-banana yogurt
- 1 medium banana, sliced and frozen

DIRECTIONS

1. Blend all the ingredients until smooth. Pour into four serving glass; serve chilled.

NUTRITION: 681 calories 36g fats 8g protein

98. Chick-fil-a's Copycat frosted lemonade

| Preparation Time: | 10' | Cooking Time: | 0' | Servings: | 4 |

Ingredients

- 2 cups vanilla ice cream
- 2 teaspoons grated lemon zest
- 2 cups lemon sorbet
- ½ cup 2% milk
- 3 ounces cream cheese, softened
- ½ teaspoon vanilla extract
- 2 tablespoons lemon drop candies, crushed
- 4 lemon slices
- 1 teaspoon sugar

Directions

1. Sprinkle the crushed lemon drop candies and sugar over a small plate or saucer. Mix well. Wet the rims of four serving glasses using 1–2 lemon slices.
2. Dash the rims of the glasses in the sugar mixture. Add all the ingredients except for the lemon slices to a blender or food processor. Blend until the mixture is smooth.
3. Pour into the serving glasses; serve chilled with the remaining lemon slices.

Nutrition: 671 calories 31g fats 6g protein

99. Panera's Copycat mango Smoothie

| Preparation Time: | 10' | Cooking Time: | 0' | Servings: | 2 |

Ingredients

- 2 cups frozen peeled mangoes, chopped
- ½ cup unsweetened pineapple juice
- ½ medium ripe banana
- 1 tablespoon honey
- ½ cup reduced-fat plain yogurt

Directions

1. Blend all the ingredients until smooth. Pour into serving glasses and serve chilled.

Nutrition: 657 calories 36g fats 6g protein

100. dIsney's CoPyCaT red aPPle freeze

PREPARATION TIME:	5-10'	SERVINGS:	4

COOKING TIME: 0'

INGREDIENTS

- ¼ cup passion fruit nectar or juice
- 1 cup heavy whipping cream, chilled
- ¼ cup mango nectar or juice
- 3 tablespoons sugar
- Slush
- 12 ounces cold water
- 3 tablespoons toasted marshmallow syrup
- 2 (12-ounce) cans frozen apple juice concentrate

DIRECTIONS

1. Add the passion fruit nectar, whipping cream, and mango nectar to a mixing bowl. Mix well. Add the sugar and beat thoroughly. Refrigerate.
2. Add the slush ingredients to a blender or food processor and blend to make a smooth mixture. Serve with the foam topping on top.

NUTRITION: 671 calories 34.9g fats 8.1g protein

Chapter 6

Soup Recipes

101. UsHlo JIru

PREPARATION TIME: 10'	COOKING TIME: 15'	SERVINGS: 4

INGREDIENTS

- 1 unit of Kombu
- 1 tablespoon of sake
- 4 cups of water
- 1 pound of Manila clams
- 2-3 strands of mitsuba
- Kosher salt as per taste

DIRECTIONS

1. De-grit the clams. Clean them thoroughly. In a saucepan, add water, clams, and the Kombu. Place the saucepan on medium flame. When the water has reached a point where it is almost boiling, take the Kombu out. Turn the flame down. Add sake to the saucepan when all the clams have opened up—season with kosher salt as per taste. Make sure you don't cook them for too long otherwise, the clams will become hard.

NUTRITION: 98 Calories 4g Carbs 17g Protein

102. JaPanese TurnIP MIso SouP

PREPARATION TIME: 10'	COOKING TIME: 15'	SERVINGS: 2

INGREDIENTS

- 1.5 cups of water
- 2 tablespoons of miso
- Half an aburaage
- 1 Japanese turnip

DIRECTIONS

1. Peel the turnip properly, and don't forget to cut off its ends. Make thin slices after cutting the turnip in half. Blanch the aburaage in boiling water for about twenty seconds, flipping a couple of times so that the oil is eliminated. After that, cut it in half, and make thin slices from only half of it.
2. Take a small-sized saucepan and, in it, add the water, aburaage, and sliced turnips. Let it boil and slightly covered. After that, allow the mixture to simmer for about five minutes, and the turnips will slowly become transparent.
3. If you prefer to have some greens, you can quickly chop the leaves of the turnip and add them too. Add the miso in the ladle, and then with the help of a fork or chopsticks, slowly mix it in the soup. Serve and enjoy!

NUTRITION: 142 Calories 22g Carbs 9.8g Protein

103. KenCHInJIru

PREPARATION TIME: 10'		**SERVINGS:** 4
	COOKING TIME: 50'	

INGREDIENTS

For the dash:
- 5 cups of water
- 1 Kombu
- 1 cup of water (for the shiitake mushrooms)
- 3 shiitake mushrooms (dried)
- For the soup,
- 2 inches of daikon radish
- Half a pack of konnyaku
- 7 ounces of firm tofu
- 3 Taro
- 1 carrot
- Half a gobo
- 2 scallions/green onions
- Japanese sansho pepper
- Shichimi Togarashi

For the seasonings:
- 2 tablespoons of soy sauce
- 3 tablespoons of sake
- 1 tablespoon of roasted sesame oil
- Half a teaspoon of kosher salt

DIRECTIONS

1. Soak the Kombu overnight in five cups of water. The next day, boil the water, and just before it arrives at the boiling point, take the Kombu out. Cover the shiitake mushrooms with water in a bowl. The mushrooms have to be submerged.
2. Cover the block of tofu with a paper towel, and in order to press it, place a plate on it for half an hour. It will drain the tofu. Cut the konnyaku into small chunks and then boil them for three minutes. Drain and keep them aside. Make small slices of carrot, daikon, and Taro. The gobo skin has to be peeled, and after slicing, soak them for five minutes in water.
3. Now, squeeze water out of the shiitake mushrooms and pass the water through a sieve. Your shiitake dashi is ready. The stem of the shiitake mushrooms will have to be discarded, and the top should be chopped into small pieces.
4. In a large-sized pot, add sesame oil and heat. Add konnyaku, gobo, Taro, carrot, and daikon, and sauté. Add the mushrooms. Add the tofu after tearing it into pieces with your fingers. Sauté everything nicely.
5. Lastly, add the kombu dashi and the shiitake dashi and boil the mixture. Simmer for ten minutes. The foam must be skimmed off. After about ten more minutes, add salt and sake. Then add soy sauce. Before serving, garnish with Sansho Pepper, Shichimi Togarashi, and chopped scallions.

NUTRITION: 67 Calories 8g Carbs 2g Protein 2g Fat

104. Corn Potage

PREPARATION TIME:	15'		SERVINGS:	4

COOKING TIME:	1 H

INGREDIENTS

- 1 cup each of Heavy whipping cream
- 1 cup Milk
- 3 cups of water
- 1 and a half teaspoons of butter (unsalted)
- Half an onion, sliced
- 1/4 teaspoon of paprika
- 1 tablespoon of olive oil
- 4 ears of corn (or 3 cups of frozen corn)
- Parsley (garnish)
- Kosher or sea salt

DIRECTIONS

1. Preheat your oven to 450 degrees Fahrenheit. Cut off the corn kernels, then transfer on a rimmed baking sheet. Save the cobs for later use.
2. Mix the paprika, salt, and olive oil with the corn kernels and spread it out evenly on the baking sheet. Grill them in the oven for about fifteen minutes and then set aside.
3. In the meantime, add some butter into a heavy-bottomed pan. When butter melts, stir in the sliced onions with some salt and sauté for a couple of minutes so that it turns translucent.
4. Add in the roasted kernels, water, and the reserved cobs. Bring the mixture to a boil. Cover and lower the heat to medium-low. Let it simmer for about fifteen minutes and then remove the cobs.
5. Blend the mixture using an immersion blender until it gets smooth and creamy and then strain it through a fine-mesh.
6. Then add milk and heavy cream into the soup and stir. Season with black pepper and salt and serve. You can add the parsley and olive oil and/or heavy cream as a garnish and serve hot or chilled.

NUTRITION: 122.6 Calories 13.7g Carbs 3.9g Protein 6.5g Fat

105. TonJiru

PREPARATION TIME: 10'	SERVINGS: 4

COOKING TIME: 40'

INGREDIENTS

For the soup:
- 7 ounces of tofu (medium-firm), cut into half-inch cubes
- 1 teaspoon of ginger, peeled and grated
- 1 piece of aburaage, cut into thin slices
- 1 Negi sliced diagonally
- 4.5 ounces of konnyaku, cut into thin rectangular pieces
- 4 ounces of carrots, peeled and cut into thin slices
- 9 ounces of daikon radish, peeled and cut into 1/8-inch slices
- 1 onion, cut into thin slices
- 8 ounces of Taro, peeled and cut into 1/3-inch slices
- 4 ounces of gobo
- 10 ounces of pork belly, sliced into one-inch pieces

For making the soup:
- 6 tablespoons of miso
- 6 cups of dashi
- 1 tablespoon of roasted sesame oil

To garnish:
- Shichimi togarashi (optional)
- 1 scallion or green onion, cut into thin small rounds

DIRECTIONS

1. Peel the outer skin of the gobo. Make a one-inch deep cross incision at one end of the gobo.
2. Rub one-fourth teaspoon of salt over the cut konnyaku pieces and leave it for five minutes. Then, place it into boiling water and cook for two to three minutes.
3. Heat sesame oil in a large pot over medium heat and add the pork belly into it. Stir fry the pork until it's no longer pinks in color. Add the onion, carrot, and daikon and stir. Add in the Taro, gobo, Negi, aburaage, and konnyaku. Stir in enough dashi to cover the ingredients.
4. Cover and let the mixture boil. Decrease the heat when boiling and remove the fat and scum from the soup. Cover and let it simmer for ten to fifteen minutes so that the root vegetables get soft.
5. Add the miso right before serving to enhance the flavor of the soup. Then, tear the tofu into pieces and add them into the soup along with the ginger. Add some green onions on the top and serve.

NUTRITION: 121 Calories 5.3g Carbs 5.5g Protein 8.4g Fat

106. maTsuTake Clear SouP

Preparation Time: 15'

Servings: 2

Cooking Time: 20'

Ingredients

- 4 stalks of Mitsuba
- 5.1 ounces of tofu (soft or silken), cut into small cubes
- 1 matsutake mushroom, cut into thin slices
- Yuzu zest
- 4 Temari Fu (optional)
- For the dashi:
- 0.4 ounces of katsuobushi
- 0.2 ounces of kombu
- 2 cups of water
- For seasoning:
- 2 teaspoons each of
- Soy sauce
- Mirin
- 1 tablespoon of sake
- Half a teaspoon of salt

Directions

1. Use a damp towel to clean the matsutake mushrooms. Remember that you shouldn't wash them. Cut off and remove a thin slice of the stem of the mushroom, then cut into thin slices.
2. Clean the dashi kombu using a clean cloth. The white powdery substance increases the flavor of the umami in the dashi, so leave it on. Don't wash the dashi.
3. Take water in a medium-sized saucepan and add the kombu in it. Slowly heat in on medium-low heat. You can also dip it in water for up to half a day if you have time. Soaking it helps bring out the kombu's flavor naturally.
4. Add in the katsuobushi when it starts boiling. Allow it to simmer for thirty seconds and then turn off the heat. Line a sieve with a paper towel and keep it over a bowl. Strain the dashi into the bowl. Twist and squeeze the paper towel and release any excess dashi into the bowl.
5. Add the dashi into a saucepan and boil it. Add in the soy sauce, mirin, sake, and salt. Then, add in the tofu and the mushrooms and cook for two to three minutes. Add the temari fu in water to allow it to hydrate. When it gets soft, squeeze out the water and transfer it into a serving bowl.
6. Take two mitsuba stalks and tie them into a knot. Before serving, add the two knotted mitsuba stalks into the soup.

Nutrition: 241 Calories 21g Carbs 4.1g Protein 16g Fat

107. Tofu and Japanese Pumpkin Soup

PREPARATION TIME: 15'   SERVINGS: 4

COOKING TIME: 45'

INGREDIENTS

- 7 ounces of mixed mushrooms, trimmed and sliced
- 3 ounces of baby spinach
- 3.5 ounces of tofu (silken firm), cut into half-inch cubes
- 2 tablespoons of mirin
- 2-4 cup of soy sauce
- 2 sachets of instant dashi powder (0.7 ounces)
- 35 ounces of butternut pumpkin, peeled and cut into half-inch cubes
- Sesame seeds (toasted) and sesame oil, to serve

DIRECTIONS

1. Add six cups of slightly salted water into a saucepan placed over medium heat. Add in the pumpkin and simmer for ten to fifteen minutes so that they just soft. Add in the mirin, soy sauce, dashi powder, and tofu and let it simmer for five minutes. Mix in the mushrooms and spinach and cook for thirty seconds so that they wilt. Take it away from the heat. Transfer the soup into serving bowls and drizzle some sesame oil and top with toasted sesame seeds.

NUTRITION: 145 Calories 20g Carbs 11g Protein 3g Fat 4g Fiber

108. Champon

PREPARATION TIME:	15′	SERVINGS:	2

COOKING TIME: 40′

Ingredients

For preparing the soup:
- 2 cups of chicken broth
- 1 tablespoon each of
- Sake
- Soy sauce
- 1/4 cup of milk (whole)
- Half a teaspoon of salt
- 1 cup of dashi
- 1 teaspoon of sugar
- 1/8 teaspoon of pepper powder (white)
- For preparing meat and the seafood:
- 2 ounces each of Pork belly (two slices) and Squid
- 11 teaspoon of soy sauce
- 2 and a half ounces of shrimp
- 1 tablespoon of sake

For the vegetables and other ingredients:
- 6 pieces of ear mushrooms (dried wood)
- 1/4 of an onion
- 1 ounce of snow pea
- 4 ounces of bean sprouts
- Black pepper (ground freshly)
- 11 ounces of Champon noodles
- 2 inches of carrot
- 5 ounces of cabbage
- A 1/3 of fish cake (kamaboko)
- 1 tablespoon of roasted sesame oil
- 1/8 teaspoon of salt

Directions

1. Add the chicken broth (two cups) and the dashi (one cup) in a pot. Combine them with a spoon. To this mixture, add soy sauce, sake, and granulated sugar (one teaspoon). Allow them to cook.
2. Once they start boiling, add the milk and white pepper. Slice the pork belly into pieces of one inch. Add soy sauce and sake (each of one teaspoon) to it. Place the shrimp, squid, and two teaspoons of sake in the bowl. Set aside for about five minutes.
3. Slice the squid by moving the knife diagonally (make parallel lines). You can make simple incisions on the flesh.
4. Take another bowl and add then the mushrooms. Pour enough water in the bowl to immerse the mushroom pieces. Rehydrate the mushrooms to soften them and then squeeze out the extra water. Slice into pieces.
5. Make thin slabs of the carrot and then half the slices vertically. Chop the onion. Discarding the core of cabbage, cut them into cubes. Cut the snow peas into halves after removing the strings from them. Make thin slices of the kamaboko fish.
6. Place a wok over moderate to high heat and add sesame oil to it. After the oil starts to boil, add pork belly pieces and cook until they brown. Add the squid and the shrimp pieces to it and cook until they become opaque.
7. Stir in carrot and onion. Add mushroom and cabbage, and keep stirring for one minute. Stir in the bean sprouts, the snow peas, and fish—Cook for an additional minute. Sprinkle pepper and then toss them to combine. Add the soup to the wok and then adjust the salt by tasting it.
8. Prepare the noodles: Cut the packet, take the noodles out, and then separate them, place a large pan over a moderate flame, and pour water. Put the noodle strips in it—Cook noodles and place in a bowl. Top the noodles with the soup and other toppings. Serve them warm.

NUTRITION: 522 Calories 93g Carbs 23g Protein 18g Fat

109. Soba Noodles WITH Sake-Poached Chicken

PREPARATION TIME:	15'		SERVINGS:	4

COOKING TIME: 50'

INGREDIENTS

- 1/4 each cup of Shiitake mushrooms and Light soy sauce
- Half a cup of sake
- 2 cups of chicken stock
- 1.5 tsps. of caster sugar
- 2 chicken breasts (6.5 oz. each)
- A bunch of bok choy
- 2 cups of enoki mushrooms
- 1 red chili (long, sliced thinly)
- 1 packed of soba noodles (9.5 ounces)

DIRECTIONS

1. Add two cups of hot water to shiitake mushrooms in a bowl. Keep them aside for five minutes and then drain them. The mushroom liquid should be reserved.
2. Now, in a saucepan, add the following ingredients – reserved mushroom liquid, chicken stock, sugar, soy sauce, and sake. Simmer on medium flame and keep stirring.
3. Then, add the chicken and keep cooking for another ten minutes. Flip the pieces of chicken and then add the bok choy— Cook for about eight minutes. Pour the bok choy and chicken to a plate.
4. Simmer the broth again. Add the shiitake mushrooms, enoki mushrooms, and the noodles. Cook them for about eight minutes. Now, divide into bowls for serving. On top of the noodles, add shredded chicken, bok choy, mushrooms, and sliced red chili. Then, use a spoon to divide the broth into the bowls.

NUTRITION: 452 Calories 57.8g Carbs 41.9g Protein 4.2g Fat 1g Fiber

COPYCAT COOKBOOK

110. Soba Noodles WITH Miso Salmon

| PREPARATION TIME: | 15' | | SERVINGS: | 4 |

| COOKING TIME: | 15' |

INGREDIENTS

- 2 bunches of broccolini (cut into halves lengthwise after trimming)
- 1 tablespoon of mirin
- 1.5 tablespoons of white miso paste
- 1 packet of soba noodles (8 oz.)
- 2 teaspoons of sake
- 1 teaspoon each of sesame oil and of caster sugar
- 17.5 oz. of salmon fillets (boned and skinned)
- 1 cup of red cabbage (sliced thinly)
- 3 cups of mesclun leaves
- For serving – mixed sesame seeds

For the ponzu dressing:
- 1/4 cup of soy sauce
- Juice of half a lemon
- 1 tablespoon each of mirin and sake

DIRECTIONS

1. In a large-sized saucepan, boil water and add some salt in it—Cook the soba noodles. Add the broccolini in the noodles just two minutes before completion. Drain and keep the noodles aside. Set your grill on high. In a small-sized bowl, combine mirin, miso, sugar, sake, and sesame oil.
2. Take a baking tray and use foil to line the tray. Place the fillets of salmon on the tray. Take the miso mixture and brush it on the fillets. Grill the salmon for about five minutes, and they should become lightly charred. Keep them aside for five minutes. Flake them roughly.
3. Now, take a large-sized bowl and combine the dressing along with the noodles and broccolini. Add the mesclun leaves too. Toss everything well and divide into serving bowls. Top with sesame seeds and grilled salmon before serving.

NUTRITION: 413 Calories 31g Carbs 13g Protein 25g Fat

111. Egg and Pork Curry Soup WITH Udon Noodles

PREPARATION TIME: 10'	SERVINGS: 2

COOKING TIME: 50'

INGREDIENTS

- 1 tablespoon of sunflower oil
- Half a cup of unsalted butter
- 2 green shallots (long, shredded green parts, chopped white parts)
- 2/3 cup of plain flour
- 8 cups of beef stock
- 1.5 tablespoons of curry powder
- 1 teaspoon of dark soy sauce
- 1 tablespoon each of sake and mirin
- 4 eggs (must be kept at room temperature)
- 5 ounces of udon noodles
- For serving – bonito flakes and nori sheets

For the pork:
- 2 tablespoons of sake
- 2 teaspoons of raw sugar
- 1 tablespoon each of dark soy sauce and mirin
- 1.5 inches of ginger (grated finely)
- 2 tablespoons of sunflower oil
- 17.5 ounces of minced pork

DIRECTIONS

1. Heat the stock and keep it aside. Take another saucepan and, in it, heat the oil—Cook the shallots for about three minutes. Then add butter and stir. Stir in flour and cook for another three minutes.
2. Add curry powder and keep stirring for a minute. Then add the hot stock into the mixture. If you can't add it at once, then add it in batches. Simmer. Add sake, soy sauce, and mirin, and mix them well in the soup.
3. It is time to prepare the pork. Heat the oil. Add ginger and pork and break the pork with the help of a spoon. Keep cooking for five minutes. Incorporate the rest of the ingredients and cook for another three minutes.
4. Add water to another saucepan and boil the water. Add the eggs and cook them to your liking. Drain the water and keep the eggs in another bowl. Peel them once they cool down.
5. Boil the soup again. Take the serving bowls and divide the soup and noodles evenly. Top the soup with halved eggs, pork mixture, nori, shredded shallot, and bonito. Serve.

NUTRITION: 508 Calories 77.5g Carbs 23.9g Protein 14.3g Fat 14.6g Fiber

COPYCAT COOKBOOK

112. Curry Udon Noodles

PREPARATION TIME: 15'	SERVINGS: 2

COOKING TIME: 40'

INGREDIENTS

- 1 spring onion
- 760ml water
- 2 tablespoons of tsuyu soup stock
- 2 packets of udon noodles (pre-cooked)
- Half each of Carrot, Potato, and Onion
- 3 blocks of Japanese curry roux

DIRECTIONS

1. Add 360ml of water to a pan. Chop the carrot, potato, and onion into small pieces and add them to the pan. Bring it to a boil. Simmer until the vegetables soften, for about 20 minutes.
2. Add three blocks of curry roux and simmer for ten minutes. Stir continuously until the curry sauce is smooth and thick.
3. Take a separate pan, add 400ml of water, and add four tbsp of tsuyu soup stock for making the noodle soup. Boil it. Boil the udon noodles and drain them after a few minutes in the colander.
4. Take a bowl and place the udon noodles, pour the noodle soup, pour the curry sauce on top. Before serving, garnish with some sliced spring onions.

NUTRITION: 340 Calories 47g Carbs 7g Protein 14g Fat

113. Kitsune Udon

PREPARATION TIME: 15'

SERVINGS: 2

COOKING TIME: 50'

INGREDIENTS

- 4 pouches of Inari Age
- 2 Servings of udon noodles
- 1 scallion or green onion, sliced thinly
- 1 tablespoon each of usukuchi soy sauce and mirin
- 2 and a quarter cups of dashi
- 1 teaspoon of sugar
- Half a teaspoon of sea salt or kosher salt
- Shichimi Togarashi (optional)
- Narutomaki (optional), cut into 1/8-inch pieces

For the homemade dashi:
- 1 and a half cups of katsuobushi
- 1 kombu
- 2 and a half cups of water

DIRECTIONS

1. You can use store-bought dashi powder or make it on your own. To make the homemade dashi, add the kombu in two and a half cups of water and let it soak for at least thirty minutes. You can also soak it for three hours or up to half a day as it helps bring out the flavor of the kombu.
2. Add the kombu and water into a saucepan and boil it over medium-low heat. Discard the kombu just before the water starts boiling. The dashi will turn bitter and slimy if you keep the kombu in the water for too long while it is boiling.
3. Add in one and a half cups of katsuobushi and boil again. Lower the heat when the dashi is boiling and let it simmer for fifteen minutes and then turn off the heat. Allow the katsuobushi to sink to the bottom of the pan and then keep it for ten to fifteen minutes. Use a fine-mesh sieve to strain the dashi into a saucepan. Your homemade dashi is now ready.
4. Add the soy sauce, sugar, mirin, dashi, and salt into a saucepan and boil the mixture. Then, cover or turn off the heat and let it simmer.
5. Add the udon noodles into a large pot of water and boil it. Once it gets cooked, transfer it into a strainer and drain all the water.
6. Add the soup and the udon noodles equally into serving bowls and add the shichimi togarashi, green onions, narutomaki, and Inari Age as a garnish.

NUTRITION: 413 Calories 58g Carbs 10g Protein 15.5g Fat

114. Momofuku Soy Sauce Eggs, Chili Chicken, and Soba Noodles

PREPARATION TIME:	15'		SERVINGS:	4

	COOKING TIME:	30'

INGREDIENTS

- 3.5 ounces of enoki mushrooms, trimmed
- 1 toasted nori sheet, torn
- 9.5 ounces of soba noodles, cooked and refreshed
- 4 eggs, hard-boiled and peeled
- 3 cups of chicken stock
- 1/3 of a cup of white miso paste
- 1 teaspoon each of ginger, finely grated and chili garlic paste
- 4 spring onions, thinly sliced, and some extra shredded onions for serving
- 7 ounces of chicken, minced
- 2 teaspoons of olive oil (extra virgin)
- 1 cup Soy sauce
- 1 cup Rice wine vinegar
- Shichimi togarashi, to serve

DIRECTIONS

1. Keep the eggs, soy sauce, and vinegar in a non-reactive bowl and chill overnight or for three to four hours.
2. Place a frying pan over high heat and add one teaspoon of oil in it. Then add the minced chicken and cook for five minutes and break the pieces using a wooden spoon. Add in the chili garlic paste when the chicken turns brown and cook for another three to four minutes so that they get brownish. Keep warm.
3. Place a saucepan over medium-low heat and heat the remaining teaspoon of oil in it. Add in the ginger and onions and cook for three to four minutes and occasionally stir so that they get tender. Add in the stock and miso and stir so that the miso dissolves.
4. Divide the nori, soup, and noodles among serving bowls. Add the extra onion, mushroom, halved eggs, and mince mixture as a topping. Sprinkle some shichimi togarashi and serve.

NUTRITION: 443.3 Calories 38g Carbs 40g Protein 16g Fat

115. Soba, Prawn, and Lemongrass Soup

PREPARATION TIME: 15'	SERVINGS: 4

COOKING TIME: 1 H 20'

INGREDIENTS

- 6 ounces of dried soba noodles
- 10.5 ounces of king prawns (medium-sized), peeled and deveined with the tails intact
- 8 cups of chicken stock
- 6-inch piece of lemongrass (only the white part), cut in half lengthwise
- 1.5-inch of ginger, thinly sliced
- 2 eschalots, thinly sliced
- 2 teaspoons Sesame oil
- 2 teaspoon Soy sauce
- 2 green shallots, thinly sliced
- 1 red chili, thinly sliced
- 1 teaspoon Sesame seeds
- 1 teaspoon Rice vinegar
- Mirin

DIRECTIONS

1. Place a large saucepan over medium-high heat and heat some sesame oil in it. Add in the ginger and eschalots and cook for three to four minutes so that the eschalots get tender. Add in the chicken stock and lemongrass and boil the mixture. Lower the heat to low and let it simmer for thirty-five to forty minutes.
2. Add in the prawns and cook for another two to three minutes. Then, add the vinegar, mirin, soy, and noodles and stir. Pour the soup into serving bowls and top with green shallots, chili, and sesame seeds.

NUTRITION: 180.6 Calories 35g Carbs 20g Protein 0.3g Fat 2.3g Fiber

116. anСienТ grains SouР

<table>
<tr><td>PREPARATION TIME:</td><td>10'</td><td></td><td>SERVINGS:</td><td>6</td></tr>
</table>

COOKING TIME: 45'

INGREDIENTS

- 1 ¾ ounces celery, diced
- 2 ½ ounces onion, diced
- 1 teaspoon fresh parsley, chopped
- 2 ½ ounces carrot, peeled & diced
- 1 ½ ounces freekeh, cooked
- 2 teaspoon garlic, crushed (approximately 2 cloves)
- 1 can tomatoes, chopped (1 pound)
- 2 ounces amaranth, cooked
- 1 ½ ounces quinoa, cooked
- ¾ tablespoon olive oil
- 14 ounces water
- ¼ teaspoon each of pepper & salt

DIRECTIONS

1. Over moderate heat in a medium casserole; heat the olive oil for a couple of minutes. Once hot, add & cook the onion together with celery, garlic, and carrot until for 3 to 5 minutes, until onion is translucent.
2. Add tomatoes (along with its accumulated juices) followed by freekeh, amaranth, quinoa & water. Increase the heat & bring the mixture to a boil. Once done, decrease the heat & let simmer for 12 to 15 more minutes, then remove the casserole from heat.
3. Carefully transfer the contents to a blender & add in the parsley. Purée until combined well. Season with pepper and salt. Serve hot & enjoy.

NUTRITION: 171 calories 28g carbs 26g protein

117. Piranha Pale ale Chili

| PREPARATION TIME: | 40' | | SERVINGS: | 8 |

| COOKING TIME: | 40' |

INGREDIENTS

- 1 pound each of ground beef & ground pork
- 2 tablespoons chili powder
- 1 bottle Piranha Pale Ale (12-ounce)
- 2 cups onion, diced
- 1 teaspoon ground black pepper
- ½ teaspoon cayenne
- 1 teaspoon garlic powder
- 2 cups water
- 1 can crushed tomatoes (15-ounce)
- ½ cup all-purpose flour
- 1 teaspoon dried thyme
- 2 cans pinto beans (15-ounce, along with the liquid)
- 1 tablespoon salt

For Garnish:
- 1 cups cheddar cheese, shredded
- ½ cup sour cream
- 1 cup Monterey Jack cheese, shredded
- ½ cup green onion, chopped

DIRECTIONS

1. Brown the ground meats over medium heat in a large saucepan. Drain any excess fat off. Add onion followed by cayenne, garlic powder, chili powder, spices, black pepper, thyme, and salt; continue to sauté for 3 to 5 more minutes.
2. Combine flour with water & add the mixture to the pan.
3. Add the leftover ingredients to the hot pan; bring the chili to a simmer & let simmer for 1 ½ hours, uncovered, stirring occasionally.
4. Serve approximately 1 ¼ cups of the prepared chili in a carved-out round of sourdough bread or in a bowl. Combine the shredded cheeses together & top the chili with approximately ¼ cup of the cheese blend followed by a tablespoon of the sour cream & garnish with a tablespoon of chopped green onions. Serve and enjoy.

NUTRITION: 175 calories 30g carbs 24g protein

118. Chicken Tortilla Soup

<table>
<tr><td>Preparation Time:</td><td>10'</td><td>Servings:</td><td>2</td></tr>
</table>

Cooking Time: 30'

Ingredients

- 1 chicken breast; chopped into small pieces
- ½ cup sweet corn
- 1 cup onion, chopped
- 3 tablespoons fresh cilantro, chopped
- 1 cup chicken broth
- Avocado to taste
- 1 can diced chilies & tomatoes (8 ounces)
- Colby jack cheese to taste
- 1 squirt of lime juice in an individual bowl
- Tortilla chips to taste
- 1 cup water

Directions

1. Over moderate heat in a large, deep pot; combine the chicken broth together with water, onion, chili, and tomatoes, corn and cilantro; bring the mixture to a boil, stirring occasionally. Add in the chicken pieces; give it a good stir, and decrease the heat to a simmer. Cook for a couple of minutes, until the chicken is cooked through. Add Tortilla chips followed by avocado & cheese to taste in serving bowls. Add soup & a squirt of lime to the bowls. Serve hot & enjoy.

Nutrition: 165 calories 34g carbs 22g protein

119. TusCan TomaTo bIsque

| PREPARATION TIME: | 10' | | SERVINGS: | 4 |

| COOKING TIME: | 20' |

INGREDIENTS

- 4 garlic cloves, crushed
- 1 can chicken broth (14 ½ ounce), undiluted
- 2 cans no-salt-added diced tomatoes (14 ½ ounce each), undrained
- 1 teaspoon olive oil
- 4 -5 teaspoons parmesan cheese, grated
- 1 tablespoon balsamic vinegar
- 2 ½ cups 1" French bread cubes (2 ½ slices)
- 1 ½ teaspoons parsley flakes, dried
- Olive oil flavored cooking spray
- 1 teaspoon oregano, dried
- ½ teaspoon pepper

DIRECTIONS

1. Arrange bread cubes on a baking sheet in a single layer & coat the bread lightly with the cooking spray.
2. Bake until dry & toasted, for 8 to 10 minutes, at 400 F.
3. Now, over medium-low heat in large saucepan; heat the olive oil.
4. Once hot, add and sauté the garlic for 2 minutes.
5. Add the leftover ingredients (except grated parmesan cheese) & bring the mixture to a boil.
6. Decrease the heat & let simmer for 10 minutes, stirring every now and then.
7. Evenly divide the croutons among 4 to 5 bowls; ladle the soup over & sprinkle with the grated parmesan cheese. Serve immediately & enjoy.

NUTRITION: 166 calories 31g carbs 22g protein

120. broCColI CHeddar SouP

PREPARATION TIME: 20'

SERVINGS: 4

COOKING TIME: 40'

INGREDIENTS

- 6 tablespoons unsalted butter
- 1 small onion, chopped
- 2 cups half-and-half
- ¼ cup all-purpose flour
- 3 cups chicken broth, low-sodium
- ¼ teaspoon nutmeg, freshly grated
- 4 (7" each) sourdough bread boules (round loaves)
- 2 bay leaves
- 4 cups broccoli florets (1 large head)
- 2 ½ cups (approximately 8 ounces) sharp white & yellow cheddar cheese, grated, plus more for garnish
- 1 large carrot, diced
- Freshly ground pepper & kosher salt to taste

DIRECTIONS

1. Over moderate heat in a large pot or Dutch oven; heat the butter until melted. Add and cook the onion for 3 to 5 minutes until tender. Whisk in the flour & continue to cook for 3 to 4 more minutes until turn golden. Slowly whisk in the half-and-half until completely smooth. Add the chicken broth followed by nutmeg and bay leaves, then season with pepper and salt; bring the mixture to a simmer. Once done, decrease the heat to medium-low & cook for 15 to 20 more minutes until thickened, uncovered.
2. In the meantime, prepare the bread bowls: Cut a circle into the top of each loaf using a sharp knife, leaving approximately 1" border all around. Remove the bread top and then hollow out the middle using your fingers or with a fork, leaving a thick bread shell.
3. Add the carrot & broccoli to the broth mixture & let simmer for 15 to 20 minutes, until tender. Discard the bay leaves. Work in batches & carefully puree the soup in a blender until smooth. Add to the pot again.
4. Add the cheese to the soup & continue to whisk over medium heat until melted. If the soup appears to be too thick, feel free to add up to ¾ cup of water. Ladle into the bread bowls & garnish with cheese. Serve immediately & enjoy.

NUTRITION: 178 calories 33g carbs 25g protein

121. Pf CHang's SPICy CHICken Noodle SouP

PREPARATION TIME: 10'

SERVINGS: 6

COOKING TIME: 20'

INGREDIENTS

- 2 quarts chicken stock
- 1 tablespoon granulated sugar
- 3 tablespoons white vinegar
- 2 cloves garlic, minced
- 1 tablespoon ginger, freshly minced
- ¼ cup soy sauce
- Sriracha sauce to taste
- Red pepper flakes to taste
- 1-pound boneless chicken breast, cut into thin 2–3-inch pieces
- 3 tablespoons cornstarch
- Salt to taste
- 1 cup mushrooms, sliced
- 1 cup grape tomatoes, halved
- 3 green onions, sliced
- 2 tablespoons fresh cilantro, chopped
- ½ pound pasta, cooked to just under package Directions and drained

DIRECTIONS

1. Add the chicken stock, sugar, vinegar, garlic, ginger, soy sauce, Sriracha, and red pepper flakes to a large saucepan. Bring to a boil, then lower the heat to a simmer. Let cook for 5 minutes.
2. Season chicken with salt to taste. In a resealable bag, combine the chicken and the cornstarch. Shake to coat.
3. Add the chicken to the simmering broth a piece at a time. Then add the mushrooms. Continue to cook for another 5 minutes.
4. Stir in the tomatoes, green onions, cilantro, and cooked pasta. Serve with additional cilantro.

NUTRITION: 218 Calories 24g Total Fat 14g Carbs 17g Protein

122. Pf CHang's HoT and Sour SouP

PREPARATION TIME: 5'

SERVINGS: 6

COOKING TIME: 5'

INGREDIENTS

- 6 ounces chicken breasts, cut into thin strips
- 1-quart chicken stock
- 1 cup soy sauce
- 1 teaspoon white pepper
- 1 (6 ounces) can bamboo shoots, cut into strips
- 6 ounces wood ear mushrooms
- ½ cup cornstarch
- ½ cup water
- 2 eggs, beaten
- ½ cup white vinegar
- 6 ounces silken tofu, cut into strips
- Sliced green onions for garnish

DIRECTIONS

1. Cook the chicken strips in a hot skillet until cooked through. Set aside. Add the chicken stock, soy sauce, pepper, and bamboo shoots to a stockpot and bring to a boil. Stir in the chicken and let cook for about 3–4 minutes.
2. In a small dish, make a slurry with the cornstarch and water. Add a bit at a time to the stockpot until the broth thickens to your desired consistency.
3. Stir in the beaten eggs and cook for about 45 seconds or until the eggs are done.
4. Remove from the heat and add the vinegar and tofu. Garnish with sliced green onions.

NUTRITION: 228 Calories 14g Total Fat 13g Carbs 13g Protein

123. dIsneyland's MonTerey Clam CHoWder

PREPARATION TIME: 15'	SERVINGS: 2

COOKING TIME: 60'

INGREDIENTS

- 5 tablespoons butter
- 5 tablespoons flour
- 2 tablespoons vegetable oil
- 1½ cups potatoes (peeled, diced)
- ½ cup onion, diced
- ½ cup red pepper
- ½ cup green pepper
- ½ cup celery
- 2¼ cups clam juice
- 1½ cups heavy cream
- 1 cup clams, chopped
- 1 tablespoon fresh thyme
- ¼–½ teaspoon salt
- 1 pinch white pepper
- 1/3–½ teaspoon Tabasco sauce
- 4 individual sourdough round breads made into bowls
- Chives for garnish (optional)

DIRECTIONS

1. Make a roux by mixing melted butter and flour over medium heat for 10 minutes. Flour burns quickly, so make sure to watch the mixture closely. Set the roux aside.
2. Sauté the potatoes, onions, peppers, and celery in the oil for 10 minutes using a soup pot.
3. Whisk the rest of the ingredients, including the roux, into the soup pot, and bring the entire mixture to a boil.
4. After the mixture has boiled, reduce the heat and let it simmer for another 5 minutes.
5. Season the soup as you like with salt and pepper. To serve, ladle the soup evenly into the prepared bread bowls and sprinkle with fresh chives if desired.

NUTRITION: 472.3 Calories 36.9g Total Fat 27.4g Carbs 9.3g Protein Sodium: 771.5 mg

124. OuTbaCk's baked PoTaTo SouP

PREPARATION TIME: 15′	SERVINGS: 2

COOKING TIME: 40′

INGREDIENTS

- 2 quarts water
- 8 medium-sized potatoes, cut into chunks
- 4 cans chicken broth
- 1 small onion, minced
- 1 teaspoon salt
- 1 teaspoon ground pepper
- 2 cups cold water
- 1 cup butter
- ¾ cup flour
- 1½ cup heavy cream
- 1½ cups jack cheese
- 2-3 thick-cut bacon slices, cooked and diced
- ¼ cup green onion, minced

DIRECTIONS

1. In a pot, add water and potatoes. Bring to a boil, reduce heat to medium, and cook potatoes for 10-15 minutes or until for tender. Drain and set aside.
2. In a separate pot, pour in broth and mix in onions, salt, pepper, and water. Simmer for 20 minutes.
3. Meanwhile, in another pot, whisk together butter and flour. Slowly add this to the pot of broth. Stir in heavy cream to the mixture and simmer for 20 minutes. Mix in potatoes to reheat.
4. Sprinkle jack cheese, bacon bits, and green onions on top. Serve.

NUTRITION: 845 Calories 49g Total Fat81g Carbs 23g Protein

125. aPPlebee's TomaTo basIl SouP

PREPARATION TIME: 15'	SERVINGS: 2

COOKING TIME: 20'

INGREDIENTS

- 3 tablespoons olive oil
- 1 small garlic clove, finely chopped
- 1 10 ¾-ounce can condense tomato soup
- ¼ cup bottled marinara sauce
- 5 ounces water
- 1 teaspoon fresh oregano, diced
- ½ teaspoon ground black pepper
- 1 tablespoon fresh basil, diced
- 6 Italian-style seasoned croutons
- 2 tablespoons Parmesan cheese, shredded

DIRECTIONS

1. Heat oil in a pan over medium heat. Add garlic and stir fry for 2 to 3 minutes or until garlic is soft and aromatic.
2. Pour tomato soup and marinara sauce into a pan and stir. Add water gradually. Toss in oregano and pepper. Once simmering, reduce heat to low. Cook for about 15 more minutes until all the flavors are combined. Add basil and stir.
3. Transfer to bowls. Add croutons on top and sprinkle with Parmesan cheese. Serve.

NUTRITION: 350 Calories 26g Total fat 28g Carbs 2g Fibers

126. CHICken EnCHIlada SouP from CHIll'

PREPARATION TIME:	15'		SERVINGS:	6

COOKING TIME: 40'

INGREDIENTS

- 1-pound chicken breast, boneless and skinless, cut in half
- 1 tablespoon vegetable oil
- ½ cup onion, chopped
- 1 garlic clove, finely chopped
- 1-quart chicken broth
- 1 cup masa harina
- 3 cups water, divided
- 1 cup enchilada sauce
- 2 cups cheddar cheese, grated
- 1 teaspoon salt
- 1 teaspoon chili powder
- ½ teaspoon ground cumin
- Crispy tortilla strips for garnish

DIRECTIONS

1. Heat oil in a pot over medium heat. Add chicken breasts and cook evenly until browned on all sides. Remove from pot. Shred, then set aside.
2. Return pot to heat and add onion and garlic. Sauté until onions are translucent. Add chicken broth.
3. Mix masa harina and 2 cups water in a bowl. Then add into pot with the onions and garlic. Add the remaining water, enchilada sauce, cheddar cheese, salt, chili powder, and cumin. Bring mixture to a boil. Add cooked chicken to the pot. Lower heat. Simmer for about 30 to 40 minutes until soup is thick. Garnish with crispy tortilla strips. Serve.

NUTRITION: 290 Calories 16g Total fat 14g Carbs 2g Fibers

127. Panera's broCColl CHeddar SouP

PREPARATION TIME:	15'	SERVINGS:	8

COOKING TIME: 50'

INGREDIENTS

- 1 tablespoon butter
- ½ onion, diced
- ¼ cup melted butter
- ¼ cup flour
- 2 cups milk
- 2 cups chicken stock
- 1½ cup broccoli florets, diced
- 1 cup carrots, cut into thin strips
- 1 stalk celery, sliced
- 2½ cups Cheddar cheese, grated
- Salt and pepper, to taste

DIRECTIONS

1. Melt 1 tablespoon of butter in a skillet and cook onion over medium heat for 5 minutes or until caramelized. Set aside.
2. In a saucepan, mix melted butter and flour, then cook on medium-low heat. Add 1 or 2 tablespoons milk to the flour to prevent from burning. Cook for at least 3 minutes or until smooth.
3. While stirring, gently pour the rest of the milk in with the flour. Mix in chicken stock. Simmer for 20 minutes or until thick and well blended. Toss in the broccoli, carrots, cooked onion, and celery. Cook for an additional 20 minutes or until vegetables turn soft.
4. Mix in cheese and stir until the cheese is completely melted. Season with salt and pepper, to taste.
5. Transfer into individual bowls. Serve.

NUTRITION: 304 Calories 23g Total Fat 11g Carbs 14g Protein

128. Cheesy Walkabout Soup

Preparation Time:	15'		Servings:	2

Cooking Time:	50'

Ingredients

- 6 tablespoons butter, divided
- 2 large sweet onions, thinly sliced
- 2 cups low sodium chicken broth
- ¼ teaspoon ground black pepper
- 2 chicken bouillon cubes
- 3 tablespoons flour
- ¼ teaspoon salt
- 1 ½ cups whole milk
- Pinch nutmeg
- ¼ cup Velveeta® cheese, cubed

Directions

1. In a large pot or Dutch oven, melt half the butter over medium heat. Add the onions. Cook, stirring occasionally, until the onions are transparent but not browned.
2. Add the chicken broth, black pepper, and bouillon cubes. Mix well and cook on low to heat through.
3. In a separate saucepan, melt the remaining butter. Add the flour and salt and cook, whisking constantly, until smooth and lightly browned. Gradually whisk in the milk and cook over medium heat until it is very thick. Mix in the nutmeg.
4. Add the white sauce to the onion soup mixture, together with the Velveeta cubes. Stir gently over medium heat until the cheese is melted, and everything is combined.

Nutrition: 260 Calories 19g Total Fat 13g Carbs 5g Protein

129. Olive Garden Chicken Gnocchi Soup

PREPARATION TIME: 15'	SERVINGS: 4

COOKING TIME: 20'

INGREDIENTS

- 4 tablespoons Butter
- 1 tablespoon extra-virgin olive oil
- 1 cup finely diced onion
- 1/2 cup finely diced celery
- 2 garlic cloves, minced
- 1/4 cup all-purpose flour
- 1/4 half-and-half
- 28 ounces chicken broth
- 1/2 teaspoon dried thyme
- 1/2 teaspoon dried parsley flakes
- 1/4 teaspoon ground nutmeg (optional)
- ½ cup carrots finely shredded
- 1 cup spinach leaves coarsely chopped
- 1 cup chicken meat cooked and diced
- 16 ounces package ready-to-use gnocchi

DIRECTIONS

1. Melt the butter in a big saucepan over medium heat. Add the onions, celery, and garlic and cook, stirring occasionally until the onions are translucent.
2. Drizzle the flour and cook for about 1 minute. Whiskey at half past one. Cook until thick.
3. Shake the chicken broth. Simmer until thick again. Stir in 1/2 teaspoon salt, thyme, parsley, nutmeg (if used), carrots, spinach, chicken, and ginger.
4. Boil with the soup until hot. Season with extra salt before serving.

NUTRITION: 369 Calories 32g Carbohydrates 11g Protein 22g Fat

130. Panera broCColi CHeese SouP

<table>
<tr><td>PREPARATION TIME:</td><td>10'</td><td>SERVINGS:</td><td>4</td></tr>
</table>

COOKING TIME: 20'

INGREDIENTS

- 1/4 cup unsalted butter
- 1/2 cup diced onions (yellow or white)
- 1 cup shredded carrots (I used matchsticks that I cut into half-inch pieces)
- 2 1/2-3 cups broccoli florets, chopped small
- 1 1/2 cups chicken broth
- 1 cup milk (I use skim/fat-free)
- 1 cup heavy whipping cream
- 1/4 cup all-purpose flour
- 1 1/2 tsp kosher salt
- 1/2 tsp black pepper
- pinch of crushed red pepper flakes (or more as desired)
- 2 cups shredded cheddar cheese

DIRECTIONS

1. Melt the butter in a large bowl over medium-high heat. Add in onions, carrots, and broccoli. Cook for about 5 minutes to soften (may vary depending on the size of your chopped vegetables)
2. Gently add the broth, milk, and cream. Sprinkle with flour and add salt, pepper, and red pepper flakes. Keep stirring and heating over medium heat until thick. This will take about 10-15 minutes.
3. When thickened, add the cheese and stir until melted and smooth. Serve the soup and enjoy!

NUTRITION: 725 Calories 55g Total Fat 40g Carbohydrates 11g Fiber

Chapter 7

aPPetIzer r ecIPes

131. bennlgan's broCColl bITes

PREPARATION TIME: 10'

SERVINGS: 4

COOKING TIME: 20'

INGREDIENTS

- Broccoli Bites
- 2 cups frozen chopped broccoli
- 3 eggs
- ¾ cup shredded Colby cheese
- ¾ cup shredded Monterey jack cheese
- 5 tablespoons real bacon bits
- 1 tablespoon diced yellow onion
- 2 tablespoons flour
- 4 cups oil, for frying
- Italian breadcrumbs, as needed
- Honey-Mustard Dipping Sauce
- ¾ cup sour cream
- 1/3 cup mayonnaise
- 1/3 cup Dijon mustard
- 1/3 cup honey
- 4 teaspoons lemon juice

DIRECTIONS

1. Drain and thaw the broccoli, then set aside. Whisk the eggs until well blended. Transfer the eggs, broccoli, cheese, bacon bits, flour, and onion in a plastic container then combine all together.
2. Let it chill for 1 hour. Heat oil at 350 degrees. Put bread crumbs in a pan. Then scoop 1 portion of broccoli mixture and form into a ball, then coat it well with bread crumbs. Fry broccoli bites and make sure they don't stick together. When cooked, place in a plate with paper towels.
3. For dipping sauce:
4. Mix sour cream, mayonnaise, and mustard. Lightly stir in some honey and lemon juice, then mix until smooth.

NUTRITION: 282.9 calories 18.9g total fats 12.8g protein

132. Chi Chi's Seafood Nachos

| Preparation Time: | 15' | Cooking Time: | 10' | Servings: | 2 |

Ingredients

- 16 large tortilla chips
- 1 (8-ounce) package Louis Kemp Crab Delights
- 1 (8-ounce) package Louis Kemp Lobster Delights
- 1 (8-ounce) thawed frozen package salad shrimp
- 1 cup shredded Monterey jack cheese

Directions

1. Place the tortilla chips on a plate. Add in the crab, lobster, and shrimp on top. Scatter some cheese, then put it in a microwave for 2 minutes. Serve.

Nutrition: 271 calories 17g total fats 13g protein

133. Chili's Boneless Buffalo Wings

| Preparation Time: | 10' | Cooking Time: | 20' | Servings: | 2 |

Ingredients

- 2 teaspoons salt
- ½ teaspoon ground pepper
- ¼ teaspoon cayenne pepper
- 1 cup flour
- ¼ teaspoon paprika
- 1 egg
- 1 cup milk
- 2 boneless skinless chicken breasts
- 2–4 cups cooking oil
- ¼ cup hot sauce
- 1 tablespoon margarine

Directions

1. Mix salt, peppers, flour, and paprika. In a different bowl, whisk egg and milk, then cut each chicken breast in bite-size pieces. Preheat the oil. Coat the chicken into the egg mixture, then with the spice mixture. Repeat to double coat.
2. When done with the breading, transfer in a plate and let it chill for 15 minutes. Then deep fry until the breading is golden brown.
3. Mix the hot sauce and margarine, then microwave until the margarine has melted. When done frying, place them on a plate with paper towels. Put the chicken in a covered container. Transfer the sauce over the chicken, cover it, and shake gently until coated with sauce.

Nutrition: 280 calories 16g total fats 11g protein

134. Chili's Chicken Fajita Nachos

Preparation Time:	15'	Cooking Time:	10'	Servings:	2

Ingredients

- 1 chicken breast strips
- 1 sliced Vidalia onion
- 1 bell pepper, cut into thin strips
- 1 envelope fajita seasoning mix
- 16 large tortilla chips
- ½ cup shredded Cheddar cheese
- ½ cup shredded Monterey jack cheese
- 16 jarred jalapeño pepper slices
- 1 cup shredded lettuce
- ½ cup thick and chunky salsa
- 2 tablespoons sour cream
- 2 tablespoons guacamole

Directions

1. Sauté chicken, onions, and bell peppers following the fajita seasoning packet. Drain and set aside. Put tortilla chips on a large plate, then layer the cooked chicken fajita on top. Put some cheese and jalapeno on top, then microwave for 3 minutes. Lastly, garnish it with lettuce, salsa, sour cream, and guacamole.

NUTRITION: 279 calories 18.1g total fats 12.4g protein

135. Chili's Southwestern Eggrolls

Preparation Time:	10'	Cooking Time:	5'	Servings:	15

Ingredients

- 1 (16-ounce) can black beans
- 1 (16-ounce) can corn
- 2 cups fresh spinach
- 2 jalapeños
- 2 garlic cloves
- ¼ cup fresh cilantro
- ¼ cup onion
- ½ teaspoon chili powder
- ½ teaspoon salt
- ¼ teaspoon black pepper
- 2 cups Mexican cheese blend
- 15 small whole-wheat tortillas
- Cooking oil
- Prepared salsa
- Sour cream

Directions

1. Mix beans, corn, spinach, jalapeños, garlic, cilantro, onion, chili powder, salt, pepper, and cheese. Stir in 2 tablespoons of mixture on each tortilla then roll. Preheat frying pan at medium-high heat, then fry the eggrolls. Drizzle with salsa and sour cream.

NUTRITION: 278 calories 17g total fats 13g protein

136. Chili's Texas Cheese fries

PREPARATION TIME: 15'   COOKING TIME: 5'   SERVINGS: 3-4

INGREDIENTS

- 1/2 (28-ounce) bag frozen steak fries
- 4 slices bacon
- 1 (8-ounce) bag shredded Cheddar cheese
- Jalapeño pepper slices, to taste
- Ranch salad dressing, for dipping

DIRECTIONS

1. Place the fries in a cookie sheet and spread evenly, then bake. In another cookie sheet, spread the bacon strips and bake until crispy. When done, take out from the oven. Stir in a thick layer of cheese and jalapenos on top of the fries, then topped with crushed bacon on top. Let it bake until the cheese melts.

NUTRITION: 277 calories 16g total fats 11g protein

137. dave and busTer's PHIlly STeak rolls

PREPARATION TIME: 10'   COOKING TIME: 20'   SERVINGS: 10

INGREDIENTS

- 1 tablespoon vegetable oil
- ½ cup diced onions
- 1 box of Steakums (7 slices)
- Salt and pepper, to taste
- 1 (15-ounce) jar of Cheez Whiz
- 10 egg roll wraps
- 2 cups vegetable oil, for frying

DIRECTIONS

1. Cook oil in a skillet over medium heat. Stir in the onion and cook until onion is translucent.
2. Mix in the Steakums with the skillet. Season well, then cook until steak is no longer pink. Set aside. Put an egg roll wrap in a diamond position.
3. Put 2 tablespoons of beef and onions in the center of an egg roll wrap, then top it with 1–2 tablespoons of Cheese Wiz. Careful, don't overfill. Fold in the corner closest to you, then flap side corners over and roll. Use egg wash to seal. Fill the pan with 1-inch oil and heat it. Carefully put the rolls into the pan and cook until golden brown. Serve.

NUTRITION: 283 calories 17.4g total fats 12.1g protein

138. Joe's Crab Shack Crab Nachos

| PREPARATION TIME: | 15' | COOKING TIME: | 10' | SERVINGS: | 3-4 |

INGREDIENTS

- 16 baked tortilla chips
- 1 (8-ounce) package of chopped imitation crabmeat
- ¼ cup sour cream
- ¼ cup mayonnaise
- 2 tablespoons chopped onion
- 1 cup shredded Cheddar cheese
- ¼ cup sliced black olives
- ¼ teaspoon paprika

DIRECTIONS

1. Put tortilla chips in a single layer on a baking sheet. Mix the crab, sour cream, mayonnaise, and onion. Portion it about 1 tablespoon on each chip. Garnish with cheese, olives, and paprika on top, then bake at 350 degrees until the cheese melts.

NUTRITION: 281 calories 16g total fats 11g protein

139. Johnny Carino's Italian Nachos

| PREPARATION TIME: | 10' | COOKING TIME: | 5' | SERVINGS: | 4 |

INGREDIENTS

- 1 (12-ounce) package wontons
- 1 (1 pound) package ground pork
- 3–4 tablespoons olive oil
- ½ cup Alfredo sauce
- 1 (6-ounce) package grilled chicken pieces
- 2 diced Roma tomatoes
- ½ cup sliced olives
- ¼ cup pepperoncini peppers
- Jalapeño peppers, to taste
- 1 cup shredded mozzarella cheese

DIRECTIONS

1. Preheat at 400 degrees. Slice wontons to form triangles. Sauté pork until brown. Stir in the wonton triangles in olive oil and put it in a single layer on the baking sheet and bake until lightly brown. Take out from the oven and drain with paper towels. Pour some alfredo sauce then mix in pork, grilled chicken, tomatoes, olives, and peppers on the wontons. Sprinkle with mozzarella, then microwave until cheese melt.

NUTRITION: 280 calories 16g total fats 10.9g protein

140. Olive Garden bread STICks

| PREPARATION TIME: 10' | COOKING TIME: 5' | SERVINGS: 4-6 |

INGREDIENTS

- 1 (10.5 ounce/6 counts) package frozen bread sticks
- 2 tablespoons olive oil
- ¼ cup Parmesan cheese

DIRECTIONS

1. Preheat at 350 degrees. Grease each bread stick with olive oil. Topped it with Parmesan cheese. Seal it in an aluminum foil. Let it bake for 12–15 minutes.

NUTRITION: 279 calories 15g total fats 9.9g protein

141. Olive Garden STuffed MusHrooms

| PREPARATION TIME: 10' | COOKING TIME: 15' | SERVINGS: 4-6 |

INGREDIENTS

- 1 (6-ounce) can clams
- 8–12 fresh mushrooms
- 1 finely minced green onion
- 1/8 teaspoon garlic salt
- ½ teaspoon minced garlic
- 1 tablespoon melted butter
- 1 teaspoon oregano leaves
- ½ cup Italian breadcrumbs
- 1 egg
- 2 tablespoons grated Parmesan cheese
- 1 tablespoon grated Romano cheese
- 2 tablespoons grated mozzarella cheese
- ¼ cup melted butter, for garnish
- ¼ cup grated mozzarella cheese, for garnish
- Fresh minced parsley, for garnish

DIRECTIONS

1. Preheat at 350 degrees. Mince the clams and save the ¼ cup of clam juice for the stuffing. Lightly grease the small baking dish. Rinse the mushrooms, then pat it dry, and cut off the stems.
2. Mix the clams, onions, garlic salt, minced garlic, butter, and oregano. Combine the bread crumbs, egg, and clam juice, then add in the cheese.
3. Place 1½ teaspoons of the stuffing mixture inside the mushroom. Transfer the stuffed mushrooms in the baking dish and drizzle with ¼ cup melted butter on the top. Seal and bake for about 35–40 minutes.
4. Take out the cover and topped it with ¼ cup of mozzarella and return it in the oven until the cheese melt. Serve with freshly diced parsley.

NUTRITION: 278 calories 14g total fats 10.9g protein

142. Olive Garden Toasted Ravioli

| Preparation Time: | 10' | Cooking Time: | 20' | Servings: | 2-4 |

INGREDIENTS

- ¼ cup water
- 2 eggs
- 1 teaspoon Italian seasoning
- 1 teaspoon garlic salt
- 1 cup plain bread crumbs
- 1 cup flour
- 1 (16-ounce) package meat-filled ravioli

DIRECTIONS

1. In a bowl, mix the water and eggs and beat well. Set aside. In another bowl, mix the Italian seasonings and garlic salt with the bread crumbs and set aside. In a third bowl, measure the flour and set aside. Heat vegetable oil in a deep fryer or skillet to 350°F for deep frying. Dip the ravioli in flour, then in the egg wash, then in bread crumbs, and carefully place in hot oil. Fry about 2–3 minutes until golden, remove from oil, and drain.

NUTRITION: 277 calories 19g total fats 14g protein

143. Olive Garden Tomato Basil Crostini

| Preparation Time: | 10' | Cooking Time: | 10' | Servings: | 4 |

INGREDIENTS

- 4 chopped medium tomatoes
- 6–8 chopped fresh basil leaves
- 6 tablespoons extra-virgin olive oil
- 8 slices of crusty bread
- 2–3 cloves of garlic

DIRECTIONS

1. In a medium bowl, mix the tomatoes, basil, and olive oil together. Grill or toast the bread. Rub the bread with garlic and top with the tomato mixture.

NUTRITION: 269 calories 15g total fats 10g protein

144. OuTbaCk STeakHouse bloomIn' OnIon

Preparation Time: 10'	Servings: 4

Cooking Time: 5'

Ingredients

Seasoned Flour
- 2 cups flour
- 4 teaspoons paprika
- 2 teaspoons garlic powder
- ½ teaspoon pepper
- ¼ teaspoon cayenne pepper

Batter
- 1/3 cup cornstarch
- 1½ cups flour
- 2 teaspoons minced garlic
- 2 teaspoons paprika
- 1 teaspoon salt
- 1 teaspoon pepper
- 24 ounces beer
- 1 Vidalia or Texas sweet onion

Directions

1. Preheat oil in a deep fryer to 375°F. In a shallow bowl, combine all seasoned flour ingredients. Prepare the batter: mix cornstarch, flour, and seasonings until well blended. Add the beer and mix well.
2. Cut about ¾" on top of onion and peel. Cut 12–16 vertical wedges, but do not cut through the bottom root end. Remove about 1" of petals from the center of the onion.
3. Dip prepared onion in seasoned flour and remove the excess by shaking. Separate the petals and dip into the batter to coat thoroughly.
4. Gently place in the fryer basket and deep-fry 1½ minutes. Turn the onion over and fry an additional 1½ minutes. Drain on paper towels. Place onion upright in a shallow bowl and remove center core with a circular cutter or apple corer.

Nutrition: 280 calories 16g total fats 11g protein

145. T.g.I. friday's baked PoTaTo SkIns

PREPARATION TIME: 10'   COOKING TIME: 15'   SERVINGS: 5

INGREDIENTS

- 10 baked potato halves
- 1 tablespoon melted butter
- Seasoned salt, to taste
- ¾ cup shredded Cheddar cheese
- 5 strips of cooked and crumbled bacon
- 1 green onion, diced

DIRECTIONS

1. Preheat oven to 375°F. Remove as much of the potato flesh as you can, leaving only the skins. Brush potato shells with butter and season with salt. Bake for 15–20 minutes, until crisp. Remove and sprinkle with cheese, bacon, and onion. Place back in the oven for 6–8 minutes until the cheese has melted. Serve with sour cream or ranch dressing.

NUTRITION: 281 calories 15g total fats 11g protein

146. PeI WeI's Crab WonTon

PREPARATION TIME: 10'   COOKING TIME: 5'   SERVINGS: 6

INGREDIENTS

- 1 (7-ounce) can white crab meat
- ½ pound cream cheese, softened
- 2–3 green onions, sliced
- ½ tablespoon garlic powder
- Splash of soy sauce
- Wonton wrappers
- Cooking oil

DIRECTIONS

1. Combine the crab, cream cheese, green onions, garlic powder, and soy sauce in a bowl. Stir until the mixture reaches a paste-like consistency.
2. Spoon a bit of the mixture into each wonton wrapper and fold. Seal around the edges with a moistened finger.

NUTRITION: 244 Calories 15g Fat 34g Carbs 87g Protein

147. Pei Wei's Vietnamese Chicken Salad Spring Roll

PREPARATION TIME:	10'		SERVINGS:	4-6

COOKING TIME: 1'

INGREDIENTS

Rice Wrappers:
- Green leaf lettuce like Boston Bibb lettuce
- Napa cabbage, shredded
- Green onions, chopped
- Mint, chopped
- Carrots, cut into 1-inch matchsticks
- Peanuts

Lime dressing:
- 2 tablespoons lime juice, about 1 lime
- 1½ teaspoons water
- 1 tablespoon sugar
- 1 teaspoon salt
- Dash of pepper
- 3 tablespoons oil

Peanut dipping sauce:
- 2 tablespoons soy sauce
- 1 tablespoon rice wine vinegar
- 2 tablespoons brown sugar
- ¼ cup peanut butter
- 1 teaspoon chipotle Tabasco
- 1 teaspoon honey
- 1 teaspoon sweet chili sauce
- 1 teaspoon lime vinaigrette

DIRECTIONS

Lime dressing:
1. Add everything but the oil to a small container or bowl and shake or stir until the sugar and salt are dissolved. Next, add the oil and shake well.

Peanut Dipping Sauce:
2. Add all the ingredients to a small bowl and mix to combine thoroughly.

Assembling:
3. In a large bowl, mix together all the salad ingredients except for the rice wrappers and lettuce.
4. Place the rice wrappers in warm water for about 1 minute to soften.
5. Transfer the wrappers to a plate and top each with 2 pieces of lettuce.
6. Top the lettuce with the salad mixture and drizzle with the lime dressing. Fold the wrapper by tucking in the ends and then rolling.
7. Serve with lime dressing and peanut dipping sauce.

NUTRITION: 178 Calories 4.4g Fat 7g Carb 68g Protein

148. Takeout dry garlic ribs

PREPARATION TIME: 15'

SERVINGS: 4-6

COOKING TIME: 2 H 15'

INGREDIENTS

- 6 pounds pork ribs
- 1½ cups broth
- 1½ cups brown sugar
- ¼ cup soy sauce
- 12 cloves garlic, minced
- ¼ cup yellow mustard
- 1 large onion, finely chopped
- ¼ teaspoon salt
- ½ teaspoon black pepper

DIRECTIONS

1. Preheat oven to 200 degrees. Season ribs with salt and pepper and place on a baking tray. Cover with aluminum foil and bake for 1 hour.
2. In a mixing bowl, stir together the broth, brown sugar, soy sauce, garlic, mustard, and onion. Continue stirring until the sugar is completely dissolved. After an hour, remove the foil from the ribs and turn the heat up to 350°F.
3. Carefully pour the sauce over the ribs. Re-cover with the foil and return to the oven for 1 hour. Remove the foil and bake for 15 more minutes on each side.

NUTRITION: 233 Calories 3.6g Fat 6.4g Carbs 65g Protein

149. abuelo's JalaPeno PoPPers

PREPARATION TIME: 10'	SERVINGS: 8

COOKING TIME: 1 H 10'

INGREDIENTS

- 30 jalapeno peppers
- 1 cup milk
- 2 packages soften cream cheese, at room temperature (8-ounces each)
- 1/8 teaspoon paprika
- 12 ounces Cheddar cheese, shredded
- 1/8 teaspoon chili powder
- 1 cup flour
- 1/8 teaspoon garlic powder
- 1 cup seasoned breadcrumbs
- ¼ teaspoon ground black pepper
- 1 quart of oil for frying
- ¼ teaspoon salt

DIRECTIONS

1. Scrape out seeds and the pith inside of the jalapeno peppers using a spoon. Combine cheddar cheese together with cream cheese in a medium-sized bowl; give them a good stir until blended well. Fill each pepper half with the prepared cream cheese blend using a spoon.
2. Add flour into a small-sized shallow bowl. Add paprika, pepper, garlic powder, chili powder, and salt. Blend into the flour until it is mixed. Pour milk into a separate medium-sized shallow bowl. Dip stuffed jalapeno into flour. Place the floured pepper on a large-sized baking sheet with a rack. Let dry for 10 minutes.
3. Pour the dried breadcrumbs into a separate bowl. Dip the floured jalapeno pepper into the milk & then into the bowl with the breadcrumbs. Place the pepper on the rack again. Preheat the oil to 350 F in advance. Dip pepper into the milk & then into the breadcrumbs. Repeat these steps until you have utilized the entire dipping peppers.
4. Work in batches and fry peppers for a minute or two, until turn golden brown. Remove from oil & place them on a baking rack to drain.

NUTRITION: 257 Calories 14.3g Fat 18.9g Carbs 21.5g Protein

150. applebee's baJa PoTaTo boaTs

PREPARATION TIME: 10'

SERVINGS: 4

COOKING TIME: 30'

INGREDIENTS

For Pico de Gallo:
- 1 ½ teaspoon fresh cilantro, minced
- 1 tablespoon canned jalapeño slices (nacho slices), diced
- 3 tablespoons Spanish onion, chopped
- 1 chopped tomato (approximately ½ cup)
- A dash each of freshly-ground black pepper & salt

For the Potato Boats:
- 2 slices Canadian bacon diced (roughly 2 tablespoons)
- Canola oil nonstick cooking spray, as required
- 1/3 cup Cheddar cheese, shredded - 3 russet potatoes, medium
- 1/3 cup Mozzarella cheese - salt as needed
- On the Side: - Salsa & sour cream

DIRECTIONS

1. Combine the entire Pico De Gallo ingredients together in a large bowl; mix well. When done, place in a refrigerator until ready to use.
2. Preheat your oven to 400 F in advance. Place potatoes in oven & bake until tender, for an hour. Set aside at room temperature until easy to handle. When done, cut them lengthwise 2 times. This should make 3 ½ to ¾" slices, throwing the middle slices away.
3. Increase your oven's temperature to 450 F. Take a spoon & scoop out the inside of the potato skins. Ensure that you must leave at least ¼ of an inch of the potato inside each skin. Spray the potato skin completely on all sides with the spray of nonstick canola oil. Put the skins, cut-side facing up on a large-sized cookie sheet. Sprinkle them with salt & bake in the preheated oven until the edges start to turn brown, for 12 to 15 minutes.
4. Combine both the cheeses together in a large bowl. Sprinkle approximately 1 ½ tablespoon of the mixture on each potato skin. Then sprinkle a teaspoon of the Canadian bacon over the cheese. Top this with a large tablespoon of the Pico de Gallo and then sprinkle each skin with some more cheese.
5. Place the skins into the oven again & bake until the cheese melts, for 2 to 4 more minutes. Remove & let them sit for a minute. Slice each one lengthwise using a sharp knife. Serve hot with some salsa and sour cream on the side.

NUTRITION: 254 Calories 24g Fat 43g Carbs 55g Protein

151. applebee's Chicken Wings

PREPARATION TIME: 15'

SERVINGS: 6

COOKING TIME: 35'

INGREDIENTS

- 35 chicken wings
- 1 ½ tablespoon flour
- 3 tablespoons vinegar
- 1 ¼ teaspoon cayenne pepper
- 1 tablespoon Worcestershire sauce
- 12 ounces Louisiana hot sauce
- ¼ teaspoon garlic powder

DIRECTIONS

1. Cook the chicken wings either by deep-frying or baking.
2. Mix the entire sauce ingredients (except the flour) together over low-medium heat in a large saucepan. Cook until warm and then add in the flour; stir well until you get your desired level of thickness.
3. When thick, cover the bottom of 9x13" baking dish with the sauce. Combine the leftover sauce with the cooked wings & place them in the baking dish. Bake until warm, for 15 to 20 minutes, at 300 F.
4. Serve with blue-cheese dressing and celery sticks. Enjoy.

NUTRITION: 189 Calories 11g Fat 35g Carbs 46g Protein

152. Panda Express's Chicken Potstickers

PREPARATION TIME: 40'

SERVINGS: 50

COOKING TIME: 30'

INGREDIENTS

- ½ cup + 2 tablespoons soy sauce, divided
- 1 tablespoon rice vinegar
- 3 tablespoons chives, divided
- 1 tablespoon sesame seeds
- 1 teaspoon sriracha hot sauce
- 1-pound ground pork
- 3 cloves garlic, minced
- 1 egg, beaten
- 1½ tablespoons sesame oil
- 1 tablespoon fresh ginger, minced
- 50 dumpling wrappers
- 1 cup vegetable oil, for frying
- 1/4 water

DIRECTIONS

1. In a mixing bowl, whisk together the ½ cup of soy sauce, vinegar, 1 tablespoon of the chives, sesame seeds, and sriracha to make the dipping sauce.
2. In a separate bowl, mix together the pork, garlic, egg, the rest of the chives, the 2 tablespoons of soy sauce, sesame oil, and the ginger.
3. Add about 1 tablespoon of the filling to each dumpling wrapper.
4. Pinch the sides of the wrappers together to seal. You may need to wet the edges a bit, so they'll stick.
5. Heat the cup of oil in a large skillet. When hot, working in batches, add the dumplings and cook until golden brown on all sides. Take care of not overloading your pan.
6. Add the water and cook until tender, then serve with the dipping sauce.

NUTRITION: 182 Calories 2.3g Fat 19g Carbs 11.2g Protein

153. Panda exPress's Cream CHeese rangoon

PREPARATION TIME: 5'

SERVINGS: 24

COOKING TIME: 5'

INGREDIENTS

- ¼ cup green onions, chopped
- ½ pound cream cheese, softened
- ½ teaspoon garlic powder
- ½ teaspoon salt
- 24 wonton wrappers
- Oil for frying

DIRECTIONS

1. Add the green onions, cream cheese, garlic powder, and salt to a medium-sized bowl and mix together.
2. Lay the wonton wrappers out and moisten the edges of the first one. Add about ½ tablespoon of filling to the center of the wrapper and seal by pinching the edges together, starting with the corners and working your way inward. Make sure it is sealed tightly. Repeat with the remaining wrappers.
3. Add about 3 inches of oil to a large pot. Heat it to about 350°F, then add the wontons a few at a time and cook until brown.
4. Remove from oil and place on a paper-towel-lined plate to drain.

NUTRITION: 193 Calories 5g Fat 100g Carbs 11g Protein

154. Panda Express's Chicken Egg Roll

PREPARATION TIME: 10'

SERVINGS: 6-8

COOKING TIME: 5'

INGREDIENTS

- 2 tablespoons soy sauce, divided
- 2 cloves garlic, minced, divided
- 2 green onions, chopped, divided
- 3 tablespoons vegetable oil, divided
- ½ pound boneless skinless chicken breasts, cooked whole & cut into pieces
- ½ head green cabbage, thinly shredded
- 1 large carrot, peeled and shredded
- 1 cup bean sprouts
- 12–16 egg roll wrappers
- 1 tablespoon cornstarch mixed with 3 tablespoons water
- Peanut Oil for frying

DIRECTIONS

1. In a resealable plastic bag, combine 1 tablespoon of the soy sauce with 1 clove of minced garlic, 1 green onion, and 1 tablespoon of the oil. Mix well. Add the cut-up chicken pieces, seal the bag, and squish it around to make sure the chicken is covered. Refrigerate for at least 30 minutes.
2. After the chicken has marinated, pour 1 tablespoon of the oil into a large skillet and heat over medium-high heat. When the oil is hot, add the chicken and cook, stirring occasionally, until the chicken is cooked through. Remove the chicken from the skillet and set aside. Pour the remaining tablespoon of oil into the skillet and add the cabbage, carrots, and remaining soy sauce. Cook and stir until the carrots and cabbage start to soften, then add the bean sprouts and the remaining garlic and green onions. Cook another minute or so.
3. Drain the chicken and vegetables thoroughly using either a cheesecloth or a mesh strainer. Getting all the excess liquid out will keep the egg rolls from getting soggy. In a large saucepan or Dutch oven, heat 3 inches of oil to 375°F. Place about 2 tablespoons of the chicken and vegetables into the center of each egg roll wrapper. Fold the ends up and roll up to cover the filling. Seal by dipping your finger in the water and cornstarch mixture and covering the edges.
4. Cook the egg rolls in batches, a few at a time, for about five minutes or until golden brown and crispy. Remove from oil to a paper-towel-lined plate to drain.

NUTRITION: 349 Calories 4g Fat 17.6g Carbs 13g Protein

155. Panda Express's Veggie Spring Roll

PREPARATION TIME:	15'	**SERVINGS:**	6-8

COOKING TIME: 5'

INGREDIENTS

- 4 teaspoons vegetable oil, divided
- 3 eggs, beaten
- 1 medium head cabbage, finely shredded
- ½ carrot, julienned
- 1 (8-ounce) can shredded bamboo shoots
- 1 cup dried, shredded wood ear mushroom, rehydrated
- 1-pound Chinese barbecue or roasted pork, cut into matchsticks
- ½ cup chopped Chinese yellow chives
- 1 green onion, thinly sliced
- 2½ teaspoons soy sauce
- 1 teaspoon salt
- 1 teaspoon sugar
- 1 (14-ounce) package egg roll wrappers
- 1 egg white, beaten
- 1-quart oil for frying, or as needed

DIRECTIONS

1. In a large skillet, heat 1 tablespoon of oil over medium-high heat.
2. When the skillet is hot, add the beaten eggs and cook until firm, then flip and cook a bit longer like an omelet. When set, remove from the pan. Cut into strips and set aside.
3. Add the remaining oil to the skillet and heat. When hot, add the cabbage and carrot and cook for a couple of minutes until they start to soften. Then add the bamboo shoots, mushrooms, pork, green onions, chives, soy sauce, salt, and sugar. Cook until the veggies are soft, then stir in the egg. Transfer the mixture to a bowl and refrigerate for about 1 hour.
4. When cooled, add about 2–3 tablespoons of filling to each egg roll wrapper. Brush some beaten egg around the edges of the wrapper and roll up, tucking in the ends first.
5. When all the wrappers are filled, heat about 6 inches of oil to 350°F in a deep saucepan, Dutch oven or fryer.
6. Add the egg rolls to the hot oil a couple at a time. When golden brown and crispy, remove from oil to a paper-towel-lined plate to drain.
7. Serve with chili sauce or sweet and sour sauce.

NUTRITION: 132 Calories 3.3g Fat 5.5g Carbs 32g Protein

156. Pf Chang's Hot and Sour Soup

PREPARATION TIME: 10'

SERVINGS: 4-6

COOKING TIME: 10'

Ingredients

- 6 ounces chicken breasts, cut into thin strips
- 1-quart chicken stock
- 1 cup soy sauce
- 1 teaspoon white pepper
- 1 (6 ounces) can bamboo shoots, cut into strips
- 6 ounces wood ear mushrooms
- ½ cup cornstarch
- ½ cup water
- 2 eggs, beaten
- ½ cup white vinegar
- 6 ounces silken tofu, cut into strips
- Sliced green onions for garnish

Directions

1. Cook the chicken strips in a hot skillet until cooked through. Set aside.
2. Add the chicken stock, soy sauce, pepper, and bamboo shoots to a stockpot and bring to a boil. Stir in the chicken and let cook for about 3–4 minutes.
3. In a small dish, make a slurry with the cornstarch and water. Add a bit at a time to the stockpot until the broth thickens to your desired consistency.
4. Stir in the beaten eggs and cook for about 45 seconds or until the eggs are done.
5. Remove from the heat and add the vinegar and tofu.
6. Garnish with sliced green onions.

NUTRITION: 345 Calories 1.2g Fat 2.2g Carbs 23.3g Protein

157. Pf Chang's Lettuce Wraps

Preparation Time:	10'	Servings:	4

Cooking Time:	10'

Ingredients

- 1 tablespoon olive oil
- 1-pound ground chicken
- 2 cloves garlic, minced
- 1 onion, diced
- ¼ cup hoisin sauce
- 2 tablespoons soy sauce
- 1 tablespoon rice wine vinegar
- 1 tablespoon ginger, freshly grated
- 1 tablespoon Sriracha (optional)
- 1 (8-ounce) can whole water chestnuts, drained and diced
- 2 green onions, thinly sliced
- Kosher salt and freshly ground black pepper to taste
- 1 head iceberg lettuce

Directions

1. Add the oil to a deep skillet or saucepan and heat over medium-high heat. When hot, add the chicken and cook until it is completely cooked through. Stir while cooking to make sure it is properly crumbled.
2. Drain any excess fat from the skillet, then add the garlic, onion, hoisin sauce, soy sauce, ginger, sriracha, and vinegar. Cook until the onions have softened, then stir in the water chestnuts and green onion and cook for another minute or so. Add salt and pepper to taste.
3. Serve with lettuce leaves and eat by wrapping them up like a taco.

Nutrition: 156 Calories 4.3g Fat 3.7g Carbs 27g Protein

158. Pf Chang's Shrimp Dumplings

Preparation Time: 20'	**Servings:** 4-6

Cooking Time: 10'

Ingredients

- 1-pound medium shrimp, peeled, deveined, washed and dried, divided
- 2 tablespoons carrot, finely minced
- 2 tablespoons green onion, finely minced
- 1 teaspoon ginger, freshly minced
- 2 tablespoons oyster sauce
- ¼ teaspoon sesame oil
- 1 package wonton wrappers

Sauce
- 1 cup soy sauce
- 2 tablespoons white vinegar
- ½ teaspoon chili paste
- 2 tablespoons granulated sugar
- ½ teaspoon ginger, freshly minced
- Sesame oil to taste
- 1 cup water
- 1 tablespoon cilantro leaves

Directions

1. In a food processor or blender, finely mince ½ pound of the shrimp.
2. Dice the other ½ pound of shrimp.
3. In a mixing bowl, combine both the minced and diced shrimp with the remaining ingredients.
4. Spoon about 1 teaspoon of the mixture into each wonton wrapper. Wet the edges of the wrapper with your finger, then fold up and seal tightly.
5. Cover and refrigerate for at least an hour.
6. In a medium bowl, combine all the ingredients for the sauce and stir until well combined.
7. When ready to serve, boil water in a saucepan and cover with a steamer. You may want to lightly oil the steamer to keep the dumplings from sticking. Steam the dumplings for 7–10 minutes.
8. Serve with sauce.

Nutrition: 244 Calories 20g Fat 57g Carbs 63g Protein

159. Pf CHang's SPICy CHICken noodle

PREPARATION TIME: 15'	**SERVINGS:** 4-6

COOKING TIME: 15'

INGREDIENTS

- 2 quarts chicken stock
- 1 tablespoon granulated sugar
- 3 tablespoons white vinegar
- 2 cloves garlic, minced
- 1 tablespoon ginger, freshly minced
- ¼ cup soy sauce
- Sriracha sauce to taste
- Red pepper flakes to taste
- 1-pound boneless chicken breast, cut into thin 2–3-inch pieces
- 3 tablespoons cornstarch
- Salt to taste
- 1 cup mushrooms, sliced
- 1 cup grape tomatoes, halved
- 3 green onions, sliced
- 2 tablespoons fresh cilantro, chopped
- ½ pound pasta, cooked to just under package directions and drained

DIRECTIONS

1. Add the chicken stock, sugar, vinegar, garlic, ginger, soy sauce, Sriracha and red pepper flakes to a large saucepan. Bring to a boil, then lower the heat to a simmer. Let cook for 5 minutes.
2. Season chicken with salt to taste. In a resealable bag, combine the chicken and the cornstarch. Shake to coat.
3. Add the chicken to the simmering broth a piece at a time. Then add the mushrooms. Continue to cook for another 5 minutes.
4. Stir in the tomatoes, green onions, cilantro, and cooked pasta.
5. Serve with additional cilantro.

NUTRITION: 100 Calories 3.7g Fat 6.7g Carbs 48g Protein

160. Pei Wei's Thai Chicken Satay

PREPARATION TIME: 20'

SERVINGS: 2-4

COOKING TIME: 10-20'

INGREDIENTS

- 1-pound boneless, skinless chicken thighs
- 6-inch bamboo skewers, soaked in water
- Thai satay marinade
- 1 tablespoon coriander seeds
- 1 teaspoon cumin seeds
- 2 teaspoons chopped lemongrass
- 1 teaspoon salt
- 1 teaspoon turmeric powder
- ¼ teaspoon roasted chili
- ½ cup coconut milk
- 1½ tablespoons light brown sugar
- 1 teaspoon lime juice
- 2 teaspoons fish sauce
- Peanut sauce
- 2 tablespoons soy sauce
- 1 tablespoon rice wine vinegar
- 2 tablespoons brown sugar
- ¼ cup peanut butter
- 1 teaspoon chipotle Tabasco
- Thai sweet cucumber relish
- ¼ cup white vinegar
- ¾ cup sugar
- ¾ cup water
- 1 tablespoon ginger, minced
- 1 Thai red chili, minced
- 1 medium cucumber
- 1 tablespoon toasted peanuts, chopped

DIRECTIONS

1. Cut any excess fat from the chicken, then cut into strips about 3 inches long and 1 inch wide. Thread the strips onto the skewers.
2. Prepare the Thai Satay Marinade and the Peanut Sauce in separate bowls by simply whisking together all the ingredients for each.
3. Dip the chicken skewers in the Thai Satay Marinade and marinate for at least 4 hours. Reserve the marinade when you remove the chicken skewers.
4. You can cook the skewers on the grill, basting with the marinade halfway through, or you can do the same in a 350-degree F oven. They taste better on the grill.
5. To prepare the Cucumber Relish, simply add all the ingredients together and stir to make sure the cucumber is coated.

Peanut sauce:

6. Whisk all ingredients until well incorporated. Store in an airtight container in the refrigerator. It will last for 3 days.
7. When the chicken skewers are done cooking, serve with peanut sauce and the cucumber relish.

NUTRITION: 298 Calories 5.4g Fat 7.5g Carbs 61g Protein

161. Chicken Lettuce Wraps

Preparation Time:	5'		Servings:	2

	Cooking Time:	25'

Ingredients

- 2 chicken breasts, boneless skinless
- 2/3 cup mushroom
- 4 -5 leaves of iceberg lettuce
- 1 teaspoon garlic, minced
- 3 tablespoons onions, chopped
- 1 cup water chestnut
- 3 tablespoons oil

For Stir Fry Sauce
- 2 tablespoons brown sugar
- ½ teaspoon rice wine vinegar
- 2 tablespoons soy sauce

For Special Sauce
- 2 tablespoons rice wine vinegar
- 1 -2 teaspoon red chili & garlic paste
- ¼ cup sugar
- 1 tablespoon lemon juice
- 2 tablespoons soy sauce
- 1 tablespoon hot mustard
- 2 tablespoons ketchup
- 1/8 teaspoon sesame oil
- ½ cup plus 2 teaspoons water

Directions

1. Dissolve sugar with water in a small sized bowl. Add in the rice wine vinegar, soy sauce, ketchup, sesame oil & lemon juice; mix well & prepare the special sauce; cover & let refrigerate until ready to serve.
2. Now, combine hot mustard with hot water; set aside. To pour over the wraps, add in the garlic chili & mustard sauce in the end to the special sauce mixture.
3. Over high heat in a large frying pan or wok; heat the oil & sauté the chicken breasts until done, for 4 to 5 minutes on each side. Remove the chicken pieces from the heat & let cool at room temperature for a couple of minutes.
4. Don't remove the oil; keep it in the pan & try to keep it hot. In the meantime, mince the mushrooms and water chestnuts to the size of small peas.
5. Now, make the stir fry sauce: In a small bowl, mix soy sauce together with rice vinegar & brown sugar; mix well. When you can handle the chicken easily and once cool, mince it as the water chestnuts and mushrooms are. Add a tablespoon of vegetable oil more to the pan & add in the garlic, chicken, onions, mushrooms & water chestnuts to the hot pan. Add in the stir fry sauce, sauté the mixture for a couple of minutes, then serve in the lettuce leaves.

Nutrition: 287 calories 6.9g carbs 59g protein

162. bbq Spare ribs

PREPARATION TIME: 15′

SERVINGS: 6

COOKING TIME: 5H 35′

INGREDIENTS

For the Marinade:
- 2 racks pork spareribs (4 to 5 pounds)
- 2 tablespoons apple cider vinegar
- 1 garlic clove, minced
- ¼ cup light brown sugar, packed
- 2 tablespoons onion, minced
- Freshly ground black pepper & kosher salt

For the Barbecue Sauce:
- 2 tablespoons Worcestershire sauce
- ½ teaspoon liquid smoke
- 3 garlic cloves, smashed
- ¼ cup tomato paste
- 2 tablespoons vegetable oil
- 1 ¾ cups apple cider vinegar
- 1 tablespoon honey
- ¼ cup molasses
- 1 cup pineapple preserves
- 2 teaspoons instant espresso powder
- 1 tablespoon mustard powder
- Freshly ground black pepper
- 1 cup ketchup
- ½ teaspoon cayenne pepper

For the Rub:
- 1 tablespoon onion powder
- 1 teaspoon each celery salt & celery seeds
- ½ cup light brown sugar, packed
- 1 tablespoon chili powder
- ¼ teaspoon cayenne pepper
- 1 tablespoon garlic powder

DIRECTIONS

1. First, prepare the marinade: In a large bowl, whisk vinegar together with the onion, brown sugar, garlic, ½ teaspoon black pepper & 1 tablespoon salt; whisk well. Place the ribs on a large cutting board, meat-side down. Begin with one end; slip a paring knife just under the membrane & loosen it with the knife and then pull it off. Coat both sides of the ribs with the prepared marinade; wrap the meat pieces in a plastic wrap & let refrigerate for overnight.
2. Now, prepare the rub: In a separate medium-sized bowl, mix the chili powder together with brown sugar, onion powder, garlic powder, celery seeds & celery salt, cayenne, 1 teaspoon black pepper & 1 tablespoon salt; mix well.
3. Soak approximately 2 cups of the hickory wood chips in water for a minimum period of half an hour, before you use them. In the meantime, preheat your grill over medium-low heat & prepare it for indirect grilling. Cover the grill's cooler side grate with foil.
4. Drain the wood chips & scatter them on top of the hot coals. Close the lid & let the smoke to build up for a minimum period of 10 minutes. Rinse the meat and remove the marinade from the ribs; pat them dry using paper towels. Rub both sides of the meat with the spice mixture using your hands.
5. Place the coated ribs on foil & over indirect heat, meat-side up. Close the lid; cook for approximately 1 hour & 30 minutes, until the meat slightly shrinks back & you can see a bit of bone, undisturbed.
6. Rotate (keep them over indirect heat and meat-side up), close the lid & continue to cook for 2 hours or a little longer; maintain the temperature of your grill by adding more of hot coals.
7. In the meantime, prepare the barbecue sauce: Over medium heat settings in a medium-sized saucepan; heat the vegetable oil. Once hot, cook the garlic for a minute, until golden, stirring occasionally. Stir in the chili powder and tomato paste for a minute, until well incorporated. Whisk in Worcestershire sauce, ¼ cup water, vinegar, the molasses, espresso powder, mustard powder, honey, cayenne, and ¾ teaspoon black pepper. Bring everything to a simmer & cook for 5 minutes, whisking occasionally.
8. Whisk in the pineapple preserves and ketchup. Bring to a moderate simmer & cook for 40 to 45 minutes, until thickened, whisking every now and then. Whisk in the liquid smoke & allow the sauce cool for a couple of minutes at room temperature & then take off the garlic.
9. Generously baste the ribs with this barbecue sauce. Close the lid; continue to cook for 20 more minutes until glazed. Transfer the meat to a large cutting board & let rest for a couple of minutes before cutting the meat into individual ribs.
10. Serve the cooked ribs with some more sauce & enjoy.

NUTRITION: 279 calories 5.9g carbs 57g protein

163. Caullflower TemPura

PREPARATION TIME: 15'	**SERVINGS:** 4

COOKING TIME: 25'

INGREDIENTS

- ½ cup plain flour
- 2 eggs, separated
- 1 cauliflower, small, cut into medium-sized florets
- 2 tablespoons plus more vegetable oil

DIRECTIONS

1. Cook the cauliflower florets for a couple of minutes in boiling water. Place them into a colander; rinse under the cold & running tap water, drain well & set aside.
2. Place the flour with a pinch of salt in a large-sized bowl. Whisk the egg yolks with ¾ cup of iced water together, and to make a smooth batter; whisk the egg yolk mixture into the flour with the oil. Whisk the egg whites in a separate, clean bowl until stiff, for a minute or two & then fold the mixture into the batter.
3. Over moderate heat settings in a large wok or deep fryer; heat the oil. Coat few pieces of cauliflower florets into the batter & then lift into the hot oil carefully using a large slotted spoon.
4. Deep-fry the coated cauliflower florets until golden & puffy for 2 to 3 minutes. Place them on kitchen towel & drain; continue cooking the cauliflower florets in batches.
5. Sprinkle salt on top of the cooked cauliflower florets & serve with some mayonnaise or aioli on the side.

NUTRITION: 279 calories 8g carbs 55g protein

164. dynamITe SHrImP

PREPARATION TIME: 5'

SERVINGS: 6

COOKING TIME: 35'

INGREDIENTS

- 15 to 20 shrimps, large, peeled & deveined
- Vegetable oil for frying

For the Batter:
- 4 tablespoon corn flour
- 1 egg, large
- ¼ teaspoon each salt & black pepper

For the Sauce:
- ½ cup mayonnaise
- 1 teaspoon rice vinegar
- 5 tablespoon hot sauce
- 1 garlic clove, minced
- 3 tablespoon tomato ketchup
- 1 teaspoon sesame oil
- ¼ teaspoon chili powder/paprika
- 1 teaspoon light honey

For Garnish:
- Spring onion, sliced

DIRECTIONS

1. Place the shrimps on paper towels; drain & mix them with all the batter ingredients. Over medium heat settings in a large frying pan; heat the oil & fry the shrimps for half a minute (ensure that the pieces of Shrimp should be wrapped up in the oil completely.

2. Immediately remove the pieces from the oil & drain them on kitchen tissues. Now, mix all the sauce ingredients together until blended well. Transfer the mixture into a cocktail glass or pudding bowl. Add in the fried pieces of shrimp; mix using a slotted spoon.

3. Garnish the shrimp pieces with the spring onions. Serve & enjoy.

NUTRITION: 284 calories 6.8g carbs 58g protein

165. norTHern-STyle SPare rIbs

PREPARATION TIME: 5'

SERVINGS: 4

COOKING TIME: 35'

INGREDIENTS

- 1 tablespoon green onion, diced
- 1 pork spareribs, rack
- ½ cup Hoisin sauce
- 1 cup light corn syrup
- 2 tablespoons onions, minced
- 1 cup ketchup
- ½ cup water
- 1 teaspoon sesame seeds
- 1/3 cup light brown sugar, packed
- 1 tablespoon rice vinegar

DIRECTIONS

1. Over medium heat settings in a medium-sized saucepan; combine all the sauce ingredients. Bring mixture to a boil, once boiling; decrease the heat settings & let simmer until thick, for 5 minutes. Remove the pan from heat & let cool for a couple of minutes at room temperature.
2. In a Dutch oven or large saucepan, heat approximately 12 to 16 cups of water & then add a few teaspoons of salt.
3. As the water boils, trim the additional meat & fat off, separating & slicing between the bones from each rib. When water starts boiling; toss the ribs in & let the ribs to boil in the brine water until the meat is no longer pink, for 10 to 12 minutes.
4. Remove the ribs to a large plate & let cool for a couple of minutes.
5. Now, over medium heat settings in a large saucepan; heat 4 cups of vegetable oil. Once hot, drop in the spare ribs, 4 to 6 at a time & fry until meat browns, for a couple of minutes.
6. Place the ribs on paper towels or rack; drain. Repeat this process with the leftover ribs, if any.
7. Now, over medium heat settings in a large skillet or wok; toss in all the ribs with the sauce until evenly coated.
8. Let the ribs to simmer in the sauce for a minute, stirring frequently & when the ribs are well coated with the sauce, dump them onto a large serving plate.
9. Sprinkle sesame seeds & a tablespoon of diced green onion on top of the cooked ribs.
10. Serve & enjoy.

NUTRITION: 279 calories 6.4g carbs 54g protein

166. Crispy green beans

PREPARATION TIME: 5'

SERVINGS: 4

COOKING TIME: 30'

INGREDIENTS

- ½ teaspoon plus more black pepper, ground
- 1-pound green beans
- 2 teaspoons plus more salt
- Vegetable oil

For the Batter
- 1 cup flour, all-purpose
- 1 cup beer
- For the Dipping Sauce
- 4 cloves garlic, chopped coarsely
- 1 cup vegan mayonnaise or any mayonnaise
- ½ teaspoon horseradish, prepared
- 6 onions, green, chopped coarsely (only whites)
- 2 ½ tablespoons Sriracha sauce

DIRECTIONS

1. Over moderate heat settings in a large saucepan; heat the vegetable oil. Combine all the batter ingredients together in a medium bowl. Dip the green beans into the batter & coat the greens with the batter using a fork, drip off any excess batter.
2. Fry the beans in hot oil until turn golden & crisp, work in batches. Remove the beans from the oil and place them on a sheet tray lined with the paper towel. Sprinkle pepper & salt to taste.
3. Finally, combine all the sauce ingredients together in a blender; blend on high settings until smooth.
4. Serve the fried green beans with some sauce on the side.

NUTRITION: 267 calories 6.3g carbs 60g protein

167. Pork dumplings

PREPARATION TIME: 30'

SERVINGS: 8

COOKING TIME: 15'

INGREDIENTS

- 2 ounces chicken broth
- ½ pound ground pork
- 1 teaspoon sugar
- 36 Dumpling Skins
- 1 teaspoon chili paste
- 3 tablespoon scallions; chopped
- ½ teaspoon sesame oil
- 1 teaspoon ground ginger
- 2 teaspoon salt

DIRECTIONS

1. Mix all the ingredients (except dumpling skins) together in a large bowl until combined well.
2. Lay the dumpling skin out on a flat surface & add approximately 2 teaspoons of filling in the center. Use some water to moisten the edges & fold the skin in half, pressing down the edges and sealing the filling inside.
3. Repeat this process until you have utilized all the filling. Steam the dumplings until cooked through for 10 to 12 minutes, or fry them in a pan. When ready, serve the dumplings with some sweet & chili dipping sauce on the side. Enjoy.

NUTRITION: 290 calories 7g carbs 58g protein

168. red SauCe WonTon's

PREPARATION TIME: 15'

SERVINGS: 4

COOKING TIME: 40'

INGREDIENTS

For Sauce:
- 1 cup chicken stock
- ½ teaspoon chili paste
- 1-ounce white vinegar
- ½ teaspoon garlic, fresh, minced
- 1-ounce sugar
- ½ ounce chili oil
- 1 cup soy sauce
- Sesame oil to taste

For Won Ton Filling:
- ¼ pound pork, trimmed, minced finely
- 2 teaspoons onion, green, minced finely
- ½ pound shrimp, washed, peeled, deveined & minced finely
- 2 teaspoons oyster sauce
- 1 teaspoon ginger, fresh, minced
- ¼ teaspoon sesame oil
- 2 teaspoons carrot, finely minced

For Garnish:
- Fresh cilantro leaves
- Green onions

DIRECTIONS

1. Combine pork & shrimp mixture together in a food processor until smooth & not lumpy.
2. Place a pea-size heap of meat mixture using a small spoon inside the won ton skin. Lightly moisten the bottom & top corners. Fold them over & seal. Arrange them on a large plate; cover & place in a refrigerator or fridge until ready to use.
3. Combine all the sauce ingredients together in a large bowl; mix well.
4. Fill a soup pot with the chicken stock & bring it to a boil. Once boiling, decrease the heat settings and let simmer slightly. Heat the batch of sauce completely. Return to the serving container. Cook won tons until the skins of the won tons are soft & they start floating to the surface for a couple of minutes in the boiling chicken stock.
5. Remove won tons into the soup bowl using a strainer. Mix the sauce well & briefly heat it. Ladle approximately 1 ounce of the hot sauce on top of the won tons.
6. Garnish with fresh cilantro & green onions; serve & enjoy!

NUTRITION: 281 calories 6.8g carbs 56g protein

169. Charred Brussels Sprouts

PREPARATION TIME: 10'		**SERVINGS:** 4

COOKING TIME: 25'

INGREDIENTS

- 1 pound or 3 ½ cups Brussels sprouts, remove any unattractive leaves
- 1 cup pineapple, fresh, diced
- 2 tablespoons olive or peanut oil
- 1 tablespoon plus 1 teaspoon honey
- ½ teaspoon salt
- ¼ cup lemon juice, freshly squeezed
- 1 tablespoon soy sauce
- 1/3 cup almonds, sliced, toasted

DIRECTIONS

1. Preheat your oven to 425 F and line a parchment paper with the rimmed sheet pan.
2. Trim the ends of your Brussels sprouts & cut them in half lengthwise. Place them with the pineapple in a large-sized bowl. Drizzle olive or peanut oil all over it & then sprinkle with a small amount of pepper and salt. Toss several times until evenly coated.
3. Whisk the oil together with the lemon juice, honey & salt in a separate bowl; set aside.
4. Spread the pineapple and Brussels sprouts onto the sheet pan lined with the parchment & place on the center rack of your preheated oven. Roast until the centers are tender and the cut side & outer leaves are nicely charred, for 15 to 20 minutes. To ensure even doneness, flip the Brussels sprouts once half way during the Cooking Time.
5. When done, drizzle the honey mixture & soy sauce on top of the hot Brussels sprouts. Gently toss to coat everything and then transfer to a large-sized serving dish. Finally, sprinkle the almonds over the top & serve immediately.

NUTRITION: 289 calories 6.3g carbs 51g protein

170. CHIna bISTro beef lo meIn

PREPARATION TIME: 10'	SERVINGS: 4

COOKING TIME: 55'

INGREDIENTS

- 1 ½ pound flank steak, partially freeze & cut into thin strips across the grain.
- 1 tablespoon soy sauce

For Marinade
- 4 tablespoons beef broth
- 1 teaspoon granulated sugar
- 2 teaspoons dark soy sauce
- 1 ½ teaspoon cornstarch
- 2 tablespoons oyster sauce

For Lo Mein
- 1 garlic clove, minced
- 8 ounces lo Mein noodles
- ¼ cup oil, or as needed
- 1 carrot, shredded coarsely
- ½ cup Chinese cabbage, shredded
- 1 teaspoon sesame oil

DIRECTIONS

1. For Marinade:
2. Thoroughly mix the soy sauce together with beef broth & oyster sauce. Whisk in the sugar & cornstarch until well blended. Place the beef strips along with the marinade mixture in a large bag, zip-top & let marinate for a minimum period of half an hour.
3. Fill a large saucepan with lightly salted water & bring it to a rolling boil. Once boiling, cook the low Mein noodles for a couple of minutes, until almost done; drain & toss the cooked noodles with sesame oil.
4. Over medium-high heat settings in a wok, heat ¼ cup of oil and then stir fry the beef until just cooked through. Using a slotted spoon, remove the fried beef; set aside.
5. Add more oil to the wok & stir fry the carrots & garlic. Keep an eye on the garlic; don't let it burn. Now, stir fry the cabbage with garlic & carrot for a minute or two more. When the vegetables are tender, stir in the already cooked beef & noodles. Thoroughly mix & stir to heat through.
6. Serve immediately with some more soy sauce on the side.

NUTRITION: 279 calories 5.9g carbs 60.3g protein

171. House-made Pork Egg rolls

INGREDIENTS

- 2 teaspoon garlic powder
- 8 egg roll wrappers (7" square)
- 2 tablespoons soy sauce
- 1-pound ground pork
- 2 tablespoons all-purpose flour
- 4 cups coleslaw
- 2 teaspoon ground ginger
- ½ teaspoon onion powder
- 2 tablespoons water
- ½ teaspoon Chinese 5 spice
- 2 tablespoons water
- 1-quart peanut oil
- 2 tablespoons sesame seeds

DIRECTIONS

1. Thoroughly mix ground pork together with garlic powder, ginger & onion powder in a large bowl. Now, over medium heat settings in a medium skillet, cook the pork mixture until pork no longer pink & is cooked through to your likings. Remove the pork from heat; set aside.
2. Over medium heat in a medium skillet, sauté the coleslaw, soy sauce, Chinese five spice & water for a minute, until tender. Add to the pork mixture; set aside. Over medium-high heat settings in a separate large skillet, heat the oil. Combine flour with 2 tablespoons of water in a small bowl until you get a paste-like consistency.
3. Now, assemble the egg rolls: For this, lay an egg roll wrapper with the corner pointed facing you. Place approximately 1/3 cup of cabbage mixture on the egg roll wrapper & fold the corner up on top of the mixture. Fold right & left corners toward the middle & continue rolling. Seal the egg roll by brushing a small amount of the flour paste onto the final corner.
4. Put egg rolls into the heated oil & fry for a couple of minutes, until turn golden brown, turning every now and then. Remove the roll from hot oil; place them on rack or paper towels to drain. Place the cooked egg roll on a large serving plate & top it with some sesame seeds. Serve with some sweet & sour sauce or soy sauce.

NUTRITION: 279 calories 6.3g carbs 61.3g protein

172. Chili-garlic green beans

PREPARATION TIME: 20'	SERVINGS: 6

COOKING TIME: 25'

INGREDIENTS

- 1 tablespoon rice vinegar
- 2 green onions, thinly chopped
- 1/8 teaspoon each black pepper & salt
- 2 tablespoon soy sauce, low sodium
- 1 teaspoon plus ¼ teaspoon red pepper flakes
- 2 pounds green beans, trimmed & cut into 2" pieces
- 1 teaspoon corn starch
- 4 garlic cloves, minced
- 1 teaspoon white granulated sugar
- 2 tablespoon sesame oil
- ¼ cup water

DIRECTIONS

1. Mix soy sauce together with corn starch, water, sugar, rice vinegar, pepper & salt in a small bowl; set aside.
2. Over medium-high heat settings in a large skillet or wok, heat the oil for half a minute & then cook the green onions, 1 teaspoon of red pepper flakes & garlic. Quickly stir fry for half a minute and then add in the green beans; stir constantly for a couple of minutes until the beans turn deep green & almost completely cooked through.
3. Push the green beans to one side of your pan, transfer the sauce into the pan, cook the sauce for half a minute over medium-high heat settings & let come to a boil. Once boiling, decrease the heat settings to low & stir several times to coat the green beans evenly with the sauce. Cook for half a minute more. Serve and enjoy!

NUTRITION: 281 calories 6.9g carbs 59.3g protein

173. buddHa's feasT VegeTable STIr-fry

PREPARATION TIME:	15'		SERVINGS:	10

COOKING TIME: 15'

INGREDIENTS

- 12 ounces broccoli, florets
- ½ cup Vegetable Stock, Homemade or canned vegetable broth, low-sodium
- 8 ounces shiitake, small or white mushrooms, stemmed & julienned
- 1 can sliced water chestnuts, drained (8 ounces)
- 2 tablespoons cornstarch
- 1 teaspoon Chinese chili paste
- 3 tablespoons soy sauce, low-sodium
- 1 tablespoon mirin
- 8 ounces firm tofu, cut into ½" cubes
- ½ head bok choy cut into 1-inch dice
- 2 garlic cloves, minced
- 1 can baby corn, drained (14 ounces)
- 4 carrots, peeled & sliced thinly on the diagonal
- Nonstick cooking spray
- Cooked brown rice, for serving

DIRECTIONS

1. Whisk stock together with cornstarch, soy sauce, chili paste & mirin in a small-sized bowl. Place half cup of the mixture in a small bowl and then add in the tofu; let sit for half an hour at room temperature. Reserve the leftover sauce. Fill ice water in a large bowl; set aside.
2. Fill a large pot with water & bring it to a boil over moderate heat settings. Cook the bok choy in boiling water for a couple of minutes. Transfer them to ice water using a large slotted spoon. Once cool down; remove them from the ice water; set them aside. Cook broccoli florets for a minute in the same pot. Transfer them to the ice water to cool as well. Remove & place them into the bowl with the bok choy; set aside.
3. Place the tofu on paper towels to drain, try keeping the sauce. Lightly coat a large skillet or wok with the cooking spray & heat it over medium heat settings. Add in the mushrooms & carrots; cook for a couple of minutes, stirring every now and then. Add in the broccoli, bok choy, tofu, baby corn, water chestnuts, & garlic. Cook for an additional minute or two. Add in the reserved sauce; cook for a couple of more minutes, until it thickens; stirring frequently. Serve immediately with some hot cooked brown rice.

NUTRITION: 280 calories 6g carbs 54g protein

174. Coconut Curry Vegetables

| Preparation Time: | 10' | | Servings: | 2 |

| Cooking Time: | 40' |

Ingredients

- 1 red bell pepper, small, cubed
- 3 cups broccoli florets
- 1 package water-packed tofu, extra firm (12 ounces), cut into cubes; drained
- ½ cup carrot, sliced thinly
- 1 onion, small, cut into ¾" cubes
- 2 tablespoons sesame or canola oil
- 1 cup mushrooms, sliced
- ½ cup whole sugar snap pea

For Coconut-Curry Sauce
- 2 tablespoons packed brown sugar
- ½ teaspoon curry powder
- 2 tablespoons soy sauce
- ½ cup coconut milk
- 2 teaspoons cider vinegar or rice vinegar, unseasoned
- ½ cup peanuts
- 2 teaspoons cornstarch

Directions

1. Fry the tofu cubes in 1 tablespoon of canola or sesame oil for a couple of minutes until brown; set aside.
2. Separately steam or blanch the broccoli, sugar snap peas & carrots in plain boiling water, until tender-crisp, for a couple of minutes.
3. Over high heat settings in a wide skillet or wok; heat the remaining canola or sesame oil; swirl & then stir-fry the onions & bell pepper for a couple of minutes until tender-crisp. Add in the mushrooms & stir for a couple of more minutes until hot. Add the tofu & blanched vegetables. Toss several times until evenly mixed.
4. Now, thoroughly mix all the sauce ingredients together in a large bowl. Taste & adjust the amount of sugar to your liking.
5. Transfer this sauce to the pan along with the veggies & bring everything to a simmer, toss again to combine everything.
6. Dissolve the cornstarch with 1 & ½ tablespoon of water; add the slurry to the pan. Stir for 8 to 10 seconds, until the sauce turns glossy.
7. Add in the peanuts & serve with some noodles, rice, or a warm loaf of bread.

Nutrition: 287 calories 6.9g carbs 53g protein

175. Korean Chicken Stir fry

PREPARATION TIME: 10'

SERVINGS: 4

COOKING TIME: 30'

INGREDIENTS

- 4 chicken thighs; sliced horizontally & then slice each piece into 2 or 3 horizontal pieces
- 1 ½ tablespoons Korean chili paste
- 1 tablespoon sesame oil
- 2 tablespoons soy sauce
- 1 ½ tablespoons sugar
- 1" piece ginger, peeled & minced
- 3 garlic cloves, minced
- 1 teaspoon Korean red chili powder
- 2 tablespoons oil
- Salt to taste

DIRECTIONS

1. Combine all the ingredients (except the chicken) in a large bowl in the Marinade, whisk well until the Korean chili paste is dissolved completely. Place the chicken thighs in the marinade & let marinate for a minimum period of an hour.
2. Grill the coated chicken thighs until completely cooked through & slightly charred. You can bake the coated chicken pieces in the oven for 20 minutes at 400 F or can pan-fry on a pan or skillet as well. Serve immediately with some steamed rice.

NUTRITION: 280 calories 6.9g carbs 57g protein

Chapter 8

OLD AND MODERN SAUCE AND DRESSING RECIPES

176. don Pablo's Prairie fire bean dip

PREPARATION TIME: 10'

SERVINGS: 6

COOKING TIME: 15'

INGREDIENTS

- 1 tablespoon oil
- ½ cup finely chopped onion
- 1 (15-ounce) can fava or pinto beans
- 2 tablespoons plain yogurt
- 2 chipotle chilis, finely chopped
- 1 tablespoon adobo sauce from the chilis
- 1 jalapeño pepper, diced
- 1 teaspoon salt
- ½ teaspoon garlic powder
- ½ teaspoon cumin
- ½ cup shredded cheddar or Monterey Jack cheese
- Additional cheese and jalapeños for topping, if desired
- Chips or soft flour tortillas cut into quarters (for serving)

DIRECTIONS

1. In a medium skillet, warm the oil over medium heat and add the onion. Cook until softened. Strain the beans and stir in the skillet. Mix in the yogurt, chilies, adobo sauce, jalapeño, salt, garlic powder, and cumin. Cook to heat through.
2. Transfer the dip to a blender and pulse until smooth. (You can leave some chunks if you like.) Transfer the dip to a heatproof serving dish and stir in the cheese. Serve warm, garnished with additional cheese and jalapeños if desired.

NUTRITION: 706 calories 50g total fats 35g protein

177. Café rIo's PICo de gallo

PREPARATION TIME: 5'

SERVINGS: 6

COOKING TIME: 0'

INGREDIENTS

- 5 ripe tomatoes, finely diced
- ½ teaspoon salt
- 1 medium sweet onion, finely diced
- 4 cloves garlic, minced
- 1 bunch cilantro, finely chopped
- 1–2 jalapeño peppers, seeded and diced
- 1 tablespoon lime juice
- 4 shakes green Tabasco sauce

DIRECTIONS

1. Mix all the ingredients. Serve at room temperature.

NUTRITION: 664 calories 48g total fats 29g protein

178. Chipotle's refried beans

PREPARATION TIME: 5'

SERVINGS: 6

COOKING TIME: 2H 1/2

Ingredients

- 1-pound dried pinto beans
- 6 cups warm water
- ½ cup bacon fat
- 2 teaspoons salt
- 1 teaspoon cumin
- ½ teaspoon black pepper
- ½ teaspoon cayenne pepper

Directions

1. Rinse and drain the pinto beans. Check them over and remove any stones. Transfer the beans in a Dutch oven and stir in the water. Bring the pot to a boil, reduce the heat, and simmer for 2 hours, stirring frequently.
2. When the beans are tender, reserve ½ cup of the boiling water and drain the rest. Heat the bacon fat in a large, deep skillet. Add the beans 1 cup at a time, mashing and stirring as you go. Add the spices and some cooking liquid if the beans are too dry.

NUTRITION: 661 calorieS 49g total fats 28g protein

179. abuelo's JalaPeño CHeesefrITTers

PREPARATION TIME: 15'	**SERVINGS:** 8

COOKING TIME: 20'

INGREDIENTS

Fritters
- 1 (8-ounce) package cream cheese, softened
- ½ cup Monterrey cheese, shredded
- ½ cup cheddar cheese, shredded
- 3 jalapeños, deseeded and finely chopped
- 1 teaspoon Lawry's seasoning
- Oil for frying

Breading
- 3 cups breadcrumbs
- ¼ cup all-purpose flour
- Egg Wash
- 2 eggs
- ¼ cup water

DIRECTIONS

1. Grease and preheat at 300 degrees. Blend all the ingredients then form the mixture into 1-inch balls (makes approximately 20 balls). Place onto the prepared sheet and set aside.
2. Beat the eggs and water together until slightly frothy; set aside. To two separate bowls, add the flour and breadcrumbs; set aside.

Assembling
3. Roll the balls in the flour first. Dunk each ball into the egg wash and then into the breadcrumbs. Toss until evenly coated. Cook the oil at 350°F and fry the balls until evenly golden brown. Drain the balls on a paper towel. Serve with your favorite dip.

NUTRITION: 636 calories 47g total fats 30g protein

180. baJa fresH's GuaCamole

PREPARATION TIME: 10'	COOKING TIME: 0'	SERVINGS: 4

INGREDIENTS

- Flesh of 3 avocados, chopped
- 2 tablespoons lime juice
- ¾ teaspoon salt
- ½ teaspoon ground cumin
- ¼ teaspoon cayenne powder
- 1 small onion, finely chopped
- 2 Roma tomatoes, seeded and diced
- 1 tablespoon chopped cilantro

DIRECTIONS

1. In a medium bowl, mash the avocados. Mix in the lime juice and Stir well. Stir in the salt, cumin, cayenne, onion, tomatoes, and cilantro.
2. Taste and adjust the seasonings to your liking. Let the guacamole sit at room temperature for about 30 minutes for the flavors to blend.

NUTRITION: 701 calories 49g total fats 31g protein

181. CHIPoTle's GuaCamole

PREPARATION TIME: 10'	COOKING TIME: 0'	SERVINGS: 6

INGREDIENTS

- 1 medium jalapeño pepper, seeded and deveined, finely chopped
- 1 cup diced red onion
- 2 tablespoons fresh cilantro, chopped finely
- 8 ripe avocados
- 8 teaspoons freshly squeezed lime juice
- 1 teaspoon kosher salt

DIRECTIONS

1. Chop avocado in half and take out the flesh. Mix in the jalapeño pepper, onion, and cilantro. Drizzle the lime juice. Season it with salt. Pound avocado with the rest of the ingredients until desired consistency is achieved. Seal it with plastic wrap before serving.

NUTRITION: 674 calories 37g total fats 26g protein

182. Chi Chi's Chili Con Queso

PREPARATION TIME: 5′	COOKING TIME: 5′	SERVINGS: 8

INGREDIENTS

- 1 block Velveeta® cheese
- ½ teaspoon granulated garlic
- 1 (4 ½-ounce) canned diced green chilies, drained
- 1 (4 ½-ounce) can pimiento peppers, drained
- 1 jalapeño pepper, minced
- Nacho chips, for serving

DIRECTIONS

1. In a microwaveable bowl, melt the Velveeta, checking and stirring often. Stir in the other ingredients. Serve warm with nacho chips.

NUTRITION: 637 calories 46g total fats 27g protein

183. Chipotle's Queso Dip

PREPARATION TIME: 15′	COOKING TIME: 2H	SERVINGS: 8

INGREDIENTS

- 1 cup cheddar, cubed
- 1 cup American cheese, cubed
- 1 cup Monterey Jack, cubed
- 1 cup heavy cream
- 2 poblano peppers
- 1 large Roma tomato, halved
- 1 teaspoon paprika
- 1 teaspoon garlic powder
- ¼ teaspoon cayenne pepper
- ½ teaspoon black pepper
- 1 tablespoon olive oil
- Tortilla chips to serve

DIRECTIONS

1. Grease the baking dish with oil and preheat at 400 degrees. Place the tomatoes and poblano pepper in the prepared baking dish and bake until the skins are blackened.
2. While the veggies are in the oven, combine the remaining ingredients in a pot and let simmer on low. Once cooked, set aside and let cool at room temperature for about 10 minutes.
3. Remove the skins and transfer to a blender. Blend until pureed. Add the pureed veggies to the cheese mixture; mix well, and continue cooking for 2 hours. Serve hot with tortilla chips.

NUTRITION: 677 calories 41g total fats 30g protein

184. don Pablo's WHITe CHili

<table>
<tr><td>PREPARATION TIME:</td><td>10'</td><td>SERVINGS:</td><td>4</td></tr>
</table>

COOKING TIME: 30'

INGREDIENTS

- 1 tablespoon olive oil
- 8 ounces chicken breast
- 1 small onion
- 3 cloves garlic
- 1 red bell pepper
- 2 (15-ounce) cans white beans
- 1 (4-ounce) can green chilies
- ½ teaspoon ground cumin
- 2 teaspoons chili powder
- 2 cups chicken broth
- 2 tablespoons lime juice
- 2 tablespoons fresh cilantro
- ½ cup salsa (optional)

DIRECTIONS

1. In a stockpot, warm the oil. Sauté the chicken pieces until they are lightly browned. Add the onion and cook to soften. Stir in the garlic and red bell pepper and cook until fragrant.
2. Add the beans, green chilies, cumin, chili powder, and broth. Heat to a simmer and cook for 15 minutes. Add the lime juice and cilantro, and serve garnished with a spoonful of salsa, if desired.

NUTRITION: 669 calories 43g total fats 30g protein

185. Chili's Original Chili

Preparation Time:	15'	**Servings:**	4

Cooking Time: 1H 30

Ingredients

Spice Blend
- ½ cup chili powder
- 1/8 cup salt
- 1/8 cup ground cumin
- 1 tablespoon paprika
- 1 teaspoon ground black pepper
- 1 teaspoon garlic powder
- 1 teaspoon of cayenne pepper

Chili
- 4 pounds chuck, ground for chili
- 3¼ cups water
- 16 ounces tomato sauce
- 1½ cups yellow onions, chopped
- 1 tablespoon cooking oil

Masa Harina
- 1 cup water
- 1 tablespoon masa harina
- Sliced green onions for garnish, if desired

Directions

1. Put all the spice blend ingredients in a bowl. Mix thoroughly and set the bowl aside. Cook the meat over medium heat in a stockpot until it is brown. While the meat is cooking, thoroughly mix together the spice mix, water, and tomato sauce.
2. Add the spice mixture to the browned meat and bring to a boil. When the chili is about to boil, sauté the onions in oil over medium heat for the meantime. When the chili is boiling, and the onions are translucent, add the onions to the chili and stir.
3. Adjust the heat to low and let the chili simmer for an hour, stirring the mixture every 15 minutes. In a bowl, mix the masa harina ingredients together. When the chili has been cooking for an hour, add the masa harina mixture to the chili and cook for another 10 minutes.
4. Transfer the chili to a bowl, garnish green onions, if desired, and serve.

Nutrition: 681 calories 48g total fats 32g protein

186. 2-IngredIenT TaHInI PasTe

PREPARATION TIME: 15'	COOKING TIME: 30'	SERVINGS: 6

INGREDIENTS

- 1 cup of hulled sesame seeds
- 3 tbsps. extra virgin olive oil (or more, if you prefer an oilier paste)

DIRECTIONS

1. Pour the sesame seeds into a pan and roast over medium-high heat, stirring regularly, until the seeds are brown.
2. Allow the seeds to cool, then place them in a blender/food processor. Drizzle in 3 tbsps. of olive oil and process until a paste is formed. Slowly add in more oil until you reach the consistency you'd prefer.
3. Thoroughly stir the paste before storing the tahini in an airtight jar/container and place it in the refrigerator. Tahini can be stored for about 3 months.

NUTRITION: 36 Calories 2g Carbs 7g Fat 1g Protein

187. SPICy MexICan barbeCue SauCe

PREPARATION TIME: 15'	COOKING TIME: 15'	SERVINGS: 12

INGREDIENTS

- 2/3 olive oil
- 1 onion, diced
- ½ tbsp garlic paste
- 1 ½ tsps. of salt
- 1 chili pepper, seeded & diced
- 2 tomatoes, peeled & chopped
- 2 tbsps. of chili powder
- 2 tbsps. of sugar
- ¼ cup of vinegar
- ¼ cup of beer

DIRECTIONS

1. Heat oil in a pan over medium heat. Drop in the onions and fry until browned.
2. Stir in the garlic, chili, chili powder, salt, and tomatoes. Allow it to simmer for 3-5 minutes until the mixture thickens.
3. Pour in the sugar, vinegar, and beer and let it simmer for 10 minutes, stirring regularly. Remove from heat and let it cool.

NUTRITION: 126 Calories 5.8g Carbs 11.6g Fat 0.7g Protein

188. Tangy frenCH remoulade SauCe

PREPARATION TIME:	15'	COOKING TIME:	15'	SERVINGS:	8

INGREDIENTS

- ¾ cup of mayonnaise
- 1 ½ tbsp of cornichon or dill relish
- 1 tsp of finely chopped capers
- 1 tbsp of lemon juice
- 1 tbsp of mustard (preferably Dijon)
- 2 tsp of chopped parsley
- 1 dash of hot sauce
- ½ tsp of salt

DIRECTIONS

1. In a bowl, mix the mayonnaise with the cornichon, capers, lemon juice, mustard, salt, and parsley together. Stir in the hot sauce and then cover with plastic wrap. Place in the refrigerator until needed.

NUTRITION: 146 Calories 1g Carbs 16g Fat

189. duCk SauCe

PREPARATION TIME:	5'	COOKING TIME:	2'	SERVINGS:	4

INGREDIENTS

- 2 teaspoons sugar
- 1 ½ tbsps. of hot water
- 3 tbsps. of apricot preservatives
- 1 salted pickled plum (pitted)
- ½ a tsp of juice from pickled plum
- 1/8 tsp of soy sauce
- ¼ tsp of rice vinegar

DIRECTIONS

1. Stir the sugar and hot water together in a bowl, until the sugar is dissolved. Add the apricot preserves and plum into the bowl and stir with a fork to break up the contents.
2. Pour in the remaining ingredients: juice from the pickled plum, soy sauce, and vinegar. Stir well and then leave the sauce to sit for 5 minutes. Stir one last time and then serve. You can store duck sauce for several months.

NUTRITION: 53 Calories 14g Carbs 1g Fat1g Protein

190. SPICY JamaICan Jerk SauCe

PREPARATION TIME:	15'	COOKING TIME:	2'	SERVINGS:	8

INGREDIENTS

- ½ cup of ground allspice
- ½ cup of brown sugar
- 6 garlic cloves
- 4-6 scotch bonnet peppers (seeded and cored)
- 1 tbsp of thyme
- 2 bunches of scallions
- 1 tsp of cinnamon
- ½ tsp of nutmeg
- salt and pepper to taste
- 2 tbsps. of soy sauce

DIRECTIONS

1. Combine all the ingredients in a blender/ food processor and blend until smooth. Enjoy!

NUTRITION: 101 Calories 25g Carbs 1g Fat 2g Protein

191. Creamy MusHroom SauCe

PREPARATION TIME:	5'	COOKING TIME:	15'	SERVINGS:	6

INGREDIENTS

- 1 tbsp of butter
- 2 tbsps. of oil
- 5 cups of portobello mushrooms, halved
- 2 sprigs of thyme
- 1 tbsp of garlic paste
- 1 cup of cream
- 1 cup of milk
- 3 tsps. of flour
- 1 tbsp of lemon juice
- salt and pepper to taste
- 2 tbsps. of parsley, chopped

DIRECTIONS

1. In a small bowl, mix together the flour and milk, until the mixture is thick and sticky. In a pan, combine the butter and oil and heat over medium heat. Once the butter has melted, add in the mushrooms and garlic and stir for about 5 minutes, ensuring that the mushrooms darken in color.
2. Pour the cream and milk into the pan and leave to simmer for 8 minutes, stirring regularly. Sprinkle in your salt, pepper, and lemon and taste, adding more if desired. Garnish with parsley and serve.

NUTRITION: 132 Calories 11g Carbs 8g Fat 5g Protein

192. Thai Satay Peanut Sauce

| Preparation Time: | 8' | Cooking Time: | 2' | Servings: | 4 |

Ingredients

- 1 cup of roasted, unsalted peanuts
- 1/3 cup of water
- 1 tbsp of garlic paste/2 cloves of garlic, minced (if you'd like a chunkier paste)
- ½ tsp of soy sauce
- 2 teaspoons sesame oil
- 1 tbsp of brown sugar
- 2 tbsps. of fish sauce (which can be substituted for 2 ½ tbsps. of soy sauce for vegetarians)
- ½ tsp of tamarind paste
- 2 tbsps. of lime juice
- ½ tsp of cayenne pepper
- 1/3 coconut milk
- ½ a green chili, chopped (if you'd like extra spice)

Directions

1. Add all the ingredients into a blender/ food processor and blend until a smooth paste. Pour in more coconut milk if you desire a thinner, runnier paste, and blend more.
2. When serving, you can drizzle a little olive oil in the center of the paste to keep the paste nice and moist.

NUTRITION: 237 Calories 17g Carbs 17g Fat 9g Protein

193. Caramel Sauce

| Preparation Time: | 8' | Cooking Time: | 8' | Servings: | |

Ingredients

- 1 ½ cups of brown sugar
- 4 tbsps. of all-purpose flour
- 1 cup of boiling water
- a pinch of salt (½ tsp)
- 2 tbsps. of butter
- 2 tbsps. of heavy cream
- vanilla (optional, to taste)

Directions

1. Heat a pan over medium-high heat and mix together the flour and sugar, stirring well.
2. Once the contents have mixed well, stir in the water & salt. Allow to cook for 6 minutes, stirring regularly so that the sugar is well blended. If the mix gets too thick, slowly mix more water in.
3. Remove from heat and mix in the butter, cream, and vanilla. Stir well to mix and melt all the ingredients together.

NUTRITION: 123 Calories 24g Carbs 3g Fat 1g Protein

194. Caramel Cream CHeese SPread

| PREPARATION TIME: | 5' | | SERVINGS: | 12 |

| COOKING TIME: | 10' |

INGREDIENTS

- 8 oz of cream cheese
- ½ a cup of toffee bits
- 5 sliced apples, pears & pretzels for serving
- 1 cup of brown sugar
- 6 tbsp of salted butter, cubed
- ½ cup of whipped cream
- pinch of cinnamon

DIRECTIONS

1. Pour the sugar into a saucepan over medium heat and whisk for around 10 minutes until the sugar melts into a golden liquid form, then remove from heat. Add the butter into the pan and slowly whisk the mixture together, ensuring that the butter melts fully.
2. Slowly add the whipped cream into the pan whilst still stirring slowly, checking the consistency. This is your homemade caramel sauce – set aside and prep the rest of your dish.
3. On a serving tray, place the cream cheese in the center. Evenly pour the caramel sauce over it – if you have leftover caramel sauce, you can either serve it in a bowl on the side or store it in the fridge for up to 2 weeks. Crumble and sprinkle your toffee bits over the top.
4. Serve with sliced apples, pears, and pretzels.

NUTRITION: 116 Calories 7.8g Carbs 9g Fat 1.5g Protein

195. baba gHanousH

PREPARATION TIME: 10′	SERVINGS: 4

COOKING TIME: 40′

INGREDIENTS

- 1 eggplant
- 2 tbsps. of lemon juice
- 2 tbsps. of tahini
- 1 garlic clove (or 1 tsp of garlic paste)
- ½ tsp of salt
- 1 tbsp of olive oil
- a sprinkle of chili flakes (optional - if you'd like a spicy kick)

DIRECTIONS

1. Preheat your oven to 400ºF.
2. Wash and poke the eggplant with a fork and place it in the oven for about 35 minutes until tender. Once done, remove from the oven and let it cool.
3. Halve the eggplant and use a spoon to scoop out the flesh. Place the flesh in a blender and add your lemon juice, tahini, garlic, oil, salt, and chili flakes. Puree the mixture for about 20 - 30 seconds.
4. Pour the mixture into a bowl/separate smaller bowls and serve with a carb such as Pita bread/chips.

NUTRITION: 106 Calories 8.7g Carbs 7.8g Fat 2.5g Protein

196. KrafT THousand Island dressIng

PREPARATION TIME: 5'   COOKING TIME: 0'   SERVINGS: 16

INGREDIENTS

- 1 cup mayonnaise
- ¼ cup ketchup
- 2 tablespoons white vinegar
- 4 teaspoons white sugar
- 2 teaspoons sweet pickle relish, minced
- 2 teaspoons white onion, finely chopped or minced
- ¼ teaspoon sea salt
- ¼ teaspoon black pepper

DIRECTIONS

1. Take a large bowl and combine all the ingredients in it. Mix well. Serve.

NUTRITION: 67 Calories 4.9g total fat 6g carbs

197. neWman OWn's Creamy Caesar Salad dressIng

PREPARATION TIME: 5'   COOKING TIME: 0'   SERVINGS: 10

INGREDIENTS

- 2 cups mayonnaise
- 6 tablespoons white vinegar, distilled
- ¼ cup Parmesan cheese, grated
- 4 teaspoons Worcestershire sauce
- 1 teaspoon lime juice
- 1 teaspoon dry mustard, ground
- 1/3 teaspoon salt, or to taste
- ½ teaspoon garlic powder
- ½ teaspoon onion powder
- ½ teaspoon black pepper, freshly ground
- 1 pinch basil, dried
- 1 pinch oregano, dried

DIRECTIONS

1. Take an electric mixer and blend all the ingredients until smooth. Chill the prepared dressing for a few hours before severing. Enjoy.

NUTRITION: 215 Calories 17.4g total fat 13.3g carbs 2.3g Protein

198. bull's eye Original bbq Sauce

PREPARATION TIME:	20'	COOKING TIME:	15'	SERVINGS:	4

INGREDIENTS

- 1½ cups tomato ketchup
- ½ cup Worcestershire sauce
- 5 tablespoons butter, melted
- ¼ cup white vinegar
- 1 tablespoon yellow mustard
- ¼ cup onions, finely minced
- 2 tablespoons hickory liquid smoke
- ½ teaspoon Tabasco sauce
- 1 cup sugar, brown
- 1 tablespoon white sugar
- Salt, to taste

DIRECTIONS

1. Combine the ingredients in a saucepan and heat it over medium heat. Simmer the ingredients for 15 minutes, stirring occasionally. Turn off the heat and let the sauce get cold. The sauce is ready.

NUTRITION: 112 Calories 13.7g total fat 20.5g carbs

199. kraft miraCle WHIP

PREPARATION TIME:	20'	COOKING TIME:	15'	SERVINGS:	2

INGREDIENTS

- 4 egg yolks
- 1/3 teaspoon salt
- 2 tablespoons powdered sugar
- 6 tablespoons lemon juice
- 2 cups oil
- 2 tablespoons cornstarch
- 2 teaspoons dry mustard
- 1 cup boiling water
- ¼ cup vinegar
- Table salt, to taste

DIRECTIONS

1. Take a blender and add egg yolks along with salt, sugar, and half of lemon juice. Blend for few seconds until combined. While the blender is running, start adding the oil, a few drops at a time.
2. Add the remaining lemon juice. Turn off the blender. In a bowl, mix together cornstarch, water, mustard, and vinegar.
3. Mix until a smooth paste is formed. Pour the bowl ingredients into a pan. Cook on low heat until thickened. Slowly add this cooked mixture into the blender.
4. Turn on the blender and combine all the ingredients well. Transfer to a jar and let cool in the refrigerator.

NUTRITION: 717 Calories 7.6g total fat 0.6g carbs

200. Hellman's Mayonnalse

Preparation Time: 15'	Cooking Time: 0'	Servings: 2

INGREDIENTS

- 3 large egg yolks
- 1 teaspoon dry mustard
- 1 teaspoon salt
- ½ teaspoon cayenne pepper
- 1½ cups canola oil
- 4–6 tablespoons lemon juice

DIRECTIONS

1. Add mustard and egg yolks into a blender and pulse until combined. While the blender is mixing, set the speed to low and start adding the oil very slowly.
2. Stop the blender and scrape down the mayonnaise. Add the lemon juice and remaining oil. Keep on blending until combined. At the end, add salt and cayenne pepper. Mix and serve.

NUTRITION: 362 Calories 39.1g total fat 3.4g Protein

201. Helnz KeTCHuP

Preparation Time: 25'	Cooking Time: 20'	Servings: 4

INGREDIENTS

- 1 cup tomato paste
- 1/3 cup light corn syrup
- ½ cup white vinegar
- 1/3 cup water
- 2 tablespoons sugar
- Salt, to taste
- 1/3 teaspoon onion powder
- ¼ teaspoon garlic powder

DIRECTIONS

1. Combine all the ingredients in a saucepan. Turn on the heat and let the liquid simmer for 20 minutes. Turn off the heat and let the mixture cool down. Store it in an airtight glass jar or serve with French fries.

NUTRITION: 78 Calories 0.2g total fat 19.3g carbs 1.4g Protein

202. Hidden Valley Original ranCH dressing

PREPARATION TIME: 10'	COOKING TIME: 0'	SERVINGS: 6

INGREDIENTS

- 1 cup mayonnaise
- 1 cup buttermilk
- 1 teaspoon parsley flakes, dried
- ½ teaspoon black pepper, ground
- 1/3 teaspoon sea salt
- ¼ teaspoon garlic powder
- ¼ teaspoon onion powder
- 2 pinches of thyme, dried

DIRECTIONS

1. Take a blender and combine all the ingredients in it. Pulse until smooth. Transfer to a glass jar and chill in the refrigerator before serving.

NUTRITION: 170 Calories 13.5g total fat 11.7g carbs 1.8g Protein

203. Sabra Hummus

PREPARATION TIME: 5'	COOKING TIME: 0'	SERVINGS: 4

INGREDIENTS

- 1 (14-ounce) can chickpeas, drained
- 1/3 cup tahini sauce
- Juice of 1 lemon
- 2 cloves garlic
- Salt and black pepper, to taste
- 1 teaspoon olive oil

DIRECTIONS

1. Use a high-speed blender to blend all the ingredients thoroughly. Serve and enjoy.

NUTRITION: 576 Calories 27g total fat 65.5g carbs 24g Protein

204. rondelé garllC & Herbs CHeese SPread

PREPARATION TIME: 5'	COOKING TIME: 0'	SERVINGS: 4

INGREDIENTS

- 18 ounces cream cheese, whipped
- 2 teaspoons fresh garlic, finely minced
- 1 teaspoon Italian seasoning
- ½ teaspoon salt
- ¼ teaspoon onion powder
- Sliced green onions for garnish

DIRECTIONS

1. Combine all the ingredients in a bowl and then transfer to a glass jar. Refrigerate for a few hours before serving and sprinkle with sliced green onions.

NUTRITION: 451 Calories 44g total fat 4.1g carbs 9.7g Protein

205. lIPTon Onlon SouP mIx

PREPARATION TIME: 5'	COOKING TIME: 0	SERVINGS: 4

INGREDIENTS

- 1½ cups dry onion flakes
- ½ cup beef bouillon powder
- 8 teaspoons onion powder
- ½ teaspoon crushed celery seeds
- ½ teaspoon dry parsley
- ½ teaspoon sugar

DIRECTIONS

1. Combine all ingredients in a jar. Store it with an airtight cover.

NUTRITION: 19 Calories 0.4g total fat 4.2g carbs

206. laWry's TaCo SeasonIngs

PREPARATION TIME: 10'

SERVINGS: 2

COOKING TIME: 0'

INGREDIENTS

- 2 tablespoons flour
- 2 teaspoons red chili powder
- 2 teaspoons paprika
- 1½ teaspoons salt, or to taste
- 1½ teaspoons onion powder
- 1 teaspoon cumin
- ½ teaspoon cayenne pepper
- ½ teaspoon garlic powder
- ½ teaspoon white sugar
- ¼ teaspoon oregano, ground

DIRECTIONS

1. Combine all the spices in a bowl and store in a glass jar.

NUTRITION: 1 Calorie 0.3g total fat 3.1g carbs 0.5g Protein

207. mrs. dasH SalT-free SeasonIng mIx

<table>
<tr><td>PREPARATION TIME:</td><td>5'</td><td>SERVINGS:</td><td>2</td></tr>
</table>

COOKING TIME: 0'

INGREDIENTS

- 2 teaspoons onion powder
- 2 teaspoons black pepper
- 2 teaspoons parsley
- 2 teaspoons dry celery seed
- 1 teaspoon dry basil
- 1 teaspoon dry bay leaf
- 2 teaspoons marjoram
- 2 teaspoons oregano
- 2 teaspoons savory
- 2 teaspoons thyme
- 2 teaspoons cayenne pepper
- 1 teaspoon coriander
- 2 teaspoons cumin
- 1 teaspoon mustard powder
- 2 teaspoons rosemary
- 2 teaspoons garlic powder
- 1 teaspoon mace

DIRECTIONS

1. Combine all the spices in a bowl and store in a glass jar. Keep it dry.

NUTRITION: 23 Calories 0.8g total fat 4g carbs 0.9g Protein

208. Old Bay Seasoning

PREPARATION TIME:	4'	SERVINGS:	4

COOKING TIME: 0'

INGREDIENTS

- ¼ cup bay leaf powder
- ¼ cup celery salt
- 2 tablespoons dry mustard
- 4 teaspoons black pepper, ground
- 4 teaspoons ginger, ground
- 4 teaspoons paprika, smoked
- 2 teaspoons white pepper, ground
- 2 Teaspoons nutmeg, ground
- 2 teaspoons cloves, ground
- 2 teaspoons allspice, ground
- 1 teaspoon crushed red pepper flakes
- 1 teaspoon mace, ground
- 1 teaspoon cardamom, ground
- ½ teaspoon cinnamon, ground

DIRECTIONS

1. Combine all the spices in a bowl and store in a glass jar. Keep it dry.

NUTRITION: 16 Calories 0.7g total fat 2.5g carbs 0.6g Protein

209. laWry's Seasoned SalT

PREPARATION TIME: 5'

SERVINGS: 1

COOKING TIME: 0'

INGREDIENTS

- 1 tablespoon salt, or to taste
- 2 teaspoons white sugar
- ¼ teaspoon smoked paprika
- ¼ teaspoon turmeric powder
- ¼ teaspoon onion powder
- ¼ teaspoon garlic powder
- ¼ teaspoon cornstarch

DIRECTIONS

1. Combine all the spices in a bowl and store in a glass jar. Keep it dry.

NUTRITION: 360mg sodium

210. KrafT STove ToP STuffIng mIx

PREPARATION TIME: 5'

SERVINGS: 8

COOKING TIME: 10'

INGREDIENTS

- 6 cups bread, cut into cubes
- 1 tablespoon parsley, flakes
- 3–4 bouillon cubes, chicken
- ¼ cup onion flakes, dried
- ½ cup celery flakes, dried
- 1 teaspoon thyme, dry
- 1 teaspoon black pepper
- ½ teaspoon sage
- ½ teaspoon salt

DIRECTIONS

1. Preheat oven to 375°F. Bake the bread in the oven for 10 minutes. Once cool, dump all the ingredients in a bowl. Shake well to combine.
2. Tip: To use the prepared mixture, mix 2 cups mixture with ½ cup water and 2 tablespoons melted butter.

NUTRITION: 57 Calories 0.7g total fat 9.3g carbs 2.9g Protein

211. Chick-fil-a Sauce

PREPARATION TIME: 5′	SERVINGS: 4

COOKING TIME: 0′

INGREDIENTS

- ¼ teaspoon onion powder
- ¼ teaspoon garlic salt
- ½ tablespoon yellow mustard
- ¼ teaspoon smoked paprika
- ½ tablespoon stevia extract, powdered
- 1 teaspoon liquid smoke
- ½ cup mayonnaise

DIRECTIONS

1. Plug in a food processor, add all the ingredients in it, cover with the lid and then pulse for 30 seconds until smooth.
2. Tip the sauce into a bowl and then serve.

NUTRITION: 183 Calories 20 g Fats

212. burger SauCe

PREPARATION TIME: 5′

SERVINGS: 12

COOKING TIME: 0

INGREDIENTS

- 1 tablespoon chopped gherkin
- ½ teaspoon chopped dill
- ¾ teaspoon onion powder
- ¾ teaspoon garlic powder
- 1/8 teaspoon ground white pepper
- 1 teaspoon mustard powder
- ½ teaspoon erythritol sweetener
- ¼ teaspoon sweet paprika
- 1 teaspoon white vinegar
- ½ cup mayonnaise

DIRECTIONS

1. Take a medium bowl, place all the ingredients for the sauce in it and then stir until well mixed.
2. Place the sauce for a minimum of overnight in the refrigerator to develop flavors and then serve with burgers.

NUTRITION: 15 Calories 7 g Fats

213.Pollo TroPICal's Curry MusTard SauCe

PREPARATION TIME: 5'		SERVINGS: 12

COOKING TIME: 0'

INGREDIENTS

- 2 teaspoon curry powder
- 4 teaspoons mustard paste
- 8 tablespoons mayonnaise

DIRECTIONS

1. Plug in a food processor, add all the ingredients in it, cover with the lid and then pulse for 30 seconds until smooth.
2. Tip the sauce into a bowl and then serve.

NUTRITION: 66 Calories 7 g Fats 1 g Protein

214. el fenlx CHIll gravy

PREPARATION TIME: 5'

SERVINGS: 28

COOKING TIME: 40'

INGREDIENTS

- 2 tablespoons coconut flour
- ½ teaspoon salt
- ½ teaspoon ground black pepper
- 1/2 teaspoon dried Mexican oregano leaves
- 1 ½ teaspoon garlic powder
- 2 teaspoons ground cumin
- ½ teaspoon ground coriander
- 2 tablespoons oat fiber
- 2 tablespoons red chili powder
- 1/8 teaspoon dried thyme leaves
- ¼ cup lard
- 2 cups beef broth

DIRECTIONS

1. Take a medium skillet pan, place it over medium heat, add lard and when it melts, stir in flour, and then cook for 3 to 5 minutes until nicely browned, frequently lifting the pan from heat to cool slightly and then bring it back onto the fire.
2. Stir in oat fiber, garlic, thyme, oregano, cumin, and coriander until mixed and cook for 2 minutes until it gets thick, stirring constantly.
3. Then whisk in the broth until smooth, switch heat to the low level, and simmer the gravy fo3 30 minutes until sauce thickens. Remove pan from heat and serve.

NUTRITION: 22 Calories 2 g Fats

215. Sweet and Smoky Chipotle Vinaigrette

PREPARATION TIME: 5'	SERVINGS: 32

COOKING TIME: 0'

INGREDIENTS

- 1 teaspoon garlic powder
- 1 teaspoon cumin
- 1 tablespoon salt
- 1 ½ tablespoon ground black pepper
- 1 teaspoon oregano leaves
- 1/3 cup liquid stevia
- ½ cup red wine vinegar
- 1 ½ cups avocado oil
- 1 tablespoon adobo sauce
- 1 tablespoon water

DIRECTIONS

1. Plug in a food processor, add all the ingredients in it except for oil, cover with the lid and then pulse for 30 seconds until smooth.
2. Blend in oil in a steady stream until emulsified and then pour the salad dressing into a medium bowl.
3. Serve straight away.

NUTRITION: 103 Calories 11.5 g Fats 0.05 g Protein 3.05 g Net Carb

216. bang bang SauCe

PREPARATION TIME: 5'

SERVINGS: 6

COOKING TIME: 0

INGREDIENTS

- ¼ cup mayonnaise
- 1 ½ tablespoon garlic chili sauce
- 1 tablespoon rice vinegar
- 2 tablespoons monk fruit Sweetener
- 1/8 teaspoon salt

DIRECTIONS

1. Plug in a food processor, add all the ingredients in it, cover with the lid and then pulse for 30 seconds until smooth.
2. Tip the sauce into a bowl and then serve.

NUTRITION: 90 Calories 10 g Fats 1 g Net Carb

217. Sweet Chili Sauce

PREPARATION TIME:	5'	SERVINGS:	6

COOKING TIME: 15'

INGREDIENTS

- 1 tablespoon garlic chili sauce
- ½ cup of water
- 2 scoops of beef bone broth collagen
- ¼ cup unseasoned rice vinegar
- 1 ½ teaspoon minced garlic
- ¼ teaspoon ground ginger
- ¼ cup erythritol sweetener
- 1 tablespoon avocado oil

DIRECTIONS

1. Take a large bowl, place all the ingredients in it except for oil and then whisk well until well combined.
2. Take a medium saucepan, place it over medium heat, add sauce mixture, and then simmer it for 15 minutes until the sauce has thickened.
3. When done, remove the pan from heat, stir in oil, let the sauce cool completely and then serve.

NUTRITION: 25 Calories 2.2 g Fats 1.2 g Net Carb

218. bIg maC SauCe

PREPARATION TIME: 5'

SERVINGS: 6

COOKING TIME: 0'

INGREDIENTS

- 1 tablespoon diced white onion
- 2 tablespoons diced pickles
- 1 teaspoon erythritol sweetener
- 1 tablespoon ketchup, low-carb
- 1 teaspoon dill pickle juice
- ½ cup mayonnaise

DIRECTIONS

1. Take a small bowl, place all of its ingredients in it and then stir well until incorporated.
2. Serve straight away or store the sauce in an air-tight container.

NUTRITION: 138 Calories 16 g Fats 1 g Net Carb

219. Caramel Sauce

<table>
<tr><td>PREPARATION TIME:</td><td>5'</td><td>SERVINGS:</td><td>8</td></tr>
</table>

COOKING TIME: 15'

INGREDIENTS

- 3 tablespoons erythritol sweetener
- 1 teaspoon vanilla extract, unsweetened
- 1/3 cup butter, salted
- 2/3 cup heavy cream

DIRECTIONS

1. Take a medium saucepan, place it over low heat, add butter and erythritol and then cook for 4 to 5 minutes until butter melts and turns golden brown.
2. Stir in cream, bring it to a gentle boil and then simmer the sauce for 10 minutes until the sauce has thickened to coat the back of the spoon, stirring constantly.
3. Remove pan from heat, stir in vanilla extract and then serve.

NUTRITION: 91 Calories 10 g Fats 1 g Protein

220. Paula deen bbq SauCe

PREPARATION TIME: 5′

SERVINGS: 32

COOKING TIME: 5′

INGREDIENTS

- 1 teaspoon onion powder
- 1 teaspoon salt
- ½ teaspoon cayenne pepper
- 1 teaspoon ground black pepper
- ¾ cup erythritol sweetener
- 2 teaspoons paprika
- ½ teaspoon cinnamon
- 2 tablespoons mustard paste
- ½ teaspoon xanthan gum
- 3 tablespoons lemon juice
- 1 ½ tablespoons liquid smoke
- ½ cup apple cider vinegar
- ¾ cup ketchup, low-carb
- 1 tablespoon Worcestershire sauce
- ½ cup of water

DIRECTIONS

1. Take a medium saucepan, place it over medium heat, add mustard, Worcestershire sauce, liquid smoke, and ketchup in it, and then pour in vinegar, lemon juice, and water.
2. Whisk until combined, cook it for 3 to 4 minutes until sauce begins to bubbles, and then whisk in xanthan gum until incorporated.
3. Then add erythritol and all the spices, whisk until combined, and remove the pan from heat.
4. Let the sauce cool completely, then serve immediately or store it in an air-tight jar or squeeze bottle.

NUTRITION: 10 Calories 2 g Fats 2 g Net Carb

221. CHorizo Queso fundIdo

PREPARATION TIME:	5'	SERVINGS:	6

COOKING TIME: 25'

INGREDIENTS

- 8 ounces Mexican chorizo
- 1 Roma tomato, cored, seeded, and diced
- 2 tablespoons minced garlic
- 1/2 of a large onion, peeled, sliced
- 1 roasted poblano pepper, seeded, cut into strips
- ½ teaspoon of sea salt
- 2 cups shredded Monterey Jack Cheese
- 1 cup Mexican cream

DIRECTIONS

1. Take a large skillet pan, place it over medium heat, add chorizo, break it up and then cook for 10 to 12 minutes until nicely brown and crisp.
2. When done, drain excess grease, transfer chorizo to a bowl, and then set it aside until required.
3. Return pan over medium heat, add onion and then cook it for 5 minutes until tender.
4. Add tomato, pepper strips, and garlic, season with salt, cook the mixture for 2 minutes until hot and then spoon the mixture into the bowl containing chorizo.
5. Remove skillet pan from the heat, pour in cream and cheese, and then blend for 5 minutes or more until cheese has melted.
6. Return the skillet pan over medium heat, add half of the chorizo mixture, stir until mixed and cook for 5 minutes until creamy.
7. Top it with the remaining chorizo mixture, place the pan under the broiler and cook for 3 minutes until the mixture begins to bubble.
8. Serve it with low-carb tortilla chips.

NUTRITION: 402 Calories 33 g Fats 22 g Protein 4 g Net Carb 1 g Fiber

222. alfredo SauCe

PREPARATION TIME: 5′	**SERVINGS:** 6

COOKING TIME: 10′

INGREDIENTS

- 1 tablespoon minced garlic
- 1/8 teaspoon salt
- 1/8 teaspoon ground white pepper
- 1/8 teaspoon ground nutmeg
- 1 ½ cups grated Parmesan cheese
- 2 cups heavy whipping cream
- ½ cup butter, unsalted
- 2 ounces cream cheese, softened

DIRECTIONS

1. Take a medium saucepan, place it over medium heat, add butter and when it melts, add garlic and then cook for 2 minutes until fragrant.
2. Then add cream cheese and heavy cream, stir until just mixed and stir in parmesan until melted.
3. Cook the sauce for 5 to 7 minutes until sauce thickens to the desired level and then stir in salt, white pepper, and nutmeg. Serve straight away.

NUTRITION: 531 Calories 53.8 g Fats 10.3 g Protein 3.7 g Net Carb

Chapter 9

OLD AND MODERN LUNCH AND DINNER RECIPES

223. P.f. CHang's CrisPy Honey CHICKen

PREPARATION TIME:	20'		SERVINGS:	4

COOKING TIME: 2 H

INGREDIENTS

Chicken:
- 1-pound chicken breast, boneless, skinless, cut into medium-sized chunks
- Vegetable oil, for frying and deep-frying

Batter:
- 4 ounces all-purpose flour
- 2½ ounces cornstarch
- 1 egg
- 6 ounces water
- 1/8 teaspoon baking powder
- 1/8 teaspoon baking soda

Chicken Seasoning:
- 1 tablespoon light soy sauce
- 1/8 teaspoon white pepper
- ¼ teaspoon kosher salt
- 1 tablespoon cornstarch

Sauce:
- ½ cup sake or rice wine
- ½ cup honey
- 3 ounces rice vinegar
- 3 tablespoons light soy sauce
- 6 tablespoons sugar
- ¼ cup cornstarch
- ¼ cup water

DIRECTIONS

1. Do the batter in advance. Combine all the batter ingredients together and refrigerate. After an hour and 40 minutes, mix all the seasoning ingredients together and mix in the chicken. Make sure that the chicken is covered entirely. Place the chicken in the refrigerator to marinate for at least 20 minutes. Except for the cornstarch and water, combine all the sauce ingredients together and set aside.

Before you begin frying your chicken:

2. Heat oil at 350 degrees. When your oil is heated, remove the chicken from the refrigerator and pour the batter all over it.
3. One by one, lower the coated chicken pieces into the heated oil. Keep them suspended until the batter is cooked (20 to 30 seconds).
4. When all the chicken is cooked, place it on the plate covered with the paper towel to cool and drain.
5. Bring the sauce mixture to a boil. While waiting for it to boil, mix the cornstarch and water in a separate bowl. Slowly pour in the cornstarch mixture into the sauce and continue cooking for 2 minutes until the sauce thickens.
6. When the sauce thickens, remove it from heat. When the chicken is cooked, pour some sauce over the entire mixture, just enough to cover the chicken. Transfer everything to a plate with rice or Chinese noodles and serve.

NUTRITION: 680.3 Calories 12g Total Fat 104.8g Carbs 30.7g Protein

224. bosTon markeT's CHICken PoT Pie

PREPARATION TIME: 10'

SERVINGS: 4

COOKING TIME: 40'

INGREDIENTS

- 1 cup half-and-half
- 1 cup chicken broth
- 3 tablespoons all-purpose flour
- 2 cups shredded chicken breast, roasted, skinless
- 2 cups mixed frozen vegetables, thawed
- 2 tablespoons fresh flat-leaf parsley, chopped
- 2 tablespoons chives, chopped
- 1 teaspoon fresh thyme, chopped
- 1 teaspoon lemon juice
- 1 teaspoon salt
- ½ teaspoon lemon zest, grated
- ½ teaspoon freshly ground black pepper
- 7 ounces ready-to-use refrigerated pie crust

DIRECTIONS

1. Get ready by: Preheating the oven to 425F; Lightly flouring a flat surface; and Bringing out 4 10-ounce ramekins.
2. Bring the half-and-half, broth, and flour to a boil while stirring with a whisk. Reduce the heat and continue to simmer for another 4 minutes while continuing to whisk the mixture. When it thickens, stir in the remaining ingredients, except for the pie crust.
3. When all the ingredients are cooked, turn off the heat and cover the pan. Set the mixture aside to work on the pie crust.
4. Place the pie crust on your floured surface and roll it into a circle with an 11-inch diameter. Cut the crust into quarters. Scoop the warm chicken mixture into each of the ramekins. Cover the tops with the pie crust, letting it drape over the edges. Slice an X into each of the tops to allow the pie to cook completely. Bake the pies for 25 minutes and remove them from the oven. Let rest 10 minutes before serving.

NUTRITION: 450 Calories 30g Total Fat 35g Carbs 10g Protein

225. P.f. CHang's beef and broccoli

PREPARATION TIME: 45'

SERVINGS: 4

COOKING TIME: 15'

INGREDIENTS

Marinade:
- 1/3 cup oyster sauce
- 2 teaspoons toasted sesame oil
- 1/3 cup sherry
- 1 teaspoon soy sauce
- 1 teaspoon white sugar
- 1 teaspoon corn starch
- Beef and Broccoli:
- ¾ pound beef round steak, cut into 1/8-inch thick strips
- 3 tablespoons vegetable oil
- 1 thin slice of fresh ginger root
- 1 clove garlic, peeled and smashed
- 1-pound broccoli, cut into florets

DIRECTIONS

1. Mix the marinade ingredients in a bowl until they have dissolved. Marinate the beef in the mixture for 30 minutes. Sauté the ginger and garlic in hot oil for a minute. When the oil is flavored, remove the garlic and ginger and add in the broccoli. Continue cooking the broccoli until tender.

2. When the broccoli is cooked, transfer it to a bowl and set aside. Pour the beef and the marinade into the pan in which you cooked the broccoli and continue cooking until beef is cooked, or about 5 minutes. Pour the broccoli back in and keep cooking for another 3 minutes. Serve.

NUTRITION: 331 Calories 21.1g Total Fat 13.3g Carbs 21.7g Protein

226. OuTbaCk's SeCreT SeasonIng MIx for STeaks

| PREPARATION TIME: | 5' | | SERVINGS: | 3 |

| COOKING TIME: | 10' |

INGREDIENTS

Seasoning:
- 4–6 teaspoons salt
- 4 teaspoons paprika
- 2 teaspoons ground black pepper
- 1 teaspoon onion powder
- 1 teaspoon garlic powder
- 1 teaspoon cayenne pepper
- ½ teaspoon coriander
- ½ teaspoon turmeric

DIRECTIONS

1. Blend all the seasoning ingredients in a bowl. Rub the spice blend into the meat on all sides and let rest for 15-20 minutes before cooking.

NUTRITION: 16.4 Calories 0.5g Total Fat 3.5g Carbs 3.5 g,

227. TaCo Bell's CHaluPa

PREPARATION TIME:	40'	**SERVINGS:**	8

COOKING TIME: 10'

INGREDIENTS

Tortillas:
- 2½ cups flour
- 1 tablespoon baking powder
- ½ teaspoon salt
- 1 tablespoon vegetable shortening
- 1 cup milk
- Oil, for deep frying

Filling:
- 1 tablespoon dried onion flakes
- ½ cup water
- 1-pound ground beef
- ¼ cup flour
- 1 tablespoon chili powder
- 1 teaspoon paprika
- 1 teaspoon salt
- Some oil for frying

For Garnishing:
- Some sour cream
- Some lettuce, shredded
- Some cheddar cheese or Monterey Jack cheese
- Some tomato, diced

DIRECTIONS

1. Combine the flour, baking powder, and salt. Stir in the vegetable shortening and mix. Then add the milk and continue mixing. Portion the dough into 8 parts, and then shape them into 8 6-inch tortillas.
2. Deep fry the tortillas until golden brown. Set aside to cool. Start making the filling. Place the onion flakes in the water and set aside for 5 minutes. Mix the rest of the filling ingredients (except the oil) together until combined. Add in the onion with the water and continue mixing. Heat the oil in a skillet and then cook the entire beef mixture until the beef browns.
3. Now, assemble your Chalupas. In the tortillas, place the following by layers:
4. Cooked beef mixture; Sour cream; Lettuce; Cheese; and lastly, Tomatoes.
5. Serve on a plate.

NUTRITION: 424.9 Calories 15.8g Total Fat 47.7g Carbs 21.6g Protein

228. Chili's baby back ribs

PREPARATION TIME: 15'

SERVINGS: 4

COOKING TIME: 3 H 30'

INGREDIENTS

Pork:
- 4 racks baby-back pork ribs

Sauce:
- 1½ cups water
- 1 cup white vinegar
- ½ cup tomato paste
- 1 tablespoon yellow mustard
- 2/3 cup dark brown sugar packed
- 1 teaspoon hickory flavored liquid smoke
- 1½ teaspoons salt
- ½ teaspoon onion powder
- ¼ teaspoon garlic powder
- ¼ teaspoon paprika

DIRECTIONS

1. Combine all the sauce ingredients and then bring to a boil. Let it simmer for 45 to 60 minutes, stir it occasionally. When it's done, preheat the oven to 300 degrees. Cover the 1 rack of ribs with aluminum foil. Put the ribs on top.
2. Take out the sauce from heat and start glazing over the ribs.
3. When it is completely covered, and transfer it on the baking pan with the foil opening facing upwards. Do it again for the remaining racks and bake it for 2½ hours. When it is almost done, prepare your grill at medium heat then cook both sides. Brush some more sauce on each side and grill for another few minutes. Don't overcook. Once done, serve with extra sauce.

NUTRITION: 645 Calories 43.8g Total Fat 10.8g Carbs 51.5g Protein

229. Applebee's Honey Barbecue Sauce WITH Riblets

PREPARATION TIME: 20'	SERVINGS: 4

COOKING TIME: 3 H 30'

INGREDIENTS

Honey Barbecue Sauce:
- 1 cup ketchup
- ½ cup corn syrup
- ½ cup honey
- ¼ cup apple cider vinegar
- ¼ cup water
- 2 tablespoons molasses
- 2 teaspoons dry mustard
- 2 teaspoons garlic powder
- 1 teaspoon chili powder
- 1 teaspoon onion powder

Meat:
- 2¼ pounds pork riblets
- Salt
- Pepper
- Garlic
- ¼ teaspoon liquid smoke flavoring
- 1 teaspoon water

DIRECTIONS

1. Season the riblets with the salt, garlic, and pepper based on your preferences, then sear them on a grill until the meat starts to separate from the bone. While doing this, preheat the oven to 275F. Mix the water and liquid smoke flavoring into a deep pan and place the ribs on an elevated rack inside—make sure that the liquid does not touch the ribs.
2. Cover the pan with two layers of foil and bake for 2 to 5 hours, depending on the strength of your oven and the number of riblets you have. The internal temperature of the meat must be at 155 degrees all throughout.
3. While waiting for the riblets to cook, prepare the sauce by mixing all the sauce ingredients together and simmering for 20 minutes. When the sauce is done cooking, transfer to a bowl, and set aside. When the ribs are done cooking, sear them on a grill until the marrow starts sizzling. Place the ribs on a plate and cover generously with the sauce.

NUTRITION: 1110 Calories 57g Total Fat 89.3g Carbs 63g Protein

230. Cracker barrel's green beans WITH baCon

| PREPARATION TIME: | 10' | | SERVINGS: | 6 |

| COOKING TIME: | 45' |

INGREDIENTS

- ¼ pound sliced bacon, cut into 1-inch pieces
- 3 cans (14.5 ounces each) green beans, with liquid
- ¼ yellow onion, peeled, chopped
- 1 teaspoon granulated sugar
- ½ teaspoon salt
- ½ teaspoon fresh ground black pepper

DIRECTIONS

1. Half-cook the bacon in a saucepan—make sure it does not get crispy. Add the green beans with the liquid to the browned bacon and season with salt, pepper, and sugar. Top the green beans with the onion and then cover the pan until the mixture boils. Lower the heat and allow the mixture to simmer for another 45 minutes before serving.

NUTRITION: 155.3 Calories 9g Total Fat 15.7g Carbs 6g Protein

231. Café rIo's Pork

PREPARATION TIME:	10'		SERVINGS:	10

COOKING TIME: 9 H

INGREDIENTS

For the Marinade:
- 3 pounds boneless pork loin
- 12 ounces Coca Cola
- ¼ cup brown sugar

For the Seasoning:
- 1 teaspoon garlic salt
- 1 teaspoon onion salt
- 1 teaspoon chili powder
- 1 teaspoon cumin, ground
- 12 ounces Coca Cola

For the Sauce:
- 12 ounces Coca Cola
- ¾ cup brown sugar
- ½ teaspoon chili powder
- ½ teaspoon ground cumin
- 1 can (4 ounces) green chili, ground
- 1 can (10 ounces) red enchilada sauce

DIRECTIONS

1. Mix the Coca Cola and sugar in an airtight container or sealable plastic bag to make the marinade.
2. Massage the marinade into the pork. Place it in the container to marinate for at least 8 hours.
3. Place the pork into a slow cooker and cover with all the seasoning ingredients in the order specified. Cook the pork on low for 7 to 9 hours.
4. After cooking, shred the pork and remove the liquid from the slow cooker. Put the shredded pork into the slow cooker again. Place all the sauce ingredients in a food processor or blender. Blend well to create the sauce. Pour the sauce over the pork, and then cook the entire mixture for another 30 minutes. Transfer to a bowl and serve.

NUTRITION: 317 Calories 7g Total Fat 31g Carbs 28g Protein

232. ruTH CHris's fileT mIgnon WITH béarnaise SauCe

PREPARATION TIME: 10'

SERVINGS: 4

COOKING TIME: 40'

INGREDIENTS

Vinegar Reduction:
- 2 tablespoons tarragon vinegar
- 2 teaspoons fresh lemon juice
- 2 teaspoons shallots, finely chopped
- 1 teaspoon dried tarragon
- Fresh ground black pepper, to taste

Sauce:
- 2 large egg yolks
- ¼ cup water
- Salt, to taste
- 2 teaspoons fresh tarragon, chopped
- 2 teaspoons fresh chervil, chopped (optional)
- ½ cup unsalted butter, melted
- Steak:
- 4 filet mignon steaks. about 8 ounces each

DIRECTIONS

1. Mix all the vinegar reduction ingredients together and bring to a boil over medium to high heat.
2. When the vinegar mixture starts to boil, lower the heat and allow the mixture to simmer until most of the liquid evaporates. When only small bubbles of liquid are left, remove the vinegar reduction from heat and set aside.
3. Let the water to simmer in the bottom part of a double boiler while whisking the egg yolks and water in the top part. Place the top part over the simmering water, making sure that the water does not touch the bottom of the bowl.
4. Pour the vinegar reduction into the egg mixture and whisk until the entire mixture reaches 284F. Remove the mixture from heat, but continue whisking. Slowly pour in the melted butter while continuing to whisk the mixture.
5. Add in the remaining sauce ingredients and continue stirring. Set the Béarnaise sauce aside, keeping it warm at 220F. Season the steaks with salt and pepper while preheating the broiler for 10 minutes. Broil the steaks to your preference (rare, medium rare, medium well, well done). Place the steaks in a warm plate, pour ¼ cup of Béarnaise sauce, and serve.

NUTRITION: 340 Calories 8g Total Fat 18g Carbs 201g Protein

233. P.f. Chang's Spare ribs

PREPARATION TIME:	5'		SERVINGS:	2

COOKING TIME: 25'

INGREDIENTS

Sauce:
- 1 cup ketchup
- 1 cup light corn syrup
- ½ cup hoisin sauce
- ½ cup water
- 1/3 cup light brown sugar, packed
- 2 tablespoons onions, minced
- 1 tablespoon rice vinegar

Ribs:
- 12 to 16 cups water
- 2 teaspoons salt
- 1 rack pork spareribs
- 4 cups vegetable oil
- 1 teaspoon sesame seeds, for garnish
- 1 tablespoon green onion, diced, for garnish

DIRECTIONS

1. Stir in all the sauce ingredients and wait for it to boil, then let it simmer for 5 minutes. Set aside. Transfer the water and salt into a large pot, then let it boil. In the meantime, clean the spare ribs and take out the excess fat.
2. When it starts to boil, transfer all the ribs into the water and continue boiling for 14 minutes. Drain and set aside. Cook the oil at 375 degrees, then put 4 to 6 ribs in it and cook for 6 minutes.
3. Do it again until all the ribs are fried. Combine the fried ribs and the sauce over medium heat. Let it simmer at least a minute. Place the ribs to a plate and serve with rice. Topped the ribs with the sesame seeds and green onions.

NUTRITION: 1344 Calories 77.2g Total Fat 113.2g Carbs 52.5g Protein

234. boston market's meatloaf

PREPARATION TIME:	10'		SERVINGS:	8

COOKING TIME:	1 H 25'

INGREDIENTS

Sauce:
- 1 cup tomato sauce
- 1½ tablespoons barbecue sauce
- 1 tablespoon sugar

Meatloaf:
- 1½ pounds lean ground sirloin
- 6 tablespoons all-purpose flour
- ¾ teaspoon salt
- ½ teaspoon onion powder
- ¼ teaspoon ground black pepper
- 1 dash garlic powder

DIRECTIONS

1. Preheat the oven to 400F, and place the ground sirloin into a bowl.
2. Mix the sauce ingredients together and bring to a simmer over medium heat. When the sauce is simmering, remove it from heat. Set aside 2 tablespoons of the sauce and pour the rest over the meat. Massage the sauce into the meat, marinating it well.
3. Add the rest of the meatloaf ingredients into the meat mixture and continue mixing and kneading until the spices are fully incorporated into the meat. Place the meat into your loaf pan and cover with foil. Bake the meat mixture for 30 minutes.
4. Remove the pan from the oven and drain the fat before cutting the meatloaf into 8 equal portions.
5. Pour the set-aside sauce over the top of the meatloaf and return it to the oven for another 25 to 30 minutes. Transfer the meatloaf to a plate and let cool before serving.

NUTRITION: 210.1 Calories 10.9g Total Fat 8.8g Carbs 18.3g Protein

235. boneflsH grlll CoPyCaT bang bang SHrlmP

PREPARATION TIME: 10'	SERVINGS: 10

COOKING TIME: 35'

INGREDIENTS

- 1 1/4 cups of mayonnaise, low fat
- 5/8 cup of chili sauce, Thai sweet
- 7 1/2 dashes of garlic-chili sauce
- 2 1/2 lbs. of shrimp, peeled
- 1/2 cup of corn starch
- 4 leaves of lettuce
- 1/4 cup of green onion, chopped

DIRECTIONS

1. Stir the sweet chili sauce and mayo together in a large-sized bowl. Add garlic-chili sauce. Stir well. Spread the corn starch into a wide, shallow dish. Press the shrimp into corn starch, giving it a fairly thin layer of coating. Heat oil in deep-fryer to 350F.
2. Deep-fry the shrimp in small batches till not transparent in the middle anymore, five minutes or so per batch. Drain on a plate lined with paper towels. Combine shrimp and mayo sauce in the sauce bowl. Stir, coating shrimp well.
3. Line medium bowl using leaves of lettuce. Add shrimp to the bowl. Garnish with the green onions. Serve.

NUTRITION: 78 Calories 0.2g total fat 19.3g carbs 1.4g Protein

236. blaCk angus STeakHouse's bbq baby baCk rlbs

PREPARATION TIME: 30'

SERVINGS: 1 SLAB

COOKING TIME: 6-8 H

INGREDIENTS

- 1 rack of pork ribs
- Your favorite barbecue sauces
- Onion powder, to taste
- Garlic powder, to taste

Marinade:
- 2 tablespoons kosher salt
- 2 tablespoons paprika
- 4 tablespoons granulated garlic
- 1 tablespoon onion powder
- 1 teaspoon cumin seeds
- 1 teaspoon Durkee Ancho pepper
- 2 teaspoons dry mustard
- 2 teaspoons black pepper

Rib Mop:
- 1 cup red wine vinegar
- 1 tablespoon garlic
- 1 cup water
- 3 tablespoons soy sauce

DIRECTIONS

1. Mix all the marinade ingredients together. Rub the marinade all over the ribs to soak them in flavor.
2. Barbecue the meat over indirect heat at 250F to 300F for 3 to 4 hours. Add soaked fruit wood to the coals for additional aroma. Make sure that the temperature remains at 250F to 300F for the entire cooking duration. While the meat is cooking, mix together the rib mop ingredients in a bowl.
3. After three to four hours, transfer the meat to an aluminum pan and brush both sides with the rib mop.
4. Cook the ribs for another hour and then remove them from heat and mop them again. Continue cooking the ribs for another 3 to 4 hours, basting them with the mop, and some barbecue sauce every hour. When the ribs are done barbecuing, sprinkle them with onion and garlic powder before wrapping them in aluminum foil. Let the ribs rest for 30 minutes.
5. Transfer the ribs to a plate and serve.

NUTRITION: 1500 Calories 30g Total Fat 108g Carbs 14g Protein

237. Texas road House's mesquiTe grilled Pork CHoPs WITH CInnamon aPPles

PREPARATION TIME: 40'

SERVINGS: 2

COOKING TIME: 40'

INGREDIENTS

Cinnamon Apples:
- 4 apples (peeled, sliced)
- 2 tablespoons butter, melted
- 1/3 cup brown sugar
- 2 tablespoons lemon juice
- ¾ teaspoon cinnamon

Pork Chop:
- 2 pork loin chops with bone, room temperature; 2 inches thick

Paste:
- 2 tablespoons extra virgin olive oil
- 2 tablespoons Worcestershire sauce
- 2 teaspoons black pepper, cracked
- 2 teaspoons chili powder
- 2 teaspoons granulated garlic powder
- 2 teaspoons kosher salt
- 1 teaspoon cumin, ground
- ½ teaspoon cinnamon, ground
- Mesquite wood chips, soaked in water for at least 30 minutes

DIRECTIONS

1. Prepare the apples by cooking all the cinnamon apple ingredients in butter until the apples soften. When they are ready, set the cooked apples aside. Reheat before serving.
2. Before you begin with the meat, you need to:
3. Soak the mesquite chips as instructed; Leave the pork loin at room temperature for 30 to 45 minutes; and Preheat the grill on high.
4. Thoroughly mix all the paste ingredients together. When the paste is done, spread it over the pork chops, covering them completely. Remove the chips from the water and place them in an aluminum foil pan.
5. Place the pan directly over the fire from the grill and cook the pork loin on both sides for about 6 minutes. When the meat is seared, lower the heat to medium. Place the pork over indirect medium heat and cook for another 25 minutes. Remove the pork from heat, wrap it in aluminum foil, and let rest for another 5 minutes. Transfer the pork to a plate with the reheated apples. Serve the entire dish.

NUTRITION: 316 Calories 22.5g Total Fat 9.1g Carbs 20.5g Protein

238. Panda Express's Grilled Teriyaki Chicken

PREPARATION TIME:	5'		SERVINGS:	4

COOKING TIME:	20

INGREDIENTS

- 2 pounds chicken thighs
- 2 tablespoons canola oil
- 2/3 cup sugar
- ¼ cup low-sodium soy sauce
- 1 teaspoon lemon juice
- ½ teaspoon garlic powder
- ¼ teaspoon ground ginger
- 1/3 cup water
- 2 tablespoons cornstarch mixed with 2 tablespoons water
- Sliced green onions for garnish

DIRECTIONS

1. In a large bowl, combine the chicken thighs and canola oil and let sit until the grill is hot. Place the chicken in a grill pan and grill for about 5 minutes on each side.
2. In a mixing bowl, combine the sugar, soy sauce, lemon juice, garlic powder, ground ginger, and water. Heat to boiling, then reduce heat and simmer for 3 minutes. Stir in the cornstarch slurry and cook on low heat until the sauce thickens.
3. Spoon sauce over grilled chicken to serve. Sprinkle with sliced green onions.

NUTRITION: 452 calories 10g Carbs 23g Protein

239. Panda exPress's SWeeT fIre CHICken breasT

| PREPARATION TIME: | 15' | SERVINGS: | 4 |

| COOKING TIME: | 15' |

INGREDIENTS

- 3 large chicken breasts, cut into 1-inch pieces
- 1 (10-ounce) bottle sweet chili sauce
- 1 medium onion, sliced
- 1 large red bell pepper, chopped
- 1¼ cup pineapple chunks
- ¼ cup pineapple juice
- 2 cloves garlic, minced
- 1 cup all-purpose flour
- 2 eggs, beaten
- Oil for frying
- 2 tablespoons oil, if needed
- Salt and pepper to taste

DIRECTIONS

1. Add the flour, salt, and pepper to a shallow dish and mix well. Dip the chicken pieces in the beaten egg followed by a dip in the flour to coat. Set aside.
2. Heat oil in a large skillet over medium-high heat. When hot, add the chicken pieces and cook until golden brown on all sides, about 6 minutes. You may have to work in batches, as you don't want the pieces to touch while cooking.
3. When done, remove the chicken from the skillet and place on a paper-towel-lined plate to drain excess oil.
4. If needed, add the rest of the oil to the skillet and heat over medium-high heat. When hot, add the onions, garlic, and peppers and cook until the onions and peppers start to soften.
5. When soft, return the chicken to the skillet along with the chili sauce, pineapple, and pineapple juice and allow to cook for about 7 minutes, stirring occasionally. Serve with a side of rice.

NUTRITION: 624 calories 11g fats 31g protein

240. Panda Express's Black Pepper Chicken

INGREDIENTS

- 6 boneless, skinless chicken thighs
- 1 green bell pepper, diced
- 1 yellow onion, sliced
- 3 celery stalks, sliced
- 2 tablespoons cornstarch
- 1 tablespoon garlic powder
- ½ tablespoon black pepper
- ½ tablespoon onion powder
- 1 teaspoon ginger powder
- 2 tablespoons peanut oil
- 2 cups cooked rice
- Sauce
- ½ cup chicken broth
- ¼ cup oyster sauce
- ¼ cup rice wine vinegar
- ½ tablespoon garlic, minced
- 1 teaspoon black pepper
- 1 teaspoon chili powder
- ½ teaspoon ginger powder

DIRECTIONS

1. Combine all the sauce ingredients, stir, and set aside. Dice the chicken into 1-inch pieces. Add the cornstarch, salt, and pepper to a mixing bowl. Toss the chicken in the mixture to coat.
2. Heat the oil over medium-high heat in a large skillet. Cook the chicken in batches to keep the pieces from touching. This lets the individual pieces cook faster and brown more easily.
3. When all the chicken has been browned, return it to the skillet along with the vegetables and cook for about 5 more minutes. Add the sauce to the chicken and vegetables and allow to simmer for 10–12 minutes. Serve with rice.

NUTRITION: 704 calories 10g fats 30g protein

241. Panda Express's Zucchini Mushroom Chicken

Preparation Time:	15'		Servings:	4

Cooking Time:	10'

Ingredients

- 1-pound boneless skinless chicken breasts, cut into bite-sized pieces
- 3 tablespoons cornstarch
- 1 tablespoon canola oil
- 1 tablespoon sesame oil
- ½ pound mushrooms, sliced
- 1 medium zucchini, cut in half lengthwise, then into ½-inch slices
- 1 cup broccoli florets
- ¼ cup soy sauce
- 1 tablespoon rice wine vinegar
- 2 teaspoons sugar
- 3 cloves garlic, minced
- 2 teaspoons minced ginger or ½ teaspoon ground ginger
- Sesame seeds, for garnish (optional)

Directions

1. Add the cornstarch to a shallow dish and season with salt and pepper. Add the chicken and toss to coat. In a large skillet, heat both the canola and sesame oil over medium-high heat. When hot, add the chicken and cook until brown on all sides.
2. Remove the chicken from the skillet and turn the heat to high. Cook the zucchini, mushrooms, and broccoli until they begin to soften, about 1 minute. Stir in the garlic and ginger and cook a bit longer. Continue to cook until the mushrooms and zucchini have softened to taste, then stir the chicken back into the skillet. When the chicken has heated up, stir in the soy sauce and the rice wine vinegar. Serve with rice.

Nutrition: 701 calories 11g fats 29g protein

242. Panda Express's Orange Chicken

Preparation Time:	15'		Servings:	4-6

	Cooking Time:	10'	

Ingredients

- 2 pounds boneless skinless chicken, chopped into bite-sized pieces
- 1 egg
- 1½ teaspoons salt
- White pepper to taste
- Oil for frying
- ½ cup cornstarch
- ¼ cup flour
- Orange sauce
- 3 tablespoons soy sauce
- ¾ cup orange juice
- ½ cup brown sugar
- Zest of 1 orange
- 1 tablespoon oil
- 2 tablespoons ginger, minced
- 2 teaspoons garlic, minced
- 1 teaspoon red chili flakes
- ½ cup green onion, chopped
- 2 tablespoons rice wine
- ½ cup water
- 2 tablespoons cornstarch
- 1 teaspoon sesame oil

Directions

1. In a shallow dish, combine the ½ cup of cornstarch and the flour. In a second shallow dish, beat together the egg, salt, pepper, and 1 tablespoon of oil. In a large skillet or deep saucepan, heat oil to 375°F.
2. Dredge the chicken pieces in the egg mixture followed by the flour mixture. Shake off any excess flour. Add the coated chicken to the hot oil and cook for about 4 minutes or until nicely browned. Transfer the chicken from the hot oil to a paper-towel-lined plate to drain.
3. In a mixing bowl, stir together the soy sauce, orange juice, brown sugar, and orange zest. In another skillet or wok, heat 1 tablespoon of oil. When hot, add the ginger, garlic, red pepper flakes, and green onions. Cook for about 1 minute or until the garlic is fragrant.
4. Stir in the rice wine and soy sauce mixture. Cook for about 1 more minute, then add the chicken. Make a slurry with the water and remaining cornstarch and gradually add to the skillet until the sauce thickens. Add sesame oil to taste. Serve with rice.

Nutrition: 725 calories 12g fats 34g protein

243. Pf CHang's Orange Peel CHICken

PREPARATION TIME:	10'		SERVINGS:	4

COOKING TIME: 30'

INGREDIENTS

- 4 boneless, skinless chicken breasts
- ¾ cup flour
- ¼ cup orange peel from 1 orange
- 2 tablespoons cornstarch
- 2 tablespoons garlic, minced
- 2 teaspoons black pepper
- 2 teaspoons Creole seasoning
- 2 teaspoons garlic powder
- 2 teaspoons onion powder
- 1 teaspoon chili powder
- Extra-virgin olive oil
- Orange peel sauce
- 1 cup tomato sauce
- 6 tablespoons orange juice
- 6 tablespoons chicken broth
- ¼ cup brown sugar
- 2 tablespoons sriracha
- 1 tablespoon soy sauce
- 1 teaspoon chili paste
- ¼ teaspoon black pepper

DIRECTIONS

1. Peel and clean an orange, removing the white pulpy part and cutting out the segments which will be used for garnish. Julienne the peel and set aside with the segments. Stir together all the sauce ingredients in a mixing bowl. Set aside.
2. Cut the chicken into bite-sized cubes. In another bowl, mix together all the spices. Toss over the chicken pieces. Stir to make sure the chicken is properly covered.
3. In a small dish, stir together the flour and cornstarch. Pour over the seasoned chicken and stir again to make sure the chicken is coated.
4. Heat the olive oil in a large skillet over medium-high heat. When hot, stir in the chicken and cook until browned on all sides. You may have to work in batches to cook the chicken faster and more evenly. When all the chicken has been cooked, remove it from the skillet.
5. Add a bit more olive oil to the pan, then toss in the orange peel slices and the garlic and cook just until garlic is fragrant. Add the sauce to the skillet and bring to a boil, then reduce heat and cook for 5 minutes or until the sauce begins to thicken. Return the chicken to the skillet and cook for 5 more minutes. Garnish with orange segments and serve with rice.

NUTRITION: 691 calories 10g fats 31g protein

244. Pf Chang's Crispy Chicken

| PREPARATION TIME: | 20' | SERVINGS: | 4 |

| COOKING TIME: | 2 H |

INGREDIENTS

Chicken
- 1-pound chicken breast, boneless, skinless, cut into medium-sized chunks
- Vegetable oil, for frying and deep-frying

Batter
- 4 ounces all-purpose flour
- 2½ ounces cornstarch
- 1 egg
- 6 ounces water
- 1/8 teaspoon baking powder
- 1/8 teaspoon baking soda

Chicken seasoning
- 1 tablespoon light soy sauce
- 1/8 teaspoon white pepper
- ¼ teaspoon kosher salt
- 1 tablespoon cornstarch

Sauce
- ½ cup sake or rice wine
- ½ cup honey
- 3 ounces rice vinegar
- 3 tablespoons light soy sauce
- 6 tablespoons sugar
- ¼ cup cornstarch
- ¼ cup water

NUTRITION: 679 calories 12g fats 32g protein

DIRECTIONS

1. Make the batter at least 2 hours in advance. Mix all the batter ingredients together and refrigerate. After an hour and 40 minutes, mix all the seasoning ingredients together and mix in the chicken. Make sure that the chicken is covered entirely.
2. Place the chicken in the refrigerator to marinate for at least 20 minutes. Mix all the sauce ingredients together - except the cornstarch and water - and set aside.
3. Before you begin frying your chicken:
4. Place a paper towel on a plate in preparation for draining the oil, and Heat your oil to 350F.
5. When your oil is heated, remove the chicken from the refrigerator and pour the batter all over it.
6. One by one, lower the coated chicken pieces into the heated oil. Keep them suspended until the batter is cooked, about 20 to 30 seconds.
7. When all the chicken is cooked, place it on the plate covered with the paper towel to cool and drain. Bring the sauce mixture to a boil. While waiting for it to boil, mix the cornstarch and water in a separate bowl.
8. Slowly pour the cornstarch mixture into the sauce and continue cooking for 2 minutes until the sauce thickens. When the sauce thickens, remove it from heat.
9. When the chicken is cooked, pour some sauce over the entire mixture, just enough to cover the chicken. Transfer everything to a plate with rice or Chinese noodles and serve.

245. Pf CHang's CHICken fried rICe

PREPARATION TIME: 10'		SERVINGS: 4

COOKING TIME: 10'

INGREDIENTS

- 2 cups prepared rice
- 1 chicken breast, cut into bite-sized pieces and seasoned with salt & pepper
- ½ cup frozen mixed vegetables
- 2 green onions, chopped
- 1 clove garlic, minced
- 1 egg
- 3 teaspoons sesame or wok oil, divided
- 2 tablespoons soy sauce

DIRECTIONS

1. In a small dish, beat together the egg and 1 teaspoon of oil. In a large skillet or wok, heat another teaspoon of the oil and cook the chicken until done. Remove from skillet and set aside.
2. Add the last teaspoon of oil to the skillet and stir in the mixed vegetables and green onions. Cook and stir until hot and tender. Then add the garlic and cook until fragrant. Using a spatula or spoon, move the vegetables to one side. Add the egg mixture and scramble until cooked, then add the chicken and stir until it is all combined.

NUTRITION: 641 calories 9g fats 34g protein

246. Pf Chang's Ginger Chicken with Broccoli

Preparation Time:	10'	**Servings:**	4

Cooking Time: 20'

Ingredients

- ½ cup egg substitute or beaten eggs
- ¼ teaspoon white pepper
- ¼ teaspoon salt
- 1-pound boneless, skinless chicken breasts, sliced
- Stir-fry sauce
- ½ cup soy sauce
- 2 tablespoons rice wine vinegar
- 1 tablespoon sugar
- ½ cup chicken broth
- 3 cups chicken broth
- ½ pound broccoli florets
- 2 tablespoons butter
- 2 tablespoons ginger, freshly minced
- 2 tablespoons green onion, minced
- 1 teaspoon garlic, minced
- ¼ cup cornstarch
- 1 teaspoon sesame oil

Directions

1. In a resealable bag, combine the eggs or egg substitute, salt, and pepper. Add the chicken pieces and seal. Place in the refrigerator for at least 3 hours or overnight. When ready to use, discard the marinade. Stir together all the ingredients for the stir-fry sauce in a mixing bowl. Mix well and set aside.
2. Add the 3 cups of chicken broth to a large skillet or wok and bring to a boil. Reduce heat to maintain a simmer. Add the chicken and cook until almost done, then remove from the pot.
3. Add the broccoli to the broth and cook until tender. Then drain the broth and transfer the broccoli to a plate. Add the butter to the skillet and heat over medium heat. When melted, stir in the ginger, green onion, and garlic and cook until the garlic is fragrant.
4. Return them to the skillet and cook until done, about 5 minutes.
5. Thicken the broth with a slurry made from the cornstarch and ½ cup of water. Cook until the sauce thickens. Serve the chicken over rice and broccoli.

Nutrition: 623 calories 11g fats 29g protein

247. Pei Wei's Spicy Chicken

PREPARATION TIME: 10'

SERVINGS: 4

COOKING TIME: 15'

INGREDIENTS

- 2 boneless skinless chicken breasts, cut into 1-inch pieces
- 1½ cups sliced carrots
- 1½ cups sugar snap peas
- 3 cups vegetable oil for frying
- Batter
- 1½ cups flour
- 1½ teaspoons salt
- 1½ teaspoons baking soda
- 2 eggs
- 2/3 cup milk
- 2/3 cup water
- Sauce
- 3 teaspoons vegetable oil
- 3 tablespoons minced garlic
- ¼ cup green onion, chopped, white parts only
- 1½ cups pineapple juice
- 3 teaspoons chili garlic paste, more if you want it spicier
- 3 tablespoons white wine vinegar
- 2 tablespoons sugar
- 2 teaspoons soy sauce
- 1 teaspoon salt
- 4 teaspoons cornstarch
- 3 tablespoons water

DIRECTIONS

1. In a mixing bowl, stir together all the ingredients for the batter. It should be smooth and without lumps. It will be thinnish. In a saucepan, bring 3 cups of water to a boil, then add the carrots and peas and cook just until tender. You want them to be a bit crispy. Drain and set aside.
2. In a deep pot or deep fryer, heat the 3 cups of oil to 375°F. Add the chicken to the hot oil a few pieces at a time. Leave it there until cooked through and golden brown, then transfer to a paper-towel-lined plate to drain.
3. In a large skillet or wok, heat 2 teaspoons of oil over medium-high heat. Add the garlic and green onion and cook for about 1 minute. In a bowl, stir together all the sauce ingredients except for the cornstarch and water.
4. Add the sauce mixture to the hot skillet and cook until it starts to bubble. Make a slurry of the cornstarch and water and add it to the bubbling sauce, and cook until the sauce starts to thicken. Add the chicken, peas, and carrots and cook until hot. Serve with rice.

NUTRITION: 684 calories 9g fats 31g protein

248. Pei Wei's Chicken Pad Thai

PREPARATION TIME:	15'	SERVINGS:	4-6

COOKING TIME: 15'

INGREDIENTS

- ½ cup low-fat coconut milk
- 6 tablespoons creamy peanut butter
- ¼ cup light soy sauce
- ¼ cup lime juice
- ½ tablespoon rice wine vinegar
- 2 tablespoons brown sugar
- 2 teaspoons grated ginger
- ½ teaspoon red pepper flakes
- Chicken stir-fry
- ½ tablespoon canola oil
- ½ tablespoon dark sesame oil
- 1–2 teaspoons curry powder (optional)
- 1-pound chicken breast, cut into bite-sized pieces
- 6–8 ounces frozen sugar snap peas
- 1 medium onion, chopped
- 2 cloves garlic, minced
- ½ pound cooked rice noodles or long thin pasta

Garnish
- ¼ cup lightly salted dry roasted peanuts, chopped
- Cilantro

DIRECTIONS

1. Stir together all the sauce ingredients in a mixing bowl. Combine well, then set aside. Cook the noodles or pasta according to the package Directions. Set aside. Heat the canola oil and sesame oil in a large skillet over medium-high heat. When hot, add the chicken and stir. Allow to cook for about 5 minutes, then stir in the garlic.
2. When the chicken is completely cooked through, add the peas and cook a bit longer to heat the peas through. Stir in the sauce and make sure the chicken is evenly coated. Add the cooked noodles and stir to make sure everything is covered in the sauce. Serve with cilantro and top with chopped peanuts.

NUTRITION: 612 calories 10g fats 33g protein

249. Pei Wei's Sesame Chicken

PREPARATION TIME: 20'

SERVINGS: 4-6

COOKING TIME: 15'

INGREDIENTS

Sauce
- ½ cup soy sauce
- 2½ tablespoons hoisin sauce
- ½ cup sugar
- ¼ cup white vinegar
- 2½ tablespoons rice wine
- 2½ tablespoons chicken broth
- Pinch of white pepper
- 1¼ tablespoons orange zest

Breaded chicken
- 2 pounds boneless skinless chicken breasts
- ¼ cup cornstarch
- ½ cup flour
- 1 egg
- 2 cups milk
- Pinch of white pepper
- Pinch of salt
- ¼ vegetable oil
- ½ red bell pepper, chunked
- ½ white onion, chunked
- 1 tablespoon Asian chili sauce
- ½ tablespoon ginger, minced
- ¼ cup scallions, white part only, cut into rings
- 1 tablespoon sesame oil
- 1 tablespoon cornstarch
- 1 tablespoon water
- Sesame seeds for garnish

DIRECTIONS

1. Prepare the sauce by whisking all the ingredients together in a small saucepan. Bring to a simmer, then remove from the heat and set aside. Whisk the eggs, milk, salt, and pepper together in a shallow dish.
2. Mix the ¼ cup of cornstarch and flour together in a separate shallow dish. Dredge the chicken pieces in the egg mixture and then in the cornstarch/flour mixture. Shake off any excess, then set aside. Heat the vegetable oil over medium-high heat in a deep skillet or saucepan.
3. When hot, drop the coated chicken into the oil and cook for about 2–4 minutes. Remove from oil and place on a paper-towel-lined plate to drain. Make a slurry out of the 1 tablespoon of cornstarch and water.
4. In a different large skillet or wok, heat 1 tablespoon of sesame oil until hot. Add the ginger and chili sauce and heat for about 10 seconds. Add the peppers and onions and cook for another 30 seconds. Stir in the chili sauce and ginger and the sauce you made earlier and bring to a boil. Once it boils, stir in the cornstarch slurry and cook until the sauce thickens.
5. When the sauce is thick, add the chicken and stir to coat. Serve with rice, and sprinkle with sesame seeds.

NUTRITION: 691 calories 10g fats 31g protein

250. Pei Wei's asian diner Caramel Chicken

Preparation Time: 20'

Servings: 6

Cooking Time: 55'

Ingredients

- 1 cup sugar
- ¼ cup water
- ¾ cup reduced-sodium chicken broth
- 3 tablespoons fish sauce
- 2 tablespoons soy sauce
- 1 whole chicken, cut into 10 pieces
- 1 teaspoon salt
- 2 tablespoons vegetable oil and more, if needed
- ¼ cup fresh ginger, chopped
- 2 tablespoons fresh garlic, chopped
- ½ large red onion, chopped
- 2 tablespoons jalapenos, chopped
- 1 English cucumber, sliced then julienned
- ½ red bell pepper, julienned lengthwise
- 1 carrot, cut diagonally
- 2 green onions, chopped
- ½ cup pineapple chunks
- ¼ cup fresh mint, chopped
- ¼ cup fresh cilantro, chopped
- ¼ cup fresh basil, chopped
- Cooked rice or rice vermicelli for serving
- Vietnamese vinaigrette
- ½ cup lime juice, plus wedges for serving
- ¼ cup light brown sugar
- 2 tablespoons Vietnamese fish sauce
- ½ teaspoon toasted sesame oil
- 4 teaspoons vegetable oil

Directions

1. Preheat oven to 325°F. Combine sugar and water in a deep sauce pot. Bring to a boil and simmer until the sugar turns a dark caramel color. Do not let it burn, and do not stir the sugar while cooking, or it may crystallize.
2. Add the chicken broth. The broth will boil quickly and spatter because of the hot sugar, so be careful! This is the reason for the deep pot. Stir in the broth and continue stirring over low heat until the sugar dissolves. Add the fish sauce and soy sauce. Set aside.
3. Combine the Vietnamese vinaigrette ingredients in a medium bowl and add cucumbers, red bell peppers, and carrots. Marinate until ready to use. Season the chicken pieces with the salt.
4. Heat the vegetable oil in a large Dutch oven and brown the chicken pieces on all sides. Set aside. In the same pan, using the extra vegetable oil if needed, sauté the ginger, garlic, red onion, and jalapeno over medium heat for 4–5 minutes until soft and fragrant.
5. Add the browned chicken pieces and the caramel sauce to the Dutch oven, turning the chicken in the caramel broth to coat all sides. Arrange the chicken, so it is all submerged in the sauce as much as possible and bring to a boil.
6. Cover the pot, put in the oven, and braise until done, about 35–45 minutes. While the chicken is cooking, assemble the green onion, pineapple chunks, and the other herbs and set aside.
7. Just before serving, add the green onions and pineapple chunks and stir well. Serve the chicken over rice or rice vermicelli. Top with a portion of Vietnamese vinaigrette slaw.

Nutrition: 697 calories 12g fats 32g protein

251. Pei Wei's Kung Pao Chicken

PREPARATION TIME: 15'

SERVINGS: 4-6

COOKING TIME: 10'

INGREDIENTS

Sauce
- 1 teaspoon red chili paste
- 2 tablespoons low-sodium soy sauce
- 1 tablespoon mirin
- 1 teaspoon seasoned rice wine vinegar
- 1 teaspoon sugar
- ¼ cup chicken broth
- 1 teaspoon cornstarch
- 1 teaspoon dark sesame oil
- **Stir-fry**
- 1½ pounds boneless, skinless chicken breasts, cut into 1-inch cubes
- 1 egg, whisked
- ¼ cup cornstarch
- ¼ cup canola oil
- ½ cup frozen crinkle-cut carrots
- 1 cup sugar snap peas
- ½ cup dry-roasted peanuts
- 10 dried red chili peppers, if you want a bit more spice, you can also add a dash of red pepper flakes
- 4 green onions, including green parts, sliced
- 3 cloves garlic, minced
- ½ cup water chestnuts, diced

DIRECTIONS

1. Beat the egg in a small shallow dish. Add the cornstarch to another shallow dish.
2. Mix together all the ingredients for the sauce in a small bowl and set aside. Bread the chicken by first dipping in the egg and then coating with cornstarch. Heat the oil over medium-high heat in a large skillet or a wok. When hot, add the coated chicken. Cook through and brown on all sides, then remove chicken to a paper-towel-lined plate to drain.
3. Add a bit more oil to the same skillet and heat. When hot, add the peas, chestnuts, and carrots. Cook for 1–2 minutes. Remove the vegetables from the skillet and place them on top of the chicken.
4. Add a bit more oil to the skillet, if needed, and quickly sauté the peanuts and chili peppers. They only need to cook for a short time. Add them to the plate with the chicken and vegetables when they are done.
5. Add the green onions and garlic to the skillet and cook just until fragrant, about 1 minute. Return everything else to the skillet, then add the sauce and stir to make sure everything is coated. Cook until the sauce starts to thicken. Serve with rice.

NUTRITION: 684 calories 9g fats 34g protein

252. Pei Wei's Chicken lo mein

PREPARATION TIME: 15'

SERVINGS: 4

COOKING TIME: 30'

INGREDIENTS

- 1½ pounds boneless, skinless chicken breast, sliced very thinly

Marinade
- 1 tablespoon soy sauce
- 1½ teaspoons cornstarch
- 2 tablespoons oyster sauce
- 2 teaspoons soy sauce
- ¼ cup beef broth
- 1 tablespoon sugar

Other ingredients
- 6 ounces linguine, cooked
- 1 teaspoon sesame oil
- ¼ cup oil
- 1 clove garlic, chopped
- 1 carrot, chopped into ½-inch pieces
- ½ cup cabbage, chopped
- 1 cup mushrooms, sliced
- 1 cup bean sprouts
- 3 green onions, both green and white parts, sliced

DIRECTIONS

1. Combine all the ingredients for the marinade in a resealable bag. Add the chicken pieces and refrigerate for at least 20 minutes. In a small mixing bowl, stir together the oyster sauce, soy sauce, beef broth, and sugar.
2. Toss the cooked noodles with the sesame oil. Add the ¼ cup of oil to a large skillet or wok and heat over medium-high heat. Add the chicken, reserve the marinade, and cook for about 5 minutes or until cooked through. Remove from the skillet and set aside.
3. Add another tablespoon of oil to the skillet if you need to. When the oil is hot, add the garlic and sauté until fragrant, then add the carrots. Cook for 1 minute. Add the cabbage and mushrooms and cook for about 2 more minutes. Stir the cooked noodles into the pan and cook for another 2 minutes.
4. Add the marinade from the resealable bag along with the cooked chicken. Allow to cook for another 3–5 minutes, then serve with rice.

NUTRITION: 691 calories 10g fats 34g protein

253. TusCan garlIC CHICken

| PREPARATION TIME: | 15′ | SERVINGS: | 4 |

COOKING TIME: 30′

INGREDIENTS

Chicken
- 1 cup all-purpose flour
- ½ cup panko bread crumbs
- 1 tablespoon garlic powder
- 2 teaspoons Italian seasoning
- 1 teaspoon sea salt
- ½ teaspoon ground black pepper
- ½ teaspoon dried basil
- ½ teaspoon dried oregano
- 3 boneless skinless chicken breasts (or 6 cutlets)
- 2 tablespoons olive oil

Pasta
- 1-pound fettuccine

Sauce
- 2 tablespoons unsalted butter
- 4 cloves garlic, minced
- 1 red bell pepper, cut into 2-inch-long thin strips
- ½ teaspoon sea salt
- ¼ teaspoon paprika
- 1/2 teaspoon ground black pepper
- 2 tablespoons all-purpose flour
- 1 cup low-sodium chicken broth
- 1 cup milk
- ½ cup half and half
- 2 cups fresh spinach, roughly chopped
- 1 cup freshly grated parmesan cheese

DIRECTIONS

1. Preheat oven to 400°F. Line a baking sheet with parchment paper. In a bowl, mix together flour, breadcrumbs, garlic powder, Italian seasoning, salt, pepper, basil, and oregano. Coat the chicken by tossing it in the mixture.
2. Heat the olive oil in a large skillet over medium heat. Carefully place the chicken in the oil. Sear for 2–3 minutes or until golden brown, making sure not to lose any of the coating. Place chicken onto a baking sheet and then into the oven for 15–20 minutes. While the chicken is baking, cook the fettuccine according to package instructions.
3. To make the sauce, melt the butter in a large skillet over medium-low heat. Add the bell pepper and cook for 3–4 minutes. Season with salt, pepper, and paprika, then add the garlic and sauté for about 1 minute.
4. Whisk in the flour, then slowly add the chicken broth, milk, and half and half. Bring the heat to medium and simmer. Add the spinach and cook until wilted. Let the sauce thicken and then mix in the parmesan cheese.
5. Remove from heat and stir until smooth. Place it in the fettuccine and toss together. Slice the chicken and place it in the fettuccine. Serve with extra parmesan cheese if desired.

NUTRITION: 487 calories 34g protein 7.3g carbs

254. Stuffed Chicken Marsala

Preparation Time: 25'

Servings: 4

Cooking Time: 45'

Ingredients

Chicken
- 4 boneless skinless chicken breasts
- ¾ cup all-purpose flour
- Salt and pepper to taste
- ½ cup olive oil
- Parsley, chopped, for garnish

Stuffing
- ½ cup smoked provolone or gouda cheese, shredded
- ½ pound mozzarella cheese, shredded
- ¼ cup parmesan cheese, grated
- ½ cup breadcrumbs
- 1 teaspoon fresh garlic, minced
- 1 teaspoon red pepper flakes
- 2 tablespoons sun-dried tomatoes, patted dry and roughly chopped
- 3 green onions, thinly sliced
- ¾ cup sour cream

Sauce
- 1 yellow onion, sliced into strings
- 1-quart dry marsala wine
- 1 cup heavy cream
- ¾ pound button mushrooms, thinly sliced

Directions

1. Combine all stuffing ingredients in a bowl. Set aside and preheat oven to 350°F. Make two slices at the thickest part of each chicken breast in order to butterfly it. Turn the chicken over and lay it flat. Cover with wax paper and pound to about ¼–½ inches in thickness.
2. Stuff each chicken breast, but do not overfill. Coat the chicken in salt, pepper, and flour. Cook the chicken in olive oil in a large skillet over medium-high heat. Once cooked, transfer to a baking dish and bake for 15–20 minutes or until the inside is cooked through.
3. Using the same large skillet, cook the onions in the chicken drippings for about 2 minutes. Add the mushrooms and continue to sauté for about 5 more minutes. Deglaze by adding wine to the skillet. Heat the wine until lightly bubbling to reduce it. Continue to cook until the sauce turns brown.
4. Heat the heavy cream in the microwave for 20 seconds. Pour it into the pan and heat until it bubbles slightly. Reduce heat to low and simmer for 5 minutes. Remove from heat when the sauce is a rich brown color.
5. Serve the sauce over the stuffed chicken and complement the meal with mashed potatoes, if desired. Sprinkle with chopped parsley.

Nutrition: 491 calories 4.6g carbs 31g protein

255. Chicken Piccata

SERVINGS: 4-6

COOKING TIME: 15'

INGREDIENTS

- 4 chicken breasts (about 2 pounds), pounded to a ¼-inch thickness
- 1 small onion
- 10 sun-dried tomatoes, cut into strips
- 1 tablespoon garlic, minced
- 1½ cups chicken broth
- Juice of ½ lemon (about 2 tablespoons)
- ¼ cup capers, rinsed
- 3 tablespoons butter
- 1/3 cup heavy cream
- Salt and pepper to taste
- ¼ cup olive oil (for frying)

DIRECTIONS

1. Season chicken breasts with salt and pepper. Cook them in a skillet with olive oil over medium-high heat until golden brown and cooked thoroughly (approximately 5–8 minutes on each side). Remove and set aside.
2. In the same skillet, sauté the onions, sun-dried tomatoes, and garlic until lightly browned. Whisk in the chicken broth, lemon juice, and capers. Reduce heat to medium-low and simmer for 10–15 minutes to reduce the sauce.
3. Remove from heat when the sauce has thickened. Add the butter and continue to whisk until melted, then add the cream. Heat for about 30 seconds, then remove. Coat chicken breast in the sauce. Serve.

NUTRITION: 501 calories 7.1g carbs 33g protein

256. Chicken alfredo

PREPARATION TIME: 10′

SERVINGS: 4

COOKING TIME: 10′

INGREDIENTS

- ¾ pound fettuccine pasta
- 2 tablespoons olive oil
- ½ cup + 2 tablespoons butter (divided)
- 2 boneless skinless chicken breasts
- 1½ teaspoons salt (divided)
- 1½ teaspoons fresh ground pepper (divided)
- 3 cloves garlic, very finely chopped
- 1½ tablespoons flour
- 2 cups heavy cream
- ¾ cup grated parmesan, plus more for topping if desired
- 2 tablespoons parsley, chopped (optional, for garnish)

DIRECTIONS

1. Cook pasta according to package instructions. Drain and set aside. Heat oil in a cast iron grill pan over high heat. Add 2 tablespoons of butter to the pan and then add the chicken breasts. Season the chicken breasts with 1 teaspoon of salt and pepper.
2. Cook the first side until golden brown. Flip, cover the pan, and reduce the heat to medium. Cook until the chicken is cooked thoroughly. Set aside and cover in foil. Once cooled, cut into strips.
3. Melt the remaining butter over medium heat in a large, deep skillet. Add garlic and cook for about 30 seconds. Reduce to medium-low heat and season with remaining salt and pepper. Add flour, whisking constantly to break up any chunks. Slowly pour the cream into the mixture. Cook until sauce is slightly thickened.
4. Stir in the parmesan until smooth. Remove from heat and set aside. Serve by tossing the pasta with the alfredo sauce. Place chicken on top and garnish with fresh parsley and parmesan, if desired.

NUTRITION: 481 calories 7.6g carbs 31g protein

257. Parmesan Crusted Chicken

Preparation Time: 15'	Servings: 4

Cooking Time: 40'

Ingredients

Breading
- 1 cup plain breadcrumbs
- 2 tablespoons flour
- ¼ cup grated parmesan cheese

For dipping
- 1 cup milk

Chicken
- 2 chicken breasts
- Vegetable oil for frying
- 2 cups cooked linguini pasta
- 2 tablespoons butter
- 3 tablespoons olive oil
- 2 teaspoons crushed garlic
- ½ cup white wine
- ¼ cup water
- 2 tablespoons flour
- ¾ cup half-and-half
- ¼ cup sour cream
- ½ teaspoon salt
- 1 teaspoon fresh flat leave parsley, finely diced¾ cup mild Asiago cheese, finely grated

Garnish
- 1 Roma tomato, diced
- Grated parmesan cheese
- Fresh flat-leaf parsley, finely chopped

Directions

1. Pound the chicken until it flattens to ½ inch thick. Mix the breading ingredients in one shallow bowl and place the milk in another. Heat some oil over medium to medium-to-low heat.
2. Dip the chicken in the breading, then the milk, then the breading again. Immediately place into the heated oil. Cook the chicken in the oil until golden brown, about 3-4 minutes per side. Remove the chicken and set aside on a plate lined with paper towels.
3. Create a roux by adding flour to heated olive oil and butter over medium heat. When the roux is done, add the garlic, water, and salt to the pan and stir. Add the wine and continue stirring and cooking.
4. Add the half-and-half and sour cream and stir some more. Add the cheese and let it melt. Finally, add in the parsley and remove from heat. Add pasta and stir to coat.
5. Divide the hot pasta between serving plates. Top each dish with the chicken, diced tomatoes, and parmesan cheese before serving.

Nutrition: 451 Calories 44g total fat 4.1g carbs 9.7g Protein

258. Chicken Giardino

Preparation Time: 10'

Servings: 4

Cooking Time: 20

Ingredients

Sauce
- 1 tablespoon butter
- ¼ teaspoon dried thyme
- ½ teaspoon fresh rosemary, finely chopped
- 1 teaspoon garlic pepper seasoning
- 1 tablespoon cornstarch
- ¼ cup chicken broth
- ¼ cup water
- ¼ cup white wine
- 1 tablespoon milk
- 1 teaspoon lemon juice
- Salt and pepper

Chicken
- 2 pounds boneless skinless chicken breasts
- ¼ cup extra virgin olive oil
- 2 small rosemary sprigs
- 1 clove garlic, finely minced
- Juice of ½ lemon
- Vegetables
- ¼ cup extra-virgin olive oil
- ½ bunch fresh asparagus (remove the bottom inch of stem, cut the remainder into 1-inch pieces)
- 1 zucchini, julienned
- 1 summer squash, julienned
- 2 roma tomatoes, cut into ½-inch pieces
- ½ red bell pepper, julienned
- 1 cup broccoli florets, blanched
- ½ cup frozen peas
- 1 cup spinach, cut into ½-inch pieces
- ½ cup carrot, julienned
- 1-pound farfalle pasta (bow ties)

Directions

1. In a saucepan, melt the butter over medium heat. Add the thyme, garlic, pepper, and rosemary. Whisk together and cook for 1 minute. In a mixing bowl, mix together the chicken broth, water, wine, milk, and lemon juice. Slowly pour in the cornstarch and whisk constantly until it has dissolved.
2. Pour the mixture into the saucepan. Whisk well and then bring to a boil. Season with salt and pepper to taste, then remove from heat.
3. Prepare the chicken by cutting into strips width-wise. In a mixing bowl, combine the olive oil, rosemary, garlic, and lemon juice. Marinate the chicken for at least 30 minutes.
4. Heat ¼ cup of olive oil over medium-high heat in a saucepan. Cook the chicken strips until the internal temperature is 165°F. Add the vegetables to the saucepan and sauté until cooked. Prepare the pasta according to package instructions. Drain. Add the pasta and pasta sauce to the sauté pan.
5. Toss to thoroughly coat pasta and chicken in sauce. Serve.

Nutrition: 481 calories 6.5g carbs 30g protein

259. Chicken and Sausage Mixed Grill

PREPARATION TIME: 10'

SERVINGS: 4

COOKING TIME: 35'

Ingredients

Marinade
- 2 teaspoons red pepper oil
- 2 tablespoons fresh rosemary, chopped
- ½ cup fresh lemon juice
- 1 teaspoon salt
- 3 bay leaves, broken into pieces
- 2 large garlic cloves, pressed
- ¼ cup extra-virgin olive oil
- Freshly shredded parmesan cheese, for serving

Skewers
- 2 pounds skinless, boneless chicken breasts
- 1-pound Italian sausage links, mild
- 1-pint cherry tomatoes
- 1 bag bamboo skewers, soaked in water for at least 30 minutes
- 3 lemons, halved
- 2 rosemary sprigs

Directions

1. To make the marinade, mix pepper oil, rosemary, lemon juice, salt, bay leaves, and pressed garlic in a baking dish. Cut the chicken breasts in half lengthwise. Pierce each chicken piece with a skewer and thread through. Add a cherry tomato at the end of the skewer. Coat each skewer with the marinade. Marinate for at least 3 hours in the refrigerator.
2. Preheat oven to 350°F. Bake sausage for 20 minutes. Let cool, then cut into 3 pieces. Grill chicken until completely cooked. Place sausages on skewers. Grill. Serve by garnishing with rosemary, lemon, and cherry tomatoes on a platter. Sprinkle with freshly shredded parmesan, if desired.

NUTRITION: 469 calories 7g carbs 32g protein

260. Chicken Gnocchi Veronese

Preparation Time: 20'	Servings: 4

Cooking Time: 25'

Ingredients

- ¼ cup extra-virgin olive oil
- 1 small vidalia onion, chopped
- 1 red bell pepper, julienned
- ½ zucchini, julienned
- Salt to taste
- 4 chicken breasts, sliced it in ½-inch strips
- 2 small sprigs rosemary
- 1 glove garlic, minced
- Juice of ½ lemon

Veronese Sauce
- 1 cup parmesan cheese, grated
- ½ cup ricotta cheese
- 14 ounces heavy cream
- **Gnocchi**

2 quarts water
- 11/3 cups all-purpose flour
- 2 eggs
- 2 pounds russet potatoes
- 2 teaspoons salt
- or
- 1-pound gnocchi (potato dumplings), cooked according to package directions

Directions

1. If using pre-made gnocchi, cook according to package instructions. If not, begin by washing potatoes and placing them in water. Cook potatoes until soft. Remove water and cool into the refrigerator. Once cooled, peel and push potatoes through a fine grater or rice grater.
2. In a mixing bowl, mix the potatoes and eggs. Slowly add flour until the dough does not stick to your hands. Divide dough into four. Roll each section into a long rope. Cut into ½-inch pieces, then create impressions by gently pushing a fork into the gnocchi.
3. Pour water into a pot and bring to a boil. Add gnocchi and cook until they begin to float. In a mixing bowl, mix the garlic, lemon juice, rosemary, and chicken slices. Marinate for 2 hours. In another bowl, mix the parmesan cheese, ricotta cheese, and heavy cream.
4. Heat the olive oil in a sauté pan over medium-high heat. Add the onion, bell peppers, and zucchini. Sauté until the onion is translucent. Add the chicken to the sauté pan and cook until brown. Reduce heat and add the sauce. Simmer. Add the gnocchi and toss to coat in the sauce. Serve with additional parmesan cheese, if desired.

Nutrition: 521 calories 5.9g carbs 31g protein

261. Chicken Parmigiana

PREPARATION TIME: 20'		SERVINGS: 4
	COOKING TIME: 25'	

INGREDIENTS

- 4 boneless, skinless chicken breasts (½ pound each)
- 2 cups flour
- ½ quart milk
- 4 eggs
- 3 cups Italian breadcrumbs
- ½ cup marinara sauce
- 1 cup mozzarella cheese
- ½ cup vegetable oil
- Parsley (to garnish)
- Cooked pasta with marinara sauce to serve

DIRECTIONS

1. Put flour in a bowl. In another bowl, mix milk and eggs together. In a third bowl, place breadcrumbs. Place chicken breasts between plastic wrap and pound to about ¼ inch in thickness. Season with salt and pepper.
2. Place chicken in flour, coating all sides. Dip into egg wash, then bread crumbs, coating each side evenly. Preheat oven to broil. In a cast iron pan, heat oil over medium heat. Fry each side of the chicken for 5 minutes or until golden brown. Drain on paper towels.
3. Place chicken on a baking dish. Top with marinara sauce and mozzarella cheese. Place in oven until cheese is melted. Garnish with parsley. Serve with a side of marinara pasta, if desired.

NUTRITION: 489 calories 6.7g carbs 34g protein

262. Chicken and Shrimp Carbonara

Preparation Time:	35'	Servings:	8

Cooking Time:	40'

Ingredients

Shrimp Marinade
- ¼ cup extra virgin olive oil
- ½ cup water
- 2 teaspoons Italian seasoning
- 1 tablespoon minced garlic

Chicken
- 4 boneless and skinless chicken breasts cubed
- 1 egg mixed with 1 tablespoon cold water
- ½ cup panko bread crumbs
- ½ cup all-purpose flour
- ½ teaspoon salt
- ½ teaspoon black pepper
- 2 tablespoons olive oil

Carbonara sauce
- ½ cup butter (1 stick)
- 3 tablespoons all-purpose flour
- ½ cup parmesan cheese, grated
- 2 cups heavy cream
- 2 cups milk
- 8 Canadian bacon slices, diced finely
- ¾ cup roasted red peppers, diced

Pasta
- 1 teaspoon salt
- 14 ounces spaghetti or bucatini pasta (1 package)
- Water to cook the pasta
- Shrimp
- ½ pound fresh medium shrimp, deveined and peeled
- 1-2 tablespoons olive oil for cooking

Directions

1. Mix all the marinade ingredients together in a re-sealable container or bag and add the shrimp. Refrigerate for at least 30 minutes.
2. To make the chicken, mix the flour, salt, pepper, and panko bread crumbs into a shallow dish. Whisk the egg with 1 tablespoon of cold water in a second shallow dish. Dip the chicken into the breadcrumb mix and after in the egg wash, and again in the breadcrumb mix. Place on a plate and let rest until all the chicken is prepared.
3. Warm the olive oil over medium heat in a deep, large skillet. Working in batches, add the chicken. Cook for 4 to 6 minutes per side or until the chicken is cooked through. Place the cooked chicken tenders on a plate lined with paper towels to absorb excess oil.
4. To make the pasta, add water to a large pot and bring to a boil. Add salt and cook the pasta according to package instructions about 10-15 minutes before the sauce is ready.
5. To make the shrimp, while the pasta is cooking, add olive oil to a skillet. Remove the shrimp from the marinade and shake off the excess marinade. Cook the shrimp until they turn pink, about 2-3 minutes.
6. To make the Carbonara sauce, in a large deep skillet, sauté the Canadian bacon with a bit of butter for 3-4 minutes over medium heat or until the bacon starts to caramelize. Add the garlic and sauté for 1 more minute. Remove bacon and garlic and set aside.
7. In the same skillet, let the butter melt and mix-in the flour. Gradually add the cream and milk and whisk until the sauce thickens. Add the cheese.
8. Reduce the heat to a simmer and keep the mixture simmering while you prepare the rest of the ingredients.
9. When you are ready to serve, add the drained pasta, bacon bits, roasted red peppers to the sauce. Stir to coat. Add pasta evenly to each serving plate. Top with some chicken and shrimp. Garnish with fresh parsley. Serve with fresh shredded Romano or Parmesan cheese.

Nutrition: 488 calories 6.7g carbs 33g proteins

263. Chicken Marsala

PREPARATION TIME:	10'		SERVINGS:	4-6

COOKING TIME: 40'

INGREDIENTS

- 2 tablespoons olive oil
- 2 tablespoons butter
- 4 boneless skinless chicken breasts
- 1 ½ cups sliced mushrooms
- 1 small clove garlic, thinly sliced
- Flour for dredging
- Sea salt and freshly ground black pepper
- 1 ½ cups chicken stock
- 1 ½ cups Marsala wine
- 1 tablespoon lemon juice
- 1 teaspoon Dijon mustard

DIRECTIONS

Chicken scaloppini
1. Pound out the chicken with a mallet or rolling pin to about ½ inch thick. In a large skillet, heat the olive oil and 1 tablespoon of the butter over medium-high heat. When the oil is hot, dredge the chicken in flour. Season with salt and pepper on both sides. Dredge only as many as will fit in the skillet. Don't overcrowd the pan.
2. Cook chicken in batches, about 1 to 2 minutes on each side or until cooked through. Remove from skillet, and place on an oven-proof platter. Keep warm in the oven, while the remaining chicken is cooking.

Marsala sauce
3. In the same skillet, add 1 tablespoon of olive oil. On medium-high heat, sauté mushrooms and garlic until softened. Remove the mushrooms from the pan and set aside.
4. Add the chicken stock and loosen any remaining bits in the pan. On high heat, let reduce by half, about 6-8 minutes. Add Marsala wine and lemon juice and in the same manner reduce by half, about 6–8 minutes. Add the mushroom back in the saucepan, and stir in the Dijon mustard. Warm for 1 minute on medium-low heat. Remove from heat, stir in the remaining butter to make the sauce silkier.
5. To serve, pour the sauce over chicken, and serve immediately.

NUTRITION: 487 calories 7.1g carbs 34g protein

264. Chicken Scampi

PREPARATION TIME: 10'

SERVINGS: 4

COOKING TIME: 20'

INGREDIENTS

- Pasta
- ½ pound uncooked angel hair pasta
- ½ teaspoon canola or olive oil
- ¼ teaspoon salt
- Chicken
- 1-pound chicken tenderloins
- ½ cup all-purpose flour
- ¼ teaspoon salt
- 1/8 teaspoon ground pepper
- ¼ teaspoon Italian seasoning
- 1/3 cup whole milk
- 2 tablespoons oil
- Vegetables and sauce
- 2 tablespoons canola or olive oil
- ½ green pepper, sliced into thin strips
- ½ red pepper, sliced into thin strips
- ½ yellow pepper, sliced into thin strips
- ½ red onion, sliced thin
- 5 tablespoons unsalted butter
- 6 cloves garlic, minced
- ¾ cup wine
- 11/3 cups chicken broth
- 2/3 cup half and half
- ¼ teaspoon ground pepper
- 1 teaspoon salt
- ¼ teaspoon Italian seasoning

DIRECTIONS

1. Cook the angel hair pasta according to package instructions. Drain and set aside.
2. To make the chicken, mix the flour, salt, pepper, and Italian seasoning in a bowl. Place the milk in a separate bowl. Lightly pound the chicken tenders, then coat them in flour. Dip into milk and dredge in flour once more.
3. In a large skillet, heat the oil over high heat. Cook each side of the chicken for about 2 minutes. Remove from heat and keep warm.
4. To make the vegetables and sauce, heat the oil in the skillet. Add the peppers and red onion. Sauté for 2 minutes over medium-high heat, stirring occasionally.
5. Add the butter and minced garlic to the vegetables. Sauté for 1 more minute. Add the wine and broth. Reduce heat to medium-low. Let cook for 5 minutes. Add half and half, salt, pepper, and Italian seasoning. Let cook for 1 minute. Add the chicken and pasta. Toss together to blend well. Simmer to warm, then serve.

NUTRITION: 489 calories 6.8g carbs 31g protein

265. Chicken Margherita

PREPARATION TIME: 35'

SERVINGS: 6

COOKING TIME: 25'

Ingredients

- **Chicken**
- 6 (4-ounce) boneless chicken breasts
- 2 cups water
- ¼ cup salt
- ¼ cup sugar
- **Pesto**
- 2 cups fresh basil
- 1 clove garlic
- 2 tablespoons pecorino romano cheese, grated
- 3–4 tablespoons extra-virgin olive oil
- 1 tablespoon pine nuts (optional)
- Lemon garlic sauce
- 2 tablespoons butter
- 2 cloves garlic, minced
- 1 tablespoon all-purpose flour
- 1 tablespoon lemon juice
- ½ cup low-sodium chicken broth
- Chicken Margherita assembly
- 6 (4-ounce) grilled boneless chicken breasts
- ½ cup prepared pesto
- 1 cup grape tomatoes, halved
- 6 ounces fresh mozzarella, sliced
- ½ cup prepared lemon garlic sauce
- Freshly shredded parmesan cheese, for garnish

Directions

1. In a Ziploc bag, combine the water, salt, and sugar. Mix well. Add the chicken and refrigerate for at least 2 hours.
2. Grill chicken until cooked thoroughly. Set aside. Blend all pesto ingredients in a food processor to achieve a smooth consistency. Add 1 tablespoon of oil, if needed. Refrigerate in a sealed container until ready to use.
3. To make the lemon garlic sauce, melt the butter in a small saucepan. Add garlic and sauté for 1 minute. Slowly add some flour and stir well. Add fresh lemon juice and chicken broth. Stir for about 3–5 minutes until the sauce begins to thicken. Keep refrigerated.
4. To assemble the Chicken Margherita, preheat oven to 425°F. Move the grilled chicken to a baking dish and top with mozzarella cheese, pesto, and halved grape tomatoes.
5. Pour the lemon garlic sauce on top. Bake until cheese melts, about 10–15 minutes. To serve, sprinkle with freshly grated parmesan cheese, if desired.

NUTRITION: 469 calories 6.3g carbs 31g protein

266. Chicken Carbonara

<table>
<tr><td>Preparation Time:</td><td>20'</td><td>Servings:</td><td>4</td></tr>
</table>

Cooking Time: 30'

Ingredients

Marinated chicken or shrimp
- 1 cup extra-virgin olive oil
- 1 cup hot water
- 1 tablespoon Italian seasoning
- 1 tablespoon chopped garlic
- 3 pounds chicken strips or large shrimp, peeled and deveined

Sauce
- 1 cup butter
- 1½ teaspoons garlic, chopped
- 3 tablespoons bacon bits
- 3 tablespoons all-purpose flour
- 1 cup parmesan cheese, grated
- 1-quart heavy cream
- 1-quart milk
- ¼ cup bacon base
- ½ teaspoon black pepper
- 1¾ pounds long pasta (spaghetti, linguine, etc.) cooked according to package Directions
- ¼ teaspoon salt

Topping
- 3 tablespoons romano cheese, grated
- 3 tablespoons parmesan cheese, grated
- 1¾ cups mozzarella cheese, shredded
- ½ cup panko breadcrumbs
- 1½ teaspoons garlic, chopped
- 1½ tablespoons butter, melted
- 2 tablespoons parsley, chopped
- Marinated chicken strips (or shrimp) as above
- 1½ cups roasted red peppers, cut into small strips
- ¼ cup bacon bits

NUTRITION: 510 calories 6.3g carbs 30g protein

Directions

1. Preheat oven to 350°F. In a mixing bowl, whisk together olive oil with hot water, Italian seasoning, and chopped garlic. Let chicken/shrimp marinate for at least 30 minutes in the refrigerator.
2. To make the sauce, melt the butter over medium heat in a large saucepan. Sauté the garlic and bacon bits for 5 minutes, stirring frequently.
3. Add the flour, parmesan cheese, heavy cream, milk, bacon base, pepper, and salt. Whisk well. Bring to a boil, then reduce heat and allow to simmer.
4. To make the topping, mix the romano cheese, parmesan, mozzarella cheese, panko, chopped garlic, melted butter, and chopped parsley in a mixing bowl. Blend well. Set aside.
5. Heat a large skillet to cook the chicken and/or shrimp. Add the red peppers and bacon bits. Cook for 3 minutes or until meat is cooked through. Add sauce and stir.
6. Add pasta. Mix well to coat the pasta evenly. Top with extra cheese, if desired. Serve.

267. Steak Gorgonzola Alfredo

PREPARATION TIME:	10'	SERVINGS:	6

COOKING TIME: 20'

INGREDIENTS

- 18 ounces rib eye or sirloin steak, cut into 2–3-inch medallions
- 1-pound fettuccine
- 4 cups baby spinach
- ½ cup sun-dried tomatoes, chopped
- ½ cup gorgonzola cheese, crumbled
- Balsamic glaze (or aged balsamic), as desired
- Alfredo sauce
- 3 tablespoons butter
- 3 tablespoons all-purpose flour
- 2 cups heavy cream
- ½ cup pecorino romano cheese, grated

DIRECTIONS

1. First, make the alfredo sauce. In a small saucepan, melt the butter over medium heat. Slowly add the flour, whisking frequently. Add the heavy cream and grated cheese. Continue to whisk until thickened.
2. Cook fettuccine according to package Directions. Drain and set aside. Grill the steak to preference in a skillet. Set aside. Place the alfredo sauce in a pot and heat on low. Add the pasta and spinach. Continue to stir until the spinach wilts. Remove from heat.
3. Place the sun-dried tomatoes, gorgonzola cheese, and steak on top of the pasta. Drizzle with balsamic glaze. Serve.

NUTRITION: 497 calories 7.9g carbs 32g protein

268. Cracker barrel's CHICken frIed CHICken

| PREPARATION TIME: | 15' | | SERVINGS: | 4 |

| COOKING TIME: | 30' |

INGREDIENTS

Chicken
- ½ cup all-purpose flour
- 1 teaspoon poultry seasoning
- ½ teaspoon salt
- ½ teaspoon pepper
- 1 egg, slightly beaten
- 1 tablespoon water
- 4 boneless skinless chicken breasts, pounded to a ½-inch thickness
- 1 cup vegetable oil

Gravy
- 2 tablespoons all-purpose flour
- ¼ teaspoon salt
- ¼ teaspoon pepper
- 1¼ cups milk

DIRECTIONS

1. Preheat the oven to 200°F. In a shallow dish, combine the flour, poultry seasoning, salt, and pepper. In another shallow dish, mix the beaten egg and water.
2. First, dip both sides of the chicken breasts in the flour mixture, then dip them in the egg mixture, and then back into the flour mixture.
3. Heat the vegetable oil over medium-high heat in a large deep skillet. A cast iron is a good choice if you have one. Add the chicken and cook for about 15 minutes, or until fully cooked, turning over about halfway through.
4. Transfer the chicken to a cookie sheet and place in the oven to maintain temperature. Remove all but 2 tablespoons of oil from the skillet you cooked the chicken in.
5. Prepare the gravy by whisking the dry gravy ingredients together in a bowl. Then whisk them into the oil in the skillet, stirring thoroughly to remove lumps. When the flour begins to brown, slowly whisk in the milk. Continue cooking and whisking for about 2 minutes or until the mixture thickens.
6. Top chicken with some of the gravy.

NUTRITION: 340 calories 28g carbs 20g protein

269. broCColl CHeddar CHICken

PREPARATION TIME: 10'

SERVINGS: 4

COOKING TIME: 45'

INGREDIENTS

- 4 skinless chicken breasts
- 1 cup milk
- 1 cup Ritz-style crackers, crushed
- 1 (10.5-ounce) can condensed cheddar cheese soup
- ½ pound frozen broccoli
- 6 ounces cheddar cheese, shredded
- ½ teaspoon salt
- ½ teaspoon pepper

DIRECTIONS

1. Preheat the oven to 350°F. Whisk the milk and cheddar cheese soup together in a mixing bowl. Prepare a baking dish by greasing the sides, then lay the chicken in the bottom and season with the salt and pepper. Pour the soup mixture over the chicken, then top with the crackers, broccoli, and shredded cheese. Bake for about 45 minutes or until bubbly.

NUTRITION: 402 calories 18g carbs 22g protein

270. Grilled Chicken Tenderloin

PREPARATION TIME:	10' and 1 H
SERVINGS:	5
COOKING TIME:	30'

INGREDIENTS

- 4–5 boneless and skinless chicken breasts, cut into strips, or 12 chicken tenderloins, tendons removed
- 1 cup Italian dressing
- 2 teaspoons lime juice
- 4 teaspoons honey

DIRECTIONS

1. Combine the dressing, lime juice, and honey in a plastic bag. Seal and shake to combine. Place the chicken in the bag. Seal and shake again, then transfer to the refrigerator for at least 1 hour. The longer it marinates, the more the flavors will infuse into the chicken.
2. When ready to prepare, transfer the chicken and the marinade to a large nonstick skillet. Bring to a boil, then reduce the heat and allow to simmer until the liquid has cooked down to a glaze.

NUTRITION: 318 calories 17g carbs 24g protein

271. Chicken Casserole

PREPARATION TIME: 10'

SERVINGS: 4

COOKING TIME: 1 H 10'

INGREDIENTS

Crust
- 1 cup yellow cornmeal
- 1/3 cup all-purpose flour
- 1½ teaspoons baking powder
- 1 tablespoon sugar
- ½ teaspoon salt
- ½ teaspoon baking soda
- 2 tablespoons vegetable oil
- ¾ cup buttermilk
- 1 egg

Filling
- 2½ cups cooked chicken breast, cut into bite-sized pieces
- ¼ cup chopped yellow onion
- ½ cup sliced celery
- 1 teaspoon salt
- ¼ teaspoon ground pepper
- 1 (10.5-ounce) can condensed cream of chicken soup
- 1¾ cups chicken broth
- 2 tablespoons butter
- ½ cup melted butter

DIRECTIONS

1. Preheat the oven to 375°F. To make the crust, in a large bowl, combine all the crust ingredients until smooth. Dump this mixture into a buttered or greased 8×8-inch baking dish. Bake for about 20 minutes, then remove from oven and allow to cool. Reduce oven temperature to 350°F.
2. Crumble the cooled cornbread mixture. Add to a large mixing bowl along with ½ cup of melted butter. Set aside. Make the chicken filling by adding the butter to a large saucepan over medium heat. Let it melt, then add the celery and onions and cook until soft.
3. Add the chicken broth, cream of chicken soup, salt, and pepper. Stir until everything is well combined. Add the cooked chicken breast pieces and stir again. Cook for 5 minutes at a low simmer. Transfer the filling mixture into 4 individual greased baking dishes or a greased casserole dish. Top with the cornbread mixture and transfer to the oven.
4. Bake for 35–40 minutes for a large casserole dish or 25–30 minutes for individual dishes.

NUTRITION: 389 calories 15g carbs 30g protein

272. Sunday CHICken

PREPARATION TIME:	10'		SERVINGS:	4

COOKING TIME:	10'

INGREDIENTS

- Oil for frying
- 4 boneless, skinless chicken breasts
- 1 cup all-purpose flour
- 1 cup bread crumbs
- 2 teaspoons salt
- 2 teaspoons black pepper
- 1 cup buttermilk
- ½ cup water

DIRECTIONS

1. Add 3–4 inches of oil to a large pot or a deep fryer and preheat to 350°F. Mix the flour, breadcrumbs, salt, and pepper in a shallow dish. To a separate shallow dish, add the buttermilk and water; stir.
2. Pound the chicken breasts to a consistent size. Dry them with a paper towel, then sprinkle with salt and pepper. Dip the seasoned breasts in the flour mixture, then the buttermilk mixture, then back into the flour.
3. Add the breaded chicken to the hot oil and fry for about 8 minutes. Turn the chicken as necessary so that it cooks evenly on both sides. Remove the chicken to either a wire rack or a plate lined with paper towels to drain. Serve with mashed potatoes or whatever sides you love.

NUTRITION: 350 calories 18g carbs 25g protein

273. Creamy Chicken and Rice

PREPARATION TIME: 10'

SERVINGS: 4

COOKING TIME: 45'

INGREDIENTS

- Salt and pepper to taste
- 2 cups cooked rice
- 1 diced onion
- 1 can cream of mushroom soup
- 1 packet chicken gravy
- 1½ pounds chicken breasts, cut into strips

DIRECTIONS

1. Preheat the oven to 350°F. Cook the rice. When it is just about finished, toss in the diced onion so that it cooks too. Prepare a baking dish by greasing or spraying with nonstick cooking spray.
2. Dump the rice into the prepared baking dish. Layer the chicken strips on top. Spread the undiluted cream of mushroom soup over the chicken.
3. In a small bowl, whisk together the chicken gravy with 1 cup of water, making sure to get all the lumps out. Pour this over the top of the casserole.
4. Cover with foil and transfer to the oven. Bake for 45 minutes or until the chicken is completely cooked.

NUTRITION: 377 calories 19g carbs 29g protein

274. CampfIre CHICken

PREPARATION TIME: 10'

SERVINGS: 4

COOKING TIME: 45'

INGREDIENTS

- 1 tablespoon paprika
- 2 teaspoons onion powder
- 2 teaspoons salt
- 1 teaspoon garlic powder
- 1 teaspoon dried rosemary
- 1 teaspoon black pepper
- 1 teaspoon dried oregano
- 1 whole chicken, quartered
- 2 carrots, cut into thirds
- 3 red skin potatoes, halved
- 1 ear of corn, quartered
- 1 tablespoon olive oil
- 1 tablespoon butter
- 5 sprigs fresh thyme

DIRECTIONS

1. Preheat the oven to 400°F. In a small bowl, combine the paprika, onion powder, salt, garlic powder, rosemary, pepper, and oregano. Add the chicken quarters and 1 tablespoon of the spice mix to a large plastic freezer bag. Seal and refrigerate for at least 1 hour.
2. Add the corn, carrots, and potatoes to a large bowl. Drizzle with the olive oil and remaining spice mix. Stir or toss to coat.
3. Preheat a large skillet over high heat. Add some oil, and when it is hot, add the chicken pieces and cook until golden brown. Lay out 4 pieces of aluminum foil and add some carrots, potatoes, corn, and a chicken quarter to each. Top with some butter and thyme.
4. Fold the foil in and make pouches by sealing the edges tightly. Bake for 45 minutes.

NUTRITION: 311 calories 11g carbs 21g protein

275. Chicken and dumPlIngs

PREPARATION TIME: 30'

SERVINGS: 4

COOKING TIME: 20'

INGREDIENTS

- 2 cups flour
- ½ teaspoon baking powder
- 1 pinch salt
- 2 tablespoons butter
- 1 scant cup buttermilk
- 2 quarts chicken broth
- 3 cups cooked chicken

DIRECTIONS

1. Make the dumplings by combining the flour, baking powder, and salt in a large bowl. Using a pastry cutter or two knives, cut the butter into the flour mixture. Stir in the milk a little at a time until it forms a dough ball.
2. Cover your countertop with enough flour that the dough will not stick when you roll it out. Roll out the dough relatively thin, then cut into squares to form dumplings.
3. Flour a plate and transfer the dough from the counter to the plate. Bring the chicken broth to a boil in a large saucepan, then drop the dumplings in one by one, stirring continually. The excess flour will thicken the broth. Cook for about 20 minutes or until the dumplings are no longer doughy.
4. Add the chicken, stir to combine, and serve.

NUTRITION: 381 calories 15g carbs 26g protein

276. Chicken Pot Pie

PREPARATION TIME: 30'

SERVINGS: 6-8

COOKING TIME: 30'

INGREDIENTS

- ½ cup butter
- 1 medium onion, diced
- 1 (14.5-ounce) can chicken broth
- 1 cup half and half milk
- ½ cup all-purpose flour
- 1 carrot, diced
- 1 celery stalk, diced
- 3 medium potatoes, peeled and diced
- 3 cups cooked chicken, diced
- ½ cup frozen peas
- 1 teaspoon chicken seasoning
- ½ teaspoon salt
- ½ teaspoon ground pepper
- 1 single refrigerated pie crust
- 1 egg
- Water

DIRECTIONS

1. Preheat the oven to 375°F. In a large skillet, heat the butter over medium heat, add the leeks and sauté for 3 minutes. Sprinkle flour over the mixture, and continue to stir constantly for 3 minutes.
2. Whisking constantly, blend in the chicken broth and milk. Bring the mixture to a boil. Reduce heat to medium-low. Add the carrots, celery, potatoes, salt, pepper, and stir to combine. Cook for 10-15 minutes or until veggies are cooked through but still crisp. Add chicken and peas. Stir to combine.
3. Transfer chicken filling to a deep 9-inch pie dish. Fit the pie crust sheet on top and press the edges around the dish to seal the crust. Trim the excess if needed.
4. In a separate bowl, whisk an egg with 1 tablespoon of water, and brush the mixture over the top of the pie. With a knife, cut a few slits to let steam escape. Bake the pie in the oven on the middle oven rack 20 to 30 minutes until the crust becomes golden brown.
5. Let the pie rest for about 15 minutes before serving.

NUTRITION: 351 calories 14g carbs 27g protein

277. green CHIli JaCk CHICken

PREPARATION TIME: 5'

SERVINGS: 2

COOKING TIME: 20'

INGREDIENTS

- 1-pound chicken strips
- 1 teaspoon chili powder
- 4 ounces green chilies
- 2 cups Monterey Jack cheese, shredded
- ¼ cup salsa

DIRECTIONS

1. Sprinkle the chicken with the chili powder while heating some oil over medium heat. Cook the chicken strips until they are half cooked, and then place the green chilies on top of the chicken. Lower the heat to low.
2. Cook for 1 to 2 minutes before adding the cheese on top. Keep cooking the chicken and cheese until the cheese melts. Serve the chicken with the salsa.

NUTRITION: 328 calories 13g carbs 29g protein

278. aPPle CHeddar CHICken

PREPARATION TIME: 10'

SERVINGS: 4-6

COOKING TIME: 45'

INGREDIENTS

- 5 cooked skinless chicken breasts, whole or cubed (Cracker Barrel uses the whole breast, but either option works just as well.)
- 2 cans apple pie filling, cut apples in third
- 1 bag extra-sharp cheddar cheese
- 1 row Ritz crackers, crushed
- 1 cup melted butter

DIRECTIONS

1. Preheat the oven to 350°F. Combine the chicken, apple pie filling, and cheddar cheese in a mixing bowl. Stir to combine. Pour the mixture into a greased casserole dish. Mix Ritz crackers with the melted butter. Spread over the casserole. Bake for 45 minutes or until it starts to bubble.

NUTRITION: 329 calories 16g carbs 27g protein

279. Cornflake CrusTed CHICken

PREPARATION TIME: 10'

SERVINGS: 4

COOKING TIME: 30'

INGREDIENTS

- 4 boneless skinless chicken breasts, cut into large strips
- 3 cups cornflakes
- 2 tablespoons melted butter
- 1 large egg, beaten
- 1 teaspoon water
- Salt
- Pepper
- Chicken poultry seasoning

DIRECTIONS

1. Preheat the oven to 400°F. Lay out the chicken breasts and season both sides with salt, pepper, and poultry seasoning. In a shallow dish, combine the water and egg.
2. In a separate shallow dish, crush the cornflakes and season with some more poultry seasoning. Dip each breast in the egg mixture, then roll it in the cornflakes. Place the chicken on a baking sheet and pat more cornflakes on top. Bake for about 30–35 minutes or until the chicken is done.

NUTRITION: 356 calories 14g carbs 28g protein

280. Turkey 'n STuffIng

| PREPARATION TIME: | 20' | SERVINGS: | 4 |

COOKING TIME: 1 H 10'

INGREDIENTS

- 4 cups day-old cornbread
- 2 cups day-old biscuits
- 1/3 cup chopped onion
- 1 cup diced celery
- 2 tablespoons dried parsley flakes
- 1 teaspoon poultry seasoning
- 1 teaspoon ground sage
- ½ teaspoon coarse ground pepper
- ¼ cup butter or margarine, melted
- 24 ounces chicken broth
- Cooking spray for greasing
- 8 cooked thick turkey breast slices
- 1 cup cranberry sauce
- Favorite sides such as green beans and mashed potatoes
- Gravy
- 3 tablespoons butter
- ½ cup diced onions
- 2 tablespoons all-purpose flour
- ¼ teaspoon salt
- ¼ teaspoon pepper
- 1/8 teaspoon dry sage flakes
- 1/8 teaspoon dry parsley flakes
- 1¼ cups milk

DIRECTIONS

1. Preheat oven to 400⅓F and spray an 8x8-inch baking dish with cooking spray. In a food processor, add the cornbread and the biscuits. Process until you get a coarse consistency. Alternatively, grate the cornbread and biscuits with a large hole hand grater.
2. In a large bowl, stir together the onion, celery, grated cornbread and biscuits, parsley, poultry seasoning, sage, and pepper. Add the butter and chicken broth to the dry stuffing and mix to combine well.
3. Spread the stuffing evenly to the prepared baking dish. Bake uncovered for 1 hour or until golden brown. Warm-up the turkey in foil in the oven for 15-20 minutes or until warmed through.
4. Prepare the gravy by whisking the dry gravy ingredients together in a bowl. Melt the butter in a saucepan over medium heat and add the onions. Stir fry over medium-low heat until fragrant and tender. Add the dry ingredients. Whisk continuously, stirring thoroughly to remove lumps. When the flour begins to brown, slowly whisk in the milk. Continue cooking and whisking for about 2-3 minutes or until the mixture thickens.
5. To serve, add two slices of turkey to each plate and top with some gravy. Add some stuffing, top with some more of the gravy. Add some cranberry sauce and favorite sides.

NUTRITION: 328 calories 16g carbs 34g protein

281. farm-raised Catfish

PREPARATION TIME: 15'

SERVINGS: 4

COOKING TIME: 10'

INGREDIENTS

- ¼ cup all-purpose flour
- ¼ cup cornmeal
- 1 teaspoon onion powder
- 1 teaspoon dried basil
- ½ teaspoon garlic salt
- ½ teaspoon dried thyme
- ¼–½ teaspoon white pepper
- ¼–½ teaspoon cayenne pepper
- ¼–½ teaspoon black pepper
- 4 catfish fillets (6–8 ounces each)
- ¼ cup butter

DIRECTIONS

1. Add the flour, cornmeal, onion powder, basil, salt, thyme, white pepper, cayenne pepper, and black pepper to a large plastic freezer bag.
2. Place the catfish fillets in the bag and gently shake to coat. Fish breaks easily, so be careful!
3. Heat a large skillet over medium-high heat. Add the butter, and when it melts, lay in the catfish. Cook, covered, for 8–10 minutes on each side, or until the fish flakes easily with a fork

NUTRITION: 329 calories 15g carbs 27g protein

282. lemon PePPer TrouT

INGREDIENTS

- 6 (4-ounce) trout fillets
- 3 tablespoons butter, melted
- 2 medium lemons, thinly sliced
- 2 tablespoons lemon juice
- Sauce
- 3 tablespoons butter
- ¼ teaspoon pepper
- 2 tablespoons lemon juice

DIRECTIONS

1. Melt the butter in a saucepan over low heat and allow it to cook until it begins to brown (don't burn it). Add the pepper and lemon juice. Brush the fish fillets with melted butter. Lay lemon slices on top of each. If cooking on a grill, use a wire grilling basket sprayed with nonstick cooking spray. Grill for about 10 minutes or until the fish flakes easily with a fork. Alternatively, you can bake in a 350°F oven for 10–15 minutes. Transfer to a serving platter and top with additional lemon slices.
2. Serve with the butter lemon sauce you made.

NUTRITION: 341 calories 17g carbs 29g protein

Chapter 10

OLD AND MODERN BREAD RECIPES

283. black and blue burger

<table>
<tr><td>PREPARATION TIME:</td><td>10'</td><td>SERVINGS:</td><td>4</td></tr>
<tr><td>COOKING TIME:</td><td>55'</td><td></td><td></td></tr>
</table>

INGREDIENTS

For Black & Blue Burger:
- 2 pounds ground beef (premium chuck 80/20 blend)
- 1 kosher dill pickle, finely sliced
- 4 soft brioche buns, cut in half
- ¼ head iceberg lettuce, finely sliced
- 12 ounces blue cheese, such as Point Reyes
- 1 heirloom tomato, finely sliced
- ½ Vidalia onion, very finely sliced
- 8 slices applewood smoked bacon, cooked crispy
- ¼ cup canola oil

For Blackening Spice:
- 1 teaspoon cayenne
- 1 tablespoon fresh ground black pepper
- 2 teaspoons ground cumin
- 1 teaspoon paprika
- 2 teaspoons granulated onion
- 1 teaspoon Italian seasoning
- ½ teaspoon chili powder
- 1 teaspoon granulated garlic
- ½ teaspoon kosher salt

For Donkey Sauce:
- 1 cup mayonnaise
- 4 dashes of Worcestershire sauce
- 1 teaspoon yellow mustard
- ¼ cup roasted garlic, minced
- 4 pinches fresh ground black pepper
- ¼ teaspoon kosher salt

For Garlic Butter:
- 4 tablespoons unsalted butter (½ stick)
- 3 tablespoons fresh flat-leaf parsley, minced
- 6 garlic cloves, minced

DIRECTIONS

1. For the blackening spice: Combine pepper together with cayenne, granulated onion, cumin, Italian seasoning, granulated garlic, chili powder, paprika & salt in a small-sized mixing bowl. Mix until blended well.
2. For the garlic butter: Over medium heat in a medium saucepan; heat the butter until melted. Add and cook the garlic for 5 to 6 minutes until fragrant. Stir in the parsley. Set aside.
3. For donkey sauce: Combine the roasted garlic together with mayonnaise, mustard, Worcestershire, pepper, and salt in a small mixing bowl; mix well. Cover & reserve. For the black & blue burger: Preheat a grill over medium-high heat.
4. Evenly divide the ground beef into eight portions; roll each into a loose ball, then flatten into a 4" patty. Place 2 ounces of the blue cheese on four of the patties. Cover with a second patty & gently seal the edges to form a stuffed patty approximately 1 ½" thick.
5. Season both sides of the stuffed patties with the blackening spice. Grill for a couple of minutes until a crust has developed on the first side, spread approximately 3" apart. Carefully flip & continue to cook the other side for 2 minutes. Put each burger with 2 slices of bacon & 1 ounce of the leftover blue cheese. Cover with a piece of foil & cook until the cheese is completely melted, for 30 more seconds. Remove the burgers to a serving tray & let rest.
6. Glaze the sides of the brioche buns lightly with garlic butter & toast on the grill for a few seconds, until crisp & golden.
7. In assembling: Coat the buns with some donkey sauce. Place the bottom buns with a burger, pickles, and onions, then layer it. Top with lettuce and tomatoes. Cover with the bun tops & secure with wooden skewers. Serve immediately & enjoy.

NUTRITION: 910 calories 61.3g total fats 42.6g protein

284. The Madlove Burger

Preparation Time: 25'

Servings: 4

Cooking Time: 1 H 20'

Ingredients

For the Maple Bacon:
- 12 slices bacon
- 1/3 cup light brown sugar, packed
- ¼ cup pure maple syrup

For the Candied Jalapenos:
- 2 large jalapeno peppers, sliced into rounds
- ¼ cup distilled white vinegar
- 1/3 cup granulated sugar

For the Burgers:
- 12 ounces ground beef chuck
- 6 ounces ground beef brisket
- 1/6 cup seltzer
- 6 ounces ground beef sirloin
- A pinch of Cajun seasoning
- 6 slices provolone cheese
- Unsalted butter, for spreading
- 6 slices mozzarella cheese
- Butter lettuce, sliced tomatoes, and sliced avocado, for topping
- 6 sesame brioche buns, split
- Freshly ground pepper & kosher salt to taste
- 6 slices Swiss cheese
- Vegetable oil, for the grill

Directions

1. For Maple Bacon: Preheat your oven to 275 F. Arrange the bacon on a rack set on a rimmed baking sheet & bake in the preheated oven for 30 minutes; brush with some maple syrup & sprinkle with the brown sugar. Continue to bake until the sugar melts & the bacon is glazed. Let cool.
2. For Candied Jalapenos: Combine jalapenos together with vinegar and granulated sugar in a small bowl; set aside.
3. For Burgers: Preheat a grill pan or grill over high heat & brush the grates with the vegetable oil. Combine beef chuck together with brisket and sirloin, Cajun seasoning, seltzer & a pinch each of pepper and salt in a large bowl. Using your hands; mix until just combined. Make six patties, approximately ½" thick from the mixture.
4. Grill the burgers for 3 ½ minutes; flip & top each with a slice of Swiss cheese, provolone, and mozzarella. Cover & cook for 2 ½ minutes more. In the meantime, butter the cut sides of the buns & grill for a minute, until warm.
5. Serve and garnish with the candied jalapenos, maple bacon, lettuce, avocado, and tomato.

Nutrition: 887 calories 59g total fats 43g protein

285. The Southern Charm burger

Preparation Time: 15'

Servings: 4

Cooking Time: 30'

Ingredients

- 2 pounds ground bison or beef
- 1 tablespoon Texas Pete or Tabasco
- 4 garlic cloves, minced
- 1 small onion, minced
- BBQ Sauce with Honey and Molasses for basting
- 8 ounces container pimento cheese spread
- 1 large green tomato, cut into 8 slices
- ¼ cup corn meal, seasoned with salt and pepper
- 1 large egg, beaten
- Pickled okra for condiments
- 8 Hearty Buns
- Nonstick cooking spray

Directions

1. Preheat the oven to 350 degrees. Mix the egg with a small amount of water in a shallow bowl & then season with pepper and salt to taste. Place the corn meal out onto a medium-sized plate.
2. Before cooking, soak the tomato slices into the egg and then press into the corn meal; ensure that the outside is nicely coated. Place the slices onto the baking sheet lightly coated with the cooking spray. Spray tops of tomatoes with the cooking spray. Bake for 12 to 15 minutes, until golden brown, turning once during the baking process.
3. Combine the ground beef together with onions, tabasco, and garlic in a large-sized mixing bowl. Season the meat well; combine thoroughly. Make 8 even-sized patties from the mixture. Baste with the BBQ Sauce & grill until you get your desired doneness.
4. Just about a minute before you remove the patties from the grill, place a portion of pimento cheese spread on top of burgers using a cookie scoop. For even melting, press the cheese down using a large spatula. Place one "fried" green tomato over each bun, top with burger, and garnish with your favorite condiments.

Nutrition: 893 calories 58g total fats 40g protein

286. a.l. PePPerCorn burger

<table>
<tr><td>PREPARATION TIME: 15'</td><td>SERVINGS: 4</td></tr>
</table>

COOKING TIME: 20'

INGREDIENTS

- Hamburger meat
- Onions
- Montreal steal seasoning
- Onion buns
- Garlic powder
- A1 peppercorn steak sauce
- Ketchup
- Mayonnaise
- Tomatoes
- Pepper jack cheese
- Bacon
- 1 large Egg
- Beer
- Pepper & salt to taste

DIRECTIONS

1. Season the hamburger meat with pepper and salt to taste; mix well or just use Red Robin's seasoning salt. Press into the shape of patties. Season the bottom and top of each patty with the garlic powder and Montreal steak seasoning.
2. Let sit at room temperature for 30 to 60 minutes. Combine ⅓ mayo with ⅓ ketchup. Add A1 peppercorn sauce to taste. Grill the burgers until you get your desired doneness.
3. Cut the onions into fine rings and then cut the tomatoes into slices. Combine 1 cup of all-purpose flour together with ½ teaspoon ground black pepper, 1 teaspoon garlic powder, 1 beaten egg & 1 ½ cups of beer; mix well. Dip the onions into the prepared beer batter.
4. Fry the batter covered onions for a couple of minutes, until turn golden brown, and then cook the bacon. Toast the onion buns. Add pepper jack cheese to the patties & let the heat from the grill until the cheese is completely melted.
5. Put a generous amount of peppercorn and brush on both slices of the bun. Load the burger patty, onion straws, bacon & tomato. Serve immediately & enjoy.

NUTRITION: 908 calories 62g total fats 43g protein

287. banzai burger

PREPARATION TIME: 15'

SERVINGS: 2

COOKING TIME: 50'

INGREDIENTS

- 1 large beefsteak tomato, cut into slices
- 2 beef patties
- 1 batch Homemade Teriyaki Sauce
- Fresh lettuce, shredded
- 4 pineapple rings
- Mayonnaise
- 2 slices of cheddar cheese
- Pepper & salt to taste

DIRECTIONS

1. Brush the beef patties on both sides with teriyaki sauce. Grill until you get your desired doneness, basting occasionally with the teriyaki sauce. Add the cheese on top near the end to melt. Brush the pineapple rings on both sides with the teriyaki sauce & grill for a minute on each side.
2. Lightly toast the hamburger buns. Place the patties over the bottom bun, place two slices of tomatoes & then two pineapple rings on top. Brush the pineapple rings with more of teriyaki sauce. Top with the shredded lettuce. Spread a generous amount of mayonnaise on the top bun & place it on the hamburger. Serve immediately and enjoy.

NUTRITION: 911 calories 60.3g total fats 41.9g protein

288. bleu ribbon burger

PREPARATION TIME: 20'	SERVINGS: 6

COOKING TIME: 40'

INGREDIENTS

- 2 pounds lean ground beef
- 1/3 teaspoon pepper
- 3 ounces cream cheese
- 2 garlic cloves, peeled & crushed
- 8 medium fresh mushrooms, sliced quite thin
- 2 teaspoons Worcestershire sauce
- 3 tablespoons blue cheese, crumbled
- ½ teaspoon salt

DIRECTIONS

1. Combine the meat together with garlic, Worcestershire sauce, pepper & salt. Make 12 thin patties approximately 4 ½" across from the meat mixture. Combine the blue cheese with cream cheese; mix well. Put cheese mixture on the patties and evenly spread to within ½" of the edges; pressing the mushroom slices into the cheese mixture.
2. Cover each patty with one of the leftover patties, seal the edges well, don't have any peek holes. Fry the patties until browned well; flip & continue to cook until the other side is cooked as well.

NUTRITION: 871 calories 56g total fats 36g protein

289. burnIn love burger

PREPARATION TIME:	10'		SERVINGS:	1

COOKING TIME: 20'

INGREDIENTS

- 1 jalapeno Kaiser cornmeal roll
- Chipotle mayonnaise
- 1/3 pound ground beef 80% lean or above, made into a patty
- Iceberg lettuce shredded
- Cayenne seasoning
- 2 slices pepper-jack cheese
- Salsa
- 1 tomato vine ripened, sliced
- Fresh Jalapeno rings or battered & fried
- Pepper & salt to taste

DIRECTIONS

For Chipotle Mayonnaise:
1. Combine the mayonnaise with pureed chipotle peppers, pepper, and salt to taste. To enhance the flavor, refrigerate for an hour.

For the Salsa:
2. Enhance your favorite store-bought salsa with fresh finely chopped tomatoes, cilantro, red onion, jalapenos, and Serrano peppers.

For the Burger:
3. Season the patty with cayenne, pepper, and salt to taste. Oil the grill grates & preheat it.
4. Grill the patty for a couple of seconds; flip and grill the other side too until cooked through. Remove the burger from grill & top with the pepper-jack cheese. Grill for two more minutes until the cheese is completely melted. Toast the bun on the grill until turn golden brown.
5. Spread the chipotle mayonnaise on both sides of your toasted bun. Place the burger on the bun & top with sliced tomato, jalapenos, salsa & shredded lettuce. Cover with the bun top; serve immediately & enjoy.

NUTRITION: 897 calories 58.9g total fats 40.9g protein

290. red robln burger

PREPARATION TIME: 30'	SERVINGS: 4

COOKING TIME: 40'

INGREDIENTS

- 4 toasted buns or 4 toast
- 1 ½ pounds lean hamburger
- 4 large eggs, fried over-medium
- Fresh coarse ground black pepper & seasoning salt to taste
- 8 slices American cheese
- ketchup
- 4 slices bacon, cooked and cut in half
- Fresh lettuce
- 4 slices tomatoes
- Mayonnaise

DIRECTIONS

1. Cook the bacon until done; set aside to cool. Once done, break into half. Make 4 even-sized patties of beef and then season with pepper and salt to taste; pan-fry or grill in a small amount of bacon fat until done.
2. Place each patty with a slice of cheese, cover lightly & set aside. Fry the eggs to your liking sunny-side up, over medium heat. Toast the buns. Once the eggs are done, set them aside. Assemble your burger in the following order:
3. Bottom bun followed by a slice of cheese, fried egg, a small amount of ketchup, 2 pieces of bacon, tomato, fresh lettuce & top the bun, spread with mayo.
4. Serve with French fries or hash browns and enjoy.

NUTRITION: 904 calories 62.4g total fats 40.1g protein

291. Sautéed Mushroom Burger

<table>
<tr><td>PREPARATION TIME:</td><td>10'</td><td>SERVINGS:</td><td>4</td></tr>
</table>

COOKING TIME: 20'

INGREDIENTS

- 1 lb. ground hamburger
- Garlic salt to taste
- Onion powder to taste
- Seasoned salt to taste
- 2 c. sliced mushrooms
- 1 tbsp. butter
- ½ onion caramelized
- 4 slices Swiss cheese
- Lettuce

DIRECTIONS

1. Preheat your grill over medium-high heat. Evenly divide the hamburger into eight balls. Flatten & season both sides with pepper & salt to taste. Grill until you get your desired doneness. Once done, remove them from the heat. Caramelize the onions & sauté the mushrooms with butter until tender; set aside. Once the burger is done, top with onions, lettuce, mushrooms, & cheese.

NUTRITION: 891 calories 58.9g total fats 37.9g protein

292. WHIsky rIver burger

PREPARATION TIME: 20'	SERVINGS: 6

COOKING TIME: 20'

INGREDIENTS

- 2 pounds 80/20 ground beef
- 6 slices of cheddar cheese
- Oil, for brushing the burgers
- 12 tablespoon mayonnaise
- Onion rings, thin & crispy
- 6 seeded hamburger buns
- Bourbon whiskey BBQ sauce
- 2 cups fresh lettuce, chopped
- 12 slices tomato

DIRECTIONS

1. Preheat the charcoal grill over high heat until it glows bright orange & ashes over.
2. In the meantime, make 6 even-sized patties from the ground beef. Lightly brush the burgers with oil.
3. Grill the burgers for a couple of minutes until turn browned & slightly charred on the first side. Flip & continue cooking until you get your desired level of doneness. Drizzle the Bourbon Whiskey BBQ Sauce over the burgers & place one slice of cheese on each burger. Cook until the cheese just starts to melt, for a minute more. Remove from the heat; set aside, and assemble the burgers.
4. Layer the cut side of both parts of the bun with approximately 1 tablespoon of mayonnaise on each half. Place the Onion Rings over the cut side of the bottom bun portion. Add the burger with cheese and sauce. Top with lettuce and tomatoes. Serve immediately & enjoy.

NUTRITION: 893 calories 57.8g total fats 40.4g protein

293. Tuscan Butter Burger

PREPARATION TIME: 15'

SERVINGS: 4

COOKING TIME: 30'

INGREDIENTS

For the Chicken Burgers
- 1 cup panko
- 1 ½ pounds ground chicken
- 4 green onions, minced
- 2 tablespoon extra-virgin olive oil
- 1 teaspoon Himalayan pink salt, black pepper, garlic blend

For the Tuscan Butter Sauce
- ¼ cup Parmesan, finely grated
- 2 tablespoon butter
- ½ cup heavy cream
- 1 tablespoon tomato paste
- ¼ teaspoon Himalayan pink salt, black pepper, garlic blend

For Assembly
- 4 seeded hamburger buns, split & lightly toasted
- 1 cup large basil leaves, fresh
- 1 jar oil-packed sun-dried tomatoes (7-ounces), drained

DIRECTIONS

1. For Chicken Burgers: Combine the chicken together with panko, green onions & 1 teaspoon Himalayan pink salt, garlic blend, black pepper in a medium bowl.
2. Cook oil over medium-high heat in a large skillet. Form 4 even-sized patties from the chicken mixture using slightly dampened hands, placing the patties carefully into the hot skillet. Cook for 8 to 10 minutes, until turn golden, flipping once during the Cooking Time. Remove the patties to a large plate; drain any excess oil.
3. For Tuscan butter Sauce: Place the skillet over medium-low heat & add butter & tomato paste. Cook for a minute, whisking frequently. Whisk in the Parmesan, heavy cream & ¼ teaspoon Himalayan pink salt, black pepper, garlic blend. Bring the mixture to a simmer. Once done, decrease the heat to low & let simmer until parmesan is melted & the sauce is reduced slightly, for a couple of more minutes. Remove from the heat.
4. Place the burger patties on the bottom buns. Spoon the Tuscan butter sauce on top of patties and then top with sun-dried tomatoes and basil. Close the sandwich with the top bun.

NUTRITION: 897 calories 60g total fats 40g protein

294. four Cheese Melt

PREPARATION TIME:	10'		SERVINGS:	4

	COOKING TIME:	30'

INGREDIENTS

- 1 cup Asiago, shredded
- 2 tablespoons extra-virgin olive oil, 2 turns of the pan
- 1 garlic clove, cracked away from the skin
- 8 slices of crusty Italian semolina bread
- 1 cup mozzarella, shredded
- ½ cup Romano or Parmesan, grated
- 1 cup provolone, shredded
- 3 tablespoons butter

DIRECTIONS

1. Over medium-low heat in a small skillet; heat the oil with butter. Once the butter is completely melted, add the garlic & gently cook for 2 to 3 minutes. Remove the garlic butter mixture from heat.
2. Now, over medium-high heat in a large nonstick skillet. Brush 1 side of 4 slices of bread with garlic oil using a pastry brush & place the buttered side down into the hot skillet. Top each slice with equal amounts of the 4 cheeses; evenly distributing them over the 4 slices. Top each sandwich with a slice more of bread brushed with garlic butter, buttered side up. Flip the grill cheese sandwiches a couple of times until cheeses are melted & gooey and the bread is toasty & golden. Cut grilled 4 cheese sandwiches from corner to corner; serve and enjoy.

NUTRITION: 904 calories 61g total fats 40.9g protein

295. Pub maC n CHeese enTree

PREPARATION TIME: 20'

SERVINGS: 4

COOKING TIME: 30'

INGREDIENTS

- 8 ounces dry pasta
- 2 tablespoon flour
- 4 tablespoon butter
- 6 ounces beer (we used an IPA)
- 1 tablespoon coarse-ground mustard
- ¼ cup milk
- 6 ounces sharp cheddar cheese, shredded
- 1 cup soft pretzel, diced into ¼" pieces
- 3 ounces Monterey jack cheese, shredded

DIRECTIONS

1. Boil the pasta per the Directions mentioned on the package Drain & set aside Now, over moderate heat in a large saucepan; heat 2 tablespoons of butter & mix in 2 tablespoons of flour; cook for a minute or two.
2. Add beer; give the ingredients a good stir until combined well. Add milk & cook until thickened slightly for 5 minutes, stirring frequently. Add mustard & cheese; decreases the heat to low.
3. Now, over moderate heat in a separate pan; heat 2 tablespoons of butter & add in the chopped pretzels, stir to coat nicely with the butter. Combine pasta with cheese sauce; transfer to an oven safe container & bake for 15 minutes at 350 F.
4. Remove from the oven & sprinkle with pretzel pieces; place into the oven again & bake for 15 minutes more. Serve hot & enjoy.

NUTRITION: 894 calories 55g total fats 37g protein

296. The boss burger

PREPARATION TIME: 15'

SERVINGS: 3

COOKING TIME: 25'

INGREDIENTS

- 1-pound ground beef
- 3 cheese slices
- Worcestershire sauce
- 3 fried eggs
- canned green chilis or Verde green sauce (any of your favorite)
- 6 bacon slices, cooked until crisp
- Pico de Gallo
- 3 burger buns
- Pepper & salt to taste

DIRECTIONS

1. Heat your grill over high heat. Season the ground beef with dashes of Worcestershire sauce, pepper & salt. Make 3 patties from the mixture & cook until you get your desired level of doneness. During the last minute of your Cooking Time, top each burger with a cheese slice. Place on a bun topped with an egg, bacon, a big scoop of Pico de Gallo & a scoop of Verde sauce.
2. Serve immediately & enjoy.

NUTRITION: 889 calories 60g total fats 40g protein

297. alex's Santa fe burger

Preparation Time: 15'

Servings: 4

Cooking Time: 15'

Ingredients

For Burgers:
- 12 yellow or blue corn tortilla chips
- 1 poblano chili, large
- 4 hamburger buns, split; toasted
- 1 ½ pounds 80% lean ground chuck or 90% lean ground turkey
- 2 ½ tablespoons canola oil
- Freshly ground black pepper & kosher salt to taste

For Queso Sauce:
- 1 tablespoon all-purpose flour
- 2 cups Monterey Jack cheese, coarsely grated (approximately 8 ounces)
- 1 tablespoon unsalted butter
- 1 ½ cups whole milk
- Freshly ground black pepper & kosher salt to taste

Directions

1. Preheat oven to 375 F. Put the chili on a rimmed baking sheet; rub with a tablespoon of the oil & then season with pepper and salt to taste. Roast in the preheated oven for 12 to 15 minutes until the skin of the chili is blackened. Remove & place the chili in a large bowl; cover using a plastic wrap & let steam for 12 to 15 more minutes. Peel, stem & seed the chili, then chop it coarsely.
2. For Queso Sauce: Heat the butter over medium heat in a small saucepan until completely melted. Whisk in the flour & cook for a minute. Add the milk; stir well and increase the heat to high; cook for 3 to 5 minutes, until thickened slightly, whisking constantly. Remove from the heat & whisk in the cheese until melted, then season with pepper and salt. Try to keep it warm.
3. Evenly divide the meat into 4 portions. Loosely form each portion into a ¾" thick burger & make a deep depression in the middle with your thumb. Season both sides of each burger with pepper and salt. Cook the burgers in the leftover oil.
4. Place the burgers on the bun bottoms & top each with chips, a few tablespoons of queso sauce & some poblano. Cover with the bun tops; serve immediately & enjoy.
5. For Toasted Burger Buns:
6. To toast a bun on a grill, griddle or grill pan; split the bun open and place it on the grill, cut side down; grill for a couple of seconds, until turn golden brown lightly.

Nutrition: 891 calories 62g total fats 41g protein

298. Chili's avoCado beef burger

PREPARATION TIME: 20'

SERVINGS: 4

COOKING TIME: 20'

INGREDIENTS

- 1-pound ground beef
- 8 sliced crispy cooked bacon
- 1 teaspoon Worcestershire sauce
- Tomato slices
- ¼ teaspoon dried thyme
- Onion Slices
- 1 teaspoon Tabasco sauce
- 4 slices of American cheese
- Mayonnaise
- 2 avocados
- Fresh Lettuce
- 4 sesame burger buns
- Pepper & salt to taste

DIRECTIONS

1. Season the ground beef with Tabasco, Worcestershire sauce, thyme, pepper, and salt. Lightly toss the ingredients using a fork until combined well. Make 4 palm-sized beef patties from the mixture.
2. Prepare your grill pan over moderate heat. When done, place the beef patty over the pan & grill until you get your desired level of doneness, for 4 to 5 minutes per side. In the meantime, mash the avocado & season with pepper and salt. Add a small amount of spice, if desired.
3. When done, layer the bottom half of the bun with the mayonnaise, onion, lettuce and tomato. Add the hot beef patty on top & then add on the cheese. Layer it with avocado & finally, a few pieces of crispy bacon. Top it off with the top of the bun; serve immediately & enjoy,

NUTRITION: 907 calories 61g total fats 40g protein

299. Chili's 1975 Soft Tacos

PREPARATION TIME: 20'		**SERVINGS:** 6

COOKING TIME: 12H 15'

INGREDIENTS

- 1 ½ pounds beef chuck pot roast, fat trimmed
- 12 corn tortillas (6" each)
- 5 teaspoons chili powder
- 2 jars mild or medium tomato-based salsa (16 ounces each)
- 3 cups fresh lettuce, shredded
- 1 avocado
- 2 tablespoons cider vinegar
- ¾ cup sour cream

DIRECTIONS

1. Spoon a cup of salsa into a small bowl & reserve. Combine the leftover salsa with chili powder and vinegar in a slow cooker. Add beef; cover & cook for 10 to 12 hours on low-heat, until the beef shreds easily. Shred the meat, using two forks & spoon into a large-sized serving bowl.
2. Preheat oven to 300 F. Stack the tortillas, wrap in foil & bake in the preheated oven for 8 to 10 minutes, until warm. Place lettuce and sour cream in bowls. Just before serving; pit, peel & dice the avocado & place in a small bowl. Put out the bowls (including the salsa) & assemble tacos at the table.

NUTRITION: 901 calories 62g total fats 42g protein

300. Spicy Shrimp Tacos

Preparation Time:	15'	**Servings:**	2

Cooking Time: 15'

Ingredients

- 6 to 8 shrimp peeled, de-veined, with tails off (3 to 4 per taco)
- 2 slices avocado
- 1/3 cup cabbage, finely shredded
- 2 flour tortillas, small
- 1 tablespoon Siracha
- 2 tablespoon mayonnaise
- ½ tablespoon Thai Sweet Chili Sauce
- 1-2 tablespoon olive oil
- A pinch each of chili powder, ground black pepper & salt

Directions

1. Wipe the surface of a grill pan with olive oil and heat it over medium-high heat. Season the shrimp with the chili powder, pepper, and salt, then grill until done, for 3 to 5 minutes.
2. Combine the mayo together with Siracha and sweet chili sauce in a small bowl.
3. Warm the tortillas & place half of the cabbage on each. Drizzle half of the sauce on each taco and then top with the shrimp. Serve immediately; garnish with the avocado & enjoy.

Nutrition: 911 calories 63g total fats 39g protein

301. ranCHero CHICken TaCos

Preparation Time: 15'		**Servings:** 8

Cooking Time: 15'

Ingredients

- Cheddar cheese, shredded
- Flour tortillas
- Chicken breast, sliced

For Ranchero Sauce

- 2 garlic cloves, chopped
- 1 Serrano or jalapeno chili, seeded & diced
- ¼ cup of chopped onion
- 3 cups tomatoes, diced
- ½ teaspoon ground chili
- 1 tablespoon oregano
- 2 tablespoons cooking oil

Directions

For Ranchero Sauce:

1. Over moderate heat in a large saucepan; heat the oil until hot & then sauté the onions, garlic, and Serrano for a couple of minutes.
2. Decrease the heat & add in the tomatoes; stir well & cook until the tomatoes have wilted for 5 to 6 minutes. Add the seasonings & let simmer for 5 minutes more.

For Quesadilla

3. Sauté or grill the chicken. Mix the chicken with the prepared sauce. Butter the outside of your tortilla. Add the chicken-ranchero sauce filling and cheese. Fold the tortilla & cook in a hot skillet. Serve hot & enjoy.

Nutrition: 869 calories 58g total fats 38g protein

302. beef baCon ranCH Quesadlllas

PREPARATION TIME: 25'	SERVINGS: 4

COOKING TIME: 35'

INGREDIENTS

- 1 package cooked bacon, finely chopped
- Ranch dressing bottled
- 1 package Mexican cheese or cheddar, shredded
- 4 chicken breasts (baked or grilled), finely chopped
- 1-2 packages whole-grain or tortillas flour

DIRECTIONS

1. While you are baking or grilling the chicken until completely cooked, brown the bacon in a large skillet until turn golden brown and cooked through; set aside at room temperature to cool.
2. Finely chop the chicken and bacon. Using low-fat cooking spray, lightly coat your heated griddle & place two tortillas down to brown. Lightly drizzle the ranch over the tortillas.
3. Sprinkle the chicken and bacon onto the ranch, top with the shredded cheese. Place a tortilla on top, smooch down with your hand to set it together, & carefully flip. Once both sides are browned, remove them from the heat and transfer them onto a large plate.
4. Once done, cut each one up into triangle sections using a super-sharp knife or pizza cutter, roughly eight triangles per tortilla.

NUTRITION: 879 calories 55g total fats 38g protein

303. Chicken Enchiladas

PREPARATION TIME: 10'	SERVINGS: 6

COOKING TIME: 30'

Ingredients

- 3 chicken breasts cooked & cubed
- 1 cup masa harina corn tortilla mix
- 2 cans chicken broth (14.5 oz each)
- 1 cup mild red enchilada sauce
- 1-2 teaspoon garlic, minced
- ½ teaspoon chili powder
- 1 teaspoon onion powder
- 16 oz Velveeta cheese, cubed
- ½ teaspoon cumin
- 3 cup water, divided
- 1 teaspoon salt

For Garnish:
- Corn tortilla strips & tomatoes

Directions

1. Sauté the garlic in a large pot for a couple of minutes. Add in the chicken broth. Whisk the masa harina with 2 cups water in a medium bowl until blended well. Add the masa mixture into the pot.
2. Add the cubed Velveeta cheese, enchilada sauce, leftover water, onion powder, cumin, chili powder & salt. Bring the mixture to a boil. Add the cubed chicken; decrease the heat & let simmer for half an hour. Garnish with tortilla strips and tomatoes; serve immediately & enjoy.

NUTRITION: 888 calories 61g total fats 39g protein

304. Chicken Fajitas

PREPARATION TIME:	15'		SERVINGS:	6

COOKING TIME:	30'

INGREDIENTS

For Vegetable Finishing Sauce:
* 2 tablespoon water
* ½ teaspoon lime juice, fresh
* 5 boneless skinless chicken breasts
* 2 large white onions sliced into ½" strips
* 3 bell peppers sliced into ½" strips
* Flour tortillas
* 2 teaspoon soy sauce
* ¼ teaspoon black pepper
* 2 tablespoon olive oil
* ¼ teaspoon salt

For Chicken Marinade:
* 1/3 cup lime juice, freshly squeezed
* 1 teaspoon garlic, minced
* ½ teaspoon liquid smoke
* 1 tablespoon white vinegar
* ½ teaspoon chili powder
* 1 tablespoon soy sauce
* ½ teaspoon cayenne pepper
* 2 tablespoon vegetable oil
* ¼ teaspoon onion powder
* 1 teaspoon salt
* 1/3 cup water
* ¼ teaspoon black pepper

For Toppings, Optional:
* Grated cheddar cheese, salsa, guacamole, sour cream, Pico de Gallo, shredded lettuce

DIRECTIONS

1. Combine the entire Chicken Marinade ingredients together in a small bowl; whisk well until completely combined. Pierce each chicken breast in several places using a large fork & then place the chicken breasts in a glass baking dish, medium-sized. Add the Chicken Marinade to the baking dish; cover & let it refrigerate overnight.
2. Over medium-high heat in a large cast iron skillet; heat the olive oil until hot & sauté the peppers for 5 to 7 minutes, then add the onions. Continue to sauté until onions & peppers turn soft, for 15 to 20 minutes more, stirring every now and then.
3. In the meantime, place a separate fry pan or skillet over medium-high heat. Place the marinated chicken breasts into the hot pan & cook for 15 to 20 minutes, until done, flipping after every 10 minutes.
4. Whisk the entire Vegetable Finishing Sauce ingredients together in a small bowl. When the onions and peppers are done; decrease the heat to medium-low and add in the Vegetable Finishing Sauce; let simmer for a couple of more minutes.
5. Once chicken breasts are cooked through, transfer them to a clean, large cutting board & slice it thinly. Place the onions, peppers, and chicken on a flour tortilla. Top with the optional topping ingredients, as desired. Serve immediately & enjoy.

NUTRITION: 891 calories 62.3g total fats 41.3g protein

305. Mushroom Jack Chicken Fajitas

Preparation Time:	10'	**Servings:**	4

Cooking Time: 45'

Ingredients

For Chipotle Garlic Butter:
- 8 garlic cloves, finely minced
- ¼ cup canned chipotle peppers
- 1 teaspoon each of ground black pepper & salt
- 1/3 cup unsalted butter, softened
- For Caramelized Onions:
- 1 ½ tablespoons white sugar
- 6 medium yellow or white onions; sliced into ¼ to ½" thick slices; separating them into rings
- 1 ½ tablespoons balsamic vinegar
- ¼ cup vegetable stock
- 1 ½ tablespoons butter, unsalted
- ½ teaspoon salt
- 1 ½ tablespoons vegetable oil

For Fajitas:
- 2 pounds chicken breast, boneless and skinless
- 1 tablespoon chipotle powder
- 2 tablespoons Cajun seasoning
- 1 teaspoon ground black pepper
- 2 cups green peppers
- 1/3 cup fresh cilantro, minced
- 2 tablespoons vegetable oil

- 1 cup Monterey Jack cheese, shredded
- 2 cups cremini mushrooms, sliced
- ½ cup green onion, minced
- Ground black pepper & salt to taste
- 2 tablespoons lime juice, freshly squeezed
- 1 ½ teaspoons salt

To Serve:
- ½ cup sour cream
- 12 corn or flour tortillas
- ¼ cup canned jalapeños, sliced
- 1 cup Monterey Jack cheese, shredded
- ¼ cup guacamole

Nutrition: 894 calories 60.9g total fats 40.9g protein

DIRECTIONS

Caramelize the Onions:
1. Over moderate heat in a shallow pan; heat the butter until melted. Scatter the sliced onions on top of the melted butter and then drizzle with the oil; slowly cook for 8 to 10 minutes, until turn translucent.
2. Decrease the heat to medium-low; give the onions a good stir and add the vinegar and sugar; toss & stir until mixed well.
3. After 10 minutes of cooking, pour in the broth. To prevent the onions from burning, don't forget to scrape up any caramelized bits from the bottom of your pan & stir every now and then.
4. Once the onions are browned well & very soft, after 10 to 15 minutes more of cooking, remove them from the heat.

Preparing the Butter:
5. Now, over medium heat in a small saucepan, heat 2 tablespoons of the butter until melted and then add the minced garlic; cook for 8 to 10 minutes, until the garlic turns fragrant and begins to brown.
6. Remove the butter from heat and place in the fridge until chilled, for 15 minutes. In a small bowl, combine the garlic butter together with softened butter, chipotle & salt.
7. Mash all the ingredients together using a large fork. Season the mixture with more salt & ground black pepper, if required. Using a plastic wrap, cover the seasoned butter & store it in the fridge until ready to use.

For the Fajitas:
8. Slice the chicken breast into ½" strips, rubbing them with the chipotle powder, Cajun seasoning, lime juice, pepper, and salt. Let rest while you heat the pan.
9. Now, over high heat in a cast iron pan; heat half of the oil until it starts to shimmer, add half of the chicken strips; cook until cooked through & well-browned. Transfer the cooked chicken to a plate & cook the leftover chicken strips.
10. Add the sliced mushrooms to the hot pan; ensure that you don't add more of oil or rinse the mushrooms. Bring the heat to medium-high & cook until the mushrooms turn brown & begin to crisp, undisturbed. Sprinkle them with a very small quantity of salt.
11. Carefully flip the mushrooms & continue to cook for 5 to 7 more minutes, until both sides turn browned & they are completely cooked. Transfer them to the plate with the cooked chicken.
12. Add the leftover oil to the hot pan. When it starts to shimmer and starts to smoke, add in the green peppers & lightly sprinkle them with a very small amount of salt, stirring occasionally.
13. When the peppers begin to soften, push them so that they sit around the edge of the pan; decrease the heat to low.
14. Add the caramelized onions to the middle of your pan, pushing them so that the peppers and onions cover any exposed portions of the pan.
15. Place the cooked chicken strips over the onions. Dot the onions, peppers, and chicken with the chipotle butter sauce.
16. Sprinkle the chicken with the shredded cheese. Layer the cooked mushrooms on top of the cheese & dot the mushrooms with ½ to 1 tablespoon more of butter.
17. Cover the pan with a lid & let it sit for 5 minutes on low heat. Once the chicken is warmed through & the cheese is completely melted, scatter the cilantro and green onions on top.
18. Serve the fajitas immediately in the cast iron pan. Warm the tortillas & serve the salsa, jalapeños, sour cream, guacamole, and extra cheese on the side.

306. game day Chili

PREPARATION TIME: 25'

SERVINGS: 13

COOKING TIME: 3H 5'

INGREDIENTS

- 1 can tomato paste (6-ounce)
- 2 pounds ground chuck
- 1 onion, medium, chopped
- 3 cans tomato sauce (8-ounce)
- 1 can beef broth (14 ½ ounce)
- 2 cans pinto beans, rinsed & drained (15-ounce)
- 1 can chopped green chilis (4.5-ounce)
- 3 - 4 garlic cloves, minced
- 1 bottle dark beer (12-ounce)
- 2 tablespoons chili powder
- 1 tablespoon Worcestershire sauce
- 2 teaspoons ground cumin
- 1 teaspoon paprika
- 1 to 2 teaspoons ground red pepper
- Pickled jalapeño pepper slices, for garnish
- 1 teaspoon hot sauce

DIRECTIONS

1. Cook ground chuck together with chopped onion and minced garlic cloves over medium heat in a Dutch oven, stirring frequently until the meat crumbles & is no longer pink from inside; drain well.
2. Combine the meat mixture with beans & the leftover ingredients (except the one for garnish) in the Dutch oven; bring everything together to a boil. Decrease the heat & let simmer until thickened for 3 hours. Garnish the recipe with pickled jalapeno pepper slices.

NUTRITION: 884 calories 58g total fats 40g protein

307. roasTed Turkey, aPPle and CHeddar

PREPARATION TIME: 5'	SERVINGS: 4

COOKING TIME: 5'

INGREDIENTS

- 8-10 ounces thick sliced roasted turkey breast
- 3 tablespoons Dijon mustard
- 1 gala apple thinly sliced
- ½ red onion, sliced thinly
- 4 ounces sharp white cheddar cheese sliced
- 8 slices Cranberry Walnut bread
- 1 tablespoon honey
- 8 pieces of lettuce about the size of bread

DIRECTIONS

1. Mix honey together with mustard and prepare the Honey mustard. Spread this mixture over the bread slices.
2. Layer 4 slices of the bread with lettuce, turkey, cheese, apple, and onion. Place the leftover slices of bread over the sandwiches, slice & serve.

NUTRITION: 817 calories 54g total fats 38g protein

308. Tuna Salad SandWICH

PREPARATION TIME: 10'

SERVINGS: 3

COOKING TIME: 10'

INGREDIENTS

- 1 can tuna, drained (6 ounces)
- 1 teaspoon Dijon-style prepared mustard
- ¼ teaspoon ground black pepper
- 1 teaspoon sweet pickle relish
- 1 teaspoon mayonnaise
- ¼ cup chopped onion
- 1 celery stalk, chopped

DIRECTIONS

1. Mash the tuna using a fork in a small bowl. Add pickle relish together with mayonnaise, celery, mustard, onion & black pepper; give everything a good stir until evenly combined. Let chill; serve & enjoy.

NUTRITION: 801 calories 51g total fats 36g protein

309. Lentil Quinoa Bowl with Chicken

| PREPARATION TIME: | 5' | SERVINGS: | 2 |

| COOKING TIME: | 15' |

INGREDIENTS

- 8 ounces cooked chicken or 2 boiled eggs
- 1 cup cooked lentils
- ½ tablespoon oil
- 1 garlic clove, minced
- ¼ teaspoon paprika
- 3 cups chicken broth
- ½ onion, chopped
- 1 cup fresh spinach
- ¼ cup sun-dried tomatoes
- 1 cup chopped kale
- ¼ cup uncooked quinoa
- 1 bay leaf
- A dash of cayenne
- ½ tablespoon Miso Paste dissolved in 1 tablespoon of Water
- Pepper and salt to Taste

DIRECTIONS

1. Over medium heat in a large saucepan; heat the oil until hot. Add onion & garlic; sauté until onions are translucent & fragrant, for a couple of minutes.
2. Add quinoa together with bay leaf, broth, sun-dried tomatoes, lentils, Miso mixture, and seasoning to the pan. Bring everything together to a boil and then decrease the heat to low. Cover & let simmer until quinoa is cooked through, for 10 to 15 minutes.
3. Just before serving, stir in the spinach and kale; let them gently wilt in the mixture. Transfer the mixture into 2 separate bowls; top each bowl with 4 ounces of chicken or a sliced egg.

NUTRITION: 863 calories 52g total fats 33g protein

310. Panera's maC & CHeese

INGREDIENTS

- 1 package rigatoni pasta (16-ounce)
- ½ teaspoon Dijon mustard
- 6 Slices white American cheese, sliced into thin strips
- ¼ cup all-purpose flour
- 8 ounces extra-sharp white Vermont cheddar, shredded
- ¼ teaspoon hot sauce
- 2 ½ cup milk
- ¼ cup butter
- 1 teaspoon kosher salt

DIRECTIONS

1. Prepare the pasta as per the directions mentioned on the package.
2. Now, over low heat in a large saucepan; heat the butter until completely melted. Whisk in the flour & cook for a minute, whisking constantly.
3. Slowly whisk in the milk; increase the heat to medium and cook, whisking until mixture starts to bubble and thickens. Remove the pan from heat.
4. Add mustard, cheeses, hot sauce, and salt; continue to stir until the sauce is smooth & cheese melts.
5. Stir in the pasta & cook over medium heat for a minute. Serve immediately & enjoy.

NUTRITION: 846 calories 55g total fats 37g protein

311. Asiago Cheese Bread

| PREPARATION TIME: | 45' | | SERVINGS: | 20' |

| COOKING TIME: | 35' |

INGREDIENTS

- 1 ½ cups shredded Asiago cheese divided
- 3 ¼ cups all-purpose flour
- 1 beaten egg, large
- 1 ¼ cups milk
- 1 teaspoon granulated sugar
- ¼ teaspoon black pepper
- 1 package Red Star Platinum Superior Baking Yeast (approximately 2 ¼ teaspoons)
- 2 tablespoons butter
- 1 ½ teaspoons salt

DIRECTIONS

1. Combine 1 ½ cups of flour together with sugar, yeast, pepper, and salt in the bowl of a stand mixer. Put the milk in a microwave safe bowl. Add the butter. Heat over moderate heat until the butter melts. Stir the milk mixture into the flour mixture & mix on low speed using the paddle attachment until completely smooth. Add in 1 ¼ cups of shredded cheese; mix until just combined.
2. Slowly add in 1 ¾ cups of flour; knead until you get a soft dough-like consistency. Knead in the stand mixer with the dough hook for 5 minutes.
3. Spray a bowl lightly with the cooking spray. Add the dough to the bowl and then turn the dough. Cover the bowl & let the dough to rise for an hour or two, until almost double, in a warm place.
4. Once done, punch the dough down & form it into two loaves. Place the loaves on a large-sized baking sheet, lightly coated with the cooking spray. Cover the loaves & let rise again for 35 to 40 minutes until doubled.
5. Preheat your oven to 375 F in advance.
6. Using a serrated knife, make a few cuts in the top of loaves. Brush the tops of the loaves with the beaten egg & then sprinkle the leftover cheese. Bake in the preheated oven until lightly browned, for 30 to 35 minutes.

NUTRITION: 840 calories 54g total fats 34g protein

312. Wild blueberry muffin

PREPARATION TIME: 10'	SERVINGS: 10

COOKING TIME: 1 H 5'

INGREDIENTS

For the Muffins:
- 1 ½ cup all-purpose flour
- 2 teaspoon baking powder
- ¾ cup granulated white sugar
- 1 large egg
- 2 teaspoon vanilla extract
- Old-fashioned buttermilk
- 1/3 cup vegetable oil
- 1 cup frozen wild blueberries
- ½ teaspoon salt

For the Topping:
- 1/3 cup raw sugar
- 4 tablespoon unsalted butter cold & cut into four pieces
- 1/3 cup all-purpose flour

DIRECTIONS

1. Line a jumbo muffin pan with 6-cup with paper liners and preheat your oven to 400 F in advance.
2. Combine coarse sugar together with cold butter and 1/3 cup flour in a small bowl. Mix the topping well using a pastry cutter until it's fine & crumbly. Store in a refrigerator until ready to use.
3. Now, whisk 1 ½ cups of flour together with baking powder, sugar & salt in a large bowl. Measure the oil in a 1-cup glass measuring cup & add the egg; whisk well. Pour in a little more than ⅓ cup of buttermilk until the liquid is approximately 8 fluid ounces. Add in the vanilla; whisk again.
4. Pour the wet mixture into the dry mixture; gently stir using a spatula or wooden spoon until just a few streaks of the flour remain. Add in the blueberries; gently mix until evenly distributed in the muffin batter.
5. Evenly divide the prepared batter among the muffin cups. Generously sprinkle the top of each muffin with the topping.
6. Bake the muffins on the center rack of your preheated oven until a toothpick comes out clean, for 28 to 30 minutes. Let completely cool. Store in an air-tight container for up to 2 days.

NUTRITION: 867 calories 56g total fats 40g protein

313. CInnamon CrunCH bagel

PREPARATION TIME: 20'

SERVINGS: 12

COOKING TIME: 30'

INGREDIENTS

For Dough:
- 2 teaspoon active dry yeast
- 1 ½ cups warm water
- 3 teaspoon cinnamon
- ¼ cup brown sugar, divided use
- 5 cups flour
- 1 ½ teaspoon salt

For Topping:
- 3 teaspoon cinnamon
- ¼ cup brown sugar
- ¼ cup sugar

DIRECTIONS

1. Combine yeast together with 3 tablespoons of brown sugar and water in the bowl of a stand mixer. Mix well & let sit until foamy for 10 minutes.
2. Add 2 cups of flour, cinnamon, and salt. Whisk well or stir with a spoon until combined well. Attach the dough hook & slowly add the flour; knead for 8 to 10 minutes until the dough comes away from the sides of the bowl.
3. Let rise for 30 to 45 minutes in a greased bowl, in a warm oven, covered.
4. Turn the dough out onto a floured counter. Evenly divide into 12 pieces & roll into balls. Poke your thumb through the center and stretch the hole a little bit to shape it like a bagel. Let sit for 10 minutes.
5. Bring a pot filled with water to a boil over high heat. Add the leftover brown sugar; work in batches and boil the bagels for 40 to 45 seconds per side. Pat dry with paper towels & arrange them 2" apart on a lined cookie sheet.
6. Combine the entire topping ingredients together & sprinkle the mixture on top of the bagels. Bake until turn golden, for 15 to 20 minutes, at 400 F. Let cool & store for 3 to 5 days at room temperature.

NUTRITION: 862 calories 53g total fats 39g protein

314. CobblesTone

PREPARATION TIME: 20'

SERVINGS: 15

COOKING TIME: 1 H 20'

INGREDIENTS

- 2 cups all-purpose flour
- 1 ¼ teaspoons salt
- 4 teaspoons baking powder
- 1 cup granulated sugar
- 2 teaspoons vanilla
- 1 ½ teaspoons cinnamon
- 1 cup kefir or 1 cup buttermilk
- 1/3 cup raisins
- 2 eggs
- 1/3 cup oil

For Streusel:
- ¼ cup butter, at room temperature
- ½ cup flour
- ¼ cup brown sugar

For Filling:
- 2 teaspoons pumpkin pie spice
- 4 Granny Smith apples, peeled cored sliced
- 1 tablespoon lemon juice
- 2 tablespoons unsalted butter
- ¼ teaspoon salt
- 3 tablespoons brown sugar

DIRECTIONS

1. Lightly grease a 15 cupcake mold and preheat your oven to 350 F in advance.
2. Now, melt the butter over medium heat in a large saucepan. Add apples together with pumpkin pie spice, brown sugar, lemon juice, and salt to the pan. Give everything a good stir & cook for 8 to 10 minutes until golden & soft.
3. Combine flour together with sugar, cinnamon, baking powder, vanilla, oil, buttermilk, eggs, and salt on medium speed with an electric mixer in a large bowl.
4. Spoon a small amount of dough batter into the bottom of each cupcake mold. Reserve approximately half of the batter.
5. To create a distinct apple layer, evenly divide the apple filling among all molds. Top off with the leftover dough batter; ensure that you fill in the sides.
6. To make the streusel, crumble the brown sugar with butter and flour with fingers. Sprinkle the mixture on top of the muffins.
7. Bake in the preheated oven for 50 minutes. Let cool in the pan for 15 minutes.

NUTRITION: 871 calories 58g total fats 41g protein

315. Cinnamon Crunch SCone

Preparation Time: 25'

Servings: 12'

Cooking Time: 10'

Ingredients

- 2 ½ teaspoons baking powder
- 1/3 cup sugar
- 3 ¼ cups all-purpose flour
- 1 ½ sticks cold butter, cubed (¾ cup)
- 1 cup buttermilk
- 2 tablespoon butter, melted
- ½ teaspoon baking soda
- 2 cups or DIY cinnamon chips or 1 package cinnamon baking chips (10 ounces)
- ½ teaspoon salt

For the Glaze:
- 5 cup powdered sugar
- ½ cup milk
- 1 tablespoon cinnamon
- 1 teaspoon vanilla extract
- pinch of salt

For Cinnamon Chips:
- 2 tablespoon vegetable shortening
- 2/3 cup sugar
- 3 tablespoon cinnamon
- 2 tablespoon light corn syrup

Directions

1. Preheat your oven to 425 F in advance.
2. Combine flour together with sugar, baking soda, baking powder, and salt in a large bowl; mix well. Cut in the butter & blend into the flour mixture using a pastry cutter or a fork until the mixture looks like coarse crumbs. Stir in the buttermilk; mix with the remaining ingredients until everything is just moist. Fold in the cinnamon chips and make sure that they are distributed evenly.
3. Turn to a slightly floured surface & start kneading the dough for 10 to 12 minutes, until the dough is no longer crumbly. Roll the dough into a long rectangle, and the dough is approximately ½" thick & cut into triangles. Place on well sprayed or well-greased baking sheets and then brush the tops with butter. Bake in the preheated oven for 12 to 15 minutes. Once done, place them on a cooling rack and let them cool before dipping into the glaze.
4. For the Glaze: Mix the powdered sugar together with vanilla extract, cinnamon, milk & a pinch of salt until a smooth glaze form. Take the cooled scones and dip into the glaze and place them on the baking sheet again. Repeat these steps until you have successfully covered the scones.
5. For the Chips: Combine sugar together with corn syrup, shortening, and cinnamon in a bowl; give everything a good stir until combined well. Preheat your oven to 200 F. Spread the mixture onto a well-greased parchment paper lined baking sheet into a rectangle that is approximately ¼" thick. Bake until the mixture is hot and melted together for 35 minutes. Let completely cool and then cut into desired pieces using a sharp knife or pizza well. Store in an airtight container until ready to serve.

Nutrition: 851 calories 58g total fats 39g protein

316. broWn beTTy

PREPARATION TIME: 5'

SERVINGS: 8

COOKING TIME: 50'

INGREDIENTS

- 1 cup white sugar
- 8 tablespoons butter
- ½ teaspoon nutmeg
- 2 large eggs, beaten
- 1 cup bread crumbs
- ½ teaspoon cinnamon
- 6 apples or peaches or pears; peeled, cored & chopped
- 1 teaspoon vanilla extract
- ½ cup brown sugar

DIRECTIONS

1. Generously coat a large-size baking dish with butter. Mix fruit with brown sugar and spices. Place the mixture into the prepared baking dish.
2. Whip eggs with vanilla in a small-sized bowl. Combine breadcrumbs with the white sugar using a fork in a separate bowl.
3. Top the fruit with crumb mixture & pour the melted butter on top; thoroughly covering. Bake for 30 to 40 minutes at 350 F.

NUTRITION: 852 calories 55g total fats 34g protein

317. PeCan brald

PREPARATION TIME: 30'

SERVINGS: 4

COOKING TIME: 25'

INGREDIENTS

- 1 package active dry yeast (¼ ounce)
- 3 beaten eggs, large
- 1 cup cold butter, cubed
- ½ cup sugar
- 5 cups all-purpose flour
- 1 cup warm water, divided (110 to 115 F)
- ½ teaspoon salt

For Filling:
- 1 cup packed brown sugar
- 1 cup butter, softened
- 1 tablespoon ground cinnamon
- 1 cup chopped pecans
- **For Glaze:**
- ½ teaspoon vanilla extract
- 1 tablespoon butter, melted
- 1 ½ cups confectioners' sugar
- 1 to 2 tablespoons milk

DIRECTIONS

1. Dissolve yeast in ¼ cup of warm water in a large bowl. Add eggs and leftover water; mix well. Combine flour together with sugar & salt in a separate bowl. Cut in the butter until crumbly. Beat into yeast mixture (ensure that you don't knead). Cover & refrigerate overnight.
2. For filling: Cream butter together with brown sugar in a small bowl. Stir in the cinnamon and pecans; set aside.
3. Turn the dough onto a lightly floured surface; evenly divide into four portions. Roll each into a 12x9" rectangle on a lightly greased baking sheet. Spread the filling lengthwise down the middle third of each rectangle.
4. One each long side, cut ¾" wide strips to the middle to within ½" of the filling. Beginning at one end, fold alternately strips at an angle across filling. Pinch ends to seal and tuck under. Cover & let rise for an hour in a warm place.
5. Bake until golden brown, for 18 to 20 minutes at 350 F. Before removing them from the pans to wire racks; let them slightly cool. Combine the entire glaze ingredients & drizzle the mixture on top of the cooled braids.

NUTRITION: 836 calories 59g total fats 36.9g protein

Conclusion

Creativity often happens when you cook at home, and you can attach a range of plant foods to a variety of colors. You are not only acquiring kilograms, antioxidants, minerals, and phytonutrients but also introducing nice textures and colors to your meals. You would be shocked by how much food in a single dish is collected.

Portion control from home can be regulated. When food is cooked for us, we tend to eat all or most of it. Try to use little dishes at home, but ensure that all good things like vegetables, fruits, whole grains, and legumes are filled. You are certainly going to be satisfied and happy.

The major advantage of trying copycat restaurant recipes is that you can save more money and use your creativity to improve the dish. You can also adjust the ingredients and add those favorite herbs to your desired taste.

You may not include some ingredients of your favorite dish when you try the copycat recipes, and it is okay. Following the recipe while recreating your favorite dish is what we are here for.

It is not hard to acquire those top-secret restaurant-quality recipes. Others may advise that you need to have culinary credentials to cook those secret recipes.

But do top secret restaurant recipes taste the way the chef served them? Perhaps. You can easily cook your favorite recipes with a little practice and patience. You would want to cook the basic formula and start adding what you think would make the recipe's flavor better after a while. You may start to think that some recipes need additional seasonings to improve your dish than the original. Nevertheless, if you wanted to prepare this dish on your own, there is still a chance.

These tricks may not seem so strong on their own but can transform how you prepare and produce food when they are all used together. These tips help you cook at home like a pro from expected spices and how you use salt to arrange it before you start cooking.

When preparing desserts at home, you can tweak the recipes as you wish. As you sample the recipes, you will know the usual ingredients and techniques in making popular sweet treats. It could inspire you to create your very own recipes. You can substitute ingredients as your taste, health, or pocket dictates. You can come up, perhaps, not with a dessert that is the perfect clone of a restaurant's recipe, but with one that is exactly the way you want it to be. Most of all, the recipes here are meant for you to experience the fulfillment of seeing the smiles on the people with whom you share your creations. Keep trying and having fun with the recipes, and you will soon be reaping your sweet rewards!

If prepared food arrives outside the home, you typically have limited knowledge about salt, sugar, and processed oils. For a fact, we also apply more to our meal when it is served to the table. You will say how much salt, sugar, and oil are being used to prepare meals at home.

Copycat recipes practically give you the ability to make great restaurant food tasting in your own home and get it the right first time and easily.

COPYCAT

RECIPES

The complete cookbook with Simple and Delicious Ideas for Beginners

William Oliver Thomas

Introduction

Are you always looking forward to making delicious foods from breakfast to dinner? Copycat recipes practically give you the ability to make great restaurant food tasting in your own home and get it the right first time and easily. Make delicious copies of the food that you always love from the restaurant's menu when dining with your family and friends.

The copycat recipes are so popular today that they are being written by several people all around the world with great content and of a high standard. Most people around the world love to eat delicious foods in a restaurant, and they hope that they will find the same recipes being served at home.

Nowadays, most people are making copycat recipes in their home when they are preparing food for their family and friends. When you are using the copycat recipe, there are a few steps that should be modified with the recipes that have already been written before.

It is important to follow the steps that have already been written before with the copycat recipe. It is essential to read the steps which have already been written before and mix the ingredients in the right proportion. Some people always feel that they will follow extra steps and modify the copycat recipe, but you should be careful when you are modifying the copycat recipe to make amazing delicious dishes at home. An individual must follow the steps correctly, and following the correct steps will make it easy for the individuals to get the recipe and make the delicious dishes in their homes. The following tips will help you to make the copycat recipes in your home with the utmost taste and enjoyment.

Get all the ingredients required for the recipe and make sure you have followed the proper quantity. You should ensure that you have the right items for your recipe and they are present in the required amount. If you are baking a cake and you are using batter, you should make sure that you have all the ingredients that you are required, and they are present in the required amount. This book has the most excellent copycat recipes from different restaurants around the world.

Chapter 1

SIDE SALAD RECIPES

1. Eggplant Parmesan

<table>
<tr><td>PREPARATION TIME:</td><td>2 h 15'</td><td>SERVINGS:</td><td>2-4</td></tr>
<tr><td>COOKING TIME:</td><td>10'</td><td></td><td></td></tr>
</table>

INGREDIENTS

- 1 medium Italian eggplant, peeled and cut into ½-inch slices
- 2 teaspoons kosher salt
- ½ cup all-purpose flour
- 1 cup eggs, beaten
- 2 cups Italian breadcrumbs
- ½ cup vegetable oil
- ¾ cup marinara sauce
- ¼ cup basil-infused olive oil
- 3 tablespoons Parmesan cheese, grated, divided
- 4 ounces mozzarella cheese, grated
- 1/8 teaspoon kosher salt
- 5 ounces angel hair pasta, cooked
- ½ teaspoon parsley, chopped

DIRECTIONS

1. Preheat the oven to broil. Line a baking sheet with paper towels. Season both sides of the eggplant circles with salt and arrange them on the pan. Cover the eggplant with another sheet of paper towel and refrigerate for 2 hours.
2. Place the flour in one bowl, the eggs in another, and the breadcrumbs in a third bowl.
3. After 2 hours, remove the eggplant from the fridge and dry the slices with a fresh paper towel. One at a time, dip the slices in flour, then in the egg, and finally in the breadcrumbs. Set them aside.
4. Cook the oil in a large skillet over medium heat. Fry the eggplant for about 2 minutes on each side and set them on a plate lined with a paper towel.
5. Cook the marinara sauce in a small saucepan and the basil oil in another small pan.
6. Place a wire rack in a baking dish and transfer the cooked eggplant slices to the rack. Sprinkle on 2 tablespoons of the Parmesan cheese and the mozzarella, then put the pan under the broiler until the cheese melts.
7. Serve the cooked pasta topped with eggplant. Pour some marinara over the top. Drizzle basil oil and sprinkle with the remaining Parmesan cheese and parsley.

NUTRITION: 230 Calories 14g Total Fat 17.1g Carbs 8g Protein

2. lasagna frITTa

PREPARATION TIME: 20'

SERVINGS: 14

COOKING TIME: 4'

INGREDIENTS

- 2/3 + ¼ cup milk (divided)
- 1 cup grated parmesan cheese, plus some more for serving
- ¾ cup feta cheese
- ¼ teaspoon white pepper
- 1 tablespoon butter
- 7 lasagna noodles
- 1 egg
- Breadcrumbs
- Oil for frying
- 2 tablespoons marinara sauce
- Alfredo sauce, for serving

DIRECTIONS

1. Place the butter, white pepper, ⅓ cup milk, parmesan, and feta cheese in a pot. Stir and boil. Make lasagna noodles as stated on the package.
2. Spread a thin layer of the cheese and milk mixture on each noodle. Fold into 2-inch pieces and place something heavy on top to keep them folded. Place in the freezer for at least 1 hour, then cut each noodle in half lengthwise.
3. In a small bowl, mix the ¼ cup milk and egg together. In another bowl, place breadcrumbs. Dip each piece into the egg wash, then the breadcrumbs. Fry the noodles at 350°F for 4 minutes.
4. Serve by spreading some alfredo sauce at the bottom of the plate, placing the lasagna on top, and then drizzling with marinara sauce. Sprinkle the grated parmesan cheese

NUTRITION: 1070 Calories 71g Total Fat 73g Carbs 35g Protein

3. fried Mozzarella

| PREPARATION TIME: | 10' | SERVINGS: | 4 |

COOKING TIME: 10'

INGREDIENTS

- 1-pound mozzarella or other cheese
- 2 eggs, beaten
- ¼ cup water
- 1½ cups Italian breadcrumbs
- ½ teaspoons garlic salt
- 1 teaspoon Italian seasoning
- 2/3 cup flour
- 1/3 cup cornstarch

DIRECTIONS

1. Slice thick cuts of the cheese. Blend together eggs and water for egg wash. Combine the breadcrumbs, garlic salt, and Italian seasoning. In another bowl, combine together flour and cornstarch.
2. Cook vegetable oil in a frying pan. Soak each piece of cheese into the flour, then egg wash, then breadcrumbs. Deep fry until golden brown. Set aside and drain on a paper towel. Serve with marinara sauce.

NUTRITION: 100.8 Calories 5.7g Total Fat 7g Carbs 4g Protein

4. Gnocchi with Spicy Tomato and Wine Sauce

PREPARATION TIME: 10'

SERVINGS: 4

COOKING TIME: 40'

INGREDIENTS

Sauce
- 2 tablespoons extra virgin olive oil
- 6 fresh garlic cloves
- ½ teaspoon chili flakes
- 1 cup dry white wine
- 1 cup chicken broth
- 2 cans (14.5 ounces each) tomatoes
- ¼ cup fresh basil, chopped
- ¼ cup sweet creamy butter, cut into 1-inch cubes, chilled
- ½ cup parmesan cheese, freshly grated

Pasta
- 1-pound gnocchi
- Salt, to taste
- Black pepper, freshly crushed, to taste

DIRECTIONS

1. Sauté the olive oil, garlic, and chili flakes in a cold pan over medium heat. When the garlic starts turning golden brown, stir in the wine and broth and let it simmer.
2. When the broth simmers down. Mix in the tomatoes and basil and then continue simmering for another 30 minutes. Once thickened, let it rest for 3 minutes.
3. After a few minutes, transfer the sauce in a blender, and stir in the butter and parmesan. Purée and set aside. Make the pasta by boiling the gnocchi in a large pot. When it is cooked, drain the pasta and blend the sauce. Serve.

NUTRITION: 320.7 Calories 22.5g Total Fat 11.6g Carbs 12.8g Protein

5. brussels SProuT n' Kale Salad

PREPARATION TIME:	5'		SERVINGS:	4-6

COOKING TIME:	1

INGREDIENTS

- 1 bunch kale
- 1-pound Brussels sprouts
- ¼ cup craisins (or dry cranberries)
- ½ cup pecans, chopped
- Maple vinaigrette
- ½ cup olive oil
- ¼ cup apple cider vinegar
- ¼ cup maple syrup
- 1 teaspoon dry mustard

DIRECTIONS

1. Cut the kale and brussels sprouts with a mandolin slicer. Transfer to a salad bowl. Add the pecans to a skillet on high heat. Toast for 60 seconds, then transfer to the salad bowl.
2. Add the craisins. Mix all the ingredients for the vinaigrette and whisk to combine. Dash the vinaigrette over the salad and toss. Refrigerate for a few hours or preferably overnight before serving.

NUTRITION: 37.8 Calories 0.26g Total Fat 7.88g Carbs 2.97g Protein 1g Fiber

6. breaded fried Okra

PREPARATION TIME: 15'

SERVINGS: 4

COOKING TIME: 10'

INGREDIENTS

- 1-pound fresh okra, rinsed and dried
- 1 cup self-rising cornmeal
- ½ cup self-rising flour
- 1 teaspoon salt
- 1 cup vegetable oil (for frying)
- Salt and pepper to taste

DIRECTIONS

1. Cook the oil in a large skillet or deep fryer. Cut the okra into ½-inch pieces. Combine the cornmeal, flour, and salt in a large bowl. Drop the okra pieces into the bowl and toss to coat. Allow to rest for a few minutes while the oil heats up.
2. Using a slotted spoon, transfer the okra from the bowl into the hot oil. Cook for about 10 minutes or until the okra has turned a nice golden color.
3. Remove from oil and place on a plate lined with paper towels to drain. Season to taste with salt and pepper.

NUTRITION: 18 Calories 3.6g Carbs 1g Protein 2g Fiber

7. Olive Garden Salad

PREPARATION TIME: 15'

SERVINGS: 4

COOKING TIME: 0'

INGREDIENTS

- ¼ cup extra-virgin olive oil
- 2 tablespoons white wine vinegar
- 3 tablespoons Miracle Whip
- 1 tablespoon fresh lemon juice
- 2 tablespoons grated parmesan cheese
- ¼ teaspoon garlic salt
- ½ teaspoon dried Italian seasoning
- 1 (10-oz.) bag American salad blend
- ¼ red onion, thinly sliced
- 4 small pepperoncini or other pickled peppers
- 1 small vine-ripened tomato, cut into wedges
- 2 tablespoons sliced black olives
- 1 tablespoon grated parmesan cheese

DIRECTIONS

1. At first, prepare the salad dressing in a blender. Add olive oil, lemon juice, Miracle Whip, garlic salt, parmesan, water, and Italian seasoning.
2. Hit the pulse button and blend the dressing until all the ingredients are well combined. Pour the dressing into a sealable jar and cover the lid.
3. Place this dressing in the refrigerator for about 1 hour. Meanwhile, prepare the salad in a salad bowl.
4. Prepare the veggies, chop the red onion, cut the tomatoes, slice the cheese, and pepperoncini, one by one on the cutting board. Add red onion, tomato, cheese, olives, and pepperoncini to the salad bowl.
5. Toss them gently with a spatula, then slowly pour in the prepared dressing while leaving half of the dressing for serving.
6. Give the salad a stir, and mix well to coat the veggies. Transfer the salad to the serving plates. Pour the reserved dressing over the salad. Garnish as desired and serve.

NUTRITION: 153 Calories 8.9g Total Fat 17g Carbs 2.9g Protein 3.5g Fiber

8. Esperanza House Salad

PREPARATION TIME:	20'	SERVINGS:	4

COOKING TIME: 0'

INGREDIENTS

- 8 cups torn lettuce/ greens - 2 cups red cabbage, shredded
- ½ cup carrots, shredded - ½ cup red onions, shredded
- ½ cup green peppers, shredded
- ½ cup mushrooms, sliced
- ½ cup mozzarella cheese, shredded
- ½ cup black olives, shredded
- ½ cup tomatoes, cubed
- ½ cup ham, cubed
- ½ cup sprouts

Esperanza Dressing
- 1 egg yolk - 1/3 cup white vinegar
- 2 tablespoons water
- 1 tablespoon Dijon mustard
- 1 teaspoon Worcestershire sauce
- 1 tablespoon dried onion flakes
- 1 teaspoon granulated garlic
- 1 teaspoon oregano
- ¾ teaspoon salt
- ¼ teaspoon black pepper
- 1 ½ cups soybean oil
- 2 tablespoons minced fresh parsley

DIRECTIONS

1. Prepare the Esperanza dressing for the salad in a small bowl.
2. Beat the egg yolk in a bowl with an electric mixer until the egg yolk turns pale in color.
3. Add vinegar, salt, black pepper, parsley, soybean oil, oregano, water, garlic, onion flakes, Dijon mustard, and Worcestershire sauce.
4. Whisk this mixture well and cover this salad dressing Transfer the salad dressing to the refrigerator Leave this dressing in the refrigerator until the salad is ready to serve.
5. Now prepare the salad ingredients and place the lettuce leaves on the cutting board.
6. Cut the lettuce leaves into thin slices and keep them aside in the salad bowl Now shred the cabbage on the cutting board and transfer to the salad bowl. Similarly, shred and chop all other vegetables, ham, and mushroom, then add them to the bowl.
7. Add ½ of the prepared dressing to the salad and preserve the other half in the refrigerator. Toss the vegetables well and garnish with olives. Serve fresh.

NUTRITION: 250 Calories 16g Total Fat 11g Carbs 12.1g Protein

9. SPInaCH aPPle Salad

| PREPARATION TIME: | 10' | SERVINGS: | 4 |

| COOKING TIME: | 0 |

INGREDIENTS

- 6 cups fresh spinach leaves
- ½ cup dried cranberries
- ½ cup feta cheese, crumbled
- ½ cup red apple, chopped
- 1/3 cup honey almonds
- Honey Poppy Seed Dressing
- 2/3 cup vegetable oil
- ½ cup honey
- 4 tablespoons apple cider vinegar
- 1 ½ tablespoons poppy seeds

DIRECTIONS

1. Prepare the honey poppy seed dressing for the salad in a small bowl Beat honey with vegetable oil in a bowl with a hand mixer Add apple cider vinegar to the honey mixture then add poppy seeds to the honey mixture
2. Whisk this mixture well and cover this salad dressing Transfer the salad dressing to the refrigerator Leave this dressing in the refrigerator until the salad is ready to serve
3. Now prepare the salad ingredients and place the spinach leaves on the cutting board
4. Cut the fresh spinach leaves into small pieces and keep them aside in the salad bowl
5. Now place the apples on the cutting board and core the apples
6. Cut the apples into small cubes then transfer to the salad bowl. Add ¼ of the prepared dressing to the salad Toss in olives and mix well. Serve fresh.

NUTRITION: 161.1 Calories 13.3g Total Fat 9.6g Carbs 4.1g Protein

10.anyTHIng and EveryTHIng Salad

PREPARATION TIME: 20′	SERVINGS: 4

COOKING TIME: 2H 10′

INGREDIENTS

- 6 eggs, beaten
- 1/3 cup sugar
- 1/3 cup apple cider vinegar
- 1 teaspoon salt, or to taste
- 4 cups of elbow macaroni, cooked
- 3 large hard-boiled eggs, peeled and diced
- 1 ¼ cup of ham, cooked
- 1 cup (4 oz.) of diced cheese, melted
- 2 celery chops, sliced thinly
- 1 medium onion, chopped
- ¾ cup sweet pickle sauce
- ¾ cup of olives stuffed with pepper
- 1/3 cup mayonnaise

DIRECTIONS

1. In a saucepan, mix eggs, beaten, sugar, vinegar, and salt cook and stir over low heat for approximately 10 minutes until the egg mixture thickens and a thermometer indicates 160° F.
2. Allow cooling completely, stirring several times. In a bowl, mix the pasta, boiled eggs, ham, cheese, celery, onion, pickle sauce, and olives. Mix the mayonnaise in the cooled egg mixture.
3. Pour over the pasta mixture. Stir to coat-cover and cool in a refrigerator for at least 2 hours.

NUTRITION: 680 Calories 39g Total Fat 17g Carbs 68g Protein 3g Fiber

11. Chili'sSalad

Preparation Time: 25'

Servings: 4

Cooking Time: 15'

Ingredients

For Pico De Gallo:
- 2 teaspoon seeded jalapeno peppers, finely diced
- ½ cup red onion finely minced
- 2 medium tomatoes diced very small
- 2 teaspoon cilantro, fresh & finely minced

For Salad:
- 4 chicken breasts skinless, boneless
- 5 ounces bag half-and-half spring mix with baby spinach
- ½ cup red cabbage chopped
- ounces bag butter bliss lettuce or romaine or iceberg lettuce
- ¾ cup raisins
- 1 cup fresh pineapple chunked
- ¼ cup teriyaki sauce
- 14 ounces can mandarin orange segments drained
- Tortilla strips
- ¼ cup water
- For Honey-Lime Dressing:
- 1 cup vanilla Greek yogurt
- ¼ cup Dijon mustard
- 1 tablespoon lime juice, freshly squeezed
- 3 tablespoon apple cider vinegar
- 1 cup honey
- 2 tablespoon sesame oil
- ½ to 1 teaspoon lime zest grated

Directions

For Pico De Gallo:
1. Combine the ingredients for Pico de Gallo together in a small bowl & let chill in a refrigerator until ready to use.

For Salad:
2. Mix the teriyaki sauce with water. Place the chicken pieces in a large-sized plastic bag or plastic bowl. Add in the prepared teriyaki mixture & let marinate for an hour or two in the refrigerator.
3. Layer the lettuce & spring mix in a large serving bowl. Add raisins and cabbage toss well.
4. Refrigerate until all ingredients are ready. After chicken has marinated, lightly coat your grill with the cooking spray and heat it over moderate heat. Remove the chicken pieces from marinade, shaking off any excess.
5. Add to the hot grill & cook until the chicken is cooked through, for 5 to 10 minutes on each side. Slice chicken down into cubes or thin strips. Set aside on the serving plate to serve.
6. For Honey-Lime Dressing:
7. Combine the entire salad dressing ingredients in a blender blend on high until blended well. Refrigerate until ready to serve.

To Assemble the Salad:
8. Remove the salad to four individual large serving plates. Place approximately ¼ cup of the mandarin orange segments & pineapple over each salad.
9. Spread a spoonful or two of Pico de Gallo onto the chicken. Drizzle with salad dressing, give the ingredients a good stir until mixed well.
10. Garnish with the tortilla strips. Serve immediately & enjoy.

Nutrition: 640 Calories 41g Total Fat 44g Carbs 24g Protein 6g Fiber

12. Cracker barrel fried apples

Preparation Time:	10'	Servings:	8

Cooking Time:	20'

Ingredients

- Melt the butter or bacon drippings in a large skillet. Evenly spread the apples at the bottom of the skillet. Sprinkle the lemon juice on top, followed by salt and brown sugar.
- Cover with the lid and cook over low heat for about fifteen minutes, or until the apples are juicy and tender. Sprinkle the nutmeg and cinnamon on top and serve. You may add a squeeze of lemon on top if desired.

Directions

1. Take a medium saucepan, place it over low heat, add butter and erythritol and then cook for 4 to 5 minutes until butter melts and turns golden brown.
2. Stir in cream, bring it to a gentle boil and then simmer the sauce for 10 minutes until the sauce has thickened to coat the back of the spoon, stirring constantly.
3. Remove pan from heat, stir in vanilla extract and then serve.

Nutrition: 78 Calories 15mg Cholestero l7g Carbs

13. Hash broWn Casserole

Preparation Time: 10'

Servings: 10

Cooking Time: 45'

Ingredients

- Nonstick cooking spray
- 2 pounds Hash browns
- 2 cups Shredded Colby cheese or cheddar cheese
- 8 oz Sour cream
- Salt and pepper
- ½ cup Minced onion
- 4 oz Butter
- 10.75 oz Condensed cream of chicken soup

Directions

1. Heat the oven to 350 degrees F. Oil a 9-by-13-inch baking pan. Spread the potatoes into the pan – season with pepper and salt. Add the butter into a microwave-safe dish and microwave until the butter gets melted.

2. Add the sour cream, onions, and sour cream into the bowl and mix thoroughly. Pour the mixture over the potatoes in the pan and sprinkle the cheese on top. Place the pan in the oven to bake for approx. 45 minutes, or until the potatoes are completely warm and the cheese starts to melt.

Nutrition: 321 Calories 8g Protein 19g Carbs 23g Fat

14. CuCumbers, TomaToes, and OnIons

PREPARATION TIME: 10'

SERVINGS: 6

COOKING TIME: 10'

INGREDIENTS

- 2 tbsp Italian dressing
- 3 Cucumbers
- 16 oz Grape tomatoes
- ½ cup Sliced white onion
- ½ cup Sugar
- 1 cup White vinegar

DIRECTIONS

1. Slice the three cucumbers into ¼-inch thin slices. Mix the Italian dressing, sugar, and vinegar in a bowl, then add the sliced onions, tomatoes, and sliced cucumbers.
2. Cover with a foil or a lid and set aside for approx. one hour for the vegetable to marinate before you serve.

NUTRITION: 120 Calories 1g Protein 24g Carbs 1g Fat

15. Old CounTry STore baby CarroTs

PREPARATION TIME: 10'

SERVINGS: 8

COOKING TIME: 45'

INGREDIENTS

- 2 lbs. Fresh baby carrots
- 1 tbsp Brown sugar
- 2 tbsp Margarine
- 1 pinch Ground nutmeg
- 1 tsp Salt

DIRECTIONS

1. Rinse the carrots and place them in a 2-quart saucepan. Add water to the pot, enough to cover the carrots. Place the lid on the pan and bring to a boil over medium heat.
2. Reduce the heat to low and simmer for about 30 to 45 minutes, or until the carrots are tender when pricked with a fork.
3. Discard half of the water in the saucepan, then add salt, sugar, and margarine into the pan. Replace the lid on the pan and cook until soft but not mushy. Add more salt if needed. Add the ground nutmeg for a little flair, if desired.

NUTRITION: 71 Calories 10g Carbs 3g Fat

16. House Salad and dressing

PREPARATION TIME: 10'

SERVINGS: 12

COOKING TIME: 0'

INGREDIENTS

- Salad
- 1 head iceberg lettuce
- ¼ small red onion, sliced thin
- 6–12 black olives, pitted
- 6 pepperoncini
- 2 small roma tomatoes, sliced
- Croutons
- ¼ cup shredded or grated Romano or parmesan cheese Dressing
- 1 packet Italian dressing mix
- ¾ cup vegetable/canola oil
- ¼ cup olive oil
- 1 tablespoon mayonnaise
- 1/3 cup white vinegar
- ¼ cup water
- ½ teaspoon sugar
- ½ teaspoon dried Italian seasoning
- ½ teaspoon salt
- ¼ teaspoon pepper
- ¼ teaspoon garlic powder

DIRECTIONS

1. To make the dressing, combine all ingredients in a small bowl. Thoroughly whisk together. Refrigerate for 1 hour to marinate. Add the salad ingredient to a salad bowl. When ready to serve, add some of the dressing to the salad and toss to coat. Add grated cheese as a garnish as desired. Store remaining dressing in an airtight container. Keep refrigerated, and it can be stored for up to 3 weeks.

NUTRITION: 435 Calories 54.8g Fat 46.4g Carbs 13.9g Protein

17. SanTa fe CrisPers Salad

<table>
<tr><td>PREPARATION TIME:</td><td>10'</td><td>SERVINGS:</td><td>4</td></tr>
<tr><td>COOKING TIME:</td><td>30'</td><td></td><td></td></tr>
</table>

INGREDIENTS

- ½ pounds boneless skinless chicken breasts
- 1 tablespoon fresh cilantro, chopped
- ¾ cup Lawry's Santa Fe Chili Marinated with Lime and Garlic, divided 1 package (10 ounces) torn romaine lettuce, approximately 8 cups
- 2 tablespoons milk
- 1 cup black beans, drained and rinsed
- ½ cup sour cream
- 1 cup drained canned whole kernel corn
- ¼ cup red onion, chopped
- 1 medium avocado, cut into chunks
- ½ cup Monterey Jack, shredded
- 1 medium tomato, cut into chunks

DIRECTIONS

1. Place chicken in a large glass dish or re-sealable marinade plastic bag. Add approximately ½ cup of the Santa Fe marinade, turn several times until nicely coated
2. Refrigerate for 30 minutes or longer.
3. Removed the chicken from marinade; get rid of the leftover marinade. Grill the chicken until cooked through, for 6 to 7 minutes per side, over medium heat; brush with 2 tablespoons of the leftover marinade. Cut the chicken into thin slices.
4. Combine the sour cream together with milk, leftover marinade, and cilantro with wire whisk in a medium-sized bowl until smooth Arrange lettuce on large serving platter.
5. Top with the chicken, avocado, corn, beans, cheese, tomato, and onion.
6. Serve with tortilla chips and dressing. Enjoy

NUTRITION: 676 Calories 86g Fat 67g Carbs 46g Protein

18. Quesadilla Explosion Salad

PREPARATION TIME:	20'		SERVINGS:	1

COOKING TIME:	20'

INGREDIENTS

- 1 vegetarian chicken patty
- 6 ounces bagged salad mix

For Chipotle Ranch Dressing:
- 1 cup 2% milk
- 1 packet ranch dressing mix
- 1 teaspoon chipotle peppers in adobo sauce
- 1 cup non-fat Greek yogurt

For Citrus Balsamic Vinaigrette
- 2 tablespoon balsamic vinegar
- ½ teaspoon orange zest
- 2 tablespoon Splenda
- ¼ cup orange juice
- A pinch of nutmeg
- For Sweet Potato Strips:
- ¼ medium sweet potato, washed, thinly sliced & cut into strips nonstick cooking spray
- ¼ teaspoon salt

For Cheese Quesadilla:
- 1 mission carb balance whole wheat fajita sized tortilla 1 ounce reduced-fat Colby Jack cheese, shredded

For Roasted Corn and Black Bean Salsa:
- 1 cup black beans, rinsed
- 2 ears of corn, roasted, kernels removed from cob ½ cup fresh cilantro, chopped
- 1 tablespoon lime juice, freshly squeezed
- ¼ red onion, chopped
- 1 jalapeno pepper, roasted, peeled, seeded, de-veined & chopped Salt to taste
- 1 red bell pepper, medium, roasted, peeled, seeded & chopped

DIRECTIONS

For Sweet Potato Strips:
1. Preheat oven to 350 F. Lightly coat the strips with nonstick cooking spray and then dust them lightly with the salt. Place on a large-sized cookie sheet in a single layer & bake for 15 to 20 minutes. Don't forget to stir the strips & turn halfway during the baking process.
2. Set aside and let cool until ready to use.

For Roasted Corn Salsa:
3. Add corn together with peppers & black beans to a large bowl and then squeeze the lime juice on top; add salt to taste. Give the ingredients a good stir & add the fresh cilantro.

For Chipotle Ranch Dressing:
4. Add yogurt and milk to the ranch dressing mix. Stir in the chipotle & store in a refrigerator.
5. For Citrus Balsamic Vinaigrette:
6. Over low heat in a large saucepan; place the entire ingredients together & cook for a minute. Set aside and let cool, then refrigerate.

For Quesadilla:
7. Place the cheese on half of the tortilla & then fold over.
8. Lightly coat the tortilla with the nonstick cooking spray & then cook over medium-high heat in a large pan. Cook until the cheese is completely melted, for a minute per side. Cut into 4 wedges.
9. Prepare the veggie "chicken" patty as per the Directions mentioned on the package & then slice into thin strips.
10. Place approximately 6 ounces of the salad mix on the plate and then top with the "chicken" strips, black bean salsa, sweet potato strips & roasted corn.
11. Place the cut quesadilla around the edge of the plate and then drizzle the salad with the prepared dressings.

NUTRITION: 245 Calories 59.8g Fat 67.3g Carbs 12.8g Protein

19. Caribbean Shrimp Salad

INGREDIENTS

- 8 cups baby spinach, fresh
- ¼ cup lime juice, freshly squeezed
- 2 tablespoons chili garlic sauce
- ½ teaspoon paprika
- 4 cups cooked shrimp
- 5 tablespoons seasoned rice vinegar, divided
- ½ teaspoon ground cumin
- 1 cup peeled mango, chopped
- ½ cup green onions, thinly sliced
- 2 garlic cloves, minced
- 1 cup radishes, julienne-cut
- ¼ cup peeled avocado, diced
- 2 tablespoons pumpkinseed kernels, unsalted 1 ½ tablespoons olive oil
- Dash of salt

DIRECTIONS

1. In a large bowl; combine the cooked shrimp together with chili garlic sauce
2. & 2 tablespoons of vinegar; toss well. Cover & let chill for an hour.
3. Now, in a small bowl, combine the leftover vinegar together with garlic cloves, oil, lime juice, lime rind, ground cumin, paprika & salt, stirring well with a whisk.
4. Place 2 cups of spinach on each of 4 plates; top each serving with a cup of the prepared shrimp mixture. Arrange ¼ cup radishes, ¼ cup mango & 1 tablespoon of the avocado around the shrimp on each plate. Top each serving with approximately 1 ½ teaspoons of pumpkinseed kernels & 2 tablespoons of green onions. Drizzle each salad with approximately 2 tablespoons of the vinaigrette. Serve and enjoy.

NUTRITION: 124 Calories 76.9g Fat 67.9g Carbs 45.8g Protein

20. SouTHWesT Caesar Salad

PREPARATION TIME:	10'	SERVINGS:	6

COOKING TIME:	20'

INGREDIENTS

- 2 tablespoons mayonnaise
- ¼ teaspoon cayenne or ground red pepper
- 6 cups fresh romaine lettuce, washed
- 1/3 cup parmesan cheese, grated
- 1 cup croutons
- ½ of a red bell pepper, cut into thin strips
- 1 cup whole kernel corn, frozen & thawed
- ½ cup fresh cilantro, chopped
- 2 tablespoons green onion, chopped
- ¼ cup olive oil
- 2 tablespoon lime juice, freshly squeezed
- 1/8 teaspoon salt

DIRECTIONS

1. Place onions together with mayo, ground red pepper, lime juice, and salt in a blender or food processor; cover & process until blended well. Slowly add the oil at the top using the feed tube & continue to process after each addition until blended well.
2. Toss the lettuce with the corn, croutons, bell peppers, cheese, and cilantro in a large bowl.
3. Add the mayo mixture; evenly toss until nicely coated. Serve immediately & enjoy.

NUTRITION: 265 Calories 62g Fat 98g Carbs 47g Protein

21. red beans from PoPeye's

| PREPARATION TIME: | 20' | | SERVINGS: | 10 |

| COOKING TIME: | 40' |

INGREDIENTS

- 3 14-ounce cans red beans
- ¾ pounds smoked ham hock
- 1¼ cups water
- ½ teaspoon onion powder
- ½ teaspoon garlic salt
- ¼ teaspoon red pepper flakes
- ½ teaspoon salt
- 3 tablespoons lard
- Steamed long-grain rice

DIRECTIONS

1. Add 2 canned red beans, ham hock, and water to the pot. Cook on medium heat and let simmer for about 1 hour.
2. Remove from heat and wait until the meat is cool enough to handle. Then remove meat from the bone.
3. In a food processor, add meat, cooked red beans and water mixture, onion powder, garlic salt, red pepper, salt, and lard. Pulse for 4 seconds. You want the beans to be cut, and the liquid thickened. Drain the remaining 1 can red beans and add to the food processor. Pulse for only 1 or 2 seconds.
4. Remove ingredients from the food processor and transfer to the pot from earlier.
5. Cook on low heat, stirring frequently until mixture is heated through. Serve over steamed rice.

NUTRITION: 445 Calories 12g Fat 67g Carbs 9g Fibers

22. Café Rio's Sweet Pork Barbacoa Salad

PREPARATION TIME: 10'

SERVINGS: 8

COOKING TIME: 8'

INGREDIENTS

- 3 pounds pork loin
- Garlic salt, to taste
- 1 can root beer
- ¼ cup water
- ¾ cup brown sugar
- 1 10-ounce can red enchilada sauce
- 1 4-ounce can green chilies
- ½ teaspoon chili powder
- 8 large burrito size tortillas
- 1½ serving Cilantro Lime Rice
- 1 can black beans, drained and heated
- 2 heads Romaine lettuce, shredded
- 1½ cups tortilla strips
- 1 cup Queso Fresco cheese
- 2 limes, cut in wedges
- ¼ cup cilantro

Dressing:
- ½ packet Hidden Valley Ranch Dressing Mix 1 cup mayonnaise
- ½ cup milk
- ½ cup cilantro leaves
- ¼ cup salsa Verde
- ½ jalapeno pepper, deseeded
- 1 plump clove garlic
- 2 tablespoons fresh lime juice

DIRECTIONS

1. Sprinkle garlic salt on pork. Put in the slow cooker with the flat side facing down.
2. Add ¼ cup root beer and water. Cover and cook on low setting for 6 hours.
3. To prepare sauce, add the rest of the root beer, brown sugar, enchilada sauce, green chilies, and chili powder in a blender. Blend until smooth.
4. Remove meat from slow cooker then transfer onto the cutting board. Shred, discarding juices and fat. Return shredded pork to slow cooker with the sauce.
5. Cook on low setting for another 2 hours. When there is only about 15 to 20
6. minutes left to cook, remove the lid to thicken the sauce.
7. To prepare the dressing, mix all dressing ingredients in a blender. Puree until smooth. Then, transfer to the refrigerator and allow to chill for at least 1 hour.
8. To assemble the salad, layer tortilla, rice, beans, pork, lettuce, tortilla strips, cheese, and dressing in a bowl. Serve with a lime wedge and cilantro leaves.

NUTRITION: 756 Calories 28g Fat 91g Carbs 7g Fibers

23.almond CrusTed Salmon Salad

PREPARATION TIME: 15'

SERVINGS: 4

COOKING TIME: 30'

INGREDIENTS

- ¼ cup olive oil
- 4 (4 -ounce) portions salmon
- ½ teaspoon kosher salt
- 1/8 teaspoon ground black pepper
- 2 tablespoons garlic aioli (bottled is fine)
- ½ cup chopped and ground almonds for crust
- 10 ounces kale, chopped
- ¼ cup lemon dressing of choice
- 2 avocados, peeled, pitted, and cut into ½-inch pieces 2 cups cooked quinoa
- 1 cup brussels sprouts, sliced
- 2 ounces arugula
- ½ cup dried cranberries
- 1 cup balsamic vinaigrette
- 24 thin radish slices
- Lemon zest

DIRECTIONS

1. In a large skillet, heat the olive oil over medium-high heat. Sprinkle the salmon with salt and pepper to season. When the skillet is hot, add the fish fillets and cook for about 3 minutes on each side or until it flakes easily with a fork. Top the salmon with garlic aioli and sprinkle with nuts.
2. Meanwhile, combine all the salad ingredients, including the quinoa, in a bowl, and toss with the dressing.
3. Serve the salad with a fish fillet on top of greens and sprinkle with radishes and lemon zest.

NUTRITION: 243 Calories 45g Fat 23g Carbs 52g Protein

24. deeP frIed PICkles from Texas roadHouse

PREPARATION TIME: 10'	SERVINGS: 4

COOKING TIME: 10'

INGREDIENTS

- Vegetable oil, for deep frying
- ¼ cup flour
- 1¼ teaspoons Cajun seasoning, divided
- ¼ teaspoon oregano
- ¼ teaspoon basil
- 1/8 teaspoon cayenne pepper
- Kosher salt
- 2 cups dill pickles, drained and sliced
- ¼ cup mayonnaise
- 1 tablespoon horseradish
- 1 tablespoon ketchup

DIRECTIONS

1. Preheat about 1½ inches oil to 375°F in a large pot.
2. In a separate bowl, make the coating by combining flour, 1 teaspoon Cajun seasoning, oregano, basil, cayenne pepper, and Kosher salt.
3. Dredge pickle slices in flour mixture. Lightly shake to remove any excess, then carefully lower into the hot oil. Work in batches so as not to overcrowd the pot. Deep fry for about 2 minutes or until lightly brown.
4. Using a slotted spoon, transfer pickles to a plate lined with paper towels to drain.
5. While pickles drain and cool, add mayonnaise, horseradish, ketchup, and remaining Cajun seasoning in a bowl. Mix well. Serve immediately with dip on the side.

NUTRITION: 296 Calories 28g Total fat 12g Carbs 1g Protein

25. Chili's Chili

Preparation Time:	10'		Servings:	8

Cooking Time:	1 h 10'

Ingredients

For Chili:
- 4 pounds ground chuck - ground for chili
- 1 ½ cups yellow onions, chopped
- 16 ounces tomato sauce
- 1 tablespoon cooking oil
- 3 ¼ plus 1 cups water
- 1 tablespoon masa harina

For Chili Spice Blend:
- 1 tablespoon paprika
- ½ cup chili powder
- 1 teaspoon ground black pepper
- 1/8 cup ground cumin
- 1 teaspoon cayenne pepper or to taste
- 1/8 cup salt
- 1 teaspoon garlic powder

Directions

1. Combine the entire chili spice ingredients together in a small bowl; continue to combine until thoroughly mixed.
2. Now, over moderate heat in a 6-quart stock pot; place & cook the meat until browned; drain. In the meantime, combine the chili spice mix together with tomato sauce & 3 ¼ cups of water in the bowl; give the ingredients a good stir until blended well.
3. Add the chili seasoning liquid to the browned meat; give it a good stir & bring the mixture to a boil over moderate heat.
4. Over medium heat in a large skillet; heat 1 tablespoon of the cooking oil & sauté the onions until translucent, for a couple of minutes. Add the sautéed onions to the chili.
5. Decrease the heat to low & let simmer for an hour, stirring after every 10 to 15 minutes. Combine the masa harina with the leftover water in a separate bowl; mix well. Add to the chili stock pot & cook for 10 more minutes

Nutrition: 143 Calories 51g Fat 63.6g Carbs 13.8g Protein

26. Ham Salad

PREPARATION TIME:	5'		SERVINGS:	2-3

	COOKING TIME:	5'

INGREDIENTS

- 3 cups Head of Lettuce, shredded
- 200 g baby spinach
- 1/2 cup Shredded Provolone Cheese
- 6 slices Black Forest Ham, cut into strips
- 1/4 cup pickled jalapeno peppers, sliced
- 1/4 cup Black olives
- 1 whole Tomato, thinly sliced or grape tomatoes 1/3 cup
- 1/4 cup ranch dressing or dressing of your choice

DIRECTIONS

1. Mix and toss all ingredients in a bowl and serve immediately

NUTRITION: 110 Calories 2.5g Fat 5g Fiber 12g Carbs 12g Protein

27. ITallan b.m.T.® Salad

| PREPARATION TIME: | 15' | | SERVINGS: | 2-3 |

| COOKING TIME: | 0' |

INGREDIENTS

- 3 cups Head of Lettuce, shredded
- 200 g baby spinach
- 1/2 cup Shredded Provolone Cheese
- 4 slices Salami Meat, cut into strips
- 4 slices Black Forest Ham, cut into strips
- 6 pieces Pepperoni
- 1/4 cup Black olives
- 1/4 cup Banana Peppers, sliced
- ¼ cup Green Pepper sliced thinly
- 1 whole Tomato
- 1/4 cup any dressing of your choice

DIRECTIONS

1. Mix and toss all ingredients in a bowl and serve immediately!

NUTRITION: 410 Calories 42g Fat 3g Fiber 10g Carbs 12g Protein

28. roasTed CHICken Salad

PREPARATION TIME:	6H OR OVERNIGHT	SERVINGS:	4-5

COOKING TIME:	20-30'

INGREDIENTS

For grilled chicken
- 2 chicken breasts, deboned
- 1 tsp salt
- 1 tbsp Italian seasoning
- 1 tbsp lemon juice
- ½ tsp msg
- ¼ tsp garlic powder
- ½ tsp onion powder
- ½ tsp black pepper

For Dressing
- 1/3 cup plain nonfat yogurt
- 1 teaspoon sugar
- 4 teaspoons lemon juice
- 4 tablespoons light mayonnaise
- Salt and pepper

For assembly
- 3 cups lettuce
- ½ cup diced celery
- 300 g baby spinach
- ½ cup diced cucumber
- 1 cup chopped red apples
- ¼ cup dried cranberries or cherries
- ¼ cup golden raisins or white grapes

DIRECTIONS

1. Prepare the chicken breast for marinating; pound each breast until even in thickness. Combine all ingredients remaining in a bowl and put in chicken breast pieces. Marinate overnight or a minimum of 6 hrs. Once the margination is done, put the chicken breast in a pan and roast in the oven for about 20-30 minutes, brushing it with the excess marinade every now and then. While waiting, prepare the dressing. Mix all ingredients under the dressing in a small bowl and chill for 15 minutes. Slices all the needed toppings and set aside. When the chicken is cooked, cut into cubes or strips.
2. Toss everything in a large bowl and serve immediately.

NUTRITION: 140 Calories 2.5g Fat 4g Fiber 11g Carbs 19g Protein

29. roasT beef Salad

PREPARATION TIME: 5'

SERVINGS: 4-5

COOKING TIME: 10'

INGREDIENTS

- 4 thinly sliced roast beef
- 3 cups lettuce
- ½ cup diced celery
- 300 g baby spinach
- ½ cup diced cucumber
- ¼ cup dried cranberries or cherries
- 1/4 cup Black olives
- 1/4 cup Banana Peppers, sliced
- ¼ cup Green Pepper sliced thinly
- 1 whole Tomato, thinly sliced or grape tomatoes 1/3 cup
- 1/4 cup any dressing of your choice

DIRECTIONS

1. Mix and toss all ingredients in a bowl and serve immediately!

NUTRITION: 150 Calories 3.5g Fat 6g Fiber 14g Carbs 21g Protein

30. STeak & CHeese Salad

PREPARATION TIME:	30-40'	SERVINGS:	3-4

COOKING TIME: 15-20'

INGREDIENTS

- 2 cloves garlic chopped
- 1/8 cup Dijon mustard
- 1/8 cup extra-virgin olive oil
- ¼ cup balsamic vinegar
- ½ tsp. Black pepper
- 1tsp.salt
- 1 1/2 lb. flank steak
- 3 cups Head of Lettuce, shredded
- 200 g baby spinach
- 1/2 cup cheese sauce
- 1/4 cup Black olives
- 1/4 cup jalapeno peppers, sliced
- ¼ cup Green Bell pepper, sliced thinly
- 1 whole Tomato, thinly sliced or grape tomatoes 1/3 cup

DIRECTIONS

1. In a bowl, mix the balsamic vinegar and mustard. Whisk in olive oil and garlic, then season with pepper and salt. Put in steak and marinate for 30 minutes or more. While waiting, prepare other ingredients for assembly of the salad.
2. After marinating, grill the steak according to your preferred doneness and let it rest before slicing. Mix all ingredients in a bowl and top off with cheese sauce.

NUTRITION: 180 Calories 8g Fat 4g Fiber 14g Carbs 17g Protein

31. SubWay Club ® Salad

PREPARATION TIME: 10'

SERVINGS: 3-4

COOKING TIME: 10'

INGREDIENTS

- 2 pcs turkey breast, cut into strips
- 2 pcs lean roast beef, cut into strips
- 2 slices Black Forest ham, cut into strips
- 400g shredded lettuce
- 1/3 cup halved cherry tomatoes
- 1 whole chopped avocado
- 1/3 cup croutons
- 2 pcs hard-boiled eggs, quartered
- ½ cup Cucumber, diced
- For the dressing:
- ¼ cup mayonnaise
- ¼ cup yellow mustard
- 1 tbsp vinegar
- Salt and pepper

DIRECTIONS

1. Make the dressing by mixing all the ingredients in a small bowl. Mix and toss everything in a bowl and serve immediately.

NUTRITION: 140 Calories 3.5g Fat 4g Fiber 12g Carbs 19g Protein

32. SubWay MelT ® Salad

PREPARATION TIME: 5'

SERVINGS: 3-4

COOKING TIME: 10'

INGREDIENTS

- 2 pcs turkey breast, cut into strips
- 4 pcs smoked bacon, cooked until crisp and crumbled
- 2 slices Black Forest ham, cut into strips
- 400g shredded lettuce
- 1/3 cup halved cherry tomatoes
- ¼ cup jalapeno peppers
- 5 pieces black olives, sliced
- 1/3 cup croutons
- 2 pcs hard-boiled eggs, quartered
- ½ cup shredded provolone cheese
- ½ cup Cucumber, diced
- 1/3 cup ranch dressing or any dressing of your choice

DIRECTIONS

1. Mix and toss everything in a bowl and serve immediately.

NUTRITION: 150 Calories 4.1g Fat 4g Fiber 15g Carbs 21g Protein

33. CHicken Teriyaki Salad

PREPARATION TIME:	5'		SERVINGS:	4-5

COOKING TIME: 5'

INGREDIENTS

- 2 boneless, skinless chicken breasts
- ½ cup store-bought teriyaki marinade

For assembly
- 8 slices of cucumber
- 1/4 cup Black olives
- 1/4 cup Banana Peppers, sliced
- ¼ cup Green Pepper sliced thinly
- ½ red onion thinly sliced
- 1 whole Tomato, thinly sliced or grape tomatoes 1/3 cup
- 300g lettuce
- 200 g baby spinach
- Sweet Onion Sauce
- 1 tablespoon red wine vinegar
- 1/3 cup light corn syrup
- 1 tablespoon white vinegar
- 2 tablespoon minced white onion
- 2 teaspoon balsamic vinegar
- ½ tsp garlic powder
- 1/4 teaspoon salt
- 4 teaspoon brown sugar
- ½ teaspoon lemon juice
- 1/8 tsp black pepper
- 1/4 teaspoon poppy seeds

DIRECTIONS

1. Put teriyaki marinade and chicken breast in a bowl and marinate for at least 30 minutes. While the chicken is marinating, prepare the sweet onion sauce by combining everything in a pan and heat them until it boils. Cool down. Slice all vegetables for the salad and set aside. Grill or panfry chicken and brush with marinade once in a while. Once cooked, slice into strips or cubes. Mix and toss everything in a bowl and serve immediately.

NUTRITION: 240 Calories 3g Fat 4g Fiber 35g Carbs 20g Protein

34. Tuna Salad

PREPARATION TIME: 10'

SERVINGS: 4-5

COOKING TIME: 15'

INGREDIENTS

For tuna mixture
- 1 can tuna (drained)
- 4tablespoons mayonnaise
- 2 teaspoon lemon juice
- salt and pepper to taste

For assembly:
- 8 slices of cucumber
- 1/4 cup Black olives
- 1/4 cup Banana Peppers, sliced
- ¼ cup Green Pepper sliced thinly
- ½ red onion thinly sliced
- 1 whole Tomato, thinly sliced or grape tomatoes 1/3 cup
- 300g lettuce
- 200 g baby spinach

DIRECTIONS

1. Mix tuna, mayo, lemon juice, salt and pepper, and chill. While waiting, prepare all remaining ingredients for assembly. Mix and toss everything in a bowl and serve immediately.

NUTRITION: 280 Calories 12g Fat1g Fiber 24g Carbs 10g Protein

35. Turkey Salad

PREPARATION TIME: 5'

SERVINGS: 3-4

COOKING TIME: 0

INGREDIENTS

- 4 slices Smoked Turkey Breast, cut into strips
- 2 pcs American Cheese, shredded
- 5 slices of cucumber
- 1/8 cup Black olives
- ¼ cup Green Pepper sliced thinly
- ¼ red onion thinly sliced
- 1 whole Tomato, thinly sliced or grape tomatoes 1/3 cup
- 300g lettuce
- 200 g baby spinach
- 1/3 cup dressing of your choice

DIRECTIONS

1. Mix and toss everything in a bowl and serve immediately

NUTRITION: 110 Calories 2g Fat 4g Fiber 12g Carbs 12g Protein

Chapter 2

OLD AND MODERN SWEET AND SAVORY SNACK RECIPES

36.roadHouse MasHed PoTaToes

PREPARATION TIME: 20'

SERVINGS: 6

COOKING TIME: 30'

INGREDIENTS

- ¼ cup Parmesan cheese, grated
- 1 whole garlic bulb
- ¼ cup sour cream
- 4 medium potatoes, peeled & quartered
- ¼ cup each of softened butter & 2% milk
- 1 teaspoon plus 1 tablespoon olive oil, divided
- ¼ teaspoon pepper
- 1 medium white onion, chopped
- ½ teaspoon salt

DIRECTIONS

1. Preheat the oven to 425 degrees. Cut off the papery outer skin from the garlic bulb; ensure that you don't separate the cloves or peel them. Remove the top from the garlic bulb, exposing individual cloves. Brush cut cloves with approximately 1 teaspoon of oil, then wrap in foil. Bake in the preheated oven for 30 to 35 minutes until cloves are soft.
2. Meanwhile, cook the leftover oil over low heat. Once done, add & cook the chopped onion for 15 to 20 minutes, until golden brown, stirring every now and then. Transfer to a food processor. Process on high until blended well; set aside.
3. Put the potatoes in a large saucepan and cover them with water. Bring to a boil. Once done, decrease the heat; cook for 15 to 20 minutes, until tender, uncovered. Drain; return to the pan. Squeeze the softened garlic over the potatoes; add butter, cheese, sour cream, milk, onion, pepper, and salt. Beat until mashed. Serve and enjoy.

NUTRITION: 220 calories 15g total fats 3g protein

37. Sweet Potatoes With Marshmallows and Caramel Sauce

PREPARATION TIME: 40'

SERVINGS: 10'

COOKING TIME: 30'

Ingredients

- ½ cup corn syrup
- 6 medium sweet potatoes, peeled & cut into 1" chunks
- ½ teaspoon ground cinnamon
- ¼ cup whole milk
- 2 tablespoons butter
- ½ cup brown sugar, packed
- Marshmallows on top
- ½ to 1 teaspoon salt

Directions

1. Put sweet potatoes in a Dutch oven; add water and ensure that the sweet potatoes are nicely covered. Bring to a boil. Once done, decrease the heat; cover & let simmer for 20 minutes.
2. Drain & transfer to a lightly greased 13x9" baking dish. Bake for 12 to 15 minutes, at 325 F, uncovered.
3. In the meantime, combine the leftover ingredients (except the marshmallows) together in a small saucepan. Bring to a boil; pour the mixture on top of the sweet potatoes. Bake until glazed, for 10 to15 more minutes, basting frequently. Just before serving, throw some marshmallows on top. Enjoy.

NUTRITION: 180 calories 12g total fats 4g protein

38. SauTéed MusHrooms

PREPARATION TIME: 20'

SERVINGS: 6

COOKING TIME: 20'

INGREDIENTS

- 1 teaspoon garlic, chopped
- 1 tablespoon butter
- 1 cup cleaned Portobello mushrooms, sliced
- 1 tablespoon thyme leaves, chopped
- 1/8 cup vegetable oil
- Freshly ground black pepper & salt to taste

DIRECTIONS

1. Warm up the oil over high heat in a large skillet until hot & smoky. Add the garlic; cook until turn fragrant, toss it constantly, and ensure that the garlic doesn't burn. Add the mushrooms; toss until mushrooms are caramelized and turn golden brown. Remove from the heat. Add butter and thyme; season with pepper and salt, to taste. Serve immediately & enjoy.

NUTRITION: 191 calories 13g total fats 5g protein

39. Ham and Cheese EmPanadas

PREPARATION TIME:	5'	SERVINGS:	6

COOKING TIME: 15'

INGREDIENTS

- 12 cooked ham feta
- 400 g mozzarella cheese
- 12 empanada tapas
- Dried oregano
- Ground chili pepper
- 1 beaten egg

DIRECTIONS

1. Cut the mozzarella cheese into 12 bars of approximately 30-35 g each. Pass the bars with oregano and floor chili pepper and area them in the center of each ham feta. Wrap the cheese with the ham, forming a bundle, and reserve. This is so that the cheese does no longer explode in the oven or while you're frying them.
2. Stretch the dough of the empanadas a touch so that they're oval and locate the applications of ham and cheese in the center of each one in all them.
3. Close the middle and locate a finger inside to push the ham even as persevering with to close the sides. This is so that the ham does not complicate your existence at the time of creating the repulse. Make the traditional repulgue and forestalls placed them in an appropriate greased baking sheet with oil. Paint the pies ham and cheese with crushed egg if desired and takes a warm oven till their golden brown.
4. If you want to fry ham and cheese empanadas, consider that the oil must be at 150-160 ° C, because if it had been hotter, they would be cooked on the outside, and inside, the cheese could no longer melt. Fry them for about 3 minutes. Remove the patties fried ham and cheese with a slotted spoon and depart them on paper towels to cast off extra oil.

NUTRITION: 188 calories 16g total fats 11g protein

40. roadHouse green beans

<table>
<tr><td>PREPARATION TIME:</td><td>10'</td><td>SERVINGS:</td><td>8</td></tr>
</table>

COOKING TIME: 20'

INGREDIENTS

- 2 cans green beans (16 ounces), drained
- 1 tablespoon sugar
- 4 ounces bacon, diced (raw) or 4 ounces ham (cooked)
- 2 cups water
- 4 ounces onions, diced
- ½ teaspoon pepper

DIRECTIONS

1. Thoroughly drain green beans using a colander; set aside. Combine pepper with sugar & water until incorporated well; set aside. Preheat your cooking pan over medium-high heat.
2. Dice the cooked ham into equal size pieces using a cutting board and a knife. Place the diced onions and ham into the preheated cooking pan. Continue to stir the onions and ham using the large spoon until the onions are tender and the ham is lightly brown.
3. Once done, add the beans and liquid mixture. Using the rubber spatula, give the mixture a good stir until incorporated well. Let the mixture boil, then lower the heat to simmer. Serve the beans as soon as you are ready and enjoy.

NUTRITION: 221 calories 16g total fats 4g protein

41. roadHouse CHeesefries

<table>
<tr><td>PREPARATION TIME:</td><td>20'</td><td>SERVINGS:</td><td>4</td></tr>
</table>

COOKING TIME: 30'

INGREDIENTS

- 6 -8 slices bacon, enough to make ½ cup once cooked
- 4 cups steak-style French fries, frozen
- ¼ teaspoon onion powder
- 2 cups sharp cheddar cheese, grated
- Oil for frying
- ¼ teaspoon each of garlic salt & seasoning salt

DIRECTIONS

1. Preheat your oven to 450 F. Cook the bacon over medium-high heat in a medium-sized frying pan. Take out the bacon when crisp & place it on a paper towel to drain.
2. Pour the bacon grease into a bowl & let slightly cool. Add onion powder, seasoned salt, and garlic salt to the grease; combine well and set aside. Assemble the fries on a greased baking sheet & bake in the preheated oven until turn slightly golden, for 10 to 15 minutes.
3. Set your oven to broil. Brush the bacon oil with the seasoning mix onto each fry. Place fries in an oven-safe bowl. Spread the cheddar cheese on top of the fries. Crumble bacon slices and then sprinkle on top of the cheese.
4. Place dish in the oven until the cheese is bubbly, for 3 to 5 minutes. Remove from the oven & let sit for a couple of minutes, then serve.

NUTRITION: 188 calories 11 total fats 4g protein

42. dInner rolls

PREPARATION TIME: 1 H

SERVINGS: 4

COOKING TIME: 15'

INGREDIENTS

For Rolls:
- 2 ¼ teaspoon or 1 packet active dry yeast
- 1 large egg, at room temperature
- 1 ¼ cup milk
- 4 tablespoons melted butter, separated
- ¼ cup honey
- 4 cups flour
- 1 teaspoon salt

For Texas Roadhouse Butter:
- ¼ cup powdered sugar
- 1 stick salted butter, at room temperature for an hour
- ¾ teaspoon cinnamon
- 1 ½ tablespoons honey

DIRECTIONS

1. For Texas Roadhouse Butter
2. Using an electric mixer, combine the entire Roadhouse butter ingredients together until smooth & creamy. Refrigerate until ready to use.
3. For Rolls:
4. Bring the milk to a boil over moderate heat. Once done, remove the pan from heat & set aside at room temperature until lukewarm.
5. Now, combine the milk with honey & yeast in a small bowl until combined well. Let sit for a couple of minutes. Combine 2 cups of flour with milk mixture, egg & 3 tablespoons of butter in a large bowl. Slowly mix until smooth. Slowly add the leftover flour & continue to mix until dough-like consistency is achieved.
6. Add salt & continue to mix for 6 to 8 more minutes. Drop the dough onto a floured surface; knead for a couple of minutes more. Grease the large bowl with the cooking spray & drop the dough inside. Using a plastic wrap, cover the bowl & let rise in a warm place for an hour.
7. Coat 2 cookie sheets lightly with the vegetable oil. Punch the dough down & roll it out on a flat, floured surface until it's approximately ½" thick. Fold it in half & gently seal. Evenly cut the dough into 24 squares & arrange them on the prepared cookie sheets. Using a plastic wrap, cover & let them rise until almost doubled in size, for 35 to 40 minutes.
8. Preheat your oven to 350 F in advance & bake until the top is a light golden brown, for 12 to 15 minutes. Heat the leftover tablespoon of butter until melted and then brush the top of the rolls.
9. Serve with Texas Roadhouse Butter and enjoy.

NUTRITION: 210 calories 14g total fats 5g protein

43. Texas red Chili

PREPARATION TIME: 2'

SERVINGS: 4

COOKING TIME: 5'

INGREDIENTS

- 2 ½ pounds boneless beef chuck, well-trimmed & cut into ¾" cubes
- 1 ½ teaspoons ground cumin seed
- 2 ounces pasilla chilis
- 1/3 cup onion, finely chopped
- 3 large garlic cloves, minced
- 2 ¼ cups water, plus more as needed
- Sour cream
- 1 tablespoon firmly packed dark brown sugar, plus more as needed
- 2 tablespoons masa harina (corn tortilla flour)
- 1 ½ tablespoons distilled white vinegar, plus more as needed
- 2 cups canned low-sodium beef broth or beef stock, plus more as required
- Lime wedges
- ½ teaspoon freshly ground black pepper
- 5 tablespoons vegetable oil, lard or rendered beef suet
- Kosher salt to taste

DIRECTIONS

1. Over medium-low heat in a straight-sided large skillet; gently toast the chilies for 2 to 3 minutes per side, until fragrant. Keep an eye on them and don't let them burn. Place the chilies in a large bowl & cover them with very hot water; let soak for 15 to 45 minutes, until soft, turning a couple of times during the soaking process.
2. Drain the chilies; split them & remove the seeds and stems. Place the chilies in a blender & then add the black pepper, cumin, ¼ cup water, and 1 tablespoon salt. Purée the mixture until a smooth, slightly fluid paste forms; feel free to add more of water as required and scrape down the sides of your blender jar occasionally. Set aside until ready to use.
3. Place the skillet over medium-high heat again & heat 2 tablespoons of lard until melted. When it starts to smoke, swirl to coat the bottom of your skillet & add half of the beef. Lightly brown on at least two sides, for 2 to 3 minutes on each side. If the meat threatens to burn, immediately decrease the heat. Transfer to a bowl & repeat with 2 more tablespoons of lard & the leftover beef. Reserve.
4. Let the skillet to slightly cool & place it over medium-low heat. Heat the leftover lard in the same skillet. Once melted, immediately add the garlic and onion; gently cook for 3 to 4 minutes, stirring every now and then. Add the stock & the leftover water; slowly whisk in the masa harina to avoid lumps. Stir in the reserved chili paste, scraping the bottom of your skillet using a spatula to loosen any browned bits. Place the reserved beef (along with any accumulated juices) & bring to a simmer over high heat. Once done, decrease the heat to maintain the barest possible simmer & continue to cook for 2 hours, until 1 ½ to 2 cups of thickened but still liquid sauce surrounds the cubes of meat & the meat is tender but still somewhat firm, stirring occasionally.
5. Thoroughly stir in the vinegar & brown sugar; add more salt to taste; let simmer gently for 10 more minutes. Switch it off and set aside for 30 minutes. If the mixture appears to be too dry, feel free to stir in the additional water or broth. Alternatively, let it simmer a couple of more minutes, if the mixture appears to be a bit loose & wet. Alter the balance of flavors with a bit of additional vinegar, sugar, or salt, if desired.
6. Gently reheat & serve in separate bowls with a dollop of sour cream on top & a fresh lime wedge on the side.

NUTRITION: 218 calories 13g total fats 4g protein

44.boneless buffalo Wings

PREPARATION TIME: 25'	SERVINGS: 2 dOzen

COOKING TIME: 2H 15'

INGREDIENTS

- 1 cup low-sodium soy sauce
- ½ teaspoon pepper
- 2 teaspoons grated orange zest
- 3 pounds boneless chicken wings
- 2 garlic cloves, minced
- 2/3 cup sugar
- 3 teaspoons chili powder
- ¾ teaspoon each of cayenne pepper & hot pepper sauce
- 2 teaspoons salt
- For Blue Cheese Dip:
- ½ cup blue cheese salad dressing
- 2 teaspoons Italian salad dressing mix
- 1 cup mayonnaise
- ⅓ cup buttermilk

DIRECTIONS

1. Combine the orange zest, sugar, soy sauce, pepper, garlic, and salt in a small bowl. Pour half of the marinade into a large re-sealable plastic bag. Mix in the chicken pieces; seal the bag & turn the pieces several times until nicely coated. Refrigerate for an hour. Using a plastic wrap, cover the leftover marinade & refrigerate.
2. Drain & discard the marinade. Transfer the chicken to a lightly greased 13x9" baking dish. Cover & bake until juices of the chicken run clear, for 1 ½ hours, at 325 F.
3. Transfer the cooked chicken to a greased 15x10x1" baking pan using a pair of tongs. Combine the pepper sauce together with chili powder, cayenne & reserved marinade in a small bowl. Drizzle on top of the chicken.
4. Bake for 30 minutes, uncovered, turning once. Whisk the entire dipping ingredients together in a small bowl. Serve with the cooked wings and enjoy.

NUTRITION: 211 calories 12g total fats 5.3g protein

45. Tater Skins

PREPARATION TIME: 5'	SERVINGS: 8

COOKING TIME: 35'

INGREDIENTS

- 4 large baking potatoes, baked
- ¼ teaspoon garlic powder
- 4 green onions, sliced
- 1 tablespoon Parmesan cheese, grated
- 1/8 teaspoon pepper
- 8 bacon strips, cooked & crumbled
- ½ cup sour cream
- 1 ½ cups cheddar cheese, shredded
- ¼ teaspoon paprika
- 3 tablespoons canola oil
- ½ teaspoon salt

DIRECTIONS

1. Preheat the oven to 475 degrees. Slice the potatoes lengthwise in half; scoop the pulp out; leaving approximately ¼" shell. Place the potato skins on a lightly greased baking sheet.
2. Combine oil with the cheese, pepper, paprika, garlic powder & salt; mix well and then brush over the skins on both sides.
3. Bake both sides until turn crisp. Sprinkle the cheddar cheese & bacon inside the skins. Bake until the cheese is completely melted. Top with onions and sour cream. Serve immediately and enjoy.

NUTRITION: 221 calories 16g total fats 5g protein

46.fried Pickles

PREPARATION TIME: 15'

SERVINGS: 8

COOKING TIME: 25'

INGREDIENTS

- ½ teaspoon garlic powder
- 32 dill pickle slices
- ½ cup all-purpose flour
- 2 large eggs, lightly beaten
- ½ teaspoon cayenne pepper
- 2 tablespoons dill pickle juice
- ½ cup Japanese (panko) breadcrumbs
- 1 tablespoon fresh dill, snipped
- ½ teaspoon salt

DIRECTIONS

1. Preheat the oven to 500 degrees. Place the pickles to stand on a paper towel until the liquid is almost absorbed.
2. In the meantime, blend the flour with salt in a shallow bowl. Whisk the eggs together with pickle juice, garlic powder, and cayenne in a separate shallow bowl. Combine the dill with panko in a third shallow bowl.
3. Dip the pickles first into the flour mixture (ensure both sides are nicely coated); shake off any excess, then dip into the egg mixture and finally into the crumb mixture, patting to help the coating to adhere. Transfer to a lightly greased wire rack in a rimmed baking sheet.
4. Bake until turn golden brown & crispy. Serve immediately & enjoy.

NUTRITION: 218 calories 14g total fats 3g protein

47. raTTlesnake blTes

<table>
<tr><td>PREPARATION TIME:</td><td>15'</td><td></td><td>SERVINGS:</td><td>6
dOzen</td></tr>
<tr><td></td><td>COOKING TIME:</td><td>35'</td><td></td><td></td></tr>
</table>

INGREDIENTS

- 2 teaspoons baking powder
- 1 cup plus 3 tablespoons all-purpose flour
- 2 cups cornmeal
- 1 ½ teaspoons sugar
- ½ teaspoon baking soda
- 1 large egg
- 2/3 cup water
- 1 small green pepper, chopped
- ½ cup butter, melted
- 2 jalapeno peppers, seeded & chopped
- ½ cup buttermilk
- 1 cup onion, grated
- Oil for deep-fat frying
- 1 teaspoon salt

DIRECTIONS

1. Combine the flour together with cornmeal, sugar, baking powder, baking soda, and salt in a large bowl. Whisk the egg with water, butter, and buttermilk in a separate bowl. Stir in the jalapenos, onion & green pepper. Stir the mixture into the dry ingredients until just moistened.
2. Now, over moderate heat in a deep-fat fryer or an electric skillet; heat the oil until hot. Using teaspoonfuls, drop the batter carefully into the hot oil, a few at a time. Fry until both sides turn golden brown. Place them on paper towels to drain. Serve warm and enjoy.

NUTRITION: 210 calories 10g total fats 4.3g protein

48. CaCTus blossom

<table>
<tr><td>PREPARATION TIME:</td><td>25'</td><td></td><td>SERVINGS:</td><td>8</td></tr>
<tr><td></td><td>COOKING TIME:</td><td>40'</td><td></td><td></td></tr>
</table>

INGREDIENTS

- 3 tablespoons dry breadcrumbs
- 1 tablespoon butter, melted
- 2 large sweet onions
- ¼ teaspoon each of pepper & salt
- 2 teaspoons Dijon mustard
- For Sauce:
- ¼ cup each of sour cream & mayonnaise, fat-free
- 1 ½ teaspoons dried minced onion
- ¼ teaspoon each of garlic powder & dill weed

DIRECTIONS

1. Slice ½" off the top of the onions using a sharp knife; peel the onions. Cut each into 16 wedges to within ½" of the root end. Place each onion on a double thickness of heavy-duty foil (approximately 12" square). Fold the foil around onions & tightly seal. Place in an ungreased 11x7" baking dish. Bake for 20 minutes at 425 F, uncovered.
2. Combine the butter with mustard in a small bowl. Carefully open the foil; fold the foil around the onions. Brush the butter mixture on top of the onions; sprinkle with breadcrumbs, pepper, and salt.
3. Bake until crisp-tender, for 20 to 22 more minutes. In the meantime, combine the entire sauce ingredients together in a small bowl. Serve with the onions.

NUTRITION: 219 calories 14g total fats 5g protein

49. Crispy Cheesy Chips

PREPARATION TIME: 10'

SERVINGS: 8

COOKING TIME: 10'

INGREDIENTS

- 1 cup whey protein isolate
- 4 cups shredded mozzarella cheese

DIRECTIONS

1. Take a medium heatproof bowl, place cheese in it, and then microwave for 1 minute until cheese melts.
2. Remove the bowl from the oven and immediately stir in whey protein until well combined and the dough comes together.
3. Spread a sheet of parchment on working space, place half of the dough on it, and then cover it with the parchment sheet of the same size.
4. Shape the dough into a thin rectangle by using hands and rolling pin and then cut out triangles by using a pizza cutter.
5. Repeat with the remaining dough to make more chips. Transfer the cheese triangles onto two large baking sheets, leaving some space between them, and then bake for 8 to 10 minutes until nicely browned.
6. When done, let the chips cool for 5 minutes and then serve with a dip.

NUTRITION: 164 Calories 0.4g Fats 36.8g Protein

50. brIned CHICken bITes

PREPARATION TIME: 10'

SERVINGS: 4

COOKING TIME: 20'

INGREDIENTS

- 1-pound chicken breast
- ½ teaspoon salt
- 2 cups pickle juice
- Avocado oil, as needed for frying

For the Coating:
- 1 tablespoon baking powder
- ½ teaspoon garlic powder
- ½ teaspoon salt
- 1 tablespoon erythritol sweetener
- ½ teaspoon ground black pepper
- ½ teaspoon paprika
- ½ cup whey protein powder

DIRECTIONS

1. Cut the chicken into 1-inch pieces, place them in a large plastic bag, add salt, pour in pickle juice, and then seal the bag.
2. Turn it upside down to coat the chicken pieces and then let marinate for a minimum of 30 minutes in the refrigerator.
3. Then remove chicken from the refrigerator, let it rest at room temperature for 25 minutes, drain it well, and pat dry with paper towels.
4. Cook the chicken and for this, take a large pot, place it over medium-low heat, pour in oil until the pot has half-full, and then bring it to 350 degrees F.
5. Meanwhile, prepare the coating and for this, take a medium bowl, place all of its ingredients in it and then stir until mixed.
6. Dredge a chicken piece into the coating mixture until thoroughly covered, arrange it onto a baking sheet lined with parchment paper and repeat with the remaining pieces.
7. Drop the prepared chicken pieces into the oil, fry for 6 minutes until thoroughly cooked, and then transfer to a plate lined with paper towels. Repeat with the remaining chicken pieces and then serve.

NUTRITION: 284 Calories 17g Fats 34g Protein 1g Carb

51. bloomin' Onion

PREPARATION TIME: 15'

SERVINGS: 4

COOKING TIME: 5'

INGREDIENTS

- 1 large sweet onion
- ½ cup coconut flour
- ½ tablespoon seasoning salt
- ½ teaspoon ground black pepper
- ½ teaspoon cayenne
- ½ tablespoon paprika
- 4 tablespoons heavy whipping cream
- 4 eggs
- 1 cup pork rind
- Avocado oil, as needed for frying

DIRECTIONS

1. Prepare the onion and for this, remove ¼ top off the onion, flip it cut-side-down and then cut it into quarters in such a way that there is only ¼-inch space from the onion nub. Cut the quarters into eights and then cut them into sixteenths.
2. Sprinkle coconut flour generously over the onion until each petal and the bottom of the onion have coated.
3. Prepare the egg wash and for this, take a medium bowl, crack the eggs in it, whisk in the cream until blended, and then spoon half of this mixture over the onion until each petal and the bottom of the onion have coated.
4. Take a separate medium bowl, place pork rind in it, add all the seasonings, stir until mixed, and then coat onion inside out with this mixture.
5. Repeat by pouring the remaining egg wash over the onion and dredge again into pork rind mixture.
6. Transfer onion onto a plate and then freeze it for 1 hour.
7. When ready to cook, take a large pot, place it over medium-high heat, fill it two-third with oil, and bring it to 300 degrees F temperature.
8. Then lower the frozen onion into the oil, petal-side-down, cook for 1 month, switch heat to medium-low level, flip the onion and fry it for 3 minutes.
9. Transfer onion to a plate lined with paper towels and let it rest for 5 minutes.
10. Serve the onion with dipping sauce.

NUTRITION: 514 Calories 30.3g Fats 47.2g Proteins 10g Carbs

52. Pepperoni Chips

<table>
<tr><td>PREPARATION TIME:</td><td>5'</td><td>SERVINGS:</td><td>2</td></tr>
</table>

COOKING TIME: 8'

INGREDIENTS

- 30 pepperoni slices

DIRECTIONS

1. Switch on the oven, set it to 400 degrees F, then set the baking rack in the middle and let it preheat. Meanwhile, take a sheet pan or two, line with parchment paper, and then spread pepperoni slices o with some spacing between each slice.
2. Bake the pepperoni slices for 4 minutes, then pat dry them with paper towels and then continue baking them for 4 minutes until nicely golden brown.
3. When done, drain the pepperoni slices on paper towels and then serve.

NUTRITION: 150 Calories 14g Fats 5g Protein 1g Carbs

53. maC 'n CHeese

PREPARATION TIME:	20'	**SERVINGS:**	12

COOKING TIME: 20'

INGREDIENTS

- 4 or 5 tablespoons flour
- ¼ teaspoon each of ground white pepper & Red-Hot Sauce
- 2 or 3 cups half and half
- ½ teaspoon Creole Seasoning or Essence
- 4 tablespoons butter, plus 2 tablespoons, plus 1 tablespoon
- 8 ½ ounces Parmigiano-Reggiano parmesan cheese, grated
- ¼ cup breadcrumbs, fresh
- 1-pound elbow macaroni
- ½ teaspoon garlic, minced
- 4 ounces each of cheddar cheese, gruyere cheese & Fontina cheese, grated
- ¾ teaspoon salt

DIRECTIONS

1. Over low heat in a heavy, medium saucepan; heat 3 or 4 tablespoons of butter until melted. Add the flour; turn to combine & cook for 3 to 4 minutes, stirring constantly. Increase the heat to medium; slowly whisk in the half and half. Cook for 4 to 5 minutes, until thickened, stirring frequently. Remove from the heat and season with 4 ounces of the grated parmesan, hot sauce, pepper, and salt. Give the ingredients a good stir until cheese is completely melted & sauce is smooth. Cover & set aside.
2. Preheat your oven to 340 F in advance.
3. Fill a pot with water; bring it to a boil. Add the macaroni and salt to taste, stir well. Bring it to a boil again. Once done, decrease the heat to a low boil & continue to cook until macaroni is al dente, for 5 minutes. Drain the macaroni in a colander and put the macaroni in the pot. Add 2 tablespoons of butter and garlic; stir until everything blends. Add the bechamel sauce; stir until combined well. Set aside until ready to use.
4. Grease a 3-quart casserole or baking dish using the leftover butter & set aside. Combine the leftover parmesan cheese together with cheddar, fontina, and gruyere cheeses in a large bowl; toss until combined well.
5. Place 1/3 of the macaroni in the prepared baking dish. Add 1/3 of the mixed cheeses on top. Top with another third of the macaroni and another third of the mixture of cheese. Repeat with the leftover macaroni & cheese mixture. Combine the breadcrumbs together with leftover grated parmesan & the Essence in a small bowl; toss until combined well. Sprinkle this on top of the macaroni and cheese.
6. Bake until the macaroni & cheese is bubbly and hot, and the top is golden brown, for 40 to 45 minutes. Remove from oven & let sit for 5 minutes before serving.

NUTRITION: 143 Calories 11g Fats 8g Protein 4g Carbs

54. red lobsTer fudge Overboard

| PREPARATION TIME: | 10′ | | SERVINGS: | 4 |

| COOKING TIME: | 15′ |

INGREDIENTS

For Pecan Brownies:
- 13 x 9 family size package of brownie mix
- Olive oil, required per the package Directions
- Egg (required as per the number mentioned on the package)
- ½ cup pecans, chopped

For Chocolate Sauce:
- ½ cup butter
- 4 unsweetened chocolate squares
- 1 can evaporated milk (12 ounces)
- 3 cups sugar
- ½ teaspoon salt
- For Whipped Cream:
- 1 can of canned whip whipped cream

DIRECTIONS

For Pecan Brownies
1. Follow the Directions mentioned on the brownie mix and then add approximately ½ cup of the chopped pecans. Pour the prepared mixture into a large pan. Bake as per the Directions mentioned on the package.

For Chocolate Sauce:
2. Over low heat in a large, heavy saucepan; melt the butter & chocolate, stirring constantly. Slowly add the sugar, alternately with evaporated milk, starting & ending with sugar; continue to stir until smooth, for 5 minutes, over medium heat. Stir in the salt.

For Whipped Cream:
3. Microwave the chocolate sauce and brownie in separate dishes; ensure it's hot. After micro-waving the brownie, place a scoop of ice cream on top. Drizzle the hot chocolate sauce on top of the ice cream and then top with the whipped cream.

NUTRITION: 169 Calories 10g Fat 19g Carbs 33g Protein

55. CHoCoLaTe Wave

PREPARATION TIME: 25'

SERVINGS: 6

COOKING TIME: 5H 15'

INGREDIENTS

- 4 organic eggs, large
- 1 cup sugar
- 2 ½ teaspoons cornstarch
- ¾ cup butter
- 4 egg yolks
- 1 cup semisweet chocolate chips
- 1 ½ teaspoon Grand Marnier

For White-Chocolate Truffle
- 3 tablespoons heavy cream
- 6 ounces white chocolate
- 2 tablespoons Grand Marnier
- 3 tablespoons softened butter

DIRECTIONS

1. Over medium-low heat in a double boiler; melt the butter. Add in the chocolate chips; continue to heat until the mixture is completely melted.
2. Combine cornstarch and sugar in a large-sized mixing bowl. Add the chocolate mixture into the sugar mixture; beat well.
3. Combine four yolks with four eggs & Grand Marnier in a separate bowl. Add this to the chocolate mixture; continue to beat until mixed well. Cover & let chill for overnight.
4. For Truffle: Over low heat in a double boiler; melt the white chocolate with heavy cream. Add Grand Marnier and butter; give the ingredients a good stir until completely smooth. Chill for overnight.
5. Lightly coat 5-ounce ramekins with butter & then dust with flour, filling approximately 1/3 of the chilled chocolate mixture. Add a rounded tablespoon of the truffle mixture. Fill to the top with the chocolate mixture.
6. Bake for 15 minutes at 450 F. Let the cakes to sit for 15 to 20 minutes before inverting. Run a knife around the edges to loosen. Serve with raspberries, chocolate sauce, and/or ice cream.

NUTRITION: 302 Calories 22g Fat 28g Carbs 35g Protein

56. Houston's Apple Walnut Cobbler

<table>
<tr><td>PREPARATION TIME:</td><td>15'</td><td>SERVINGS:</td><td>6</td></tr>
</table>

COOKING TIME: 30'

INGREDIENTS

- 3 large Granny Smith apples, peeled and diced
- 1½ cups walnuts, coarsely chopped
- 1 cup all-purpose flour
- 1 cup brown sugar
- 1 teaspoon cinnamon
- Pinch of nutmeg
- 1 large egg
- ½ cup (1 stick) butter, melted
- Vanilla ice cream
- Caramel sauce, for drizzling

DIRECTIONS

1. Preheat oven to 350°F. Lightly grease an 8-inch square baking dish. Spread diced apple over the bottom of the baking dish.
2. Sprinkle with walnuts. In a bowl, mix together flour, sugar, cinnamon, nutmeg, and egg to make a coarse-textured mixture.
3. Sprinkle over the apple-walnut layer. Pour melted butter over the whole mixture. Bake until fragrant and crumb top is browned (about 30 minutes). Serve warm topped with scoops of vanilla ice cream.
4. Drizzle with caramel sauce.

NUTRITION: 611 Calories 36g Fat 69g Carbs 8g Protein

57. PaPa JoHn's CInnaPle

PREPARATION TIME:	5'		SERVINGS:	12

COOKING TIME:	12'

INGREDIENTS

- 1 whole pizza dough
- 1 tablespoon melted butter
- 2 tablespoons cinnamon, or to taste

Topping
- ¾ cup flour
- ½ cup white sugar
- 1/3 cup brown sugar
- 2 tablespoons oil
- 2 tablespoons shortening

Icing
- 1½ cups powdered sugar
- 3 tablespoons milk
- ¾ teaspoon vanilla

DIRECTIONS

1. Preheat oven to 460°F. Grease or spray a pizza pan or baking sheet.
2. Brush the dough evenly with melted butter. Sprinkle with cinnamon. Place the ingredients for the topping in a bowl and toss together with a fork.
3. Sprinkle topping over the dough. Bake until fragrant and lightly browned at the edges (about 10–12 minutes). Mix the icing ingredients together in a bowl. If too thick, gradually add in a little more milk. Drizzle icing over warm pizza

NUTRITION: 560 Calories 90g Carbs 19g Fat 8g Protein

58. Ollve Garden's Cheese ZITI al forno

| Preparation Time: | 10' | | Servings: | 8 |

| Cooking Time: | 35' |

Ingredients

- 1 lb. Ziti
- 4 tbsp Butter
- 2 cloves Garlic
- 4 tbsp All-purpose flour
- 2 cups Half & Half
- A dash of Black pepper
- Kosher salt (as desired)
- 3 cups Marinara
- 1 cup - grated Parmesan - divided
- 2 cups Shredded mozzarella - divided

Other Shredded Cheese:
- ½ cup Fontina
- ½ cup Romano
- ½ cup Ricotta
- ½ cup Panko breadcrumbs

The garnish:
- Fresh Parsley

Directions

1. Warm the oven to reach 375° Fahrenheit.
2. Spritz the casserole dish with cooking oil spray. Prepare a large pot of boiling - salted water to cook the ziti until al dente. Drain and set it to the side.
3. Mince the garlic. Shred/grate the cheese and chop the parsley.
4. Make the alfredo. Heat the skillet using the medium temperature setting to melt the butter. Toss in the garlic to sauté for about half a minute. Whisk in flour and simmer until the sauce is bubbling (1-2 min.).
5. Whisk in the Half-and-Half and simmer. Stir in ½ cup parmesan, pepper, and salt. Cook it until the sauce thickens (2-3 min.). Stir in the marinara, one cup of mozzarella, Romano, fontina, and ricotta. Fold in the pasta. Dump it into the casserole dish.
6. Combine ½ cup of the parmesan and the breadcrumbs. Sprinkle it over the top of the dish. Set the timer and bake until browned as desired and bubbly (30 min.). Garnish with parsley and serve.

Nutrition: 272 Calories 20g Fat 25g Carbs 23g Protein

59. CHIPoTle's refrled beans

PREPARATION TIME: 5'

SERVINGS: 6

COOKING TIME: 5'

INGREDIENTS

- 1-pound dried pinto beans
- 6 cups warm water
- ½ cup bacon fat
- 2 teaspoons salt
- 1 teaspoon cumin
- ½ teaspoon black pepper
- ½ teaspoon cayenne pepper

DIRECTIONS

1. Rinse and drain the pinto beans. Check them over and remove any stones. Place the beans in a Dutch oven and add the water. Bring the pot to a boil, reduce the heat, and simmer for 2 hours, stirring frequently.
2. When the beans are tender, reserve ½ cup of the boiling water and drain the rest. Heat the bacon fat in a large, deep skillet. Add the beans 1 cup at a time, mashing and stirring as you go. Add the spices and some of the cooking liquid if the beans are too dry.

NUTRITION: 100 Calories 18g Carbs 1g Fat 6g Protein

60. loW faT Veggle Quesadllla

PREPARATION TIME: 10'

SERVINGS: 2

COOKING TIME: 5'

INGREDIENTS

- ½ tablespoon canola oil
- ½ cup mushrooms, chopped
- ½ cup carrot, grated
- 1/3 cup broccoli, sliced
- 2 tablespoons onion, finely chopped
- 1 tablespoon red bell pepper, finely chopped
- 1 teaspoon soy sauce
- 1 dash cayenne pepper
- 1 dash black pepper
- 1 dash salt
- 2 flour tortillas
- ¼ cup cheddar cheese, grated
- ¼ cup mozzarella cheese, grated
- ¼ cup sour cream
- ¼ cup salsa, medium or mild to taste
- ¼ cup shredded lettuce

DIRECTIONS

1. Heat oil in a large skillet. Add mushrooms, carrots, broccoli, onion, and bell pepper. Stir-fry over medium-high heat for about 5 minutes. Pour in soy sauce, then season with cayenne, salt, and pepper. Transfer vegetables onto a plate. Set aside.
2. In the same skillet, heat first tortilla. Top with cheddar and mozzarella cheeses, followed by the cooked vegetables. Cover with the second tortilla. Cook for about 1 minute on each side or until cheeses are runny. Cut into slices. Serve hot with sour cream, salsa, and shredded lettuce on the side.

NUTRITION: 186 Calories 12g Fat 18g Carbs 25g Protein

61. Garlic Mashed Potatoes

PREPARATION TIME: 20'	**SERVINGS:** 4

COOKING TIME: 1 H

INGREDIENTS

- 1 medium-sized bulb garlic, fresh
- 2 pounds red-skinned potatoes
- ½ cup milk
- ½ cup heavy cream
- ¼ cup butter
- Salt and pepper to taste

DIRECTIONS

1. Preheat the oven to 400°F. Wrap whole garlic bulb with aluminum foil and bake it for 45 minutes, until the garlic softens. Remove it from the oven and let it cool in its wrapping.
2. Once cool, unwrap the garlic, peel off the outer layer, and squeeze the cooked pulp out. Set it aside. In the meantime, cut the potatoes and wash them, don't remove the skin and put them in a saucepan. Add water just to cover the potatoes. Boil until it cooks thoroughly for about 20 minutes.
3. Drain the water and add the other ingredients. Use the hands to mash. Lumps can be left, depending on your preference. Serve.

NUTRITION: 254 Calories 16g Fat 24g Carbs 31g Protein

62. VegeTable Medley

PREPARATION TIME: 15'

SERVINGS: 4

COOKING TIME: 10'

INGREDIENTS

- ½ pound cold, fresh zucchini, sliced in half-moons
- ½ pound cold, fresh yellow squash, sliced in half-moons
- ¼ pound cold red pepper, julienned in strips ¼-inch thick
- ¼ pound cold carrots, cut into ¼-inch strips a few inches long
- ¼ pound cold red onions, thinly sliced
- 1 cold, small corn cob, cut crosswise in 1" segments
- 3 tablespoons cold butter or margarine
- 1 teaspoon salt
- 1 teaspoon sugar
- ½ teaspoon granulated garlic
- 1 teaspoon Worcestershire sauce
- 1 teaspoon soy sauce
- 2 teaspoons fresh or dried parsley

DIRECTIONS

1. Wash, peel, and cut your vegetables as appropriate. In a saucepan, heat the butter over medium-high heat. Once it is hot, add salt, sugar, and garlic. Add the carrots, squash, and zucchini, and when they start to soften, add the rest of the vegetables and cook for a couple of minutes.
2. Add the Worcestershire sauce, soy sauce, and parsley. Stir to combine and coat the vegetables. When all the vegetables are cooked to your preference, serve.

NUTRITION: 276 Calories 21g Fat 22g Carbs 30g Protein

63.Mega Mango SmooTHIe

PREPARATION TIME: 10'

SERVINGS: 4

COOKING TIME: 1H 10'

INGREDIENTS

- 1 can of brownie mix
- Ice cream, vanilla, to serve
- Hot Caramel sauce, to serve

DIRECTIONS

1. Set the oven's temperature to exactly 350° F; cut the foil strips to line the giant muffin tin cups;
2. Lay the strips in crisscross-layer form for use as a handle for lifting when the brownies are made. Spray the foil in the kitchen spray pan; Prepare the brownie batter as indicated. Divide the batter between the muffin pans. The muffin cups can be about ¾ full;
3. Set the muffin pan on a heating sheet with the edges and start baking in the preheated oven for 40 to 50 minutes approximately; Remove the muffin pan from your oven and let it cool in the mold for 5 minutes approximately, then take to a rack to cool for another 10 minutes;
4. To loosen the sides of each brownie, you can use an icing spatula or a knife and then use the handles to lift the muffin pan. Serve a hot brownie on a plate with hot caramel sauce and a scoop of vanilla ice cream.

NUTRITION: 206 Calories 24g Fat 24g Carbs 29g Protein

64. lasagna WITH feTa and blaCk Ollves

PREPARATION TIME: 10'

SERVINGS: 4

COOKING TIME: 15'

INGREDIENTS

- 8 lasagna sheets
- 600 gr of diced tomatoes
- Dried basil and oregano
- Salt and black pepper
- 1 sugar
- +/- 300 ml of béchamel
- 1 jar of pitted kalamata black olives
- +/- 150 gr of block feta
- A little grated cheese to brown
- A mixture of dried Greek herbs and Olive oil

DIRECTIONS

1. Heat a touch olive oil in a saucepan or frying pan. Add the diced tomatoes, sugar, dried basil and oregano, salt and pepper (dose in step with your taste). Let simmer for at least 1/2 hour. Prepare your béchamel as you commonly do. Drain the olives and dice the feta.
2. Spread a little tomato and béchamel sauce within the bottom of a gratin dish, location 2 sheets of lasagna, tomato sauce, béchamel, black olives, and diced feta. Continue identically till all the ingredients are used up. Finish with béchamel, sprinkle with grated cheese, and sprinkle with Greek herbs.
3. Finally, bake at 180 ° C for 30 to 40 minutes and serve immediately.

NUTRITION: 270 calories 16g total fats 11g protein

65. Easy CoPyCaT MonTerey's liTTle MexICo Queso

PREPARATION TIME: 15′	SERVINGS: 6

COOKING TIME: 10′

INGREDIENTS

- 1/2 cup of chopped yellow onion
- 1/2 cup of finely chopped celery
- 2 large green peppers such as Anaheim or Hatch, finely diced
- 2 tablespoons of butter
- 1 pound of American cheese
- 1/3 cup milk

DIRECTIONS

1. The real mystery of flavored cheese is to fry vegetables till they're almost wholly cooked when you begin adding a little crunch in your American cheese.
2. Place the chopped onion, thinly sliced celery, and diced pepper in a casserole over medium warmness, upload tablespoons of oil, and cook until the onion is transparent. Put in a medium bowl, American cheese, sautéed onions, and milk. Heat until low or medium warmness melts the cheese.

NUTRITION: 226 Calories 4g Carbohydrates 9g Protein 18g Fat

66. fried KeTo CHeese WITH MusHrooms

| PREPARATION TIME: | 10' | SERVINGS: | 4 |

COOKING TIME: 20'

INGREDIENTS

- 300 g mushrooms
- 300 g halloumi cheese
- 75 g butter 10 green olives
- salt and ground black pepper
- 125 ml mayonnaise (optional)

DIRECTIONS

1. Rinse and trim the mushrooms and chop or slice them. Heat the right quantity of butter in a pan in which they match and halloumi cheese and mushrooms.
2. Fry the mushrooms over medium heat for 3-5 minutes till golden brown. If vital, add extra butter and fry the halloumi cheese for a few minutes on every side. Stir the mushrooms occasionally.
3. Lower the warmness towards the end. Serve with olives.

NUTRITION: 169 calories 17g total fats 10g protein

67. MusHroom reCIPe STuffed WITH CHeese, SPInaCH, and baCon

PREPARATION TIME: 10'	SERVINGS: 4

COOKING TIME: 15'

INGREDIENTS

- 18 large mushrooms
- 4 strips of bacon cut into small cubes
- 2 butter spoons
- 2 tablespoons chopped onion
- ¾ cup grated fontina cheese
- 150 g spinach leaves chopped into large pieces
- Kosher Salt and freshly ground black pepper

DIRECTIONS

1. Preheat the oven to 200 ° C. Cover a baking sheet with parchment paper. Wash the mushrooms. Remove the stems and locate the lids with the rounded sides down at the baking sheet. Chop the stems and reserve.

2. In a skillet over medium warmness, fry the bacon reduce into small cubes until crispy, drains. Leave approximately a tablespoon of bacon inside the pan. Add tablespoons of butter to the pan and add the chopped mushroom stems and chopped onion. Cook until the onion is translucent.

3. Add the spinach to the pan and cook until 3 minutes. Drain and transfer the aggregate to a bowl to cool. Add the bacon and half of a cup of cheese to the slightly cooled spinach aggregate. Stir to combine the components.

4. Try and upload Salt and freshly ground black pepper. Fill the mushrooms and cover each one with a touch extra fontina cheese. Bake for 15 minutes or until cheese melts and browns slightly.

NUTRITION: 164 calories 18g total fats 12g protein

68. Shrimp Nachos with Avocado and Tomato Salsa

Preparation Time:	5'		Servings:	6

Cooking Time:	15'

Ingredients

Salsa
- 2 ripe Hass avocados, diced ¼ inch
- 1 large ripened tomato, free of stems and seeds, cut into ¼-inch dice
- 2 tablespoons fresh lime juice
- 1 tablespoon finely chopped fresh coriander leaves
- 1 garlic clove, minced or garlic press
- ½ teaspoon ground cumin
- Kosher Salt
- Freshly ground black pepper
- 1 ear of sweet corn, peeled
- Extra virgin olive oil
- ½ teaspoon ground cumin
- ¼ teaspoons chipotle chili powder
- 20 jumbo shrimps (count of 21/30), shelled and deveined, without the tail
- 170 grams tortilla chips
- 225 grams of coarsely grated sharp cheddar cheese
- 4 green onions (white and pale green parts only), thinly sliced, green and white parts separated
- 1 small jalapeño pepper, seeded, finely chopped
- 1 tablespoon chopped fresh coriander

Directions

1. Combine the components for the salsa sauce. Season with ½ tsp. Salt and ¼ tsp. Of pepper.
2. Set the grill at 350 to 450 degrees and preheat the perforated grill for 10 mins.
3. Lightly brush the corn with oil, then grill directly on the cooking grids over medium warmth, with the lid closed and turning it if necessary, till it is browned in places and tender, eight to 12 mins. Leave to cool, then cut the grains from the cob.
4. Mix the cumin, the chili powder, ½ tsp. Salt and ¼ tsp. Of pepper. Brush the shrimp with oil, then sprinkle the spice aggregate lightly. Divide the shrimp in a single layer on the baking sheet and grill over medium direct heat, with the lid closed and turning once till they're firm to the touch and opaque inside the center, 2 to 4 minutes. With protecting barbeque gloves, do away with the baking sheet and the shrimp from the warmth and transfer the shrimp to a piece surface. Cut every shrimp in 1/2 crosswise, crosswise. Prepare the grill for oblique cooking over medium warmness (350 to 450 ° F).
5. Spread the tortilla at the bottom of a 12-⅓n⅓h solid iron skillet. Scatter cheese calmly over potato chips, then corn, the white part of green onions, and jalapeño pepper. Cook over indirect medium warmth, with the barbecue lid, closed, for 8 to 10 minutes, till the cheese has melted. During the final 2 mins of cooking, upload the shrimp on the nachos. Remove from warmth and garnish with the inexperienced a part of the green onions and the coriander. Serve warm with salsa.

Nutrition: 204 calories 18.1g total fats 12g protein

69. Mimosa Eggs WITH Truffle

| PREPARATION TIME: | 5' | | SERVINGS: | 6 |

| COOKING TIME: | 15' |

INGREDIENTS

- 6 Eggs
- 1/2 cup Mayonnaise
- 2 c. tablespoons Chives finely chopped
- 1-2 tsp. tablespoon truffle oil of excellent quality
- 2-3 slices crispy bacon, crumbled
- Salt and pepper
- Pastry bag or Ziploc bag

DIRECTIONS

1. Boil the eggs for approximately 8 minutes. Let cool and peel the shell. Cut in 1/2 lengthwise, cast off the yolk with a small spoon, and place in a bowl with mayonnaise, truffle oil, salt, pepper, and half of the chives. Mash the mixture with a fork or use a small blender. Put all the mixtures in a piping bag or a Ziploc bag. Arrange the egg whites on a pleasing plate and fill them with the combination. Garnish with the rest of the chives and bacon. You can end with a little fleur de sel and a touch extra truffle oil, if necessary.

NUTRITION: 125 Calories 18g total fats 10.9g protein

70. SHrlmP TemPura

PREPARATION TIME: 10'

SERVINGS: 6

COOKING TIME: 5'

INGREDIENTS

- 1/2 kg clean shrimp
- Garlic and salt to season shrimp
- 4 whole eggs
- 5 tablespoons of flour
- 1 Red Seasonal Envelope or Seasonal for Fish Oil for frying

DIRECTIONS

1. Season the smooth shrimp with garlic and salt and set aside. Beat whole eggs till soft, upload a pinch of Salt, the seasoning and flour, and beat appropriately with a fork until smooth.
2. Gradually dip the shrimp on this batter and fry in warm oil. When browning the dough, take away with a slotted spoon and drain on an absorbent paper towel. Serve warm as it tastes or maybe with white rice and shrimp sauce.

NUTRITION: 170 calories 14g total fats 10g protein

71. Copycat Chili's Southwest Egg rolls

Preparation Time: 5'

Servings: 4

Cooking Time: 15'

Ingredients

- 8 oz chicken breast
- 1 teaspoon of olive oil vegetable oil is fine
- 1 tablespoon of olive oil vegetable oil is fine
- 1/4 cup chopped red bell pepper
- 1/4 cup chopped spring onions
- 1/2 cup frozen corn
- 1/2 cup canned black beans
- 1/4 cup frozen spinach
- 2 tsp of pickled jalapeno pepper
- 1 teaspoon of taco spice
- 3/4 cup of grated Monterey Jack cheese
- 8/7-inch flour tortillas
- 1/4 cup mashed fresh avocados (about half an avocado)
- 1 pack of Ranch Dressing Mix
- 1/2 cup milk
- 1/2 cup mayonnaise
- 2 tablespoons of chopped tomatoes
- 1 tablespoon of chopped onions

Directions

1. Season with salt and black pepper to the fowl. Brush the fowl breast with olive oil. Grill on a grill with medium heat. Cook on each side for five to 7 mins. Cut the hen into tiny pieces. Set apart the fowl.
2. Sauté till tender red pepper. Refer to the aggregate of the green onion, rice, black beans, spinach, and pickled jalapenos. Attach the seasoning of taco. Via the sun.
3. Place the tortillas in the same quantities of the filing, identical amounts of chicken, and pinnacle with cheese. Fold and roll-up on the ends of the tortilla. Make positive the tortillas are very tight to roll. To defend the pin with toothpicks.
4. We are growing enough vegetable oil in a big pot to cover the pan's backside through 4 inches. Heat up to 350°C. Deep fry the rolls of the eggs until golden brown. It ought to take seven to eight mins. When extracting golden from oil, growing it on a rack of wire.
5. Prepare a container of mayonnaise half-cup ranch dressing mix and buttermilk half of cup. Remove the aggregate 1/4 cup of mashed avocado. In a blender, pump the combination till the sauce is mixed.

Nutrition: 502 Calories 42g Carbohydrates 19g Protein 28g Fat

72. Ham and Cheese Grinders

PREPARATION TIME:	10′		SERVINGS:	2

COOKING TIME:	5′

INGREDIENTS

- 300 g of refrigerated pizza dough
- 2 cloves of garlic
- 2 tablespoons olive oil
- 1 teaspoon Italian seasoning
- ¼ cup grated Parmesan cheese
- 1 cup shredded mozzarella cheese
- 250 g sliced ham
- 1 egg
- Chopped fresh parsley
- Marinara sauce

DIRECTIONS

1. Gather all the elements to make ham and cheese grinders.
2. Preheat the oven to 180 ° C. Add the chopped garlic and the Italian seasoning to the olive oil.
3. Spread the chilled pizza dough in a large rectangle and reduce the choppy edges if desired.
4. Distribute the olive oil combination over the dough and sprinkle the grated Parmesan cheese and 1/2 of the grated mozzarella cheese over the dough floor.
5. Cowl the surface of the cheese with cooked ham and sprinkle the surface with the rest of the grated mozzarella cheese. Roll the dough as you could see inside the image.
6. Seal the edges of the dough through becoming a member of the dough and cut into nine parts. Place the ham and cheese grinders on a baking sheet lined with parchment paper.
7. Beat the egg with a teaspoon of warm water until well mixed. Brush the egg on the top and sides of the grinders.
8. Bake the grinders for 15 to twenty minutes or till they're fluffy and golden brown.
9. Cover the grinders with chopped fresh parsley and serve right away with marinara sauce.

NUTRITION: 190 calories 17g total fats 11g protein

73. Mozzarella Cheese Sticks Recipe

PREPARATION TIME: 5′

SERVINGS: 10

COOKING TIME: 5′

INGREDIENTS

- ¼ cup flour
- 1 cup breadcrumbs
- 2 eggs
- 1 tablespoon milk
- 500 g mozzarella cheese
- 1 cup of vegetable oil
- 1 cup marinara sauce

DIRECTIONS

1. Gather all the elements of mozzarella cheese sticks then mix eggs and milk together in a medium bowl. Cut the mozzarella into sticks 2 x 2 cm thick.
2. Cover each mozzarella cane with flour. Then dip them inside the egg and then within the breadcrumbs.
3. Dip the mozzarella sticks lower back into the egg and skip them in breadcrumbs.
4. Take to the freezer earlier than frying. Heat the oil within the pan and prepare dinner the mozzarella cheese sticks for approximately a minute on every aspect or until well browned.
5. Drain the cheese sticks on paper napkins and serve with marinara sauce or pizza sauce.

NUTRITION: 168 calories 19g total fats 12g protein

74. Copycat Mac and Cheese with Smoked Gouda Cheese and Pumpkin

Preparation Time: 5'

Servings: 2

Cooking Time: 15'

Ingredients

- 1 1/2 tbsp olive oil
- 120 grams of fresh baguette torn into small pieces
- 2 teaspoons fresh thyme leaves
- 1/4 cup grated Parmesan
- 450 grams of spiral pasta (or penne)
- 4 tablespoons salted butter
- 4 tablespoons of flour
- 3 cups room temp milk
- 1 cup canned pumpkin puree
- 2 cups smoked and chopped gouda cheese
- 2 cups cut sharp cheddar
- Kosher Salt

Directions

1. Preheat oven to 190°C. Grease a large pan with nonstick cooking spray.
2. In a massive bowl, combine the cornbread, olive oil, thyme, and ½ tsp kosher Salt. Put in greased pan and bake till golden brown (12 to 15 minutes). Remove from oven, incorporate grated Parmesan, and set aside.
3. In a large pan of boiling salted water, cook the pasta al dente in line with package deal Directions. Drain the water and set aside the pasta.
4. Melt butter in a pan over medium heat. Incorporate the flour and cook dinner, continually stirring, till the aggregate starts to thicken (about one to mins).
5. Gradually include the milk, continually mixing until it paperwork a lightly thickened sauce (five to six minutes). Add the mashed pumpkin and two teaspoons of kosher salt. Beat till included adequately into the sauce. Lower the warmth and location, the gouda and cheddar cheeses, mixing nicely until melted.
6. Incorporate the cooked pasta into the sauce. Transfer the whole lot to a prepared baking sheet. Sprinkle with toasted breadcrumbs. Put in oven and let till golden and blistered (about 20 mins). Serve immediately.

Nutrition: 159 calories 15g total fats 12g protein

75. baked buffalo meatballs

PREPARATION TIME: 5'

SERVINGS: 4

COOKING TIME: 20'

INGREDIENTS

- 350 gram of ground chicken meat
- 1 clove of minced garlic
- 1/4 cup of ground bread
- 2 tablespoons grated parmesan
- 2 teaspoons fresh celery leaves
- 1 egg
- 1/4 cup flour
- salt and pepper to taste
- 1/2 cup botanica sauce (Valentina or buffalo botanica)
- 2 tablespoons melted butter
- 1 tablespoon apple cider
- vinegar
- garlic powder and celery salt to taste for blue cheese dressing
- 1/3 cup of mayonnaise
- 1/3 cup sour cream
- 1 tablespoon lemon juice
- 1/4 cup blue cheese salt and pepper to taste

DIRECTIONS

1. Preheat the oven to 190ºC Mix the chook with the garlic, the ground bread, the Parmesan, the celery, the egg, and the flour. Form balls together with your arms and region them on a tray with foil; bake for 18 mins.
2. Mix the botanica sauce with the melted butter and season with garlic powder and celery salt, bathe on this sauce every meatball as quickly as they go away the oven.
3. To make the dressing, blend the cream, mayonnaise, lemon, and half of the blue cheese; upload the relaxation of the crumbled cheese and season to taste. Serve the meatballs with chopsticks observed via blue cheese dressing.

NUTRITION: 170 calories 16g total fats 13g protein

Chapter 3

OLD AND MODERN FRUIT SALAD RECIPES

76. aPPle PomegranaTe Salad: Wendy's™ CoPyCaT

PREPARATION TIME:	25'		SERVINGS:	8

COOKING TIME:	0'

INGREDIENTS

- 1 bunch/8 cups romaine
- ½ cup Pomegranate seeds
- ½ cup Toasted and chopped walnuts/ pecans
- ½ cup Shredded parmesan cheese
- 1 Granny Smith apple
- 1 tbsp Lemon juice
- ¼ cup Olive oil
- ¼ cup White wine vinegar
- 2 tbsp Sugar
- ¼ tsp Salt

DIRECTIONS

1. Tear the romaine into pieces and combine with the pecans, pomegranate seeds, and cheese in a salad bowl. Chop and toss in the apple with lemon juice. Whisk the rest of the fixings until blended in a small mixing container. Toss it together and serve.

NUTRITION: 300 calories 17.8g fats 2.4g protein

77. Cranberry fruIT Salad: THe famous luby's CafeTerIa™ CoPyCaT

PREPARATION TIME: 20'

SERVINGS: 8-10

COOKING TIME: 0'

INGREDIENTS

- 1 Apple
- 12 oz Fresh cranberries
- 1 Banana
- 1 Orange
- 1 cup Broken walnuts/pecans

DIRECTIONS

1. Peel the banana. Rinse and sort the cranberries and peel the orange removing the pith.
2. Whisk the sugar and water in a saucepan until the crystals are dissolved. Dump the cranberries into the pan and lower the heat once it's boiling. Simmer until most of the cranberries have popped or for four to five minutes, stirring occasionally.
3. Transfer the pan of cranberries from the burner and set the pan to the side to cool for a few minutes. Quarter the apple, core, and chop, adding it to the cooled cranberries.
4. Chop the banana and orange, adding it to cranberries with the nuts. Mix and pop it into the fridge until time to eat (at least four hours or - even better - overnight).

NUTRITION: 289 calories 16g fats 4g protein

78. fuJi aPPle CHICken Salad: Panera bread™ CoPyCaT

| Preparation Time: | 15' | | Servings: | 4 |

| Cooking Time: | 10' |

INGREDIENTS

- 10 oz mix of spring mix salad and chopped romaine
- ½ Red onion
- 2-3 Vine-ripened tomatoes
- 2 Chicken breasts
- 2 cups Apple chips
- ¾ cup Roasted pecan halves
- ½ cup Crumbled Gorgonzola cheese
- ¾ cup Vinaigrette - Panera™ Bread Fuji Apple

DIRECTIONS

1. Do the prep. Thinly slice the onion and chop the salad. Shred the chicken. Combine each of the fixings in a large salad dish. Evenly distribute the salad and serve!

NUTRITION: 250 calories 16g fats 3g protein

79. Market Salad: Chick-fil-a™ Copycat

PREPARATION TIME: 10'	SERVINGS: 1-2

COOKING TIME: 10'

INGREDIENTS

- 1 cup Chicken breast
- 1 head Romaine lettuce
- 8 oz Baby greens
- ½ cup Red cabbage
- ½ cup Carrots
- Optional: Crumbled goat/blue cheese
- 1 Red apple
- 1 Green apple
- 1-pint Strawberries
- ¼ cup Blueberries

DIRECTIONS

1. Do the prep. Cook and cool the chicken. Then chop/shred it. Tear the lettuce apart. Shred the carrots and cabbage. Cut the apples into chunks, and quarter the strawberries.
2. Combine each of the fixings in a salad bowl and serve with the vinaigrette.

NUTRITION: 270 calories 15g fats 4g protein

80. STraWberry PoPPyseed Salad: Panera™ CoPyCaT

PREPARATION TIME: 30'

SERVINGS: 10

COOKING TIME: 0'

INGREDIENTS

- ¼ cup Sugar
- 1/3 cup Slivered almonds
- 8 cups Torn romaine lettuce
- 1 small Halved - thinly sliced onions
- 2 cups Halved fresh strawberries

The Dressing:
- 2 tbsp Sugar
- ¼ cup Mayo
- 1 tbsp Sour cream
- 1 tbsp 2% milk
- 2 ¼ tsp Cider vinegar
- 1 ½ tsp Poppy seeds

DIRECTIONS

1. Pour the sugar into a small heavy skillet. Cook it and stir using the med-low temperature setting until melted and caramel-colored or for about ten minutes. Stir in the almonds until coated. Smear the mixture onto a layer of foil to cool.
2. Toss the romaine, onion, and strawberries in a large salad serving container. Combine the dressing fixings and toss them with the salad. Break the candied almonds into pieces and sprinkle over salad. Serve immediately.

NUTRITION: 249 calories 16.9g fats 3.1g protein

81. Sweet Carrot Salad: Chick-fil-a™ Copycat

PREPARATION TIME: 35'

SERVINGS: 8

COOKING TIME: 0'

INGREDIENTS

- 1 lb. Grated carrots
- 1 cup Crushed pineapple
- ½ cup Raisins
- 1 tbsp Honey
- 2 tbsp Mayonnaise
- 1 dash Lemon juice

DIRECTIONS

1. Grate the carrots and mix in with the raisins, pineapple, and the rest of the fixings until evenly coated. Pop into the fridge to chill for about half an hour to meld the flavors before serving.

NUTRITION: 239 calories 16.4g fats 12g protein

82. Waldorf Salad: Texas Luby's Cafeteria™ Copycat

PREPARATION TIME:	15' + 2H - CHILLING TIME	SERVINGS:	8

COOKING TIME:	0'

INGREDIENTS

- 4 cups Granny Smith apples
- 2 cups Canned pineapple tidbits
- 1 cup Celery
- ½ cup Mayonnaise
- ¼ cup Whipping cream
- 1 drop Vanilla extract
- 1 tbsp Powdered sugar
- 1 tbsp Chopped walnuts or pecans

DIRECTIONS

1. Drain the pineapple, chop the celery, and cube the apples. Combine the pineapple, apples, celery, and mayo in a large mixing container, tossing gently.
2. In another mixing container, whip the cream using the high-speed setting with an electric mixer to create stiff peaks. Blend in the vanilla, sugar, and fruit. Cover in plastic and chill for a minimum of two hours. When it's time to serve, sprinkle with the nuts.

NUTRITION: 259 calories 17.3g fats 5g protein

83. Cottage Cheese and Poppy Seed Mousse with Cherry Water

PREPARATION TIME: 90'

SERVINGS: 6

COOKING TIME: 0'

Ingredients

- 50 g ground poppy seeds
- 6 tbsp Cherry water (at will)
- 5 sheets white gelatin
- 1 pack vanilla sugar
- 150 g sugar
- freshly squeezed juice of 1 lemon
- 250 g cream
- 500 g low-fat quark

Directions

1. Roast the poppy seeds in a non-fat pan over medium-high heat, stirring, until they smell. Deglaze with 60 ml water and possibly 3 tbsp cherry water, let the liquid boil down completely. Let the poppy seeds cool.
2. In the meantime, soak the gelatin in water according to the package. Mix the vanilla sugar, sugar, lemon juice, any remaining cherry water, and 50 g of cream until the sugar has dissolved. Add the curd and poppy seeds and stir until smooth. Whip the rest of the cream until stiff.
3. Squeeze out the gelatin and dissolve in a small saucepan over low heat. Add 1 tablespoon of curd cream, stir well, add a spoon and stir well again, then stir the gelatin quickly with a whisk under the remaining curd, fold in the cream. Cover the mousse and let it set in the fridge in about 5 hours.
4. Cut off the mousse with a tablespoon of cams and serve - for example, with spiced cherries or cassis pears.

NUTRITION: 280 calories 16g fats 3g protein

84. good Mood fruiT Salad

PREPARATION TIME: 30'

SERVINGS: 4

COOKING TIME: 0'

INGREDIENTS

- 1 Apple
- 150 g grapes
- 1 kiwi
- 1 banana
- 1 orange
- 2 tbsp dried cranberries (dried fruit shelf)
- 2 tbsp Agave syrup

DIRECTIONS

1. Wash the apple and grapes. Peel the kiwi, banana, and orange. Cut everything into small pieces. (Bananas stay firmer if you quarter them lengthways and then cut them into thumb-thick slices - that makes cubes.) Mix the fruit and cranberries with the agave syrup.

NUTRITION: 145 calories 14g fats 5g protein

85. fruIT Salad WITH Lemon foam

PREPARATION TIME: 30'

SERVINGS: 4

COOKING TIME: 0'

INGREDIENTS

- 4th ripe nectarines
- 200 g Raspberries
- 1 tbsp Pistachio nuts
- 4th very fresh egg yolk (size M)
- 4 tbsp sugar
- Juice of 1 lemon
- 1/8 l prosecco (or non-alcoholic sparkling wine)

DIRECTIONS

1. Peel the nectarines with a small sharp knife and cut the pulp into slices from the stone. Read out the raspberries, wash them carefully, and drain them on kitchen paper. Spread the fruit mixed in four glasses or on dessert plates. Roughly chop the pistachios.
2. Prepare a saucepan with a suitable metal mixing bowl for a hot water bath, pour approx. 5 cm of water into the saucepan and heat. Mix the egg yolks in the bowl with the sugar and whisk for 3-4 minutes with the whisk of the hand mixer.
3. Place the bowl over the hot water bath and pour the lemon juice and prosecco into the egg yolk cream while stirring continuously until an airy foam form. Pull out the bowl from the water bath and continue to beat the foam for 1-2 minutes until it is only lukewarm.
4. Pour the lemon foam over the fruit salads and sprinkle the pistachios. Serve the dessert immediately.

NUTRITION: 225 calories 17.1g fats 4g protein

86. Vegan Amaranth Pudding with fruit Salad

PREPARATION TIME: 60'

SERVINGS: 4

COOKING TIME: 0'

INGREDIENTS

- 200 g Amaranth grains
- 1 l soy milk
- 6 Apricots
- 2 tbsp Walnut kernels
- 4 tbsp Pomegranate seeds
- 60 g sugar
- Cinnamon powder
- 3 tbsp food starch
- 2 pack Bourbon vanilla sugar
- 1 pinch salt
- 300 g cold soy cream
- 1 pack Cream fixer

DIRECTIONS

1. For the pudding on the evening before, cover the amaranth with sufficient water and let it swell for 12 hours. Pour into a colander the next day and drain. Boil the amaranth and soy milk in a saucepan, then cover and simmer over low heat for 25 minutes.
2. In the meantime, wash, halve, stone and cut the apricots for the fruit salad and cut them into wedges. Roughly chop the walnut kernels. Mix the apricot slices, nuts, pomegranate seeds, and 1 tablespoon of sugar, season with a pinch of cinnamon.
3. Mix the starch, vanilla sugar, remaining sugar, salt, and ½ tsp cinnamon. Stir the mix into the amaranth and let simmer for about 2 minutes. Let the pudding mixture cool lukewarm in the pot.
4. Whisk the soy cream with the hand mixer until foamy. Sprinkle in the cream fixer and continue beating until the cream is firm and foamy. Fold the whipped cream under the pudding mixture. Fill the pudding in four glasses and arrange the fruit salad on it.

NUTRITION: 248 calories 14g fats 6g protein

87. QuICk fruIT Salad WITH Sabayon

PREPARATION TIME:	30'	SERVINGS:	4

COOKING TIME:	0'

INGREDIENTS

- 2nd fully ripe figs
- 1 kiwi
- 100 g each seedless blue and green grape
- 100 g Strawberries
- 1 pear
- 6 tbsp freshly squeezed lime juice
- 2nd Egg yolks
- 1 tbsp sugar
- grated peel of 1 organic lime
- 1 tbsp chopped almonds

DIRECTIONS

1. Wash the figs and quarter them lengthways. Peel the kiwi, quarter lengthways and slice transversely. Wash the grapes, pluck from the stems and cut in half.
2. Briefly rinse, clean, and halve the strawberries. Quarter the pear, core, peel, and cut into fine slices. Arrange the fruit decoratively on four plates, drizzle with 2 tablespoons of lime juice.
3. Mix the egg yolks with the sugar, 2 tablespoons of warm water, and the remaining lime juice and the grated lime peel in the kettle and beat in a hot, non-boiling water bath until the mixture is thick and creamy.
4. Remove from the water bath, continue to beat for 1-2 minutes next to the stove and spread lukewarm over the fruit. Sprinkle with the almonds.

NUTRITION: 135 calories 14g fats 5g protein

88. TroPICal fruIT Salad WITH CoConuT Cream

PREPARATION TIME: 60'

SERVINGS: 4

COOKING TIME: 0'

INGREDIENTS

- 150 g small strawberries
- 100 g Raspberries
- 1 pear
- 1 Apple
- 1 banana
- 2nd Kiwi fruit
- 1 1/2 tbsp lemon juice
- 2 tbsp sugar
- 4 tbsp Grated coconut
- 150 g cream

DIRECTIONS

1. Wash the strawberries carefully and cut out the sepals. Pick raspberries. Peel the pear, apple, banana, and kiwi fruit. Quarter the pear and apple, core, and cut into wedges. Slice the banana. Quarter the kiwis lengthways, separate the stalk from the center and cut the kiwis into thin slices.
2. Mix the lemon juice with 1 tablespoon of sugar, mix in the fruit and let marinate for 15-30 minutes.
3. Mix the grated coconut with 1 teaspoon of sugar in a pan and roast without fat while stirring over medium heat until golden yellow. Be careful not to burn them! Put on a plate.
4. Do not whip the cream until stiff, pour in the remaining sugar, and mix in the coconut flakes. Spread the fruit salad on plates and garnish with the coconut cream.

NUTRITION: 295 Calories 14g fats 3.1g protein

89. Exotic fruit Salad with Coconut-lime Yoghurt

PREPARATION TIME: 30'	SERVINGS: 4

COOKING TIME: 0'

INGREDIENTS

- 3rd Tangerines
- 1 papaya
- 300 g Pineapple pulp
- 50 ml orange juice
- 5 tbsp Lime juice
- honey
- 300 g Greek or Turkish yogurt (10% fat)
- 50 g coconut cream

DIRECTIONS

1. Peel the tangerines, divide them into individual segments, and divide them crosswise. Peel and halve the papaya, remove the seeds and dice the pulp. Dice the pineapple pulp as well.
2. Mix all the prepared fruits, add the orange juice, and 1 tablespoon of lime juice, and season with a little honey.
3. Place the yogurt with coconut cream and 4 tablespoons of lime juice in a blender jar and puree until smooth. Season the cream with honey to taste. Divide the coconut-lime yogurt into four deep plates and arrange the fruit on it.

NUTRITION: 175 calories 16g fats 4.3g protein

90.gIngerfruIT Salad WITH VanIlla SauCe

PREPARATION TIME: 60-90'

SERVINGS: 6

COOKING TIME: 0'

INGREDIENTS

- 1 Vanilla bean
- 1/4 l milk
- 250 g cream
- 1 tbsp food starch
- 2nd fresh egg yolk
- 60 g sugar
- 1 ripe mango
- 3rd ripe peaches
- 1 small ripe honeydew melon
- 250 g Strawberries
- 1-piece fresh ginger (approx. 4 cm)
- 4th Stems of mint
- 1 Organic lime
- 70 g powdered sugar

DIRECTIONS

1. Slice the vanilla pod for the sauce, scrape out the pulp. Put both in a saucepan with 200 ml milk and the cream and simmer for 5 minutes, stirring occasionally, over low heat.
2. In the meantime, mix the starch well with the egg yolks, remaining milk, and sugar. Pour into the pot while stirring and bring to the boil once, stirring constantly. Take it from the stove and let it cool off. (Fish out the pod before serving!)
3. For the salad, peel the mango thinly, cut diagonally from the core, and dice finely. Wash, halve, core, and dice peaches. Cut the melon into wedges, remove the seeds with a spoon, cut the pulp from the skin, and dice. Wash and clean the strawberries and quarter or halve them depending on their size.
4. Peel and finely chop the ginger. Wash the mint, pluck the leaves, and cut them into strips.
5. Wash the lime hot. Rub the peel finely, squeeze out the juice and mix both with sugar, ginger, and mint. Mix gently under the fruit and cover and let the salad cover in the refrigerator for 25-30 minutes.

NUTRITION: 280 calories 14.1g fats 2.6g protein

91. fruIT Salad WITHVanIlla SauCe

PREPARATION TIME: 30'		SERVINGS: 10

COOKING TIME: 0'

INGREDIENTS

- 400 g Cream pudding with vanilla flavor
- 400 ml milk
- 1 kg fresh fruit (e.g., orange, banana, apple, berries, kiwi, grapes)

DIRECTIONS

1. For the sauce, simply stir the cream pudding into the cold milk.
2. Wash and clean the fresh fruit. Halve or quarter larger fruits. Mix the fruit and eat with the sauce.

NUTRITION: 135 calories 15.1g fats 5.1g protein

92. fruIT Salad WITH VogHurT Cream

PREPARATION TIME: 30'

SERVINGS: 4

COOKING TIME: 0'

INGREDIENTS

- 1 Charentais melon
- 500 g soft seasonal fruit
- 50 g Pine nuts
- 2 tbsp Coconut flakes
- 1 cup Cream (200 ml)
- 1 parcel vanilla sugar
- 1 cup Vanilla Yogurt (150 g)

DIRECTIONS

1. Divide the melon once, remove the seeds and scrape out the pulp with an ice cream spoon so that the peel is not destroyed. Cut the pulp into 1 cm cubes.
2. Wash the rest of the fruit well and cut it into small pieces. Mix all the fruit well in a large bowl and arrange it in the melon bowls. What no longer fits in the small bowls.
3. Roast the pine nuts briefly in a non-fat pan, add coconut flakes for a few seconds. Spread both evenly over the fruit salad.
4. For the yogurt cream, whip the cream stiffly together with the vanilla sugar using the hand mixer. Stir in the vanilla yogurt and let it flow in slowly just before the cream becomes really stiff. Serve with fruit salad.

NUTRITION: 405 calories 14.9g fats 5.1g protein

Chapter 4

OLD AND MODERN DESSERT RECIPES

93. maPle buTTer blondie

PREPARATION TIME: 15′

SERVINGS: 9

COOKING TIME: 35′

INGREDIENTS

- 1/3 cup butter, melted
- 1 cup brown sugar, packed
- 1 large egg, beaten
- 1 tablespoon vanilla extract
- ½ teaspoon baking powder
- 1/8 teaspoon baking soda
- 1/8 teaspoon salt
- 1 cup flour
- 2/3 cup white chocolate chips
- 1/3 cup pecans, chopped (or walnuts)
- Maple butter sauce
- ¾ cup maple syrup
- ½ cup butter
- ¾ cup brown sugar
- 8 ounces cream cheese, softened to room temp
- ¼ cup pecans, chopped
- Vanilla ice cream, for serving

DIRECTIONS

1. Preheat the oven to 350°F and coat a 9x9 baking pan with cooking spray.
2. In a mixing bowl, combine the butter, brown sugar, egg, and vanilla, and beat until smooth. Sift in the baking powder, baking soda, salt, and flour, and stir until it is well incorporated. Fold in the white chocolate chips.
3. Bake for 20–25 minutes. While those are in the oven, prepare the maple butter sauce by combining the maple syrup and butter in a medium saucepan.
4. Cook over low heat until the butter is melted. Add the brown sugar and cream cheese. Stir constantly until the cream cheese has completely melted, then remove the pot from the heat. Remove the blondies from the oven and cut them into squares.
5. Top with vanilla ice cream, maple butter sauce, and chopped nuts.

NUTRITION: 40g carbs 14g fats 3g protein

94. aPPle CHImI CHeeseCake

PREPARATION TIME: 10'

SERVINGS: 2

COOKING TIME: 10'

INGREDIENTS

- 2 (9 inches) flour tortillas
- ¼ cup granulated sugar
- ½ teaspoon cinnamon
- 3 ounces cream cheese, softened
- ½ teaspoon vanilla extract
- 1/3 cup apple, peeled and finely chopped
- Oil for frying
- Vanilla ice cream (optional)
- Caramel topping (optional)

DIRECTIONS

1. Make sure your tortillas and cream cheese are at room temperature; this will make them both easier to work with. In a small bowl, combine the sugar and cinnamon.
2. In another mixing bowl, combine the cream cheese and vanilla until smooth. Fold in the apple. Divide the apple and cheese mixture in two and place half in the center of each tortilla. Leave at least an inch margin around the outside.
3. Fold the tortilla top to the middle, then the bottom to the middle, and then roll it up from the sides. Heat about half an inch of oil in a skillet over medium heat.
4. Place the filled tortillas into the skillet and fry on each side until they are golden brown. Transfer them to a plate lined with paper towels to drain any excess oil, then immediately coat them with the cinnamon and sugar. Serve with a scoop of ice cream.

NUTRITION: 43g carbs 12g fats 5g protein

95. Triple Chocolate Meltdown

Preparation Time: 1H		**Servings:** 8

Cooking Time: 30'

Ingredients

- 2 cups heavy cream, divided
- 1 cup white chocolate chips
- 1 cup semi-sweet chocolate chips
- 1-pound bittersweet chocolate, chopped
- ½ cup butter, softened
- 6 eggs
- 1 ½ cups of sugar
- 1 ½ cups all-purpose flour
- Ice cream, for serving

Directions

1. Preheat the oven to 400°F.
2. Prepare 8 ramekins by first coating the inside with butter and then sprinkling them with flour so the bottom and sides are covered. Place them on a baking tray.
3. In a saucepan, bring 1 cup of heavy cream to a simmer. Remove it from the heat and add the white chocolate chips, stirring until the chocolate is melted and the mixture is smooth. Allow it to cool for about half an hour, stirring occasionally.
4. Repeat with the other cup of cream and the semi-sweet chocolate chips. In a double boiler, combine the bittersweet chocolate with the softened butter and stir until the chocolate is melted and the mixture is smooth. Remove the bowl from the heat and allow it to cool for about 10 minutes.
5. In a mixing bowl, beat the eggs and the sugar together for about 2 minutes, or until the mixture is foamy. Use a rubber spatula to fold in the bittersweet chocolate mixture. Turn the mixer to low and beat in the flour half a cup at a time, being careful not to overmix the batter.
6. Pour the batter evenly into the prepared ramekins and place the baking tray in the oven. Bake for about 18 minutes. When done, the cakes should have a slight crust but still be soft in the middle. Remove them from the oven when they have reached this look. If you cook them too long, you won't get the lava cake effect.
7. Let the ramekins sit on the tray for 2–3 minutes and then invert them onto serving plates. Drizzle some of both the semi-sweet and white chocolate sauces over the top and serve with a scoop of ice cream.

Nutrition: 39g carbs 15g fats 6g protein

96. CHoColaTe mousse dessert SHooTer

PREPARATION TIME: 30'

SERVINGS: 4

COOKING TIME: 0'

INGREDIENTS

- 2 tablespoons butter
- 6 ounces semi-sweet chocolate chips (1 cup), divided
- 1 teaspoon vanilla
- 2 eggs, separated, at room temperature
- 2 tablespoons sugar
- ½ cup heavy cream
- 8 Oreo® cookies
- ½ cup prepared fudge sauce
- Canned whipped cream

DIRECTIONS

1. Melt the butter and all but 1 tablespoon of the chocolate chips in a double boiler. When they are melted, stir in the vanilla and remove from the heat. Whisk in the egg yolks.
2. Beat the egg whites until they form soft peaks, and then fold them into the chocolate mixture. Beat the sugar and heavy cream in a separate bowl until it forms stiff peaks or is the consistency that you desire. Fold this into the chocolate mixture.
3. Crush the remaining chocolate chips into small pieces and stir them into the chocolate. Crush the Oreos. (You can either scrape out the cream from the cookies or just crush the entire cookie.)
4. Spoon the cookie crumbs into the bottom of your cup and pat them down. Layer the chocolate mixture on top. Finish with whipped cream and either more chocolate chips or Oreo mixture. Store in the refrigerator until ready to serve.

NUTRITION: 45g carbs 12g fats 5g protein

97.deadly CHoColaTe SIn

| PREPARATION TIME: | 12' | | SERVINGS: | 12 |

| COOKING TIME: | 10' |

INGREDIENTS

- 1-2 tablespoons butter for greasing or cooking spray
- 6 ounces semisweet chocolate
- 1 cup unsalted butter
- 1 teaspoon vanilla extract
- 4 eggs, at room temperature
- 4 egg yolks, at room temperature
- ½ cup brown sugar, firmly packed
- 6 tablespoons cornstarch
- 1 (10 ounces) package frozen raspberries in a heavy syrup, thawed
- 1-pint fresh raspberries
- 2 ounces bitter chocolate
- 12 triangular cookies or chocolate pieces
- 12 sprigs fresh mint

DIRECTIONS

1. Preheat the oven to 375°F. Prepare 12 (4 ounces) ramekins by buttering or spraying them with non-stick cooking spray. Combine the chocolate, unsalted butter, and vanilla in a double boiler and melt the chocolate, stirring to combine. In a large mixing bowl, beat together the eggs, egg yolks, and brown sugar. Mix this on high for 5–7 minutes, or until the volume almost doubles.
2. Set the mixer to low and add the cornstarch one tablespoon at a time, beating after each addition. Turn the mixer back to high and beat another 5 minutes or until soft peaks form.
3. Now, fold the chocolate into the egg mixture, making sure to scrape the bottom and sides of the bowl.
4. Pour the batter into the prepared ramekins and bake for 10 minutes. After 10 minutes, remove the ramekins from the oven and allow them to cool. Store in the refrigerator, covered with plastic wrap, until ready to serve.
5. When ready to serve, run a knife around the edges to loosen the cake, then invert the cake on serving plates.
6. Purée the thawed raspberries in a blender, then ladle them over the top of each cake. Top with fresh raspberries, chocolate pieces, and mint. Serve

NUTRITION: 40g carbs 10g fats 6g protein

98. Orange CreamsICle Cake

PREPARATION TIME: 30'		**SERVINGS:** 8-10

COOKING TIME: 30-35'

INGREDIENTS

- 1 (18.25 ounce) box orange cake mix
- 1 (3 ounces) package orange-flavored gelatin
- 1 cup boiling water
- 1 (3.4 ounces) package instant vanilla pudding mix
- 1 cup milk
- 1 teaspoon vanilla extract
- 1 teaspoon orange extract
- 1 (8 ounces) tub Cool Whip®, thawed
- White chocolate shavings, to garnish

DIRECTIONS

1. Preheat the oven to 350°F and prepare two 9-inch round cake pans by greasing and dusting them with flour. In a large bowl, prepare the packaged cake mix according to the package Directions. Divide the batter evenly between the prepared cake pans.
2. Bake for 35–45 minutes or until a toothpick inserted in the center comes out clean. Remove the cakes from the oven. While they are still hot, use the handle end of a wooden spoon to poke holes throughout.
3. Prepare the gelatin with one cup of hot water, and when it is dissolved completely, pour it over the hot cake, making sure the gelatin goes into all the holes.
4. Let the cake sit and cool completely. (You can put it in the refrigerator to speed up the process if you like.) Prepare the vanilla pudding using only one cup of milk. Fold in the Cool Whip, making sure it is well incorporated.
5. Put a layer of the pudding mixture between the cake layers and use the remaining to completely frost the cake. Garnish with chocolate shavings and grated orange peel if desired. Refrigerate until ready to serve.

NUTRITION: 41g carbs 12g fats 3g protein

99.Cinnamon Apple Turnover

PREPARATION TIME: 10'

SERVINGS: 4-6

COOKING TIME: 25'

INGREDIENTS

- 1 large Granny Smith apple, peeled, cored, and diced
- ½ teaspoon cornstarch
- ¼ teaspoon cinnamon
- Dash ground nutmeg
- ¼ cup brown sugar
- ¼ cup applesauce
- ¼ teaspoon vanilla extract
- 1 tablespoon butter, melted
- 1 sheet of puff pastry, thawed
- Whipped cream or vanilla ice cream, to serve

DIRECTIONS

1. Preheat the oven to 400°F. Prepare a baking sheet by spraying it with non-stick cooking spray or using a bit of oil on a paper towel.
2. In a mixing bowl, mix together the apples, cornstarch, cinnamon, nutmeg, and brown sugar. Stir to make sure the apples are well covered with the spices. Then stir in the applesauce and the vanilla.
3. Lay out your puff pastry and cut it into squares. You should be able to make 4 or 6 depending on how big you want your turnovers to be and how big your pastry is.
4. Place some of the apple mixture in the center of each square and fold the corners of the pastry up to make a pocket. Pinch the edges together to seal. Then brush a bit of the melted butter over the top to give the turnovers that nice brown color.
5. Place the filled pastry onto the prepared baking pan and transfer to the preheated oven. Bake 20–25 minutes, or until they become a golden brown in color. Serve with whipped cream or vanilla ice cream.

NUTRITION: 43g carbs 13g fats 4g protein

100. burger King's HersHey's Sundae Pie

PREPARATION TIME: 20'

SERVINGS: 8

COOKING TIME: 10'

INGREDIENTS

Crust
- 1½ cups crushed chocolate wafers
- 2 tablespoons sugar
- ½ cup melted butter

Cream cheese layer
- 8 ounces cream cheese
- ¾ cup powdered sugar
- 8 ounces Cool Whip or cream, plus more for topping
- 1 teaspoon vanilla extract

Chocolate layer
- 1 (3½-ounce) box chocolate pudding
- 1½ cups milk
- Chocolate syrup, for drizzling
- Chocolate chips, for topping

DIRECTIONS

1. Preheat oven to 350°F. Meanwhile, prepare the crust. Place ingredients in a food processor or blender and pulse until well-blended. Spread and press into a 9-inch pie pan. Bake until fragrant and set (about 10 minutes). Place on a wire rack to cool.
2. Prepare the cream cheese layer. Beat the cream cheese until softened. Beat in sugar, Cool Whip, and vanilla until well-blended. Spread evenly over cooled crust.
3. Use 1½ cups milk to prepare pudding (follow packaging instructions) and spread over cream filling.
4. Top with dollops of Cool Whip, drizzle with chocolate syrup and sprinkle with chocolate chips.
5. Let chill to set.

NUTRITION: 420 Calories 27.8g Total Fat 39.1g Carbs 5.2g Protein

101. Chili's Chocolate Brownie Sundae

Preparation Time: 20'		**Servings:** 8

Cooking Time: 30'

Ingredients

- ½ cup flour
- 1/3 cup cocoa
- ¼ teaspoon salt
- ¼ teaspoon baking powder
- ½ cup margarine, melted
- 1 cup white sugar
- 2 eggs
- 1 teaspoon vanilla
- ½ cup chocolate chips
- ½ gallon vanilla ice cream, slightly softened
- 1 (6-ounce) jar fudge topping
- Whipped cream, for topping (optional)
- ½ cup walnuts, coarsely chopped
- 8 maraschino cherries, for garnish

Directions

1. Preheat oven to 350°F. Grease a 9×9 baking pan. Sift together flour, cocoa, baking powder, and salt in a bowl. Set aside.
2. Combine melted margarine, sugar, eggs, and vanilla, blending well. Add flour mixture, stirring briefly to moisten. Stir in chocolate chips. Do not over-mix.
3. Pour into prepared pan. Bake until fragrant and corners begin to separate from the pan (about 30 minutes). If over-baked, the result will be cakey instead of fudgy.
4. Cool slightly before cutting into 8 bars. Place a scoop of ice cream on top of each brownie and drizzle with fudge sauce. Top with whipped cream (optional) and sprinkle with chopped walnuts.
5. Garnish with cherries.

Nutrition: 1290 Calories 61g Total Fat 195g Carbs 14g Protein

102. ben & Jerry's CHerry garCla Ice Cream

PREPARATION TIME: 4 H	SERVINGS: 4-8

COOKING TIME: 0'

INGREDIENTS

- ¼ cup Bing cherries, fresh or frozen (thawed), drained well and roughly chopped
- 2 cups thick cream
- 1 cup milk
- ¾ cup sugar
- 2 large eggs
- 1½ teaspoons vanilla extract (optional)
- ¼ cup semisweet chocolate, broken into bits

DIRECTIONS

1. Chill cherries until ready for use. In a saucepan, whisk together cream, milk, sugar, and eggs. Whisk while heating gently to 165°F. Remove from heat. Strain into a bowl. Cover and let chill for about 2 hours. Place in ice cream maker and let churn. It should be ready in about 20 minutes. Add cherries and chocolate just before the ice cream is done. Transfer to containers, cover, and freeze well (about 4 hours). Serve and enjoy.

NUTRITION: 250 Calories 14g Total Fat 26g Carbs 4g Protein

103. P.f. CHang's CoConuT PineaPPle Ice Cream WITH banana SPring rolls

PREPARATION TIME:	5'		SERVINGS:	6

	COOKING TIME:	30'

INGREDIENTS

Ice Cream
- 1 (13½-ounce) can coconut milk
- 1 cup granulated sugar
- 1½ cups heavy cream
- 1 teaspoon coconut extract
- 1 (8-ounce) can crushed pineapple, drained
- 1/3 cup shredded coconut

Banana Spring Rolls
- 3 ripe bananas (preferably plantains), halved horizontally
- 3 rice paper or wonton wrappers
- 1–3 tablespoons brown sugar
- 1 teaspoon cinnamon
- Oil, for frying
- Caramel sauce, for drizzling (optional)
- Paste for sealing wrappers
- 2 tablespoons water
- 2 teaspoons flour or cornstarch

DIRECTIONS

1. Make the ice cream. Place coconut milk and sugar in a mixing bowl. Mix with an electric mixer until sugar is dissolved. Mix in remaining ingredients until well-blended. Place in ice cream maker to churn (follow manufacturer's instructions) until ice cream holds when scooped with a spoon (about 30 minutes). Transfer to a container with lid and freeze for at least 2 hours or until desired firmness is reached.
2. Make the banana spring rolls. Lay the wrapper on a flat surface. Position a banana slice near the edge of the wrapper closest to you (the bottom). Sprinkle with about 1 teaspoon to 1 tablespoon brown sugar, depending on how sweet you want it. Sprinkle with a pinch or two of cinnamon. Roll up like a burrito, tucking in the sides. In a small bowl, stir the paste ingredients together. Brush the paste on the edge of the wrapper and seal the roll. Place roll, sealed side down, on a plate, and repeat with the remaining bananas. Heat oil, about 1–1½ inches deep, over medium to high heat. Fry the rolls until golden brown (1–2 minutes on each side). Place on paper towels to drain.
3. Serve the rolls with scoops of ice cream and drizzle with caramel sauce, if desired.

NUTRITION: 146 Calories 11g Total Fat 33g Carbs 5g Protein

104. Tgl friday's Oreo Madness

PREPARATION TIME:	10' + 2H FREEZING TIME	SERVINGS:	18

COOKING TIME:	0'

INGREDIENTS

- 1 (14-ounce) package Oreo cookies
- ½ cup (1 stick) butter, melted
- 5 cups vanilla ice cream
- For drizzling:
- Hot fudge and caramel toppings

DIRECTIONS

1. Line muffin pans with cupcake liners. If needed, let ice cream stand at room temperature to soften a little for easier spreading. Place Oreos in a blender or food processor and pulse to break into crumbs.
2. Transfer to a bowl and stir in melted butter. Mix well. Press about 2 tablespoons each of crumb mixture into muffin tins. Top each with about ¼ cup ice cream, smoothening down with a spatula.
3. Cover with another 2 tablespoons of crumbs. Cover and freeze until set (about 2 hours). Remove from muffin tins. Drizzle with toppings and serve.

NUTRITION: 287 Calories 14g Total Fat 38.1g Carbs 2.6g Protein

105. Ben & Jerry's CHunky Monkey Ice Cream

Preparation Time:	20' + 8H FREEZING TIME	Servings:	4-8

Cooking Time: 30'

Ingredients

- 3 medium ripe bananas, peeled and cut into bite-size pieces
- ⅓ cup brown sugar, packed
- 1 tablespoon butter, diced
- 1½ cups whole milk
- 2 tablespoons granulated sugar
- ½ teaspoon vanilla extract
- 1½ teaspoons freshly-squeezed lemon juice
- ¼ teaspoon coarse or sea salt
- ¼ cup walnuts, coarsely chopped
- ¼ cup chopped dark chocolate or dark chocolate chips

Directions

1. Preheat oven or oven-type toaster to 400°F. In a shallow baking dish, coat the banana slices with brown sugar and sprinkle with butter.
2. Bake until sugar is caramelized, and bananas are browned (about 30–40 minutes), stirring occasionally. Let cool slightly and then combine with milk, sugar, vanilla, lemon juice, and salt.
3. Use a blender or food processor to make a smooth puree. Cover with plastic wrap and chill for about 4 hours. Transfer to ice cream maker and let churn, following manufacturer's instructions.
4. Stir in walnuts and chocolate. Freeze for about 4 hours or until of desired consistency.

Nutrition: 290 Calories 17g Total Fat 30g Carbs 4g Protein

106. JaCk In THe box's Oreo Cookle SHake

PREPARATION TIME: 5'

SERVINGS: 2

COOKING TIME: 0'

INGREDIENTS

- 3 cups vanilla ice cream
- 1½ cups milk, cold
- 8 Oreo cookies, without filling, broken into small pieces
- Whipped cream, for topping (optional)
- 2 cherries, for garnish (optional)

DIRECTIONS

1. Place ice cream and milk in a blender. Pulse gently until smooth. Continue blending at low speed and add Oreos. Blend until cookies are pureed (about 10 seconds). Pour into 2 cups or glasses. Top with whipped cream and cherries (optional).

NUTRITION: 722 Calories 36.4g Total Fat 83.7g Carbs 18.7g Protein

107. dalry Queen's Candy Cane Chill

PREPARATION TIME: 5'

SERVINGS: 2

COOKING TIME: 0'

INGREDIENTS

- 4 large scoops vanilla ice cream
- 1 cup Cool Whip, thawed or frozen
- ¼ cup milk
- 3 regular sized candy canes, broken into small pieces
- ¼ cup chocolate chunks

DIRECTIONS

1. Place all ingredients in a blender. Blend to desired consistency. (Add more ice cream, if needed.) Pour into 2 glasses or mugs.

NUTRITION: 536 Calories 26.6g Total Fat 68.5g Carbs 6.6g Protein

108. dairy Queen's blizzard

PREPARATION TIME: 5'

SERVINGS: 1

COOKING TIME: 0'

INGREDIENTS

- 1 candy bar, of your choice
- ¼ to ½ cup milk
- 2½ cups vanilla ice cream
- 1 teaspoon fudge sauce

DIRECTIONS

1. Place the candy bar of your choice into the freezer to harden it. Break the candy bar into multiple tiny chunks and place all the ingredients into a blender.
2. Keep blending until the ice cream becomes thicker, and everything is mixed completely.
3. Pour into a cup and consume.

NUTRITION: 953 Calories 51.6g Total Fat 108.8g Carbs 15.1g Protein

109. Applebee's Maple Butter Blondie

Preparation Time: 10'

Servings: 6

Cooking Time: 25'

Ingredients

- 1/3 cup butter, melted
- 1 cup brown sugar, packed
- 1 egg, beaten
- 1 tablespoon vanilla extract
- 1 cup all-purpose flour
- ½ teaspoon baking powder
- 1/8 teaspoon baking soda
- 1/8 teaspoon salt
- ½ cup white chocolate chips
- ½ cup walnuts or pecans, chopped

Maple Cream Sauce:
- ½ cup maple syrup
- ¼ cup butter
- ½ cup brown sugar
- 8 ounces cream cheese, softened
- Walnuts for garnish, chopped; optional
- Vanilla ice cream for serving

Directions

1. Preheating the oven to 350F, and Greasing an 8×8 baking pan.
2. Dissolve the sugar in the melted butter. Whip in the egg and the vanilla and set the mixture aside.
3. In another bowl, mix together the flour, baking powder and soda, and salt.
4. Slowly pour the dry mixture into the butter mixture and mix thoroughly.
5. Make sure the mixture is at room temperature before folding in the nuts and chocolate chips.
6. Transfer the mixture into the baking pan and bake for 20 to 25 minutes.
7. While waiting for the blondies to bake, combine the syrup and butter over low heat. When the butter has melted, mix in the sugar and cream cheese. Take the mixture off the heat when the cream cheese has melted and set aside.
8. Let the blondies cool a little and then cut them into rectangles. Serve with the syrup, top with walnuts and vanilla ice cream, if desired, and serve.

Nutrition: 1000 Calories 54g Total Fat 117g Carbs 13g Protein

110. Houston's apple Walnut Cobbler

PREPARATION TIME: 15'	SERVINGS: 6

COOKING TIME: 30'

INGREDIENTS

- 3 large Granny Smith apples, peeled and diced
- 1½ cups walnuts, coarsely chopped
- 1 cup all-purpose flour
- 1 cup brown sugar
- 1 teaspoon cinnamon
- Pinch of nutmeg (optional)
- 1 large egg
- ½ cup (1 stick) butter, melted
- Vanilla ice cream
- Caramel sauce, for drizzling (optional)

DIRECTIONS

1. Preheat oven to 350°F. Lightly grease an 8-inch square baking dish. Spread diced apple over the bottom of the baking dish. Sprinkle with walnuts.
2. In a bowl, mix together flour, sugar, cinnamon, nutmeg (optional), and egg to make a coarse-textured mixture. Sprinkle over the apple-walnut layer.
3. Pour melted butter over the whole mixture. Bake until fragrant and crumb top is browned (about 30 minutes). Serve warm topped with scoops of vanilla ice cream. Drizzle with caramel sauce (optional).

NUTRITION: 611 Calories 36g Total Fat 69g Carbs 8g Protein

111. melTIngPoTCHoColaTefondue

<table>
<tr><td>PREPARATION TIME:</td><td>10'</td><td>SERVINGS:</td><td>4</td></tr>
<tr><td>COOKING TIME:</td><td>5'</td><td></td><td></td></tr>
</table>

INGREDIENTS

- 8 ounces semi-sweet or dark chocolate chips
- 1 cup heavy cream
- 1 tablespoon unsalted butter
- 2 tablespoons chunky peanut butter or Nutella (optional)
- Possible complements: strawberry, banana, grapes, cherries, brownies, cream puffs, rice puffs, marshmallows, or cheesecake, cut into bite-size pieces

DIRECTIONS

1. Heat cream in a saucepan to a simmer. Stir in butter, chocolate, and peanut butter or Nutella (if using). Let sit to allow the chocolate to melt (about 2 minutes). Whisk until smooth and serve immediately with desired complements.

NUTRITION: 667 Calories 32g Total Fat 84g Carbs 9g Protein

112. P.f. CHang's gInger Panna CoTTa

PREPARATION TIME: 10'

SERVINGS: 3

COOKING TIME: 4H 10'

INGREDIENTS

Panna Cotta:
- ¼ cup heavy cream
- ½ cup granulated sugar
- 1 tablespoon grated ginger
- 1½ tablespoons powdered gelatin
- 6 tablespoons warm water

Strawberry Sauce:
- 2 pounds ripe strawberries, hulled
- ½ cup granulated sugar
- 2 teaspoons cornstarch
- ½ lemon, juice
- 1 pinch salt

DIRECTIONS

1. Place the cream, sugar, and ginger in a saucepan and cook over medium-low heat, until the sugar dissolves. Remove the mixture from heat and set aside.
2. In a medium-sized bowl, mix the water and the gelatin together. Set aside for a few minutes. After the gelatin has rested, pour the sugar mixture into the medium-sized bowl and stir, removing all lumps.
3. Grease your ramekins and then transfer the mixture into the ramekins, leaving 2 inches of space at the top.
4. Place the ramekins in your refrigerator or freezer to let them set for at least 4 hours.
5. While the panna cottas are setting, make the strawberry sauce by cooking all the sauce ingredients in a medium-sized pan for 10 minutes. Stir the mixture occasionally, then remove from heat.
6. When the panna cottas are ready, flip over the containers onto a plate and allow the gelatin to stand. Drizzle with the strawberry sauce and serve.

NUTRITION: 346 Calories 30g Total Fat 16g Carbs 4g Protein

113. Starbucks' Cranberry bliss bars

| PREPARATION TIME: | 35' | | SERVINGS: | 6 |

| COOKING TIME: | 20' |

INGREDIENTS

- 2¼ cups all-purpose flour
- 1½ teaspoons baking powder
- ¼ teaspoon salt
- 1/8 teaspoon ground cinnamon
- ¾ cup butter, melted
- 1½ cups light brown sugar, packed
- 2 large eggs
- ¾ teaspoon vanilla extract
- ½ cup dried cranberries
- 6 ounces white baking chocolate, coarsely chopped
- White Chocolate Frosting
- 1 (8-ounce) package cream cheese, cubed, softened
- 1 cup powdered sugar
- 1 tablespoon grated orange zest, or to taste
- 6 ounces white baking chocolate, melted, divided
- ½ cup dried cranberries, chopped

DIRECTIONS

1. Preheat oven to 350°F. Grease a 9×13-inch baking pan. In a bowl, combine flour, baking powder, salt, and cinnamon. Set aside. In a mixer bowl, combine the still-warm melted butter with sugar. Let cool slightly.
2. While mixing continuously, add eggs one at a time. Mix in vanilla. Add flour mixture and mix to incorporate and to make a thick batter. Stir in cranberries and chopped chocolate.
3. Spread evenly in prepared pan. Bake until the toothpick inserted in the center comes out clean (about 18–20 minutes). Let cool completely on a wire rack.
4. Meanwhile, prepare the frosting. Beat cream cheese, powdered sugar, and orange zest until well-blended. Gradually add half of the melted white chocolate and mix until smooth.
5. Spread the frosting over the cooled blondies. Sprinkle with cranberries and drizzle with the remaining melted chocolate. Cut into bars or triangles and serve.

NUTRITION: 198 Calories 8g Total Fat 28g Carbs 2g Protein

114. Olive Garden's Tiramisu

PREPARATION TIME: 10'

SERVINGS: 9

COOKING TIME: 2 H 40'

INGREDIENTS

- 4 egg yolks
- 2 tablespoons milk
- 2/3 cup granulated sugar
- 2 cups mascarpone cheese
- ¼ teaspoon vanilla extract
- 1 cup heavy cream
- ½ cup cold espresso
- ¼ cup Kahlua
- 20–24 ladyfingers
- 2 teaspoons cocoa powder

DIRECTIONS

1. Bring water to a boil, then reduce the heat to maintain a simmer. Place a heatproof bowl over the water, making sure that the bowl does not touch the water. In the heatproof bowl, whisk together the egg yolks, milk, and sugar for about 8 to 10 minutes.
2. When the mixture has thickened, remove the bowl from heat and then whisk in the vanilla and mascarpone cheese until the mixture becomes smooth. In another bowl, whisk the cream until soft peaks are formed.
3. Using a spatula, fold the whipped cream into the mascarpone mixture, making sure to retain the fluffiness of the whipped cream. In another bowl, mix the espresso and Kahlua.
4. Dip the ladyfingers into the espresso mixture one by one. Dip only the bottom, and dip them quickly so as not to make them soggy. Cover the bottom of an 8×8 pan with half of the dipped ladyfingers, cracking them if necessary.
5. Pour half of the mascarpone mixture over the ladyfingers. Place another layer of ladyfingers over the mixture. Pour the rest of the mixture over the second layer of ladyfingers and smooth out the top.
6. Dust some cocoa powder over the top and then place it in the refrigerator. Slice the cake and serve when set.

NUTRITION: 289 Calories 14g Total Fat 34.4g Carbs 4g Protein

115. maple butter blondie

<table>
<tr><td>PREPARATION TIME:</td><td>15'</td><td>SERVINGS:</td><td>9</td></tr>
</table>

COOKING TIME: 35'

INGREDIENTS

- 1/3 cup butter, melted
- 1 cup brown sugar, packed
- 1 large egg, beaten
- 1 tablespoon vanilla extract
- ½ teaspoon baking powder
- 1/8 teaspoon baking soda
- 1/8 teaspoon salt
- 1 cup flour
- 2/3 cup white chocolate chips
- 1/3 cup pecans, chopped (or walnuts)
- Maple butter sauce
- ¾ cup maple syrup
- ½ cup butter
- ¾ cup brown sugar
- 8 ounces cream cheese, softened to room temp
- ¼ cup pecans, chopped
- Vanilla ice cream, for serving

DIRECTIONS

1. Preheat the oven to 350°F and coat a 9x9 baking pan with cooking spray. In a mixing bowl, combine the butter, brown sugar, egg, and vanilla, and beat until smooth.
2. Sift in the baking powder, baking soda, salt, and flour, and stir until it is well incorporated. Fold in the white chocolate chips. Bake for 20–25 minutes.
3. While those are in the oven, prepare the maple butter sauce by combining the maple syrup and butter in a medium saucepan.
4. Cook over low heat until the butter is melted. Add the brown sugar and cream cheese. Stir constantly until the cream cheese has completely melted, then remove the pot from the heat.
5. Remove the blondies from the oven and cut them into squares. Top with vanilla ice cream, maple butter sauce, and chopped nuts.

NUTRITION: 40g carbs 12g fats 4g protein

116. Chef John's Zabagllone

PREPARATION TIME: 10'

SERVINGS: 2

COOKING TIME: 1H 25'

INGREDIENTS

- ½ cup Strawberries
- 3 tbsp and 1 tsp White sugar
- 3 Egg yolks
- ¼ cup Dry Marsala wine

DIRECTIONS

1. Remove the hulls, slice the strawberries into halves, and mix them with the sugar (1 tsp.). Cover the bowl and let it rest on the countertop for about one hour. Portion fruit into two serving bowls of choice.
2. Toss the yolks of the eggs, sugar, and marsala into a metal mixing container. Heat it using the low-temperature setting. As it heats, whisk until it forms loose peaks (6-8 min.) and warm to the touch.
3. Scoop the custard over the berries and serve warm.

NUTRITION: 44g carbs 11g fats 5g protein

117. Chocolate Mousse Dessert Shooter

Preparation Time: 30'		**Servings:** 4

Cooking Time: 0'

Ingredients

- 2 tablespoons butter
- 6 ounces semi-sweet chocolate chips (1 cup), divided
- 2 eggs
- 1 teaspoon vanilla
- 8 Oreo® cookies
- ½ cup prepared fudge sauce
- 2 tablespoons sugar
- ½ cup heavy cream
- Canned whipped cream

Directions

1. Melt the butter and all but 1 tablespoon of the chocolate chips in a double boiler.
2. When they are melted, stir in the vanilla and remove from the heat.
3. Whisk in the egg yolks.
4. Beat the egg whites until they form soft peaks, and then fold them into the chocolate mixture.
5. Beat the sugar and heavy cream in a separate bowl until it forms stiff peaks or is the consistency that you desire. Fold this into the chocolate mixture.
6. Crush the remaining chocolate chips into small pieces and stir them into the chocolate. Crush the Oreos. (You can either scrape out the cream from the cookies or just crush the entire cookie.)
7. Spoon the cookie crumbs into the bottom of your cup and pat them down. Layer the chocolate mixture on top. Finish with whipped cream and either more chocolate chips or Oreo mixture.
8. Store in the refrigerator until ready to serve.

NUTRITION: 41g carbs 12g fats 2g protein

118. Cinnamon Apple Turnover

PREPARATION TIME: 10'

SERVINGS: 4-6

COOKING TIME: 25'

INGREDIENTS

- 1 large Granny Smith apple, peeled, cored, and diced
- ½ teaspoon cornstarch
- ¼ teaspoon cinnamon
- Dash ground nutmeg
- ¼ cup brown sugar
- ¼ cup applesauce
- ¼ teaspoon vanilla extract
- 1 tablespoon butter, melted
- 1 sheet of puff pastry, thawed
- Whipped cream or vanilla ice cream, to serve

DIRECTIONS

1. Preheat the oven to 400°F. Prepare a baking sheet by spraying it with non-stick cooking spray or using a bit of oil on a paper towel.
2. In a mixing bowl, mix together the apples, cornstarch, cinnamon, nutmeg, and brown sugar. Stir to make sure the apples are well covered with the spices. Then stir in the applesauce and the vanilla.
3. Lay out your puff pastry and cut it into squares. You should be able to make 4 or 6 depending on how big you want your turnovers to be and how big your pastry is.
4. Place some of the apple mixture in the center of each square and fold the corners of the pastry up to make a pocket. Pinch the edges together to seal. Then brush a bit of the melted butter over the top to give the turnovers that nice brown color.
5. Place the filled pastry onto the prepared baking pan and transfer to the preheated oven. Bake 20–25 minutes, or until they become a golden brown in color. Serve with whipped cream or vanilla ice cream.

NUTRITION: 42g carbs 13g fats 4g protein

119. Cherry Chocolate Cobbler

Preparation Time: 10'

Servings: 8

Cooking Time: 45'

Ingredients

- 1½ cups all-purpose flour
- ½ cup sugar
- 2 teaspoons baking powder
- ½ teaspoon salt
- ¼ cup butter
- 6 ounces semisweet chocolate morsels
- ¼ cup milk
- 1 egg, beaten
- 21 ounces cherry pie filling
- ½ cup finely chopped nuts

Directions

1. Preheat the oven to 350°F. Combine the flour, sugar, baking powder, salt, and butter in a large mixing bowl. Use a pastry blender to cut the mixture until there are lumps the size of small peas.
2. Melt the chocolate morsels. Let cool for approximately 5 minutes, then add the milk and egg and mix well. Beat into the flour mixture, mixing completely. Spread the pie filling in a 2-quart casserole dish. Randomly drop the chocolate batter over the filling, then sprinkle with nuts.
3. Bake for 40–45 minutes. Serve with a scoop of vanilla ice cream if desired.

Nutrition: 45g carbs 14g fats 3g protein

120. Pumpkin Custard with Gingersnaps

Preparation Time:	30'		Servings:	8

	Cooking Time:	35'

Ingredients

- Custard
- 8 egg yolks
- 1¾ cups (1 15-ounce can) pure pumpkin puree
- 1¾ cups heavy whipping cream
- ½ cup sugar
- 1½ teaspoons pumpkin pie spice
- 1 teaspoon vanilla

Topping
- 1 cup crushed gingersnap cookies
- 1 tablespoon melted butter

Whipped Cream
- 1 cup heavy whipping cream
- 1 tablespoon superfine sugar (or regular sugar if you have no caster sugar)
- ½ teaspoon pumpkin pie spice

Garnish
- 8 whole gingersnap cookies

Directions

1. Preheat the oven to 350°F. Separate the yolks from 8 eggs and whisk them together in a large mixing bowl until they are well blended and creamy.
2. Add the pumpkin, sugar, vanilla, heavy cream, and pumpkin pie spice and whisk to combine. Cook the custard mixture in a double boiler, stirring until it has thickened enough that it coats a spoon.
3. Pour the mixture into individual custard cups or an 8×8-inch baking pan and bake for about 20 minutes if using individual cups or 30–35 minutes for the baking pan, until it is set and a knife inserted comes out clean.
4. While the custard is baking, make the topping by combining the crushed gingersnaps and melted butter. After the custard has been in the oven for 15 minutes, sprinkle the gingersnap mixture over the top.
5. When the custard has passed the clean knife test, remove from the oven, and let cool to room temperature. Whisk the heavy cream and pumpkin pie spice together with the caster sugar and beat just until it thickens. Serve the custard with the whipped cream and garnish each serving with a gingersnap.

Nutrition: 44g carbs 14g fats 3g protein

121. baked apple dumplings

PREPARATION TIME: 20′

SERVINGS: 2-4

COOKING TIME: 40′

INGREDIENTS

- 1 (17½ ounce) package frozen puff pastry, thawed
- 1 cup sugar
- 6 tablespoons dry breadcrumbs
- 2 teaspoons ground cinnamon
- 1 pinch ground nutmeg
- 1 egg, beaten
- 4 Granny Smith apples, peeled, cored, and halved
- Vanilla ice cream for serving

Icing
- 1 cup confectioners' sugar
- 1 teaspoon vanilla extract
- 3 tablespoons milk

Pecan Streusel
- 2/3 cup chopped toasted pecans
- 2/3 cup packed brown sugar
- 2/3 cup all-purpose flour
- 5 tablespoons melted butter

DIRECTIONS

1. Preheat the oven to 425°F. When the puff pastry has completely thawed, roll out each sheet to measure 12 inches by 12 inches. Cut the sheets into quarters. Combine the sugar, breadcrumbs, cinnamon, and nutmeg together in a small bowl.
2. Brush one of the pastry squares with some of the beaten egg. Add about 1 tablespoon of the breadcrumb mixture on top, then add half an apple, core side down, over the crumbs. Add another tablespoon of the breadcrumb mixture.
3. Seal the dumpling by pulling up the corners and pinching the pastry together until the seams are totally sealed. Repeat this process with the remaining squares. Assemble the ingredients for the pecan streusel in a small bowl.
4. Grease a baking sheet or line it with parchment paper. Place the dumplings on the sheet and brush them with a bit more of the beaten egg. Top with the pecan streusel.
5. Bake for 15 minutes, then reduce heat to 350°F and bake for 25 minutes more or until lightly browned. Make the icing by combining the confectioners' sugar, vanilla, and milk until you reach the proper consistency.
6. When the dumplings are done, let them cool to room temperature and drizzle them with icing before serving.

NUTRITION: 43g carbs 13g fats 3.1g protein

122. PeaCH Cobbler

PREPARATION TIME: 10'

SERVINGS: 4

COOKING TIME: 45'

INGREDIENTS

- 1¼ cups Bisquick
- 1 cup milk
- ½ cup melted butter
- ¼ teaspoon nutmeg
- ½ teaspoon cinnamon
- Vanilla ice cream, for serving

Filling
- 1 (30-ounce) can peaches in syrup, drained
- ¼ cup sugar

Topping
- ½ cup brown sugar
- ¼ cup almond slices
- ½ teaspoon cinnamon
- 1 tablespoon melted butter

DIRECTIONS

1. Preheat the oven to 375°F. Grease the bottom and sides of an 8×8-inch pan. Whisk together the Bisquick, milk, butter, nutmeg, and cinnamon in a large mixing bowl. When thoroughly combined, pour into the greased baking pan.
2. Mix together the peaches and sugar in another mixing bowl. Put the filling on top of the batter in the pan. Bake for about 45 minutes.
3. In another bowl, mix together the brown sugar, almonds, cinnamon, and melted butter. After the cobbler has cooked for 45 minutes, cover evenly with the topping and bake for an additional 10 minutes. Serve with a scoop of vanilla ice cream.

NUTRITION: 41g carbs 13g fats 4g protein

123. CampfIre S'mores

Preparation Time: 15'

Servings: 9

Cooking Time: 40'

Ingredients

Graham Cracker Crust
- 2 cups graham cracker crumbs
- ¼ cup sugar
- ½ cup butter
- ½ teaspoon cinnamon
- 1 small package brownie mix (enough for an 8×8-inch pan)

Brownie Mix
- ½ cup flour
- 1/3 cup cocoa
- ¼ teaspoon baking powder
- ¼ teaspoon salt
- ½ cup butter
- 1 cup sugar
- 1 teaspoon vanilla
- 2 large eggs

S'mores Topping
- 9 large marshmallows
- 5 Hershey candy bars
- 4½ cups vanilla ice cream
- ½ cup chocolate sauce

Directions

1. Preheat the oven to 350°F.
2. Mix together the graham cracker crumbs, sugar, cinnamon, and melted butter in a medium bowl. Stir until the crumbs and sugar have combined with the butter.
3. Line an 8×8-inch baking dish with parchment paper. Make sure to use enough so that you'll be able to lift the baked brownies out of the dish easily. Press the graham cracker mixture into the bottom of the lined pan.
4. Place the pan in the oven to prebake the crust a bit while you are making the brownie mixture.
5. Melt the butter over medium heat in a large saucepan, then stir in the sugar and vanilla. Whisk in the eggs one at a time. Then whisk in the dry ingredients, followed by the nuts. Mix until smooth. Take the crust out of the oven, pour the mixture into it, and bake for 23–25 minutes. When brownies are done, remove from oven and let cool in the pan.
6. After the brownies have cooled completely, lift them out of the pan using the edges of the parchment paper. Be careful not to crack or break the brownies. Cut into individual slices.
7. When you are ready to serve, place a marshmallow on top of each brownie and broil in the oven until the marshmallow starts to brown. You can also microwave for a couple of seconds, but you won't get the browning that you would in the broiler.
8. Remove from the oven and top each brownie with half of a Hershey bar. Serve with ice cream and a drizzle of chocolate sauce.

Nutrition: 41g carbs 12g fats 4g protein

124. banana Pudding

PREPARATION TIME:	15'+ 1H 30' CHILLING TIME
SERVINGS:	8-10
COOKING TIME:	0'

INGREDIENTS

- 6 cups milk
- 5 eggs, beaten
- ¼ teaspoon vanilla extract
- 11/8 cups flour
- 1½ cups sugar
- ¾ pound vanilla wafers
- 3 bananas, peeled
- 8 ounces whipped cream

DIRECTIONS

1. In a large saucepan, heat the milk to about 170°F.
2. Mix the eggs, vanilla, flour, and sugar together in a large bowl. Very slowly add the egg mixture to the warmed milk and cook until the mixture thickens to a custard consistency.
3. Layer the vanilla wafers to cover the bottom of a baking pan or glass baking dish. You can also use individual portion dessert dish or glasses.
4. Layer banana slices over the top of the vanilla wafers. Be as liberal with the bananas as you want.
5. Layer the custard mixture on top of the wafers and bananas. Move the pan to the refrigerator and cool for 1½ hours. When ready to serve, spread Cool Whip (or real whipped cream, if you prefer) over the top. Garnish with banana slices and wafers if desired.

NUTRITION: 45g carbs 14g fats 3g protein

125. Chili's new York STyle CHeeseCake

PREPARATION TIME: 35'

SERVINGS: 12

COOKING TIME: 1H 25'

INGREDIENTS

- 15 graham crackers (each 3 by 5"), broken into pieces
- 2 ½ pounds cream cheese (five 8-ounce bars), room temperature
- 1 teaspoon packed lemon zest, finely grated plus 1 tablespoon fresh juice
- 1/3 cup dark-brown sugar, packed
- 1 1/3 cups granulated sugar
- 1 cup sour cream, at room temperature
- 5 large eggs, at room temperature
- 1 ¼ teaspoons coarse salt
- 6 tablespoons softened butter, unsalted, melted, plus more for pan
- 1 teaspoon pure vanilla extract

DIRECTIONS

1. Preheat oven to 350 F. Finely grind the crackers in a food processor. Add in the brown sugar, melted butter, zest & ½ teaspoon of salt; continue to pulse until you get wet sand-like texture. Evenly press into the bottom & halfway up sides of a buttered 9" spring form pan. Bake in the preheated oven for 12 to 15 minutes until set. Let cool.
2. Decrease your oven temperature to 325 F. Beat the cream cheese until smooth, on medium speed. Slowly beat in the granulated sugar for 2 to 3 minutes until light & fluffy. Beat in the lemon juice & leftover salt. Slowly beat in the eggs and then the vanilla and sour cream until completely smooth.
3. Place the pan in the middle of a double layer of foil. Lift the edges of foil up, tightly wrapping it around the sides of your pan & fold it in under itself until flush with the top of the pan.
4. Pour the filling into pan & smooth the top using a small offset spatula.
5. Place the springform pan in a roasting pan; transfer to the oven. Pour enough boiling water into the roasting pan to come halfway up sides of the springform pan. Bake in the preheated oven 1 hour 45 minutes to 2 hours until the cake is puffed & turn slightly wobbly in the center and golden brown on top.
6. Remove the springform pan from roasting pan; let cool for 20 minutes on a wire rack. Remove the foil and run a paring knife around the sides of the pan to loosen. Let completely cool. Drape the pan with a plastic wrap; refrigerate for overnight until cold. Remove the cake from pan; serve & enjoy.

NUTRITION: 44g carbs 12g fats 3.9g protein

126. STarbuCk's CoPyCaT Cranberry CHoColaTe bliss bars

PREPARATION TIME: 10'

SERVINGS: 3 DOZEN

COOKING TIME: 55'

INGREDIENTS

- 3/4 cup of cubed butter, unsalted
- 1 1/2 cups of brown sugar, light, packed
- 2 eggs, large
- 3/4 tsp. of vanilla extract, pure
- 1 1/2 tsp. of baking powder
- 2 1/4 cups of flour, all-purpose
- 1/4 tsp. of salt, kosher
- 1/8 tsp. of cinnamon, ground
- 1/2 cup of cranberries, dried
- 6 oz. of chopped baking chocolate, white
- Frosting, 1 container prepared

DIRECTIONS

1. Preheat the oven to 350F. In a large-sized microwave-safe bowl, melt butter. Add and stir in brown sugar. Cool a bit.
2. Beat in vanilla and eggs. In a separate bowl, whisk flour, kosher salt, cinnamon, and baking powder together. Stir in the chocolate and cranberries, making a thick batter. Spread into buttered 13" x 9" pan. Bake till golden brown, 18 to 20 minutes or so. Completely cool on wire rack. Slice and serve.

NUTRITION: 42g carbs 13g fats 3.4g protein

127. CHoColaTe PeCan

PREPARATION TIME: 10'

SERVINGS: 8

COOKING TIME: 50'

INGREDIENTS

- 3 eggs
- ½ cup sugar
- 1 cup corn syrup
- ½ teaspoon salt
- 1 teaspoon vanilla extract
- ¼ cup melted butter
- 1 cup pecans
- 3 tablespoons semisweet chocolate chips
- 1 unbaked pie shell

DIRECTIONS

1. Preheat the oven to 350°F. Beat together the eggs and sugar in a mixing bowl, then add the corn syrup, salt, vanilla, and butter. Put the chocolate chips and pecans inside the pie shell and pour the egg mixture over the top. Bake for 50–60 minutes or until set. Serve with vanilla ice cream.

NUTRITION: 41.9g carbs 5.1g fats 3.1g protein

128. Peanut butter Kisses

<table>
<tr><td>PREPARATION TIME: 5'</td><td>SERVINGS: 22</td></tr>
</table>

COOKING TIME: 1 H 20'

INGREDIENTS

- 1 ½ cups of smooth, unsweetened peanut butter
- 1 cup of coconut flour
- ¼ cup of keto sweetener (Swerve)
- a pinch of salt
- 1 tsp of vanilla extract
- 2 cups of dark chocolate
- 1 tbsp of coconut oil
- ¼ cup of nuts, chopped finely
- 4 tbsps. of peanut butter for drizzling

DIRECTIONS

1. Place the 1 ½ cups of peanut butter in a microwave safe dish and heat it for about 15 seconds to melt.
2. Pour the peanut butter, coconut flour, sweetener, vanilla extract, and salt in a medium bowl and mix until a smooth, thick paste is formed.
3. Prepare a baking tray and line it with parchment paper (make sure that this tray can fit in your freezer).
4. Use an ice cream scoop (preferably) to scoop the peanut butter mixture and place dollops of small circles of the mixture onto the baking tray (you should have about 20 scoops' worth). Place the tray in the freezer and allow the mixture to freeze for about 1 hour until firm.
5. When the peanut butter balls are almost ready, place the dark chocolate in a microwave safe bowl and microwave the chocolate until it has melted, then allow it to cool to room temperature.
6. Add the melted chocolate into a medium bowl, along with the coconut oil and the chopped nuts. Place the remaining 4 tbsps. of peanut butter into a microwave safe bowl and melt the peanut butter.
7. When the peanut butter balls are firm, use a fork to dip the balls into the chocolate mixture and place them back on the baking tray. Drizzle the peanut butter over the balls. Place the tray back into the freezer for another 10 minutes and enjoy cold.

NUTRITION: 259 Calories 19g Carbohydrates 18g Fat 8g Protein

129. Peanut butter & Pecan nut Cheesecake

Preparation Time:	30' + 4H CHILLING TIME
Servings:	10'

Cooking Time: 3 H

Ingredients

For the crust:
- 3 tbsps. of butter
- 1 ½ cups of pecan nuts
- 2 tbsps. of powdered erythritol
- 2 tbsps. of sultanas

For the filling:
- 12 tbsps. of butter
- 32 oz of cream cheese
- 1 cup of powdered erythritol
- ½ cup of whipping cream
- 4 teaspoons vanilla extract
- ½ tsp of cinnamon
- 4 eggs

For the topping:
- a handful of sultanas
- ¼ cup of crushed pecan nuts
- 1 tbsp of cinnamon
- 2 tbsps. of honey

Nutrition: 6g Calories 606 Carbohydrates 61g Fat 9g Protein

1. Preheat the oven to 325°F and prepare a springform/cake dish about 9" in size. Lightly grease the pan with a small dollop of butter.
2. Place the 3 tbsps. of butter into a small bowl and place it in the microwave for 10 seconds to melt the butter. Then set the butter aside to cool to room temperature.
3. Place the pecan nuts into a food processor and pulse until it's a fine, grounded texture.
4. Add the ground pecan nuts into the bowl with the melted butter, and pour the powdered erythritol and sultanas into the mixture. Mix the contents well in the bowl to combine the ingredients, then evenly pour the mixture into the base of the springform dish and use your fingers to firmly press in the pecan nut mixture. This should form a firm base with no cracks or spaces.
5. Place the crust in the oven for 10 minutes, then remove and set the dish aside to cool down. Keep the oven's temperature at 325°F as you'll be using it again soon.
6. For the filling, pour the remaining 12 tbsps of butter into a medium saucepan over medium-high heat and stir, while the butter melts. Once the butter has melted, and it starts to brown a little, remove it from the heat and set aside.
7. Pour the cream cheese into a medium bowl and slowly mix it to soften it, using a hand mixer. Once the cream cheese is soft and fluffy, add the remaining 1 cup of erythritol, heavy cream, cinnamon, and vanilla extract into the bowl and gently mix the ingredients together.
8. Crack the eggs into the bowl and then pour in the butter, while still slowly mixing to combine the ingredients, until well combined.
9. Use aluminum foil to wrap the sides and base of the springform pan, twice, then pour the filling into the pan, covering the base.
10. Place the springform pan on a baking tray and place it into the oven.
11. Pour water into the baking tray, so that it covers a few inches surrounding the springform pan.
12. Bake the cake for 1 hour and 10 minutes.
13. Remove the cake from the oven and the baking tray filled with water. Place the springform pan on a dry/cooling rack for 10 minutes, then use a spatula/butter knife to loosen the edges of the cake from the pan.
14. Separate the cake from the pan and allow the cake to cool for another hour at room temperature, then cover the cake with a lid/plastic wrap and place it in the refrigerator to set. This should preferably be left in the refrigerator overnight or for at least 4 hours to allow the cake to fully set.
15. When the cake has set, mix the honey and remaining cinnamon in a cup, stirring well to mix the ingredients. Lightly drizzle a loose design over the top of the cake with the honey mixture. Sprinkle the sultanas and crushed pecan nuts on top.

130. THREE-INGREDIENT CHOCOLATE MACADAMIA FAT BOMBS

PREPARATION TIME: 5'

SERVINGS: 4

COOKING TIME: 30'

INGREDIENTS

- 1 oz of dark chocolate chips/dark chocolate shavings
- 1 ½ oz of macadamia nuts, halved
- 1 tbsp of coconut oil
- ½ tsp of cinnamon
- a pinch of salt

DIRECTIONS

1. Prepare a tray that will work well for making truffles, i.e., a truffle mold or a mini muffin pan that has cup sizes of about 2x1" each. Make sure that this tray can also fit in your freezer.
2. In a microwave safe bowl, add the chocolate into the bowl and place it in the microwave for 30 seconds-1 minutes, until the chocolate has melted. Set the chocolate aside to cool down for a few seconds.
3. Add 3 macadamia nut halves into each cup (should be about 8 cups) and set aside. Return back to the bowl with the melted chocolate, and add in both the coconut oil and a pinch of salt and cinnamon, then mix until well combined.
4. Spoon the chocolate mixture evenly into each cup of the tray, covering the macadamia nut base.
5. Use the spoon to level out the surfaces of the cups and then place the tray in the freezer for 30-40 minutes until the chocolate has solidified.

NUTRITION: 167 Calories 2g Carbohydrates 16g Fat 2g Protein

131. Goat Cheese WITH STeWed blaCkberrIes

Preparation Time:	10'	Servings:	4

Cooking Time: 12'

Ingredients

- 20 oz of goat cheese
- 9 oz of blackberries
- 1 tbsp of erythritol
- ½ tsp of cinnamon
- 2 tbsps.' of paprika
- 1 mint leaf
- 1 oz of pistachio nuts
- 2 thin slices of orange

Directions

1. Preheat the oven to 350ºF and prepare an oven tray.
2. In a microwave safe, small bowl, mix the blackberries, erythritol, 1 tbsp of water, and cinnamon together. Place the bowl in the microwave for 20-30 seconds to lightly warm the mixture. Stir the mixture once more. Slap the mint leaf to awaken the aromas and add the leaf into the bowl. Cover the bowl and set it aside, allowing the flavors to infuse together.
3. Place the goat cheese on the baking tray and place it in the oven to bake for about 10 minutes until the cheese starts to get a yellowish tint. Remove the cheese from the oven and evenly sift the paprika spice over the cheese, then place the cheese back in the oven for 2 more minutes, so that the spice infuses itself into the cheese.
4. Place a small frying pan on medium-high heat and add the chopped pistachios into the pan. Lightly roast the nuts for 2 minutes, then set aside.
5. Serve the cheese topped with the berry mixture, pistachio nuts. Slightly drizzle a little of the orange juice from the slices over the berry mix, then garnish the cheese with the leftover orange slices.

Nutrition: 584 Calories 4g Carbohydrates 46g Fat 33g Protein

132. rHubarb TarT

<table>
<tr><td>PREPARATION TIME:</td><td>10'</td><td>SERVINGS:</td><td>8</td></tr>
<tr><td>COOKING TIME:</td><td>45'</td><td></td><td></td></tr>
</table>

INGREDIENTS

For the crust:
- 6 oz of almond flour
- 1/2 cup of erythritol
- ¾ oz of shredded coconut
- 3 oz of butter
- 1 tsp of cinnamon

For the filling:
- 4 ½ oz of butter
- ½ cup of erythritol
- 1 ¾ cups of almond flour
- 3 eggs
- 1 tsp of vanilla extract
- 7 oz of rhubarb
- 1 tsp of cinnamon
- ¼ cup of berries
- 2 tbsps. of sultanas (optional)

DIRECTIONS

1. Preheat the oven to 360°F and prepare a tart dish of about 9" in size by lightly greasing it with a dollop of butter.
2. In a small, microwave safe bowl, add the 3 oz of butter into the bowl and place it in the microwave for a few seconds so that the butter melts. Set it aside to cool down.
3. In a medium bowl, pour in the almond flour, erythritol, coconut, and cinnamon. Mix the contents together until well combined.
4. Once the butter has cooled, pour it into the dry ingredient bowl whilst still stirring.
5. Spoon the dough mixture into the tart dish and use your hands to press the dough around the sides of the tart dish to form a pie crust. Press the dough firmly into the tart dish to ensure that there are no cracks and that the crust is as even as possible, then place it into the oven to bake for 10 minutes.
6. While the crust is baking, prepare the filling. Microwave the 4 ½ oz of butter in a microwave safe bowl for about 10 seconds so that the butter softens.
7. Pour the softened butter into a medium bowl, along with the erythritol, and beat the mixture until it's light and fluffy.
8. Pour the flour and vanilla into the bowl and crack the eggs into the mixture, while still beating the contents to mix the ingredients well. Cover the dish and set it aside.
9. In a separate bowl, use a vegetable peeler to cut long, thin strips of rhubarb and add the strips into the bowl. Add the 1 tsp of cinnamon, berries, and sultanas into the bowl and mix the contents together.
10. Remove the tart crust from the oven and spoon the flour filling into the crust, and even it out using a spoon. Then layer on the berry and rhubarb mixture.
11. Place the tart back into the oven for 35 more minutes.

NUTRITION: 515 Calories 3g Carbohydrates 49g Fat 11g Protein

133. Saffron Panna CoTTa

PREPARATION TIME:	20' + 2H CHILLING TIME	SERVINGS:	6

COOKING TIME: 10'

INGREDIENTS

- ½ tbsp of plain gelatin
- 2 cups of heavy cream
- ¼ tsp of vanilla extract
- 1 tbsp of honey
- a pinch of saffron
- a pinch of cinnamon
- 1 tbsp of chopped almonds
- 12 raspberries
- 1 slice of lemon
- ½ tsp of lemon rind

DIRECTIONS

1. In a medium bowl, mix the gelatin with water (generally 1 tsp of gelatin needs 1 tbsp of water, but follow the instructions of your specific brand of gelatin, to make sure the mixture is correct). Mix well and set it aside.
2. Place a small saucepan over medium-high heat and add the cream, vanilla, saffron, and cinnamon into the pan. Mix the contents and bring to a light boil, then reduce the heat to a simmer for about 3 minutes so that the spices infuse well into the contents.
3. Remove the pan from the heat and pour the gelatin mixture into the pan, stirring it well to incorporate it.
4. Prepare 6 glasses/short serving bowls and evenly pour the mixture into the bowls. Sprinkle the lemon zest over the tops of the desserts, then cover the glasses with plastic wrap and place the desserts in the refrigerator for a minimum of 2 hours.
5. When the desserts are almost ready, place the almonds into a frying pan and lightly roast them for 3-5 minutes.
6. Sprinkle the almonds onto the panna cotta, then top each dessert with a few raspberries.
7. Lastly, squeeze the slice of lemon's juice over the desserts, and generously sprinkle the lemon zest over the top. Keep the dessert in the refrigerator until ready to serve.

NUTRITION: 271 Calories 2g Carbohydrates 29g Fat 3g protein

Chapter 5

OLD AND MODERN PASTRY RECIPES

134. Chess Pie

PREPARATION TIME: 6 H

SERVINGS: 8

COOKING TIME: 1 H

INGREDIENTS

- 1 Pie crust
- 4 Eggs
- 1 ½ cup Granulated sugar
- ½ cup Butter - melted and cooled slightly
- ¼ cup Milk
- 1 tbsp White vinegar
- 2 tsp Pure vanilla extract
- ¼ cup Cornmeal
- 1 tbsp All-purpose flour
- ½ tsp Kosher salt

DIRECTIONS

1. Warm the oven at 425° Fahrenheit. Roll out the pie crust and arrange it into the pie dish. Trim and crimp edges, and poke the center of the crust using a fork. Pop it into the freezer to chill for at least 15 minutes.
2. Arrange a layer of parchment baking paper inside the pie crust. Weigh it down using something such as dried beans to keep it flat. Bake until golden (15 min.). Carefully remove the parchment and pie weights and bake ten minutes more. Cool it while making the pie filling.
3. Adjust the oven temperature to 325° Fahrenheit. Whisk the eggs and sugar in a large mixing container. Melt and add the butter, milk, vinegar, and vanilla, whisking until incorporated. Mix in the cornmeal, flour, and salt until combined.
4. Dump the filling into the pie crust and bake until just set in the middle (50 min.). Cool the pie at room temperature for at least four hours. Then pop it into the fridge until ready to serve. Dust with powdered sugar before serving.

NUTRITION: 43g carbs 14g fats 3g protein

135. Coconut Cream Pie bars

PREPARATION TIME: 40'

SERVINGS: 15
VARIES

COOKING TIME: 20'

INGREDIENTS

Crust Ingredients:
- 1 cup Butter
- 2 cups A-P flour
- ½ cup Powdered sugar

Filling Ingredients:
- 3 cups Half-and-Half
- 4 Eggs
- 3 cups Coconut milk
- 1 ½ cup White sugar
- ½ tsp Salt
- 2/3 cup Cornstarch
- 1 ½ cup Flaked coconut
- ½ tsp Coconut extract
- ½ tsp Vanilla extract

Topping Ingredients:
- 2 cups Heavy whipping cream
- 1 tbsp cold Water
- 1 tsp Gelatin
- 3-4 tbsp Powdered sugar
- 1 cup Coconut - for toasting

DIRECTIONS

1. Make the crust. Warm the oven at 350° Fahrenheit. Prepare the baking dish with a foil sling (if desired).
2. Combine the powdered sugar and flour. Dice and mix in the butter using a food processor (pulse it about 6-10 times) and press the mixture into the pan. Bake until light brown (18-20 min.) and cool it on a wire rack.
3. Toast the coconut. Spread one cup of the coconut flakes onto a baking tray and bake in the oven along with your shortbread crust for three to six minutes, stirring every minute or so until the coconut is golden brown. Spread it out on a plate to thoroughly cool.
4. Prepare the cream filling. Whisk the coconut milk, half-and-half, eggs, sugar, cornstarch, and salt in a large saucepan. Once boiling, adjust the temperature setting to med-low, whisking c until it's thick and bubbling (15-30 min.).
5. Add in the coconut and vanilla extracts and the 1.5 cups of untoasted coconut. Stir and dump the filling over the crust. Cool it on the countertop a short time and pop it into the refrigerator to chill about two to four hours until it's firm.
6. Prepare the topping. Measure and add one tablespoon cold water in a small bowl and sprinkle the gelatin evenly over the top. Let it soften for two minutes before microwaving it for 30 seconds and whisking to dissolve the gelatin.
7. Use a chilled bowl and beater to whisk two cups of heavy cream and powdered sugar until the cream forms stiff peaks. Stop and add the gelatin mixture about halfway through. Plop the cream over the bars and gently spread it around. Sprinkle on toasted coconut.
8. Pop it into the fridge to chill until serving time. Pull the bars out of the dish by slicing with a sharp knife to enjoy.

NUTRITION: 40g carbs 12g fats 4g protein

136. Creamy Hazelnut Pie

PREPARATION TIME: 10'

SERVINGS: 8

COOKING TIME: 40'

INGREDIENTS

- 8 oz Room Temp cream cheese
- 1 cup Confectioner's sugar
- 1 ¼ cup Nutella - divided
- 8 oz Thawed - frozen whipped topping
- 9-inch crust Chocolate crumb

DIRECTIONS

1. Cream the sugar, cream cheese, one cup of Nutella, and the confectioner's sugar. Fold in the topping and add the mixture to the crust. Warm the rest of the Nutella in a microwave for 15-20 seconds and drizzle it over the pie. Pop the pie into the fridge for at least four hours or overnight for the best results.

NUTRITION: 47 carbs 15g fats 6g protein

137. The famous Woolworth Icebox Cheesecake

PREPARATION TIME: 10'

SERVINGS: 6

COOKING TIME: 1 h

INGREDIENTS

- 3 oz Lemon Jell-O
- 1 cup Boiling water
- 8 oz Cream cheese
- 1 cup Granulated sugar
- 5 tbsp Lemon juice
- 12 oz Evaporated milk - well chilled - ex. Carnation
- Graham crackers - crushed

DIRECTIONS

1. Dissolve Jell-O in boiling water. Cool slightly until it's thickened. Combine the cream cheese, sugar, and lemon juice with an electric mixer until smooth. Add in the thickened Jell-O and mix. In another container, beat the milk until fluffy. Add the cream cheese mixture and blend well using the mixer. Line the baking tray with crushed crackers. Dump the filling into the pan and top with more crushed crackers and chill.

NUTRITION: 40g carbs 10g fats 5g protein

138. frozen banana SPLIT Pie

PREPARATION TIME: 25'

SERVINGS: 8

COOKING TIME: 50'

INGREDIENTS

- 3 tbsp Hard-shell ice cream topping - chocolate
- 9-inch Graham cracker crust
- 2 Bananas
- ½ tsp Lemon juice
- ½ cup Pineapple ice cream topping
- 1 quart Softened strawberry ice cream
- 2 cups Whipped topping
- ½ cup Toasted walnuts
- Chocolate syrup
- 8 Maraschino cherries with stems

DIRECTIONS

1. Pour the chocolate topping into the crust and pop it into the freezer until chocolate is solid (5 min.). Slice and arrange the bananas in a bowl to toss with the juice. Place the bananas over the chocolate topping and layer using the pineapples, ice cream, whipped topping, and chopped nuts. Use a layer of plastic to cover the pie and freeze it until firm. Transfer it to the countertop to thaw for about 15 minutes before slicing it to serve. Top it off using the chocolate syrup and stemmed cherries.

NUTRITION: 38g carbs 12g fats 6g protein

139. frozen PeaCH PIe

PREPARATION TIME:	30'		SERVINGS:	2

COOKING TIME:	1 H

INGREDIENTS

- 2 ½ cups Graham cracker crumbs
- ½ cup and 2 tbsp Melted butter - divided
- ¼ cup Sugar
- 14 oz Sweetened condensed milk
- ¼ cup Orange juice
- ¼ cup Lemon juice
- 16 oz Frozen unsweetened sliced peaches
- 1 tbsp Grated lemon zest
- 1 ½ cups Heavy whipping cream
- Optional: Sweetened whipped cream (as desired)

DIRECTIONS

1. Warm the oven at 350° Fahrenheit. Crumble and combine the cracker crumbs, sugar, and butter onto the bottom and up the sides of the two pie plates. Bake the pies until lightly browned (10-12 min.). Cool on wire racks.
2. Measure and add the milk, lemon juice, orange juice, peaches, and lemon zest into a blender and mix until smooth. Dump it into a mixing container. In another container, beat the cream until stiff peaks form and fold it into the peach mixture.
3. Scoop the filling into the crusts. Cover and freeze for at least four hours or until firm. Transfer the delicious pie to the table about 15 minutes before serving and top with whipped cream if desired.

NUTRITION: 47g carbs 13g fats 9g protein

140. Key Lime Pie

PREPARATION TIME: 20'

SERVINGS: 8

COOKING TIME: 45'

INGREDIENTS

- ¼ cup Boiling water
- 0.3 oz Sugar-free lime gelatin
- 2 (6 oz) Key lime yogurt
- 6 oz Reduced-fat graham cracker crust
- 8 oz Frozen fat-free whipped topping

DIRECTIONS

1. Boil the water and add it to the gelatin. Stir for about two minutes until it's dissolved. Whisk in the yogurt and topping. Pour it into the crust and pop in the fridge. Chill the pie for at least two hours and serve.

NUTRITION: 45g carbs 13g fats 8g protein

141. STraWberry Lemonade freezer Pie

PREPARATION TIME: 15'	SERVINGS: 8

COOKING TIME: 50'

INGREDIENTS

- 2 ½ cups Frozen & thawed - sliced sweet strawberries
- 3.4 oz Instant lemon pudding mix
- 8 oz Frozen - thawed whipped topping
- 9-inch Graham cracker crust
- Optional: Additional fresh berries & whipped topping

DIRECTIONS

1. Combine the strawberries (with juices) and pudding mix in a large mixing container. Wait for about five minutes and fold in the whipped topping. Spread the filling into the crust. Freeze the pie for at least eight hours to overnight. Let it stand for five to ten minutes before serving.

NUTRITION: 40g carbs 16g fats 7g protein

142. Sweet Potato Pie

PREPARATION TIME:	2H	SERVINGS:	8

COOKING TIME: 1H

INGREDIENTS

- 1 ¼ cup A-P flour
- 4 tbsp Leaf lard
- 4 tbsp Good-quality butter
- ¼ tsp Kosher salt
- 3-4 tbsp Ice water

The Potato Filling:
- 2 large Orange-fleshed California sweet potatoes
- ½ cup White sugar
- 2 lightly whisk Large eggs
- ¼ cup Half & Half - heavy cream
- ¾ tsp Cinnamon
- ¼ tsp Nutmeg - freshly grated
- ½ cup Light brown sugar
- 7 tbsp Unsalted butter
- Kosher salt

DIRECTIONS

1. Cut the butter and lard into small pieces. Mix each of the dough components (omit the water) in a large mixing container. Knead the mixture until crumbly with a few lumps in it. Drizzle the mixture using the ice water and work the dough.
2. Shape the dough and wrap it in plastic wrap to chill it for one hour. When cold, scoop the dough onto a well-floured surface. Dust flour over the top. Knead the dough, adding flour as needed. Work the dough until it extends over the edges of the pie pan.
3. Warm the oven at 400° Fahrenheit. 'Blind-bake' the pie dough for 15 minutes.
4. Thoroughly cool it in the pan on a rack for about half an hour. Lower the oven temperature to 350° Fahrenheit.
5. Make the filling. Warm a pot of water using the high-temperature setting. Peel and slice the potatoes into one-inch cubes. Lower the setting to medium and toss in the potatoes to cook until (20 to 25 min.). Drain and rinse using cold water.
6. Toss them into a food processor to create a creamy purée. Measure and return 2.5 cups into the food processor. Whisk and add the eggs, butter, granulated sugar, half-and-half, nutmeg, cinnamon, and brown sugar. Mix until smooth and dump into the pie shell, smoothing the top.
7. Place the pie pan on a baking sheet and set a timer to bake until the crust is lightly golden and filling is almost set with a slight jiggle in the center (1 hr.).
8. Cool thoroughly on a wire rack. Place a layer of foil over the pie and pop in the fridge until it's time to serve.

NUTRITION: 45g carbs 17g fats 7g protein

143. blueberry Sour Cream Pound Cake

PREPARATION TIME: 35'

SERVINGS: 12

COOKING TIME: 1 H

INGREDIENTS

- 3 cups and 2 tbsp A-P flour - divided
- ½ tsp Baking soda
- 3 cups Sugar
- ½ tsp Salt
- 1 cup room temp - unsalted butter
- 1 cup Sour cream
- 6 Eggs
- 1 tsp Vanilla
- 2 cups Blueberries
- To Dust: Powdered sugar

DIRECTIONS

1. Set the oven temperature setting at 325° Fahrenheit. Butter and flour a Bundt pan. Sift/whisk three cups of flour, salt, and baking soda to remove lumps. Set it to the side for now.
2. Mix the sugar and butter using an electric mixer until it is creamy. Add in sour cream and beat until it's combined. Alternate adding flour mixture and eggs, beating until just combined. Quickly mix in the vanilla.
3. Gently toss the blueberries and two tablespoons flour. Fold the blueberries into the batter. Dump the batter into the prepared pan and bake until golden and a toothpick inserted into the center comes out clean (1 ¼ hr.).
4. Cool it in the Bundt pan for at least ten minutes before turning onto a wire rack to cool completely. Once cool, dust it using a bit of powdered sugar.

NUTRITION: 40g carbs 10g fat 5g protein

.144 Carrot Cake delight

PREPARATION TIME: 25'	SERVINGS: 2 (-INCH ROUNDS)
COOKING TIME: 2 H	

INGREDIENTS

- 6 cups Grated carrots
- 1 cup Raisins
- 1 cup Brown sugar
- 4 Eggs
- 1 ½ cup White sugar
- 1 cup Vegetable oil
- 2 tsp Vanilla extract
- 1 cup Drained crushed pineapple
- 1 tsp Salt
- 3 cups A-P flour
- 1 ½ tsp Baking soda
- 4 tsp Ground cinnamon
- 1 cup Chopped walnuts

DIRECTIONS

1. Grate the carrots and mix with the brown sugar. Set aside for about one hour and stir in the raisins. Warm the oven at 350° Fahrenheit. Grease and flour the cake pans. Whisk the eggs until light and mix in the white sugar, vanilla, and oil. Fold in the pineapple.
2. Sift or whisk the flour, cinnamon, baking soda, and salt, and fold into the wet mixture until absorbed. Lastly, fold in the carrot mixture and nuts. Pour into the prepared pans.
3. Bake for 45 to 50 minutes until the cake tests are completed using a toothpick. (Stick the center of the cakes; when done, it's clean. Transfer the pans to the countertop to cool for ten minutes before removing from the pan.
4. Wait for them to cool to frost with frosting and serve.

NUTRITION: 41g carbs 13g fats 6g protein

145. four layer Pumpkin Cake with frosting

Preparation Time: 30'

Servings: 16

Cooking Time: 1 H

Ingredients

- ½ tsp Fine sea salt
- 3 cups A-P flour
- 2 tsp Baking powder
- 1 tsp Chinese five-spice powder
- 1 tsp Baking soda
- 2 sticks room temp - unsalted butter
- 2 cups Golden brown sugar - packed
- 3 room temp eggs
- 15 oz Pure pumpkin
- 1/3 cup Whole milk

The Icing:
- 1 cup Unsalted – room temp butter
- 8 oz room temp cream cheese
- 1 tbsp Orange peel - finely grated
- 3 cups Powdered sugar - sifted
- ¼ cup Orange juice
- Walnut halves/chopped - toasted

Directions

1. Position the rack in the bottom third of the oven, warming it to reach 350° Fahrenheit. Spray the pans using a spritz of baking oil spray. Line the bottoms using a layer of parchment baking paper (lightly greasing the paper too).
2. Whisk the baking powder and soda, flour, salt, and 5-spice powder. Use an electric mixer to combine the butter and brown sugar in another large bowl until creamy. Mix in the eggs one at a time.
3. Fold in the pumpkin and dry fixings in three additions - alternately with milk in two additions. Dump the prepared batter into the baking trays.
4. Bake the cakes until the tester inserted into the center comes out clean (40 min.). Cool in pans on a rack for about 15 minutes. Loosen the edges with a small spatula and invert the cakes on cooling racks. Remove the parchment. Flip the cakes over onto racks and leave until thoroughly cooled.
5. Prepare the frosting using an electric mixer to mix the butter in a large mixing container until smooth. Mix in the cream cheese and orange peel, beating until creamy. Fold in and mix the powdered sugar (low speed).
6. Trim the rounded tops from cakes. Use a long-serrated knife to cut each cake horizontally in half. Arrange one cake layer, cut side up, onto a large platter. Spoon about 2/3 cup of frosting onto the cake - spreading to the edges.
7. Continue two more times with the cake and frosting. Top with the remaining cake layer with the cut side down. Decorate it using the rest of the frosting. Top it off using walnuts before serving.

Nutrition: 41g carbs 11g fats 5g protein

146. Georgia Peach Pound Cake

PREPARATION TIME: 20′

SERVINGS: 8

COOKING TIME: 1 H

INGREDIENTS

- 4 Eggs
- 1 cup Softened butter/margarine
- 3 cups A-P flour
- 2 cups White sugar
- ½ tsp Salt
- 1 tsp Baking powder
- 1 tsp Vanilla extract
- 2 cups Fresh peaches

DIRECTIONS

1. Set the oven at 325°Fahrenheit. Butter a ten-inch tube pan and sprinkle with white sugar. Cream the sugar with the butter until it's fluffy. Whisk and fold in the eggs - one at a time - whisking after each addition. Mix in the vanilla.
2. Set aside ¼ of a cup of flour for later, and sift the rest of the flour with the baking powder and salt. Slowly mix it into the creamed mixture. Toss the reserved flour over the chopped peaches, and mix thoroughly into the batter. Dump the batter into the prepared pan.
3. Bake the cake for one hour and about 15 minutes. Leave the cake in the pan for about ten minutes, before placing it onto a wire rack to cool completely. For the sauce, puree a portion of the peaches, add two tablespoon cornstarch, and cook using the low-temperature setting until thickened. Serve the mixture as a sauce over the cake.

NUTRITION: 45g carbs 12g fats 5g protein

147. Pineapple Pecan Cake with frosting

Preparation Time: 40'	Servings: 8

Cooking Time: 15'

Ingredients

The Cake:
- 2 cups Sugar
- 2 tsp Baking soda
- 2 cups Flour
- 2 Eggs
- 20 oz Crushed pineapple with juice
- Optional: 1 cup Chopped pecans

The Icing:
- 1 stick Room Temp - softened butter
- 8 oz Cream cheese - softened
- 2 cups Confectioners' sugar
- 1 tbsp Vanilla

Directions

1. Whisk the sugar, flour, and baking soda in a large mixing container. Butter the baking pan and set the oven temperature setting at 350°Fahrenheit. Whisk and mix in the eggs, pineapple, and juice with the pecans. Mix just until moistened.
2. Dump the batter into the buttered pan. Set the timer to bake until done (30-35 min.). Transfer it to the countertop and wait for it to cool thoroughly. Prepare the icing by combining the butter, cream cheese, vanilla, and confectioners' sugar. Beat until smooth. Decorate the cake and serve.

Nutrition: 40g carbs 12g fats 4g protein

148. red VelveT Cake

PREPARATION TIME: 20'

SERVINGS: 6 INCH CAKE

COOKING TIME: 30'

INGREDIENTS

The Cake:
- 1 ¼ cup A-P flour
- ¾ tsp Baking soda
- 1 tbsp Unsweetened cocoa powder
- ½ tsp Kosher salt
- ½ cup Coconut oil
- 1 cup Sugar
- 1 large Egg
- 1 tbsp Red food coloring
- ½ tsp Vinegar
- 1 ½ tsp Vanilla bean paste/extract
- ½ cup Buttermilk

The Frosting:
- ½ cup room temp - unsalted butter
- 4 oz room temp - cream cheese
- 2 cups Powdered sugar
- 1 tsp Vanilla bean paste or extract
- 1/8 tsp Kosher salt

DIRECTIONS

1. Warm the oven to 350° Fahrenheit. Lightly grease the pans and set them aside for now. Whisk the salt, flour, baking soda, and cocoa powder. Prepare the mixer. Cream the coconut oil and sugar until fluffy (3-4 min.). Whisk and add the egg, food coloring, vanilla, and vinegar.
2. Mix in the dry components and buttermilk in two to three alternating additions and beat until just combined. Portion the batter between the cake pans and bake until a toothpick inserted into the center comes out clean (25 minutes).
3. Gently press down the top of the cakes to even them out while they're still hot. Cool them for ten minutes in their pans and turn them onto a wire rack to cool completely. Prepare the Frosting: Cream the butter and cream cheese in the stand mixer until combined. Add in the salt, powdered sugar, and vanilla.
4. To Assemble: Stack up the cooled cake layers with a thick layer of frosting in between. Frost and serve.
5. Note: For the oil, unrefined provides a hint of coconut flavor or use refined for no coconut flavor.

NUTRITION: 45g carbs 13g fats 6g protein

149. PumPkIn CHeeseCake

PREPARATION TIME: 30' + 8H CHILLING TIME

SERVINGS: 8-10

COOKING TIME: 1 H 45'

INGREDIENTS

- 2 ½ cups graham cracker crumbs
- ¾ cup unsalted butter, melted
- 2 ¾ cups granulated sugar, divided
- 1 teaspoon salt, plus a pinch
- 4 (8-ounce) blocks cream cheese, at room temperature
- ¼ cup sour cream
- 1 (15-ounce) can pure pumpkin
- 6 large eggs, room temperature
- 1 tablespoon vanilla extract
- 2 ½ teaspoons ground cinnamon
- 1 teaspoon ginger, ground
- ¼ teaspoon cloves, ground
- 2 cups whipped cream, sweetened
- 1/3 cup toasted pecans, roughly chopped

DIRECTIONS

1. Preheat the oven to 325°F and grease a 12-inch springform pan.
2. In a mixing bowl, combine the graham cracker crumbs, melted butter, ¼ cup of the sugar, and a pinch of salt. Mix until well combined and press the mixture into the prepared springform pan. Bake for about 25 minutes.
3. While the crust is baking, begin making the filling by beating together the cream cheese, sour cream, and pumpkin.
4. Add the rest of the sugar, and slowly incorporate the beaten eggs and vanilla. Add the remaining salt, cinnamon, ginger, and cloves.
5. Fill a large baking pan (big enough to hold your springform pan) with about half an inch of water. Place it in the oven and let the water get hot.
6. Put foil around the edges of your springform pan, then add the filling and place the pan in the oven inside the water bath you made with the baking pan.
7. Bake for 1 hour and 45 minutes or until the center is set. You can turn the foil over the edges of the cake if it starts to get too brown. Remove the pan from the oven and place it on a cooling rack for at least one hour before removing the sides of the springform pan.
8. After it has cooled, remove sides of the pan and refrigerate the cheesecake for at least 8 hours or overnight. Serve with whipped cream and toasted pecans.

NUTRITION: 45g carbs 12g fats 5g protein

150. Reese's Peanut Butter Chocolate Cake Cheesecake

| PREPARATION TIME: | 2H + 6H CHILLING TIME | | SERVINGS: | 8-10 |

| COOKING TIME: | 1H 15' |

INGREDIENTS

Cheesecake
- 4 (8-ounce) packages cream cheese, softened
- 1 ¼ cups sugar
- ½ cup sour cream
- 2 teaspoons vanilla extract
- 5 eggs
- 8 Chocolate Peanut Butter cups, chopped
- 1 (14-ounce) can dulce de leche

Chocolate Cake
- 1 ¾ cups all-purpose flour
- 2 cups sugar
- ¾ cup cocoa
- 2 teaspoons baking soda
- 1 teaspoon salt
- 2 eggs, room temp
- 1 cup buttermilk
- ½ cup butter, melted
- 1 tablespoon vanilla extract
- 1 cup black coffee, hot

Peanut Butter Buttercream
- ¾ cup butter
- ¾ cup shortening
- ¾ cup peanut butter
- 1 ½ teaspoons vanilla
- 4-5 cups powdered sugar

Ganache
- 2 cups semi-sweet chocolate chips
- 1 cup heavy cream
- 1 teaspoon vanilla

NUTRITION: 42g carbs 13g fats 5g protein

1. Preheat the oven to 350°F and grease a 9-inch springform pan. Make the cheesecake. Preheat the oven to 475°F. Fill a large baking pan (your springform pan with have to fit in it) with half an inch of water and place it in the oven while it preheats.
2. Beat the cream cheese in a large bowl until it is fluffy. Gradually incorporate the sugar, sour cream, and vanilla, and mix well.
3. Add the eggs one at a time and beat until just combined. Fold in the peanut butter cups and pour the batter into the springform pan. Bake at 475°F for 15 minutes, then reduce the heat to 350°F and bake for 60 minutes or until the center is completely set.
4. Remove the cake from the oven and let it cool for 60 minutes before taking off the sides of the springform pan. When it is completely cool, refrigerate the cheesecake for at least 6 hours, but 8 hours to overnight would be better. When it is completely cold, cut the cheesecake in half to make two layers.
5. Meanwhile, make the chocolate cake: mix the flour, sugar, cocoa, baking soda, and salt together in a large bowl. Mix in the eggs, buttermilk, melted butter, and vanilla, and beat until it is smooth. Slowly incorporate the coffee.
6. Grease and flour two 9-inch round cake pans. Pour the batter evenly into each pan and bake for 30–35 minutes. When fully cooked, remove the cakes from the oven and cool for 15 minutes before taking them out of the pans. When fully cooled, wrap each cake in plastic wrap and refrigerate until ready to assemble the cake.
7. Make the buttercream frosting by beating together the butter and shortening, then add the peanut butter and vanilla. Mix in the powdered sugar one cup at a time until you achieve the desired sweetness and consistency.
8. To assemble, put one layer of chocolate cake on a cake plate. Drizzle half of the dulce de leche over the top of the cake. Top that with a layer of cheesecake, and spread peanut butter frosting over the top of the cheesecake. Repeat to make a second layer. When assembled, place the whole cake in the freezer for about an hour to fully set.
9. Make the ganache by melting chocolate chips with heavy cream and vanilla in a small saucepan. When the cake is completely set, pour ganache over the top. Refrigerate until ganache the sets.

151. White Chocolate Raspberry Swirl Cheesecake

Preparation Time:	45' + 5H REFRIGERETION	Servings:	8-10

Cooking Time:	1H 45'

Ingredients

Crust
- 1 ½ cups chocolate cookie crumbs, such as crumbled Oreo® cookies
- 1/3 cup butter, melted

Filling
- 4 (8-ounce) packages cream cheese
- 1 ¼ cups granulated sugar
- ½ cup sour cream
- 2 teaspoons vanilla extract
- ½ cup raspberry preserves (or raspberry pie filling)
- ¼ cup water
- 5 eggs
- 4 ounces white chocolate, chopped into chunks

Optional Garnish
- 2 ounces shaved white chocolate (optional)
- Fresh whipped cream

Directions

1. Preheat the oven to 475°F. In a food processor, crumble the cookies and add the melted butter. Press the mixture into a greased 9-inch springform pan, and place in the freezer while you make the filling.
2. Pour half an inch of water in a large baking pan (it needs to fit your springform pan) and place it in the oven. In a mixing bowl, beat together the cream cheese, sugar, sour cream, and vanilla. Scrape the sides of the bowl after the ingredients have been well combined.
3. Beat the eggs in a small bowl, then add them slowly to the cream cheese mixture.
4. In another small dish, mix the raspberry preserves and water. Microwave for 1 minute. If you want to remove the raspberry seeds, you can run the hot liquid through a mesh strainer.
5. Remove the crust from the freezer and cover the outside bottom of the pan with aluminum foil. Sprinkle the white chocolate over the crust, then pour half of the cheesecake batter into the springform pan. Next, drizzle half of the raspberry preserves over the top of the batter. Then add the rest of the batter with the rest of the drizzle.
6. Place the springform pan into the water bath and bake for 15 minutes at 475°F, then reduce the heat to 350°F and bake about 60 more minutes more, or until the center of the cake is set and cake is cooked through.
7. Remove from oven and cool it completely before removing sides of the pan, then move to the refrigerator for at least 5 hours. Serve with extra white chocolate and fresh whipped cream.

Nutrition: 41g carbs 12g fats 4g protein

152. Carrot Cake CHeeseCake

| PREPARATION TIME: | 20' + 5H CHILLING TIME | SERVINGS: | 8 |

| COOKING TIME: | 50-60' |

INGREDIENTS

Cheesecake
- 2 (8-ounce) blocks cream cheese, at room temperature
- ¾ cup granulated sugar
- 1 tablespoon flour
- 3 eggs
- 1 teaspoon vanilla

Carrot Cake
- ¾ cup vegetable oil
- 1 cup granulated sugar
- 2 eggs
- 1 teaspoon vanilla
- 1 cup flour
- 1 teaspoon baking soda
- 1 teaspoon cinnamon
- 1 dash salt
- 1 (8-ounce) can crushed pineapple, well-drained with juice reserved
- 1 cup grated carrot
- ½ cup flaked coconut
- ½ cup chopped walnuts

Pineapple Cream Cheese Frosting
- 2 ounces cream cheese, softened
- 1 tablespoon butter, softened
- 1 ¾ cups powdered sugar
- ½ teaspoon vanilla
- 1 tablespoon reserved pineapple juice

NUTRITION: 40g carbs 11g fats 6g protein

DIRECTIONS

1. Preheat the oven to 350°F and grease a 9-inch springform pan. In a large bowl, beat together the cream cheese and the sugar until smooth. Then beat in the flour, eggs, and vanilla until well combined. Set aside.
2. In another large bowl, beat together the ¾ cup vegetable oil, sugar, eggs, and vanilla until smooth. Then add the flour, baking soda, cinnamon, and salt and beat until smooth. Fold in the crushed pineapple, grated carrot, coconut, and walnuts.
3. Pour 1 ½ cups of the carrot cake batter into the prepared pan. Drop a large spoonful of the cream cheese batter over the top of the carrot cake batter. Then add a spoonful of carrot cake batter over the top of the cream cheese batter. Repeat with the remaining batter.
4. Bake the cake for 50–60 minutes, or until the center is set. Remove it from the oven and cool for about an hour before taking out the sides of the springform pan. Refrigerate for at least 5 hours.
5. While the cake is cooling, make the frosting. Beating together all the frosting ingredients. Frost the cake when it is completely cold.

153. OrIgInal CHeeseCake

| PREPARATION TIME: | 4 H 15' | | SERVINGS: | 12 |

| COOKING TIME: | 1 H 5' |

INGREDIENTS

- **Crust:**
- 1 ½ cups graham cracker crumbs
- ¼ teaspoon ground cinnamon
- 1/3 cup margarine, melted

Filling:
- 4 (8-ounce) packages cream cheese, softened
- 1 ¼ cups white sugar
- ½ cup sour cream
- 2 teaspoons vanilla extract
- 5 large eggs

Topping:
- ½ cup sour cream
- 2 teaspoons sugar

DIRECTIONS

1. Preheat the oven to 475°F and place a skillet with half an inch of water inside. Combine the ingredients for the crust in a bowl. Line a large pie pan with parchment paper, and spread crust onto the pan. Press firmly. Cover it with foil, and keep it in the freezer until ready to use.
2. Combine all the ingredients for the filling EXCEPT the eggs in a bowl. Scrape the sides of the bowl while beating, until the mixture is smooth. Mix in eggs one at a time, and beat until fully blended.
3. Take the crust from the freezer and pour in the filling, spreading it evenly. Place the pie pan into the heated skillet in the oven, and bake for about 12 minutes.
4. Reduce the heat to 350°F. Continue to bake for about 50 minutes, or until the top of the cake is golden. Remove it from the oven and transfer the skillet onto a wire rack to cool.
5. Prepare the topping by mixing all ingredients in a bowl. Coat the cake with the topping, then cover. Refrigerate for at least 4 hours. Serve cold.

NUTRITION: 41g carbs 11g fats 2g protein

154. UlTImaTe red VelveT CHeeseCake

| PREPARATION TIME: | 3h 30' | SERVINGS: | 16 |

| COOKING TIME: | 1h 15' |

INGREDIENTS

Cheesecake:
- 2 (8-ounce) packages cream cheese, softened
- 2/3 cup granulated white sugar
- Pinch salt
- 2 large eggs
- 1/3 cup sour cream
- 1/3 cup heavy whipping cream
- 1 teaspoon vanilla extract
- Non-stick cooking spray
- Hot water, for water bath

Red velvet cake:
- 2 ½ cups all-purpose flour
- 1 ½ cups granulated white sugar
- 3 tablespoons unsweetened cocoa powder
- 1 ½ teaspoons baking soda
- 1 teaspoon salt
- 2 large eggs
- 1 ½ cups vegetable oil
- 1 cup buttermilk
- ¼ cup red food coloring
- 2 teaspoons vanilla extract
- 2 teaspoons white vinegar

Frosting:
- 2 ½ cups powdered sugar, sifted
- 2 (8-ounce) packages cream cheese, softened
- ½ cup unsalted butter, softened
- 1 tablespoon vanilla extract

NUTRITION: 39g carbs 12g fats 4g protein

Directions

1. For the cheesecake, preheat the oven to 325°F. Beat the cream cheese, sugar, and salt for about 2 minutes, until creamy and smooth. Add the eggs, mixing again after adding each one. Add the sour cream, heavy cream, and vanilla extract, and beat until smooth and well blended.
2. Coat a springform pan with non-stick cooking spray, then place parchment paper on top. Wrap the outsides entirely with two layers of aluminum foil. (This is to prevent water from the water bath from entering the pan.)
3. Pour the cream cheese batter into the pan, then place it in a roasting pan. Add boiling water to the roasting pan to surround the springform pan. Place it in the oven and bake for 45 minutes until set.
4. Transfer the springform pan with the cheesecake onto a rack to cool for about 1 hour. Refrigerate overnight.
5. For the red velvet cake, preheat the oven to 350°F. Combine the flour, sugar, cocoa powder, baking soda, and salt in a large bowl. In a separate bowl, mix the eggs, oil, buttermilk, food coloring, vanilla, and vinegar. Add the wet ingredients to dry ingredients. Blend for 1 minute with a mixer on medium-low speed, then on high speed for 2 minutes.
6. Spray non-stick cooking spray in 2 metal baking pans that are the same size as the springform pan used for the cheesecake. Coat the bottoms thinly with flour. Divide the batter between them.
7. Bake for about 30–35 minutes. The cake is made when only a few crumbs are attached to a toothpick when inserted in the center. Transfer the cakes to a rack and let them cool for 10 minutes. Separate the cakes from the pans using a knife around the edges, then invert them onto the rack. Let them cool completely.
8. To prepare the frosting, mix the powdered sugar, cream cheese, butter, and vanilla using a mixer on medium-high speed, just until smooth.
9. Assemble the cake by positioning one red velvet cake layer onto a cake plate. Remove the cheesecake from the pan, peel off the parchment paper, and layer it on top of the red velvet cake layer. Top with the second red velvet cake layer.
10. Coat a thin layer of prepared frosting on the entire outside of the cake. Clean the spatula every time you scoop out from the bowl of frosting, so as to not mix crumbs into it. Refrigerate for 30 minutes to set. Then coat the cake with a second layer by adding a large scoop on top, then spreading it to the top side of the cake then around it. Cut into slices. Serve.

155. STraWberry SHorTCake

Preparation Time: 5'

Servings: 16

Cooking Time: 2h 15'

Ingredients

Sugared Strawberries:
- 2 cups strawberries (sliced)
- ¼ cup granulated sugar

Whipped Cream:
- 4 cups heavy cream
- ½ cup powdered sugar
- ¼ teaspoon vanilla

Shortcake Biscuit:
- 4 ½ cups all-purpose flour
- ½ cup sugar
- 5 tablespoons baking powder
- 2 teaspoons salt
- 1 ¾ cups butter
- 2 cups heavy cream
- 2 cups buttermilk
- 2 scoops vanilla ice cream

Directions

1. Preheat the oven to 375°F. In a bowl, combine the sliced strawberries with the sugar. Stir, cover, and refrigerate for 2 hours. Chill a mixing bowl and beat the heavy cream, powdered sugar, and vanilla until soft peaks form. Don't over beat or you will lose the fluffy consistency. Refrigerate.
2. In a mixing bowl, mix together the flour, sugar, baking powder, and salt. Stir to combine. Using two butter knives, cut the butter into the flour mixture until it becomes crumbly. Add the cream and the buttermilk and mix gently until the batter forms.
3. Turn out the dough onto a floured surface, and roll it to form biscuits about half an inch thick. Take care not to turn the cutter as you remove it from the dough. Place the biscuits on a non-stick cookie sheet and bake for about 15 minutes. They should at least double in size.
4. When they cool, assemble the shortcake by cutting each biscuit in half, topping the bottom half with strawberries and ice cream, and placing the top half of the biscuit on top of the ice cream. Top with more strawberries and whipped cream.

Nutrition: 40g carbs 12g fats 5g protein

156. lemonCello Cream TorTe

INGREDIENTS

- 1 box yellow cake mix
- Limoncello liqueur (optional)
- 1 package ladyfinger cookies
- 1 (3-ounce) package sugar-free lemon gelatin
- 1 cup boiling water
- 1 (8-ounce) package cream cheese, softened
- 1 teaspoon vanilla extract
- 1 (13-ounce) can cold milnot (evaporated milk), whipped

For the glaze:
- 1 cup confectioner's sugar
- 1–2 tablespoons lemon juice

DIRECTIONS

1. Preheat the oven to 350°F. Prepare the yellow cake mix according to the Directions on the package. Use two 9-inch round cake pans, or you can use a springform pan and cut the cake in half after it is baked.
2. When the cake is made and cooled, you can soak the layers lightly with some limoncello. Do the same with the ladyfingers. Bring one cup of water to a boil and stir in the lemon gelatin. Refrigerate until it gets thick, but don't let it set.
3. Mix together the cream cheese and vanilla, then mix in the thickened gelatin. Fold the whipped milnot into the mixture until combined. To assemble the cake, place the bottom layer of the cake back in the pan. This will help you get even layers. Top the cake with about half an inch of the lemon filling. Place ladyfingers on top of the filling, then top with another layer of the filling. Place the other half of the cake on the top.
4. Place the cake in the refrigerator to set. Make a drizzle with some lemon juice and confectioner's sugar, and drizzle over the cake.

NUTRITION: 45g carbs 16g fats 5g protein

157. Oreo Cookie CheeseCake

PREPARATION TIME:	10' + 4-6H CHILLING TIME	**SERVINGS:**	8-10

COOKING TIME: 60'

INGREDIENTS

- 1 package Oreo cookies
- ⅓ cup unsalted butter, melted
- 3 (8-ounce) packages cream cheese
- ¾ cup granulated sugar
- 4 eggs
- 1 cup sour cream
- 1 teaspoon vanilla extract
- Whipped cream and additional cookies for garnish

DIRECTIONS

1. Preheat the oven to 350°F. Crush most of the cookies (25-30) in a food processor or blender, and add the melted butter. Press the cookie mixture into the bottom of a 9-inch springform pan and keep it in the refrigerator while you prepare the filling.
2. In a mixing bowl, beat the cream cheese until smooth, and add the sugar. Beat in the eggs in one a time. When the eggs are mixed together, beat in the sour cream and vanilla.
3. Chop the remaining cookies and fold them gently into the filling mixture. Pour the filling into the springform pan and bake at 350°F for 50–60 minutes. Ensure the center of the cake has set.
4. Let the cake cool for 15 minutes, then carefully remove the sides of the springform pan. Transfer to the refrigerator and refrigerate for 4–6 hours or overnight.

NUTRITION: 47g carbs 18g fats 8g protein

158. banana Cream CHeeseCake

| PREPARATION TIME: | 20' | | SERVINGS: | 4 |

| COOKING TIME: | 1H 30' |

INGREDIENTS

- 20 vanilla sandwich cookies
- ¼ cup margarine, melted
- 3 (8-ounce) packages cream cheese, softened
- 2/3 cup granulated sugar
- 2 tablespoons cornstarch
- 3 eggs
- ¾ cup mashed bananas
- ½ cup whipping cream
- 2 teaspoons vanilla extract

DIRECTIONS

1. Preheat the oven to 350°F. Crush the cookies in either a food processor or blender. When they have turned to crumbs, add the melted butter. Place the mixture in a springform pan and press to entirely cover the bottom and up the sides of the pan. Refrigerate this while you prepare the filling.
2. Beat the cream cheese until it is smooth, and add the sugar and corn starch. When the cheese mixture is well blended, add in the eggs one at a time. When the eggs are incorporated, add the bananas, whipping cream, and vanilla, beating until well combined.
3. Pour the filling into the springform pan and bake at 350°F for 15 minutes. Reduce the heat to 200°F and bake until the center of the cheesecake is set, about 1 hour and 15 minutes.
4. When the center is set, remove the cake from the oven. Pop the spring on the pan, but don't remove the sides until the cheesecake has cooled completely. When it is cool, transfer it to the refrigerator. Refrigerate for at least 4 hours before serving. Serve with whipped cream and freshly sliced bananas.

NUTRITION: 46g carbs 11g fats 5g protein

159. blaCkouT Cake

PREPARATION TIME: 30'

SERVINGS: 8-10

COOKING TIME: 35-45'

INGREDIENTS

For the Cake:
- 1 cup butter, softened
- 4 cups sugar
- 4 large eggs
- 4 teaspoons vanilla extract, divided
- 6 ounces unsweetened chocolate, melted
- 4 cups flour
- 4 teaspoons baking soda
- ½ teaspoon salt
- 1 cup buttermilk
- 1 ¾ cups boiling water

For the Chocolate Ganache:
- 12 ounces semisweet chocolate, chips or chopped
- 3 cups heavy cream
- 4 tablespoons butter, chopped
- 2 teaspoons vanilla
- 1 ½ cups roasted almonds, crushed (for garnish)

DIRECTIONS

1. Preheat the oven to 350°F. Prepare two large rimmed baking sheets with parchment paper (or grease and dust with flour 3 8-inch cake pans).
2. In a large bowl or bowl for a stand mixer, beat together the butter and sugar until well combined. When the sugar mixture is fluffy, add the eggs and 2 teaspoons of vanilla. When that is combined, add the 4 ounces of melted chocolate and mix well.
3. In a separate bowl, stir together the flour, baking soda, and salt. Gradually add half the flour mixture to the chocolate mixture. When it is combined, add half of the buttermilk and mix until combined. Repeat with remaining flour mixture and buttermilk. When it is completely combined, add the boiling water and mix thoroughly. (The batter should be a little thin).
4. Divide the batter evenly between the two large baking sheets that you prepared earlier (or 3 8-inch cake pans).
5. Transfer to the oven and bake for 20–30 minutes for the baking sheets or 25-35 minutes for the cake pans, or until a toothpick inserted in the center comes out clean.
6. Remove from the oven and let cakes cool for about 10 minutes. With the pastry ring, make 3 cakes from each of the baking sheets. When they are completely cool down. If using cake pans, turn them out onto a cooling rack and let them cool completely and then cut horizontally into two to make 6 cake layers.
7. Make the ganache by mixing the chocolate chips and cream in a heat-safe glass bowl. Place the bowl over a pot of boiling water. Reduce heat to medium-low and let simmer gently. Stir constantly with a wooden spoon until the chocolate is all melted. Add-in the butter and vanilla and stir until well combined. Let cool for a few minutes, cover with plastic wrap, and refrigerate until the ganache holds its shape and is spreadable, about 10 minutes.
8. To assemble the cake, place the first cake layer on a serving plate and spread some of the ganache on the top. Place the second cake layer on top and spread some of the ganache on top. Repeat until all 6 layers are done. Use the remaining ganache to frost the top and sides of the cake, then cover the sides with crushed almonds (if desired) by pressing them gently into the chocolate ganache. Refrigerate before serving.

NUTRITION: 41g carbs 10g fats 4g protein

160. Molten lava Cake

PREPARATION TIME: 20'

SERVINGS: 5-6

COOKING TIME: 10'

INGREDIENTS

For the Cakes:
- Six tablespoons unsalted butter (2 tablespoons melted, four tablespoons at room temperature)
- 1/2 cup natural cocoa powder (not Dutch process), plus more for dusting
- 1 1/3 cups all-purpose flour
- One teaspoon baking soda
- 1/2 teaspoon baking powder
- 1/2 teaspoon salt
- Three tablespoons milk
- 1/4 cup vegetable oil
- 1 1/3 cups sugar
- 1 1/2 teaspoons vanilla extract
- Two large eggs, at room temperature

For the Fillings and Toppings:
- 8 ounces bittersweet chocolate, finely chopped
- 1/2 cup heavy cream
- Four tablespoons unsalted butter
- One tablespoon light corn syrup
- Caramel sauce, for drizzling
- 1-pint vanilla ice cream

NUTRITION: 546 Calories 5g Protein 61g Carbohydrate 31g Fat

DIRECTIONS

1. Oven preheats to 350 degrees F. Make the cakes: Brush four one 1/4-cup brioche molds (jumbo muffin cups or 10-ounce ramekins) with the butter melted in 2 tablespoons. Clean the cocoa powdered molds and tap the excess.
2. In a small bowl, whisk in the flour, baking soda, baking powder, and salt. Bring 3/4 cup water& the milk and over medium heat to a boil in a saucepan; set aside.
3. Use a stand mixer, combine vegetable oil, four tablespoons of room-temperature butter and sugar and beat with the paddle attachment until it's fluffy at medium-high speed, around 4 minutes, scrape the bowl down and beat as desired. Add 1/2 cup cocoa powder and vanilla; beat over medium velocity for 1 minute. Scrape the pot beneath. Add one egg and beat at medium-low speed for 1 minute, then add the remaining egg and beat for another minute.
4. Gradually beat in the flour mixture with the mixer on a low level, then the hot milk mixture. Finish combining the batter with a spatula of rubber before mixed. Divide the dough equally between the molds, each filling slightly more than three-quarters of the way.
5. Move the molds to a baking sheet and bake for 25 to 30 minutes, until the tops of the cakes feel domed, and the centers are just barely set. Move the baking sheet to a rack; allow the cakes to cool for about 30 minutes before they pull away from the molds.
6. How to set up the Cake: Make the Filling: Microwave the sugar, butter, chocolate, and corn syrup in a microwave-safe bowl at intervals of 30 seconds, stirring each time, until the chocolate starts to melt, 1 minute, 30 seconds. Let sit for three minutes and then whisk until smooth. Reheat, if possible, before use.
7. Using a paring knife tip to remove the cakes gently from the molds, then invert the cakes onto a cutting board.
8. Hollow out a spoon to the cake; save the scraps. Wrap the plastic wrap and microwave cakes until steaming, for 1 minute.
9. Drizzle the caramel plates, unwrap the cakes, then put them on top. Pour three tablespoons into each cake filling.
10. Plug in a cake scrap to the door. Save any leftover scraps or discard them.
11. Top each cake, use an ice cream scoop. Spoon more chocolate sauce on top, spread thinly so that it is coated in a jar.

161. White Chocolate raspberry nothing bundt Cakes

PREPARATION TIME: 20′

SERVINGS: 5-6

COOKING TIME: 10′

INGREDIENTS

- Chopped into small cubes, 200g butter, plus extra for greasing
- 100g white chocolate, broken into pieces
- Four large eggs
- 200g caster sugar
- 200g self-rising flour
- 175g raspberries, fresh or frozen

For the ganache
- 200g white chocolate, chopped
- 250ml double cream
- A little icing sugar, for dusting

DIRECTIONS

1. Heat oven to fan/gas 4, 180C/160C. Grease and line the 2 x 20 cm round base with loose-bottomed cake tins. In a heat-proof mixing bowl, place the butter and chocolate, set over a pan of barely simmering water, and allow to melt gradually, stirring occasionally.
2. Once butter and chocolate have melted, remove from heat and cool for 1-2 minutes, then beat with an electric whisk in the eggs and sugar. Fold and raspberries in the starch.
3. Pour the mixture gently into the tins and bake for 20-25 minutes or until golden brown and a skewer inserted in the center is clean (Don't be fooled by their juiciness, the raspberries leave a residue on the skewer). Pullout the cakes from the oven & allow for 10 minutes of cooling in the tins before placing on a wire rack.
4. To make the ganache, place the chocolate over a pan of barely simmering water in a heatproof bowl with 100ml of the cream on top. Remove until the chocolate has melted into the sugar, and leave a smooth, shiny ganache on you. You need to leave the ganache at room temperature to cool, then beat in the rest of the cream.
5. Sandwich them together with the chocolate ganache after the cakes have cooled. Just before serving, sprinkle them with icing sugar.

NUTRITION: 489 Calories 3.9g Protein 59g Carbohydrate 28g Fat

162. Caramel roCksllde broWnles

PREPARATION TIME: 25'

SERVINGS: 5-6

COOKING TIME: 25'

INGREDIENTS

- 1 cup butter (2 sticks)
- 2 cups of sugar
- Four eggs
- Two teaspoons vanilla extract
- 2/3 cup unsweetened natural cocoa powder
- 1 cup all-purpose flour
- 1/2 teaspoon salt
- One teaspoon baking powder
- 1/2 cup semisweet chocolate chips
- 1 cup (plus more for drizzling over the top) caramel topping
- 3/4 cup chopped pecans (plus more for sprinkling on top)

DIRECTIONS

1. Preheat to 350 degrees on the oven. On a medium saucepan, melt butter over medium heat.
2. Clear from heat the pan and whisk in sugar. Whisk in the vanilla extract & the eggs. Mix the cocoa, baking powder, flour, salt and in a separate dish. Drop the dry ingredients into the saucepan and combine them until they have just been added. Add chocolate chips.
3. Pour the batter into two nine by 9-inch baking pans that are evenly split, sprayed with nonstick spray, and lined with parchment paper.
4. Bake for 25-28 minutes and leave to cool.
5. Use the parchment paper edges to lift the whole brownie out of one of the pans, and chop into 1/2-inch cubes.
6. Pour 1 cup of caramel over the brownies still in the saucepan, then add the chopped pecans and brownie cubes.
7. Press down to make the caramel stick to the brownie cubes. If desired, drizzle with extra caramel and sprinkle with a few more chopped pecans.
8. If needed, serve with ice cream and excess sugar, and chopped pecans.

NUTRITION: 509 Calories 5g Protein 67g Carbohydrate 32g Fat

163. Cornbread Muffins

PREPARATION TIME: 10'

SERVINGS: 6-7

COOKING TIME: 25'

INGREDIENTS

- ½ cup butter softened
- 2/3 Cup white sugar
- ¼ cup honey
- Two eggs
- ½ teaspoon salt
- 1 ½ cups all-purpose flour
- ¾ cup cornmeal
- ½ teaspoon baking powder
- ½ cup milk
- ¾ cup frozen corn kernels, thawed

DIRECTIONS

1. Preheat oven to 400 grades F (200 grades C). Grease or 12 cups of muffins on deck.
2. Cream the butter, sugar, honey, eggs, and salt together in a big pot. Add in rice, cornmeal, and baking powder, blend well. Stir in corn and milk. Pour the yield into prepared muffin cups or spoon them.
3. Bake for 20 to 25 minutes in a preheated oven until a toothpick inserted in the center of a muffin comes out clean.

NUTRITION: 141 Calories 6g Protein 22g Carbohydrate 18g Fat

164. CHoColaTe mousse Cake

<table>
<tr><td>PREPARATION TIME:</td><td>10'</td><td>SERVINGS:</td><td>6-7</td></tr>
<tr><td>COOKING TIME:</td><td>25'</td><td></td><td></td></tr>
</table>

INGREDIENTS

- 1 (18.25 ounce) chocolate cake mix pack
- 1 (14 ounces) can sweeten condensed milk
- 2 (1 ounce) squares unsweetened chocolate, melted
- ½ cup of cold water
- 1 (3.9 ounces) package instant chocolate pudding mix
- 1 cup heavy cream, whipped

DIRECTIONS

1. Preheat oven up to 175 degrees C (350 degrees F). Prepare and bake cake mix on two 9-inch layers according to package Directions. Cool off and pan clean.
2. Mix the sweetened condensed milk and melted chocolate together in a big tub. Stir in water slowly, then pudding instantly until smooth. Chill in for 30 minutes, at least.
3. Remove from the fridge the chocolate mixture, and whisk to loosen. Fold in the whipped cream and head back to the refrigerator for at least another hour.
4. Place one of the cake layers onto a serving platter. Top the mousse with 1 1/2 cups, then cover with the remaining cake layer. Frost with remaining mousse, and cool until served. Garnish with chocolate shavings or fresh fruit.

NUTRITION: 324 Calories 8g Protein 32g Carbohydrate 50g Fat

165. blaCkberry and aPPles Cobbler

PREPARATION TIME: 10'

SERVINGS: 6

COOKING TIME: 30'

INGREDIENTS

- ¾ cup stevia
- 6 cups blackberries
- ¼ cup apples, cored and cubed
- ¼ teaspoon baking powder
- 1 tablespoon lime juice
- ½ cup almond flour
- ½ cup of water
- 3 and ½ tablespoon avocado oil
- Cooking spray

DIRECTIONS

1. In a bowl, mix the berries with half of the stevia and lemon juice, sprinkle some flour all over, whisk and pour into a baking dish greased with cooking spray.
2. In another bowl, mix flour with the rest of the sugar, baking powder, the water, and the oil, and stir the whole thing with your hands.
3. Spread over the berries, introduce in the oven at 375° F, and bake for 30 minutes. Serve warm.

NUTRITION: 221 Calories 6.3g Fat 3.3g Fiber 6g Carbohydrates 9g Protein

166. blaCk Tea Cake

| PREPARATION TIME: | 10' | SERVINGS: | 8 |

| COOKING TIME: | 35' |

INGREDIENTS

- 6 tablespoons black tea powder
- 2 cups almond milk, warmed up
- 1 cup avocado oil
- 2 cups stevia
- 4 eggs
- 2 teaspoons vanilla extract
- 3 and ½ cups almond flour
- 1 teaspoon baking soda
- 3 teaspoons baking powder

DIRECTIONS

1. In a bowl, combine the almond milk with the oil, stevia, and the rest of the ingredients and whisk well.
2. Pour this into a cake pan lined with parchment paper, introduce in the oven at 350° F and bake for 35 minutes. Leave the cake to cool down, slice, and serve.

NUTRITION: 200 Calories 6.4g Fat 4g Fiber 6.5g Carbohydrates 5.4g Protein

167. Quinoa Muffins

<table>
<tr><td>Preparation Time:</td><td>10'</td><td>Servings:</td><td>12</td></tr>
</table>

Cooking Time: 30'

Ingredients

- 1 cup quinoa, cooked
- 6 eggs, whisked
- Salt and black pepper to the taste
- 1 cup Swiss cheese, grated
- 1 small yellow onion, chopped
- 1 cup white mushrooms, sliced
- ½ cup sun-dried tomatoes, chopped

Directions

1. In a bowl, combine the eggs with salt, pepper, and the rest of the ingredients and whisk well.
2. Divide this into a silicone muffin pan, bake at 350 degrees F for 30 minutes and serve for breakfast.

Nutrition: 123 Calories 5.6g Fat 1.3g Fiber 10.8g Carbohydrates 7.5g Protein

168. figs Pie

PREPARATION TIME: 10'

SERVINGS: 8

COOKING TIME: 1 H

INGREDIENTS

- ½ cup stevia
- 6 figs, cut into quarters
- ½ teaspoon vanilla extract
- 1 cup almond flour
- 4 eggs, whisked

DIRECTIONS

1. Spread the figs on the bottom of a springform pan lined with parchment paper.
2. In a bowl, combine the other ingredients, whisk and pour over the figs,
3. Bake at 375° F for 1 hour, flip the pie upside down when it's done and serve.

NUTRITION: 200 Calories 4.4g Fat 3g Fiber 7.6g Carbohydrates 8g Protein

Chapter 6

SOFT DRINK RECIPES

169. lemon and berry SlusH

PREPARATION TIME: 5'

SERVINGS: 7

COOKING TIME: 0'

INGREDIENTS

- 1 cup soda, lemon and lime flavored
- 2 cups strawberries, cut into half
- 1/3 cup lemon juice
- 1/4 cup sugar
- 3 cups of ice cubes

DIRECTIONS

1. Put all the ingredients and fill it to the max water line, then blend until smooth. Plug in a food processor, place all the ingredients in the order as mentioned in the ingredients list and then pulse for 1 to 2 minutes until frothy.
2. Divide the slush evenly between four glasses and then serve.

NUTRITION: 110 Calories 29.7 g Carbohydrates 0.25 g Fiber 29 g Sugars

170. Taco bell's Pena Colada drink

PREPARATION TIME:	5'	**SERVINGS:**	4

COOKING TIME: 0'

INGREDIENTS

- ½ cup lemon and lime soda pop
- 1 cup Pina colada mix
- 1 cup crushed ice
- 2 slices of lime

DIRECTIONS

1. Plug in a food processor, place all the ingredients in it except for lime slices and then pulse for 1 to 2 minutes until frothy.
2. Divide the drink evenly between two glasses, top with lime slices, and then serve.

NUTRITION: 245 Calories 2.7g Fat 32g Carbohydrates 0.4g Fiber 21.5g Sugars

171. Chickfil-a lemonade

PREPARATION TIME: 5'

SERVINGS: 4

COOKING TIME: 0'

INGREDIENTS

- 1 ¾ cup lemon juice
- 5 cups water, cold
- 1 cup of sugar

DIRECTIONS

1. Take a large jug or a pitcher, pour in lemon juice, and then stir in sugar until dissolved.
2. Pour in water, stir until mixed, and then chill it in the refrigerator for a minimum of 1 hour before serving.

NUTRITION: 217 Calories 1 g Fat 57 g Carbohydrates 1 g Fiber 53 g Sugars 1 g Protein

172. dairy Queen blizzard

PREPARATION TIME: 5'	SERVINGS: 2

COOKING TIME: 0'

INGREDIENTS

- 8 Oreo Double Stuff cookies
- 4 cups vanilla ice cream
- 8 mini Oreo cookies

DIRECTIONS

1. Take a large bowl, place ice cream in it, and then beat it until creamy.
2. Break Oreo cookies into chunks, add to the ice cream and then fold by using a spoon until mixed.
3. Divide evenly between two glasses, top with mini Oreo cookies, and then serve.

NUTRITION: 580 Calories 24 g Fat 80 g Carbohydrates 1 g Fiber 67 g Sugars 15 g Protein

173. Watermelon and Mint Lemonade

Preparation Time:	5'	Servings:	6

Cooking Time:	0'

Ingredients

- ½ cup chopped mint leaves
- 4 cups water, chilled
- 1 cup of sugar
- 2 cups watermelon juice
- 1 ½ cups lemon juice

Directions

1. Take a large jug or a pitcher, pour in lemon juice, stir in sugar until dissolved, and then stir in mint leaves.
2. Pour in the water, stir until mixed, and then stir in watermelon juice.
3. Let the lemonade chill for 1 hour in the refrigerator and then serve.

Nutrition: 220 Calories 55 g Carbohydrates 12 g Fiber 53 g Sugars

174. SonIC OCean WaTer

PREPARATION TIME: 5'	SERVINGS: 2

COOKING TIME: 0'

INGREDIENTS

- 2 limes, juiced
- 1 teaspoon coconut extract, unsweetened
- 1 tablespoon sugar
- 2 tablespoons water
- 1 teaspoon blue food coloring
- 2 bottles of Sprite, each about 12 ounces
- ½ cup crushed ice

DIRECTIONS

1. Take a small bowl, place it water, stir in sugar until dissolved, and then let it cool until chilled.
2. Fill two glasses evenly with crushed ice and then pour in the sprite.
3. Add coconut extract into the chilled sugar mixture, stir until mixed, and then stir in food color.
4. Add the coconut extract mixture evenly into each glass, stir until mixed, and then serve.

NUTRITION: 116 Calories 30.2 g Carbohydrates 30.2 g Sugars

175. rainforesT Café's STraWberry lemonade

PREPARATION TIME: 5'

SERVINGS: 8

COOKING TIME: 5'

INGREDIENTS

- ¾ cup of sugar
- 1-pound strawberries, fresh, diced
- 6 cups water, chilled
- 1 lemon, zested
- 6 lemons, juiced

DIRECTIONS

1. Take a small saucepan, place it over medium-high heat, and then add berries in it. Pour in 1 cup water, stir in lemon zest and then bring the mixture to a boil.
2. Transfer strawberry mixture into a pitcher, add remaining water along with lemon juice and then stir until combined. Taste to adjust sweetener if needed and then let it chill for 1 hour in the refrigerator before serving.

NUTRITION: 487 Calories 132 g Carbohydrates 5 g Fiber 122 g Sugars

176. Chick-fil-a's frozen lemonade CoPyCaT

PREPARATION TIME: 10'

SERVINGS: 3

COOKING TIME: 0'

INGREDIENTS

- 1/2 c. freshly squeezed lemon juice
- 1/2 c. sugar
- 2 c. water
- 6 c. vanilla ice cream
- sliced lemons, for garnish

DIRECTIONS

1. Dissolve the sugar in lemon juice. Add water and chill to dilute.
2. Stir lemonade and ice cream into a blender. Mix until smooth, and split between 3 cups. Garnish with lemon slices, and serve.

NUTRITION: 470 calories 3g fiber 120g sugar

177. dunkIn donuT's mInT HoT CHoColaTe CoPyCaT

PREPARATION TIME: 5'

SERVINGS: 53

COOKING TIME: 0'

INGREDIENTS

- 7-1/2 cups instant chocolate drink mix
- 1 package (25.6 ounces) nonfat dry milk powder
- 2-1/2 cups confectioners' sugar
- 1 cup powdered nondairy creamer
- 25 peppermint candies, crushed
- Miniature marshmallows

Each Servings:
- 1 cup hot whole milk

DIRECTIONS

1. Combine the initial 5 ingredients. Divide into gift bags, or growing them in an airtight tub, adding as desired miniature marshmallows. Mixing can take up to 6 months to store in a cold, dry location.
2. To make hot cocoa: place 1/3 cup cocoa mix in a mug. Incorporate hot milk until blended. Fill in as many marshmallows as you wish.

NUTRITION: 420 calories 3g fiber 112g sugar

178. Tim Horton's Hot Apple Cider Copycat

PREPARATION TIME: 2H 5'

SERVINGS: ABOUT 2 QUARTS

COOKING TIME: 0'

INGREDIENTS

- 8 whole cloves
- 4 cups apple cider or juice
- 4 cups pineapple juice
- 1/2 cup water
- 1 cinnamon stick (3 inches)
- 1 teabag

DIRECTIONS

1. Place the cloves on a double cheesecloth thickness; bring up cloth corners and tie to form a bag with kitchen string. Place the rest of the ingredients into 3-qt. Slow cooker; add a bag of spices.
2. Cover and cook for 2 hours on medium, or until the ideal temperature hits cider. Until serving, remove the spice packet, cinnamon stick, and teacup.

NUTRITION: 401 calories 6g fiber 110g sugar

179. New Orleans' famous Hurricanes Copycat

PREPARATION TIME: 10'	SERVINGS: 6

COOKING TIME: 0'

INGREDIENTS

- 2 cups passion fruit juice
- 1 cup plus 2 tablespoons sugar
- 3/4 cup lime juice
- 3/4 cup light rum
- 3/4 cup dark rum
- 3 tablespoons grenadine syrup
- 6 to 8 cups ice cubes
- Orange slices, starfruit slices, and maraschino cherries

DIRECTIONS

1. Combine the fruit juice, sugar, lime juice, rum, and grenadine into a pitcher; whisk until sugar is dissolved.
2. Pour into ice-cold glasses filled with hurricane or highball. Serve with slices of orange, starfruit, and cherries.

NUTRITION: 403 calories 3.8g fiber 103g sugar

180. ruby Tuesday's raspberry Iced Tea CoPyCaT

PREPARATION TIME: 25'

SERVINGS: 15

COOKING TIME: 0'

INGREDIENTS

- 4 quarts water
- 10 tea bags
- 1 (12 ounces) frozen unsweetened raspberries
- 1 cup sugar
- 3 tbsp lime juice

DIRECTIONS

1. Let the 2 quarts of water boil in a saucepan; remove from heat. Add tea bags; steep, sealed, on taste for 5-8 minutes. Discard the bags for tea.
2. In a large saucepan, put the raspberries, sugar, and remaining water; bring to a boil, stirring to dissolve sugar. Reduce heat; simmer for 3 minutes, uncovered. Push the mixture into a bowl through a fine-mesh strainer; discard the pulp and seeds.
3. Combine the tea, raspberry syrup, and lime juice into a large pitcher. Cover, refrigerate, until cold.

NUTRITION: 120 calories 4g fiber 104g sugar

181. mike'sHard lemonade CoPyCaT

PREPARATION TIME: 5'

SERVINGS: 2

COOKING TIME: 0'

INGREDIENTS

- 2-1/4 cups sugar
- 5 cups water, divided
- 1 tablespoon grated lemon zest
- 1-3/4 cups lemon juice
- 1 cup light rum or vodka
- 6 to 8 cups ice cubes

Garnish:
- Lemon slices

DIRECTIONS

1. Combine the sugar, 1 cup of water, and lemon zest into a large saucepan. Cook over medium heat and stir until sugar dissolves, about 4 minutes. Out of heat strip. Stir in the juice of the lemon and the remaining vapor. Offer in a 2-qt. Pitcher; leave to cool until chilled.
2. Stir the rum in. Place 3/4 to 1 cup of ice in a highball glass for each serving. Pour lemonade into the glass. Garnish as desired, with lemon slices.

NUTRITION: 402 calories 4.9g fiber 104.3g sugar

182. Chick-fil-a's frosted lemonade Copycat

PREPARATION TIME: 10'

SERVINGS: 4

COOKING TIME: 0'

INGREDIENTS

- 2 tbsp lemon drop candies
- 1 tsp sugar
- 1/2 small lemon
- 1/2 cup milk
- 2 cups vanilla ice cream
- 2 cups lemon sorbet
- 3 ounces cream cheese
- 2 tsp lemon zest
- 1/2 tsp vanilla extract

DIRECTIONS

1. Mix the crushed lemon drops and the sugar in a shallow dish. Moisten the rims of four glasses using 1 or 2 lemon slices; dip the edges into a candy mixture.
2. Place the remaining ingredients in a blender (minus lemon slices); cover and process until smooth. Pour into prepared glasses; immediately serve with remaining slices of lemon.

NUTRITION: 411 calories 6g fiber 112g sugar

183. Crystal Light's Berry Sangria Mix Copycat

PREPARATION TIME: 15'

SERVINGS: 10

COOKING TIME: 0'

INGREDIENTS

- 1 bottle (750 ml) sparkling white wine
- 2-1/2 cups white cranberry juice
- 2/3 cup light or coconut rum
- 1/3 cup each fresh blackberries, blueberries, and raspberries
- 1/3 cup chopped fresh strawberries
- Ice cubes

DIRECTIONS

1. Mix wine, juice, and rum in a large saucepan; add fruit. Refrigerate to a total of 2 hours; serve over ice.

NUTRITION: 403 calories 4.9g fiber 117g sugar

Chapter 7

PRACTICAL ADVICE FOR BEGINNERS TO CANNING AND PRESERVING YOUR FAVORITE FOODS

There are a few safety tips that you should follow when you start canning and preserving foods from home. Canning is a great way to store and preserve foods, but it can be risky if not done correctly. However, if you follow these tips, you will be able to can foods safely.

Choose the Right Canner

The first step to safe home canning is choosing the right canner. First off, know when to use a pressure canner or a water bath canner.

Use a pressure canner that is specifically designed for canning and preserving foods. There are several types of canner out there, and some are just for cooking food, not for preserving food and processing jars. Be sure that you have the right type of equipment.

Make sure your pressure canner is the right size. If your canner is too small, the jars may be undercooked. Always opt for a larger canner as the pressure on the bigger pots tends to be more accurate, and you will be able to take advantage of the larger size and can more foods at once!

Before you begin canning, check that your pressure canner is in good condition. If your canner has a rubber gasket, it should be flexible and soft. If the rubber is dry or cracked, it should be replaced before you start canning. Be sure your canner is clean, and the small vents in the lid are free of debris. Adjust your canner for high altitude processing if needed.

Once you are sure your canner is ready to go and meets all these guidelines, it is time to start canning!

Opt for a Screw Top Lid System

There are many kinds of canning jars that you can choose to purchase. However, the only type of jar approved by the USDA is a mason jar with a screw-top lid. These are designated "preserving jars" and are considered the safest and most effective option for home preserving uses.

Some jars are not thought to be safe for home preservation despite being marketed as canning jars. Bail Jars, for example, have a two-part wire clasp lid with a rubber ring in between the lid and jar. While these were popular in the past, it is now thought that the thick rubber and tightly closed lid does not provide a sufficient seal, leading to a higher potential for botulism. Lightening Jars should not be used for canning as they are simply glass jars with glass lids, with no rubber at all. That will not create a good seal!

Reusing jars from store-bought products is another poor idea. They may look like they're in good condition, but they are typically designed to be processed in a commercial facility. Most store-bought products do not have the two-part band and lid system, which is best for home canning. The rubber seal on a store-bought product is likely not reusable once you open the original jar. You can reuse store-bought jars at home for storage but not for canning and preserving.

Check Your Jars, Lids, and Bands

As you wash your jars with soapy water, check for any imperfections. Even new jars may have a small chip or crack and need to be discarded. You can reuse jars again and again as long as they are in good condition.

The metal jar rings are also reusable; however, you should only reuse them if they are rust free and undented. If your bands begin to show signs of wear, consider investing in some new ones.

Jar lids need to be new as the sealing compound on the lid can disintegrate over time. When you store your jars in damp places (like in a basement or canning cellar), the lids are even more likely to disintegrate. Always use new lids to ensure that your canning is successful.

Check for Recent Canning Updates

Canning equipment has changed over the years, becoming higher-tech and, therefore, more efficient at processing foods. In addition to the equipment becoming more advanced, there have also been many scientific improvements, making canning safer when the proper steps are taken. For example, many people used to sterilize their jars before pressure canning. While this is still okay to do, it is unnecessary as science has shown that any bacteria in the jars will die when heated to such a high temperature in a pressure canner. Sterilization is an extra step that you don't need!

Make sure that your food preservation information is all up to date and uses current canning guidelines. Avoid outdated cookbooks and reassess "trusted family methods" to make sure they fit into the most recent criteria for safe canning. When in doubt, check with the US Department of Agriculture's Complete Guide to Home Canning, which contains the most recent, up-to-date canning tips.

Pick the Best Ingredients

When choosing food to can, always get the best food possible. You want to use high quality, perfectly ripe produce for canning. You will never end up with a jar of food better than the product itself, so picking good ingredients is important to your final product's taste. Also, products that past their prime can affect the ability to handle it. If strawberries are overripe, your jam may come out too runny. If your tomatoes are past their prime, they may not have a high enough pH level to be processed in a water bath. Pick your ingredients well, and you will make successfully preserved foods.

Clean everything

While you may know that your jars and lids need to be washed and sanitized, don't forget about the rest of your tools. Cleaning out your canner before using it is essential, even if you put it away clean. Make sure to wipe your countertop well, making sure there are no crumbs or residue. Wash your produce with clean, cold water, and don't forget to wash your hands! The cleaner everything is, the less likely you are to spread bacteria onto your jarred foods.

Follow Your Recipe

Use recipes from trusted sources, and be sure to follow them to the letter. Changing the amount of one or two ingredients may alter the balance of acidity and result in unsafe canning (especially when using a water bath canner). Use the ingredients as directed and make very few changes—none if possible.
Adhere to the processing times specified by your recipe. Sometimes the times may seem a little long, but the long processing time makes these products safe to store on the shelf. The processing time is the correct amount of time needed to destroy spoilage organisms, mold spores, yeast, and pathogens in the jar. So, as you may have guessed, it is extremely important to use the times written in your recipe as a hard rule.

Cool the Jars

Be sure that you give your jars 12 hours to cool before testing the seal. If you test the seal too early, it may break as the jar is still warm, making it pliable. Be sure to cool the jars away from a window or fan as even a slight breeze may cause the hot jars to crack. Once cool, remove the metal band, clean it and save it for your next canning project.

Conclusion

Creativity often happens when you cook at home, and you can attach a range of plant foods to a variety of colors. You are not only acquiring kilograms, antioxidants, minerals, and phytonutrients but also introducing nice textures and colors to your meals. You would be shocked by how much food in a single dish is collected.

Portion control from home can be regulated. When food is cooked for us, we tend to eat all or most of it. Try to use little dishes at home, but ensure that all good things like vegetables, fruits, whole grains, and legumes are filled. You are certainly going to be satisfied and happy.

The major advantage of trying copycat restaurant recipes is that you can save more money and use your creativity to improve the dish. You can also adjust the ingredients and add those favorite herbs to your desired taste. Now you have saved your money and restaurant-quality dishes for your family as well.

You may not include some ingredients of your favorite dish when you try the copycat recipes, and it is okay. Following the recipe while recreating your favorite dish is what we are here for.

It is not hard to acquire those top-secret restaurant-quality recipes. Others may advise that you need to have culinary credentials to cook those secret recipes. Yet, we can gather those ingredients ourselves and cook an elaborate meal that tastes like the real deal.

But do top secret restaurant recipes taste the way the chef served them? Perhaps. You can easily cook your favorite recipes with a little practice and patience. You would want to cook the basic formula and start adding what you think would make the recipe's flavor better after a while. You may start to think that some recipes need additional seasonings to improve your dish than the original. Nevertheless, if you wanted to prepare this dish on your own, there is still a chance.

With just a few simple tricks and tips, you can also cook quality cuisine in your kitchen. These tricks may not seem so strong on their own but can transform how you prepare and produce food when they are all used together. These tips help you cook at home like a pro from expired spices and how you use salt to arrange it before you start cooking.

When preparing desserts at home, you can tweak the recipes as you wish. As you sample the recipes, you will know the usual ingredients and techniques in making popular sweet treats. It could inspire you to create your very own recipes. You can substitute ingredients as your taste, health, or pocket dictates. You can come up, perhaps, not with a dessert that is the perfect clone of a restaurant's recipe, but with one that is exactly the way you want it to be. Most of all, the recipes here are meant for you to experience the fulfillment of seeing the smiles on the people with whom you share your creations. Keep trying and having fun with the recipes, and you will soon be reaping your sweet rewards!

If prepared food arrives outside the home, you typically have limited knowledge about salt, sugar, and processed oils. For a fact, we also apply more to our meal when it is served to the table. You will say how much salt, sugar, and oil are being used to prepare meals at home.

Copycat recipes practically give you the ability to make great restaurant food tasting in your own home and get it the right first time and easily.

CPSIA information can be obtained
at www.ICGtesting.com
Printed in the USA
BVHW051213150221
600147BV00009B/624